DAY BY DAY

Rowland Purton

DAY BY DAY

Stories and prayers for every day of the year

Oxford . Basil Blackwell

Reprinted 1974

ISBN 0 631 14680 6

TO MY WIFE

Printed in Great Britain by
Western Printing Services Ltd, Bristol
and bound at the Kemp Hall Bindery, Oxford

Day by day,
Dear Lord, of thee three things I pray:
To see thee more clearly,
Love thee more dearly,
Follow thee more nearly,
Day by day.

ST. RICHARD OF CHICHESTER

Contents

Introduction

DAY BY DAY has been prepared mainly for the Head Teacher who is seeking material for school assemblies which can be used over a long period of time. Many existing useful books are limited in value because of their smaller number of stories. This book contains material enough to be used over a period of at least two years without repetition and contains stories and prayers appropriate to most school, community or national situations.

It is considered that the outlines could be used in junior, middle or secondary schools and that they might prove useful out of school too in the hands of preachers or youth leaders. Moreover, reference to the general index will reveal that this is also a comprehensive mine of information on many subjects.

For school assemblies, the material may be used in any of three ways.

1. By topics

The stories have been grouped in fives so that a theme for a week may be followed. Some of these, particularly those on pages 107–141, are more directly applicable to certain seasons of the year but the majority can be taken at any time as desired. Each story within the theme stands on its own and can be used independently of the others. This means that if a school has only four assemblies because of taking the B.B.C. service, or for any other reason, one story can be omitted without detriment to the theme.

Some themes, such as The Christian Year and the stories of saints may lend themselves more than others for casual use when a week may include only a couple of assemblies as at half-term or end of term.

After two years, when the themes have been exhausted, one can begin to work through them again.

2. By date

Every story has some association with a particular date and there is a story for every day of the year (see page xxxii). Some are the stories of saints told on their feast days; some are the stories of great men and women on the anniversaries of their birth, death or particular achievement; and some recount great events. Most important anniversaries are spotlit, though a few are passed by, e.g. Trafalgar Day, because Nelson is mentioned in another context. This is inevitable when finding a story for every day.

If used in this way, stories can be told as appropriate in the first year. In the second year some can still be used in this way—stories which in the previous year fell on week-end days, holidays or other days when no story was taken in assembly. On the remaining days, stories can be taken which normally fall during holiday periods.

After two years there could be a short break and then the stories told again as in 1.

3. At random

It has been mentioned already that each story is independent of others and there is therefore no reason why they cannot be taken in any order that the Head may desire. It is, however, felt that this is probably the least effective method.

SAINTS

Since a number of the stories are of saints and make reference to the feast day, it would be advisable at an early stage to explain what a saint is and what we mean by a feast day.

In the main, these saints are those who have been *canonized* by the Roman Catholic Church after an extensive consideration of their life and work. The feast day on which they are remembered is, in most instances, the date of death. (See also page 122.) It follows that many good Christians are not called 'Saint' if they were not members of the Roman Catholic Church. This does not mean that these are inferior.

Recently certain saints have been 're-examined' and their status reduced or their names removed from the canon. Some well-known ones, such as St. George and St. Christopher, have nevertheless been included in this book.

Each unit consists of a story, often incorporating a Bible reading. It is followed by a prayer and a suggested closing prayer or Benediction. In most cases the prayers follow the theme of the story; but occasionally a prayer is one written by a person who is the subject of the story.

Some of these prayers are drawn from traditional sources and the dependence upon other works will be obvious from a glance at the list of sources. Most prayers, however, have been written by the author especially for this purpose and are marked*.

Prayers taken from other sources are, of course, reproduced in their original or traditional form: those written for this book are written using 'you' rather than 'thou' to make them more intelligible to the children and to avoid any impression that there is a special language for church services, which must therefore be somewhat removed from the everyday world.

The prayer supplement (page 401) includes prayers suitable for the opening of worship, closing prayers and Benedictions (to which reference is made after each story), prayers for the school and those for special occasions. These, with the prayers printed after the stories, form a comprehensive anthology of prayers on most subjects likely to be needed in school. Reference should be made to the prayer index.

Bible readings have been included where appropriate but no attempt has been made to include a reading just for the sake of doing so. Some readings introduce the stories; some find a place within the story; and others prove appropriate conclusions. Where no Bible reading is indicated, it might make an interesting variation to use one as part of the opening act of worship or associated with the prayer. Some suggested readings for this purpose are indicated on page 427. Of course, it is not necessary to have a Bible reading in every service and poems or readings from other sources can sometimes be used very effectively.

It will be appreciated that the outlines given here do not form complete services but perhaps the second half. It is important that every service should begin on a note of praise or thanksgiving and perhaps prayers of a more general nature should come early in the service (see page xii). A few opening prayers are included in the prayer section but there are numerous other sources of prayers of this kind, some of which may be included in the children's hymn books, thus enabling them actively to participate.

Introduction   xi

Some suggested orders of service are as follows:

Opening sentences	Prayer
Hymn	Hymn
Prayers	Bible Reading
Lesson (Bible Reading	Story
and story)	Prayer
Prayer	Hymn or verse
Hymn or sung verse	Benediction
Prayer	

Sometimes the hymn and first prayer may be chosen with the general theme in mind but sometimes they may be chosen mainly for worship and thanksgiving.

It is a good idea to adopt a general pattern for the service as children (and adults too) feel more secure in a pattern that can be recognized. It is suggested, for example, that the children might stand for the opening of worship, hymn and prayers, then sit for the Bible reading and story, standing again for the closing prayers.

This does not mean that the service should follow too rigid a pattern. There can be many variations. The prayers in the first part of the service serve as an example. There is no need to take the Lord's Prayer every day: it becomes monotonous. On the days when the Lord's Prayer is included, it may sometimes be sung, sometimes spoken and sometimes repeated after the leader who is taking assembly. There may be one or two other prayers which the children learn, such as a prayer for the school (page 413). There is a lot to be said too for encouraging children to write prayers themselves and for those children to read their prayers in assembly.

Thus, if two prayers are included near the beginning of the service, there can be variety through the week. Here is just one example:

Day 1   A prayer of thanksgiving (by leader)
        The Lord's Prayer spoken together

Day 2   A child's prayer of thanksgiving
        A prayer for forgiveness (page 405)

Day 3   A prayer of thanksgiving (read together)
        A prayer for the school

Day 4   A child's prayer
        The Lord's Prayer sung

Day 5   Responsive prayer (litany)

At the end of the service, the printed prayer and the suggested closing prayer may be separated by a sung verse or a hymn, or the closing prayer may follow immediately on the other if both are used.

The prayers and Bible readings have been selected with care so that they are suitable for the purpose. Many prayers on the subjects were not used because the language seemed too far removed from the children. At the same time, some traditional prayers have been included because of their beauty, their appropriateness or their traditions ('Our closing prayer is one that has been said by Christian people for over a thousand years . . .'). There may be criticism that a few prayers are a little beyond the children's understanding. This I accept. But do adults always know the full meanings of prayers they use? And is not worship itself something that involves more than the mind and the intelligence?

Some of the tried prayers of the Church have an appeal of majesty and feeling similar to that which is aroused by the Authorized Version of the Bible, a feeling which is sometimes lost in the more easily understood modern translations.

For the Bible readings it is suggested that the New English Bible or the Jerusalem Bible be used but the A.V. or R.S.V. can be used sometimes for variety and indeed there are some passages which read better in the words of the A.V.

Again, it is a good idea for older children to read the Bible passages at times but it is essential that the reading should be well rehearsed. There is nothing more able to destroy the atmosphere of the service than a Bible reading mumbled unintelligibly and unheard by the majority of the children.

The atmosphere attained in the assembly is vital if it is not to become a meaningless daily duty. This atmosphere can be created in many ways—by the appearance of the hall, by music and flowers, and by carefully planning the services. It will be obvious that this book should be used wisely and not just reached for at the last moment and thumbed through for a story that has not been used lately. There should be that degree of thought and careful preparation which is necessary in all school work but even more so when bringing children before God.

ROWLAND PURTON

Acknowledgments

Prayers from various sources have been used. The pages on which the undermentioned prayers may be found are indicated in the list of prayer sources on page 419.

Some of the ancient prayers for which the original source is shown are also to be found in the *Book of Common Prayer*.

The text of the Authorized Version of the Bible, and of the 1662 *Book of Common Prayer*, is Crown Copyright and the extracts used herein are reproduced by permission.

An extract from the *Prayer book as Proposed in 1928* is printed with the permission of the holders of the copyright.

The author and publishers would like to thank the following for permission to reproduce copyright material.

Lady Collins for two prayers from *Prayers for Young People* by Dr. William Barclay.

Messrs. J. M. Dent & Sons Ltd., for a prayer by John Hunter from *Devotional Services for Public Worship*.

The Girl Guides Association for a prayer from *The Guide Law* compiled by Miss Marjory Campbell.

The Girls' Brigade for six prayers from *Devotions for Company and Camp* by Rev. A. E. Shakeshaft.

Messrs. Hodder and Stoughton Ltd., for a verse by Rev. G. A. Studdert-Kennedy (page 277) and an extract from *The Ascent of Everest* by John Hunt (page 19).

A prayer from *Gitanjali* by Rabindranath Tagore is printed by permission of the Trustees of the Tagore Estate and Macmillan, London and Basingstoke.

Messrs. John Murray (Publishers) Ltd., for a prayer from *A Chain of Prayer Across the Ages* compiled by Selina Fox; and for an extract from *Scott's Last Expedition* by R. F. Scott (page 113).

Messrs. Thomas Nelson & Sons Ltd., for a prayer by Geoffrey Clifton from *The Junior Hymn Book*.

The Oxford University Press for a prayer from *Prayers and Hymns for Little Children*; for five prayers from *The Daily Service Revised Edition*; for two prayers from *The Kingdom, the Power and the Glory*; and for permission to use as part of a prayer a verse from the hymn 'When a knight won his spurs' by Jan Struther (1901–1953) from *Enlarged Songs of Praise*.

Pergamon Press Ltd., for two prayers from *Junior Worship*

edited by Ernest H. Hayes and J. Kenneth Meir (1956) published by Religious Education Press.

The Headmaster of Rydal School for two prayers from *Rydal School Hymnal*.

Student Christian Movement Press Ltd., for nine prayers by Dr. William Barclay from *Epilogues and prayers* (1963); and five prayers from *A Book of Prayers for Schools* (1958) by Rev. H. Bisseker, Mr. A. E. Pite and Rev. E. M. Venables.

The Society for Promoting Christian Knowledge, for a prayer by S. M. E. Trood from *Service Book for Youth*; for a prayer from *The Splendour of God*; and for a verse by Christina Rossetti (page 99).

The Headmaster of Uppingham School, Mr. J. C. Royds, for four prayers from *Prayers in use at Uppingham School*.

The material for this book has been collected during a long period of time and, despite all efforts, it has not been possible to trace all original sources. If, therefore, any copyright has been unwittingly infringed, the author extends his sincere apologies. Any such omissions will, if notified, be gladly corrected in any future editions.

Table of Contents by Theme

Table of contents by theme   xix

Table of contents by theme   xxi

4. THE CHRISTIAN CHURCH   143

Table of contents by theme

Table of Contents by Date

Most of the stories are associated with a certain date. This list is provided for those who would like to use the stories as 'anniversary' stories instead of by weekly topics. There is one story for every day of the year.

Table of Contents by Date   xxxiii

1 Home, Friends and Relationships

This series of six themes is concerned with familiar and personal things, right relationships and attitudes.

| *Home* | *Schools* | *Living together* |
| *Teamwork* | *Friends* | *Names and reputations* |

Each theme consists of five topics, with the exception only of *Teamwork* which has four printed. It is suggested that the fifth might be one of the Commemorative days on pages 184–186 if not being taken later in the year.

In these, as with other themes which follow, there may frequently be additional snippets of information of a local or topical nature which can profitably be added to the printed material for added interest. In At Home (1), for example, the opening paragraph can be more specifically related to the school catchment area; Schools (1) provides for local school information; while Names and Reputations (1) could be enhanced by reference to current 'pop' or film idols.

If taken as themes, it is suggested that *'At Home'* might be the opening theme of one school year and *Schools* the first in the following year.

At home (1)

Duke of Marlborough

What kind of house do you live in? Is it a house, a flat, a bungalow or a cottage? Is it old or is it new? Is yours the only family to live there, or do you share it with someone else? Would you change it for another kind of house if you had the chance?

Do you think you would like to live in a palace? Perhaps you have paid a visit to a great house that belongs to an important family and have seen huge rooms with ornate carving and plaster work, filled with tapestries and works of art. You may have thought that it was more like a museum than a place to live in. Certainly there is a lot of history attached to these palaces.

Blenheim Palace, for example, was built at Woodstock near Oxford for John Churchill, the First Duke of Marlborough, in the time of Queen Anne. Marlborough had won such an outstanding victory against the French at the Battle of Blenheim, that Parliament began to build Blenheim Palace for the Duke at a cost of a quarter of a million pounds. When the Duke died on 16th June, 1722, Blenheim Palace was only partially completed and his widow found the rest of the money that was needed to complete it.

Most people dream at times of living in a palace, yet they find their smaller homes more convenient and would not exchange them for palaces even if they had the opportunity.

Home, after all, is the place where you can feel most comfortable and contented. And that depends as much upon the people who live in it as it does on the kind of building. Home is what we help to make it.

O God our Father, we thank you for our homes and families. May our homes be places of contentment and peace. Help us always to be loving, kind and helpful and to do nothing to spoil our home life; through Jesus Christ our Lord. *Amen.**

Closing prayer No. 3

At home (2)

St. Francis Xavier

Just imagine living in a castle! You might think that with a home like that you would not want to venture far. Yet many a person born in a castle has left it for a very different kind of life.

One of these, Francis Xavier, was born in 1506 into a noble family living in Castle Xavier, Spain. His family expected him to become a soldier as his ancestors had been but Francis chose to be a scholar and had plans to become a lecturer or professor.

However, while he was studying in Paris, Francis met a young man named Ignatius Loyola, who persuaded him to join with a small band of men who became known as the Society of Jesus. Francis hesitated. He knew what Jesus said to those who would be disciples.

Bible Reading: St. Luke 9: 57–62

At last he decided to give up everything in the service of God. The work was difficult and involved long journeys. Francis did things that he would never have dreamed of, looking after the sick and incurable, washing the sores of beggars, sleeping in cattle sheds and begging for food.

Later he went to India, a journey which took thirteen months in the cramped quarters of a small ship. There he worked among the Portuguese colonists as well as among the Indian villagers and fishermen before going even further afield to Ceylon, Singapore, New Guinea and Japan. He hoped also to reach China but he died before being able to do so.

The man who baptized thousands of people in Asia and who underwent many hardships on his journeys, is remembered as St. Francis Xavier and 2nd December is kept as his feast day. [*see note on page* x]

A prayer of St. Ignatius Loyola, who persuaded St. Francis Xavier to serve God in this way:

Teach us, good Lord, to serve thee as thou deservest; to give and not to count the cost; to fight and not to heed the wounds; to toil and not to seek for rest; to labour and not to ask for any reward save that of knowing that we do thy will. *Amen.*

Benediction No. 54

At home (3)

St. Dunstan

Dunstan was born near Glastonbury, in Somerset, only a few years after the death of King Alfred the Great. If Alfred earned the title 'the Great' for his wise rule, Dunstan deserves a similar title for his service to God, the Church and the country.

A relative of the royal family of Wessex, he was given a good education at Glastonbury. There he learned to appreciate the way in which the monks lived and decided that this was the life for him. He liked the idea of men living together in a community in which they worked and worshipped together. Later, as Abbot of Glastonbury, Dunstan introduced stricter rules for the monks, then went on to begin or renew the work at other abbeys, such as Bath, Westminster and Exeter.

Most of the kings of Wessex turned to him for help and advice. King Edgar made him Archbishop of Canterbury and when, in 973, Edgar was recognized not only as King of Wessex but of all England, Dunstan crowned him at Bath. The coronation ceremony which Dunstan prepared for this is the one on which British coronations since then have been based.

Dunstan had other talents too, for he was also recognized as a clever writer, iron-worker and musician.

But above all, Dunstan's life in the monastery had taught him how to live with God. A writer of his day wrote that when Dunstan sang at the altar, 'he seemed to be talking with the Lord face to face'.

He died at Canterbury in A.D. 988, on 19th May, on which day he is still remembered as St. Dunstan.

O Lord our God, help us to know you not as a God who is afar off but as one to be met and spoken with day by day. Give us a sense of your nearness even now as we pray and help us to know that as we leave this place we do not leave your presence but we take you with us into all the activities of the day. Hear us and help us for the sake of Jesus Christ our Lord. *Amen.**

Closing prayer No. 23

At home (4)

St. Anthony

You would probably not think very much of the idea of living in a cave, yet many people have done so and not just people long ago in the Stone Age.

We read in the Bible of people who lived in the wilderness and had only a cave for shelter. Here is part of one story about Elijah for instance:

Bible Reading: 1 Kings 19: 9–13a

In the early days of the Christian Church, there were many who put aside all they owned and went away into lonely places where they could pray and think about God.

Some of these were known as the 'desert fathers', since their dwellings were huts, caves or abandoned dwellings in the lands of the Middle East. Much of their time was spent in prayer and meditation but they also did some manual work, such as making mats or baskets, in order to obtain money for food, which was usually very simple fare.

On 17th January, the Christian Church remembers St. Anthony, who was born about two hundred and fifty years after the time of Jesus. His home was in Egypt and it was there, when he was twenty years old, that he began to live alone. Forty years later, he moved to a cave on Mount Kolzim, near the north-west corner of the Red Sea and there he spent the remainder of his long life. He lived to be over one hundred years old.

His whole life was given to the service of God, and he was known far and wide for his wisdom. People of many walks of life sought his advice, which was readily given.

Teach us, O Lord, not to think only of ourselves but to give up some of our time for others:
To help those who are less able than we are;
To do little jobs for people older than ourselves;
To visit those who cannot leave their homes.

Above all, teach us to spend time with you so that we may know what is your will for us; through Christ our Lord. *Amen.**

Closing prayer No. 36

At home (5)

Dr. Nansen and Refugees

There may be times when we wish that our homes were a little better, perhaps with more room or in a different neighbourhood. We may sometimes envy those with better homes than ours. If we do, we should remember millions of people with few of the comforts that we have and many with no home at all.

Among those who have worked to help the homeless and the refugees is Dr. Fridtjof Nansen, a great Norwegian explorer and a man of courage and determination, who succeeded on several occasions in doing what others said was impossible.

His adventures had included travelling on skis across Greenland, drifting in the Arctic with his ship held fast in the ice, sailing toward the North Pole, encounters with walruses and bears, falls into icy water and a stay of four months with one companion in an ice hut through the long cold winter months.

When he retired from exploring, Nansen was called upon to solve another task which people thought to be impossible. After the war of 1914–18, half a million prisoners were stranded in the north of Russia. The League of Nations, responsible for such problems, asked the help of Dr. Nansen. It was a tremendous task but he succeeded.

The rest of his life was spent in helping other groups of refugees to settle down to a new life. He died on 13th May, 1930, having worn himself out in the service of the homeless people of the world.

Almighty God, our heavenly Father, we thank you for the comforts of home and the love of families and friends. We bring to you in prayer the people of many lands, who have lost all they had and must live as refugees in other places. Bless all who work to help them until men shall learn to live in peace with their neighbours and share the good things of this world; through Jesus Christ our Lord. *Amen.**

Closing prayer No. 39

Schools (1)

Each morning during term time you set off for school. Some of you are pleased to come and look forward to what you are going to do during the day: others may wish that they could stay at home instead. However we may feel about school, we have to attend because it is the law that all children must do so.

Had you lived a little more than a hundred years ago, you would possibly have loved the chance to learn because only a few children had the opportunity. In fact, many children had to go out to work before they were as old as you are now. Then, in 1870, a law was passed which laid down that schools were to be provided for all children. School Boards were set up to build the schools that were necessary. Since then schools have been built wherever they were needed.

[A brief summary of facts regarding our own school]

Schools now are very different from those of a hundred years ago. A lot has happened in a century of state education. These changes have come about as a result of the thought and work of a great many people to whom we owe a great deal.

Today we have greater opportunities than ever in the past but it is up to each one of us to make the most of them—to be attentive to our work so that we may learn all we can; to learn to live with others and when to give and take; and to acquire for ourselves wisdom and understanding.

An Old Testament writer tells of the value of wisdom and understanding.

Bible Reading: Proverbs 3: 13–18

Our Father, bless our school and all who come here every day. Bless our teachers and those who clean our school and keep it warm, and those who prepare and serve our meals. Help us all to praise and serve thee. May we be strong to do thy will, brave to tackle hard and unpleasant tasks, loyal to our friends and forgiving to our enemies; through Jesus Christ our Lord. *Amen.*

Junior Worship

Closing prayer No. 58

Schools (2)

Robert Raikes

Bible Reading: St. Matthew 19: 13–15

Long before there were schools for many children, Robert Raikes, the smartly dressed, middle-aged editor of the *Gloucester Journal* watched from his window some children at play. Most of them were dressed in rags; their language was shocking; and frequently their games ended in fighting. How different they were from his own children.

Raikes began to ask questions about these children, and found they spent most of their time working in factories. Then he decided to open a school for them on Sundays when they had their day off from the factory, to teach them to become good citizens and give them something useful to do.

People laughed at him. Sunday schools had been started by others but they had soon closed. But Raikes had his supporters too, including a woman who was willing to teach the children in her home.

It was an up-hill battle. Some boys only came for fun; some jeered at younger boys who tried to sing the hymns. But even the roughest boys seemed to like Robert Raikes and took notice of him. Some of them actually came to Sunday school with clean hands and faces and with their hair combed. That in itself was an achievement.

At last, after about three years, Raikes realized that he was winning. His Sunday school was a success. Now he must encourage others to start them too.

On 3rd November, 1783, Raikes used his newspaper to launch an appeal for more schools. The result was remarkable. From all over the country people wrote to Robert Raikes—the 'father of Sunday Schools'—for help.

O Lord Jesus Christ, who blessed the children, we praise you for those who have tried to help children to grow into better citizens of our land and to learn your holy ways. Bless all who work among children today and help them to see the fruits of their labours; for the sake of Jesus Christ our Lord. *Amen.**

Closing prayer No. 14

Schools (3)

Thomas Hughes

Thomas Hughes died on 22nd March, 1896, leaving behind him a book which became famous—*Tom Brown's Schooldays*. In the book we read how Tom Brown made his journey by coach from Berkshire to Rugby, the very journey which Thomas Hughes must have made himself when he first left his Berkshire home on the stage which was to take him to Rugby School.

In fact, we are left wondering how much of Tom Brown was actually a reflection of Tom Hughes, and how many of Tom's adventures were ones which the author saw for himself during the years he spent at the school. Certainly the book is one of the finest pictures of life at a public school at that time.

If sometimes we think school life is difficult today, we do well to remember what schooldays were like then. The book tells of bullying, thrashings, and even small boys being 'toasted' in front of the fire.

However, the days when Thomas Hughes was at Rugby were ones when many changes were taking place and people were anxious to make conditions better. Much of this change was due to the headmaster of Rugby School, Dr. Thomas Arnold, who had a much better understanding of boys than many others had. The changes which he introduced at Rugby spread to other schools too.

Most of the boys at Rugby had the greatest respect for Dr. Arnold—a wise man who did a great deal for education in Britain.

Many young people have learned how to live a good life following the example of older people whom they have come to respect.

Bible Reading: Proverbs 2: 20–22

A prayer of Dr. Arnold (adapted)

Let thy blessing, O Lord, rest upon our work this day. Teach us to seek after truth, and enable us to attain it; but grant that as we increase in the knowledge of earthly things, we may grow in the knowledge of thee; through Jesus Christ our Lord. *Amen.*

Closing prayer No. 5

Schools (4)

                                       Friedrich Froebel

Bible Reading: Proverbs 2: 1–6

Friedrich Froebel loved the countryside and became greatly interested in trees and flowers. When he left school he began to study forestry, land surveying and other things to do with the land in his native Germany.

But, after he had attended university, he spoke one day to the headmaster of a school in Frankfurt, who told him that he should give up his plans for forestry and become a teacher. So, at the age of twenty-three, Froebel became a teacher.

He recalled that as a boy he had been taught by two teachers, one who taught uninteresting facts and beat any boy who could not remember them and one who showed a tremendous amount of patience and kindness. Froebel knew what kind of teacher he ought to try to be.

He always made lessons as interesting as he could and sometimes he took the boys out of school for their lessons. He became interested in new methods of teaching that were being put forward by a Swiss man named Pestalozzi. Some people criticized Froebel's work but he certainly gained good results.

Later in life, Froebel became convinced that education should begin at an early age and he started school for those between the ages of three and seven. This school he called a Kindergarten.

Froebel died on 1st June, 1852, but he is far from forgotten. Kindergarten schools are still found in many lands and the name Froebel holds an honoured place in the story of education for a great step forward toward better methods of teaching and much happier schools.

We humbly thank thee, O Almighty God, for the blessings which thou hast bestowed upon us in this school. Help us to use these in thy service and teach us to serve thee not only in word and prayer, but in everything that we do; and this we ask for Jesus Christ's sake, our blessed Lord and Saviour. *Amen.*

Prayers in use at Uppingham School

Benediction No. 43

Schools (5)

Margaret McMillan

Bible Reading: St. Luke, 2: 39–47

From this story, it seems that Jesus made good use of the opportunities of learning that were available in his day. It is an example that we should do well to copy. We have many opportunities for learning; we have good schools to attend; but in the days when Margaret McMillan was born, on 20th July, 1860, education was not compulsory and many children had no school at all.

Margaret McMillan herself was fortunate. She was born of Scottish parents in New York State and was educated in Scotland and in Switzerland. Eventually she went to live in Bradford, Yorkshire, where, in 1894, she was elected to the School Board, which was responsible for the education of the children of Bradford. It was there that she arranged for the first ever medical inspection of school children.

In 1902, she joined her sister Rachel to open a children's open-air clinic at Bow, in east London. Several years later, she founded an open-air school at Deptford.

It was not long before people were taking an interest in the idea of nursery schools for children under the age of five and, when a Nursery School Association was formed in 1923, Margaret McMillan was chosen to be its first president.

In 1917, Margaret McMillan was awarded the C.B.E. in recognition of her great service to education. Like other pioneers, her work has helped to build up the system which we have today.

O God our Father, we have so much to be thankful for; for people who have given us schools and books, and for those teachers who have found interesting ways of teaching. Help us today to make full use of our opportunities, so that we may grow in knowledge and in wisdom to become good citizens of our land; through Jesus Christ our Lord. *Amen.**

Benediction No. 51

Living together (1)

One of the most difficult lessons to learn is the art of living together. Too often we are ready to quarrel or start a fight so that we can have our own way. One Bible story tells how Abraham avoided a quarrel.

Bible Reading: Genesis 13: 5–9

Quarrels which are not settled sometimes lead to war. War is a sad affair but it seems so much worse when it is civil war in which people fight their own countrymen and sometimes even their own relatives.

It is now over three hundred years since the terrible Civil War broke out in England, with the King and his followers on one side and Parliament and its supporters on the other.

On the one side, King Charles I, like his father before him, believed that God gave him the right to rule and no one could tell him how to do so. On the other side, Parliament insisted that the King should do as he was told. It became clear that neither side would give an inch. Both became very angry and gathered around them those who thought the same as they did. The stage was set for war.

The first great battle of the Civil War was fought at Edgehill, on 23rd October, 1642, between the King's supporter's, who became known as Cavaliers, and the Parliamentary troops, to be known as Roundheads. Neither side won. It was the first of many battles to be fought during the next four years.

The tragedy of this, as with so many wars, is that it might have been avoided with a little give and take. We should guard against thinking that we are always right and that others must be wrong if they disagree with us.

Take from us, O God, the pride which makes us think that we are right and therefore that those who disagree with us must be wrong. Help us to be ready to see the points of view of others. Keep us from greed, hatred, envy and any attitude that causes bad feeling; and make us more truly your children: for Jesus Christ's sake. *Amen.**

Closing prayer No. 7

Living together (2)

St. Valentine's Day

Learning how to live with others is very important. One day you will be choosing the person with whom you wish to set up home. Then, if your home is to be happy, there will have to be plenty of giving as well as taking.

You may already have thought what kind of person you would like to live with and may, perhaps, have amused yourself by sending a Valentine.

Nowadays, fewer people send or receive Valentines than they did about a hundred years ago, when a young lady would be judged successful or otherwise, according to the number of cards she received. In fact, some of them sent cards to themselves to make sure that they had several to show!

But what had St. Valentine to do with lovers? Nothing at all. In fact, all we know of him is that he was a priest in Rome, who was imprisoned, beaten and then beheaded. Later a church was built at the place where he died. It was just that his day, 14th February, fell at the time when people believed that birds began to mate and young people might be looking for a partner to marry. So for hundreds of years, St. Valentine's Day has been a happy day for many young people.

In the meanwhile, you can practise living at peace with others by being kind and considerate in your own home. Here is some advice given by St. Paul.

Bible Reading: Ephesians 6: 1–3

O God, our Father, we ask you to bless those whom we love and those who are especially dear to us.

Bless our parents, and help us to live in such a way that we may never bring anxiety or sorrow to them.

Bless those whom we love, and help us to live in such a way that we may never be untrue, unfaithful or disloyal to them. *Amen.*

Dr. William Barclay

Closing prayer No. 3

Living together (3)

Every year, thousands of people get married and they cannot do too much for each other. But how many can say after a year has passed that they have never quarrelled?

Long ago, probably during the reign of King Stephen, a prize was offered to any couple who could swear that, for a year and a day, not an angry word had passed between them. The prize was a flitch of bacon—a flitch being the whole side of a hog. This flitch was to be obtained from the Prior of Dunmow, in Essex.

In the few hundred years that followed, only a handful of people succeeded in proving their claim. The custom was dropped about two hundred years ago, but, in 1855, awards were made again to those who could satisfy a jury of six single men and six single women.

Nowadays, on 7th June, which people believe is the anniversary of the day on which the award was first made, people can still claim the Dunmow Flitch, but the whole matter is treated in a very light-hearted way.

However, it is still interesting to notice how few people have been able to claim not to have quarrelled.

When St. Paul wrote to the people who lived at Colossae in Greece, he offered advice on how to get on well together. Here are his words:

Bible Reading: Colossians 3: 12–15

Most quarrels are caused by thinking too much of ourselves and too little of others.

Throughout today, O God, help me
To say nothing that will hurt anybody,
To do nothing that is unkind or harmful,
To think only the best of other people,
To repeat nothing that is best forgotten,
To treat others as I would like to be treated myself;
    This I ask for Jesus Christ's sake. *Amen.**

Closing prayer No. 6

Living together (4)

In the summer of 1608, Samuel de Champlain, the French explorer, sailed slowly up the great St. Lawrence River to find a suitable place to land and build a settlement from which he could explore the rivers, lakes and forests of the land we now call Canada.

At last, on July 3rd he discovered an ideal place at the foot of a cliff. He called it Quebec, just as the Indians had done before him. The name is almost certainly from an Indian word meaning 'the river gets narrow here'.

Soon the settlers were busy cutting down trees to build their homes. They also worked together to build a high fence, or stockade, for their protection and to make their settlement prosper.

As time passed, the settlement became too small for all who would live there and a new, larger settlement was built on the cliff top. Champlain could hardly have imagined the great city which stands there today, a reminder of those first settlers who lived and worked together to make a success of their new home.

The Bible has a story of some people who learned to work together for something important.

Bible Reading: Acts 4: 32–35

It was because those people worked together that the Christian Church began to grow. In the same way, by working together for good and forgetting ourselves, we can help to improve our school, our town and any organizations to which we belong.

O Lord, our God, we remember how your Church began with a handful of people who followed Jesus. We praise you for these and for all pioneers in the faith, who began to sow the seeds of the Gospel in far away places of the earth. Make us ready to sow such seeds as we may, remembering that it is others who will see the rewards of our labours; through Jesus Christ our Lord. *Amen.**

Closing prayer No. 27

Living together (5)

St. Bruno

In the Old Testament, we find a story of some men, servants of God, who wanted to make a new home for themselves because their old one was too small.

Bible Reading: 2 Kings 6: 1–4

We notice from this story that they were working together and everyone had his part to play in cutting and shaping the wood.

Many hundreds of years later, another little group of men set out to make a new home for themselves where they could worship and work together. Their leader was Bruno, son of a rich nobleman of Cologne, who had been educated at the cathedral school, had become a priest and had been superintendent of all the schools around the city of Rheims.

Bruno decided to leave the city life behind him to go and live in the quietness of the country. With six companions, he found a wild lonely place known as the Chartreuse. There in the narrow valley, they built themselves a small church and a number of scattered huts to live in.

Their life was a very simple one of worship and work. They wore the coarsest clothes, ate very simple food and denied themselves all luxuries. In spite of this, others joined them.

Bruno founded other similar places, where men, who became known as Carthusian monks, could live and work together.

Each year, on October 9th, the Christian Church remembers St. Bruno, the man who found God in the quietness of the mountains about nine hundred years ago.

Help us, O God, in these days of noise and bustle to remember how Jesus spoke with you in the quietness of the wilderness. May we, too, seek you in the quietness, so that we may be aware of your presence, understand your will, and be filled with your peace. This we ask for Jesus Christ's sake. *Amen.**

Benediction No. 55

Teamwork (1)

Crimean War

Some people appear to muddle their way through life without seeming to have any particular aim or ambition. You may have heard it said of someone that his right hand does not know what his left hand is doing.

A little over a hundred years ago, a war was fought in which many people seemed quite unaware of what they should be doing. In fact it was one great muddle from start to finish. The war was the Crimean War, which broke out on 28th March, 1854.

None of the soldiers had ever fired an angry shot. None of the generals had ever commanded an army. It was hardly surprising that mistakes were made. They even disagreed among themselves after the first battle and so gave the enemy time to build powerful defences. One army, the Light Brigade, was sent by mistake to almost certain death.

Soldiers suffered from the cold because no warm clothing was sent. Others were half-starved, while food rotted on a nearby beach because there were no wagons in which to move it. Soldiers were dying because even the simplest of medical supplies did not arrive. At last, people began working together so that matters improved.

In the Bible we read how Nehemiah was frequently attacked by enemies as his people rebuilt the walls of Jerusalem. He organized his people so that they could work together and protect each other.

Bible Reading: Nehemiah 4: 16–21

Most successful people are those who have learned to co-operate with others and so help one another.

Guide us, O God, in all our thinking and in all our actions so that we may learn how to work well with others. Make us honest in our dealings, careful in our speaking and concerned for the feelings of others so that they may find us pleasant to know and easy to work with; through Jesus Christ our Lord. *Amen.**

Closing prayer No. 58

Teamwork (2)

Everest climbed

The most overworked word in the English language is 'I'. How often do we say 'Look what *I* have done' or 'See how successful *I* am', forgetting that we are only successful because we have been helped by a great number of other people.

On 29th May, 1953, Edmund Hillary and a Sherpa named Tensing pulled themselves up to the snowy summit of Mount Everest. They were the first men to stand on the highest point on earth, with the world stretching out below them in every direction. Of that thrilling moment, Hillary wrote:

'I looked at Tensing. In spite of the balaclava helmet, goggles, and oxygen mask—all encrusted with icicles—that concealed his face, there was no disguising his grin of delight as he looked all around him. We shook hands, and then Tensing threw his arm around my shoulders and we thumped each other on the back until we were almost breathless. It was 11.30 a.m.'

It had been a hard and strenuous climb and had been achieved only by teamwork. Sir John Hunt, leader of the expedition, wrote:

'The greatness of climbing on the highest hills lies in the fact that no single man is capable of reaching a summit by his own efforts.'

Hillary and Tensing felt 'on top of the world'—as indeed they were—thanks to a great team.

Life has many mountains to be climbed and the path may often seem difficult, but what a wonderful feeling it is when we have triumphed. And then let us remember to say not 'Look what *I* have done' but 'Look what *I* have been able to do through the help of other people.'

Bible Reading: Romans 12: 3–5

As we go through life, O God, help us to face our problems with courage and determination. May we never be discouraged, but press on in spite of all difficulties until our aim is achieved. Help us willingly to accept the help of others and always to acknowledge the help received from them and from you, the strength of all who trust you; through Jesus Christ our Lord. *Amen.**

Closing prayer No. 13

Teamwork (3)

Two great conductors

Bible Reading: 1 Corinthians 12: 12–18

Your body is a most amazing structure, having, among other things, feet to walk, hands to feel, eyes to see, ears to hear, a nose for smelling, a tongue for tasting and a voice for speaking—all of which are controlled by your brain. Without any of these, your body cannot work perfectly. All have their part to play.

Some of the finest music in the world is that played by an orchestra, in which each instrument has a particular part to play—strings, woodwind, brass, percussion and sometimes other instruments too.

To ensure that all the instruments play at the correct time and with the correct volume, the orchestra has a conductor. Each member of the orchestra has his own piece of music, but the conductor has the complete score—the music for every instrument that is being played.

There have been many famous conductors, two British ones sharing the same birthday. Sir Thomas Beecham was born on 29th April, 1877 and Sir Malcolm Sargent on 29th April, 1895.

Both conductors played in many countries of the world. Sir Thomas Beecham was particularly renowned for conducting without the score in front of him. Sir Malcolm Sargent will be remembered among other things for conducting some of the Promenade concerts in London and especially the last of each series.

A successful conductor can work wonders with an orchestra. If all the instrumentalists obey the conductor, they play in harmony, just as the people of the world could live in harmony if they kept the laws of God and followed the leadership of Jesus Christ.

O God, Creator of the world, help us to live in harmony in your world. Help us to realize that we must work with others; make us aware of our own particular responsibilities and help us to perform them to the best of our ability as we follow the example of our leader, Jesus Christ. *Amen.**

Benediction No. 47

Teamwork (4)

Gilbert and Sullivan

On March 14th, 1885, the curtain was raised at the Savoy Theatre in London for the first performance of the new comic opera, *The Mikado*—a most unlikely story of the son of the Mikado, or Emperor of Japan, who ran away disguised as a wandering minstrel, almost got himself beheaded, and eventually married Yum-Yum to live happily ever after.

The opera was the work of two men, Sir W. S. Gilbert, who wrote the words, and Sir Arthur Sullivan, who wrote the music.

People had already enjoyed previous operas which the two had written, *H.M.S. Pinafore*, *The Pirates of Penzance* and others, but *The Mikado*, was to become the best known of them all.

Gilbert and Sullivan were an odd pair. Gilbert loved humour and was able to work out the strangest of plots, which always seemed to come right in the end. Sullivan was more seriously minded and composed other songs, hymn tunes and pieces of music for the orchestra. Within a few years, they had composed several other operas, *Ruddigore*, *The Yeomen of the Guard* and *The Gondoliers*.

In some ways they seemed to be perfect partners, yet they quarrelled frequently over little things and parted company after a quarrel about a carpet.

Gilbert and Sullivan operas are still enjoyed today. What a pity that two such gifted men were unable to work together for much longer!

Here are some words of advice, given by St. Paul. People with the qualities he mentions are unlikely to fall out over little things.

Bible Reading: Galatians 5: 21–26

O God, Father of us all; help us always
To be ready to work with other people;
To see the points of view of others;
To recognize that we are not always right;
To be willing to give as well as to take;
To be co-operative, thoughtful and considerate;
   In the Name of Jesus Christ our Lord. *Amen.**

Benediction No. 41

Making and losing friends (1)

St. Paul and Timothy

Some of the happiest people are those with the good fortune to be blessed with many friends, especially friends who are loyal and understanding. Friends who are only out for what they can get are easy to find: those who are loyal, come what may, are worth their weight in gold. It has been said that 'a friend is someone who knows all about you and loves you just the same'.

St. Paul found a loyal young friend in Timothy, whom he met in Lystra, a town in which Paul was stoned and left for dead. When next Paul visited the town, Timothy joined Paul on his travels. From that time, he became Paul's trusted companion and friend. At times he travelled with Paul; at other times he went on special missions. Often Paul's letters include greetings also from Timothy.

We know that Timothy was a great comfort and help to Paul, especially during his times of imprisonment. When others failed, Timothy remained true. Here is what Paul wrote about him.

Bible Reading: Philippians 2: 19–24

In later years, Timothy was given special work to do in the city of Ephesus, where he almost certainly became the first bishop. To encourage him in his work, Paul wrote two letters, which we find in our Bible. Those were difficult days and tradition says that Timothy was eventually beaten to death.

It seems fitting that these two friends, who worked so closely together, should be remembered together today, St. Timothy on 24th January and St. Paul on 25th January.

O Lord Jesus Christ, who counted many men and women as your friends, help us to make friends and to be friends. Help us to enjoy our friendships and to be the kind of friends whom others can enjoy, kind, warm-hearted, considerate, sympathetic and thinking more of our friends than we do of ourselves, remembering that you loved your friends enough to die for them. *Amen.**

Benediction No. 52 (the words of St. Paul)

Making and losing friends (1)

Making and losing friends (2)

As Jesus walked by the Sea of Galilee and called the fishermen to follow him, he chose those who were to become his closest friends and, of these, it is possible that John became the closest of all, for he shared the greatest experiences with Jesus and is generally believed to be the disciple who is referred to as 'the disciple whom Jesus loved'.

Perhaps Jesus liked some of the fire that appeared in his character. Jesus nicknamed John and his brother James 'the Sons of Thunder', no doubt because of their quick tempers and, at least once, he had to point out that they still had much to learn about the ways of the Kingdom of God.

John was there on the mountain on that wonderful occasion when Jesus appeared different, in what we call the transfiguration; he was close to Jesus at the last supper; he was the disciple whom Jesus told from the cross to look after his mother; he was the first to reach the tomb on Easter morning; and he was the first to recognize Jesus some time later by the Sea of Galilee, early in the morning while they were fishing.

Later, with Peter, John was recognized as one of the leaders of the church at Jerusalem before being sent as a prisoner to the island of Patmos. He is believed to have written the Gospel and epistles that bear his name and also the book of the Revelation.

St. John, remembered on 27th December, is sometimes referred to as 'the apostle of love', for he told people, just as Jesus had done, that they should love one another. Here are some of his words.

Bible Reading: 1 John 4: 7–12

O God our Father, grant us
The love which is always ready to forgive;
The love which is always eager to help;
The love which is always happier to give than to get.
    And so grant that living in love, we may live like Jesus. *Amen.*

Dr. William Barclay

Closing prayer No. 24

C

Making and losing friends (3)

St. Francis of Assisi

There is an old proverb, *A friend in need is a friend indeed.* It is not difficult to find friends when all is going well. True friends are those who are ready to help even when we have little to offer in return.

One who decided that he would be a friend to anyone he could, was Francis, the son of a rich merchant who lived in Assisi.

Like other young men of his day, he was full of fun and up to all manner of pranks. Then he went to war and was taken prisoner. It was after a bout of sickness that he became so dissatisfied with his way of life that he determined to change it completely.

One day, in a small church, he gave his whole life to God and vowed that he would always do God's will. Soon he began to give away his possessions and his fine clothing to those in need, until his father disowned him.

Francis remembered how Jesus sent out his disciples, telling them to take nothing with them. Here are the words of Jesus as recorded in St. Luke's Gospel.

Bible Reading: St. Luke 10: 1–9

Francis decided that this was how he would live. He dressed in the simple, coarse tunic worn by the humblest of peasants and set out to go where God led him. Soon others joined him and became known as *friars* (brothers).

There were many who had cause to thank the friars, who became friends in need to the sick and the distressed in the name of Jesus.

St. Francis, himself, died in Italy, praising God to the end. He is remembered on 4th October.

A prayer of St. Francis of Assisi:

Eternal God, the Father of all mankind: we commit to thee the needs of the whole world: where there is hatred, give love; where there is injury, pardon; where there is distrust, faith; where there is sorrow, hope; where there is darkness, light; through Jesus Christ our Lord. *Amen.*

Closing prayer No. 31

Making and losing friends (4)

Sir Walter Raleigh

Once Sir Walter Raleigh had had many friends and could have counted the Queen of England among their number. Those were the days when he had been a dashing young courtier, soldier, scholar and writer, whose sense of humour and gallantry had endeared him to many.

Now he sat in his prison cell knowing that he was to be put to death to please the Spanish king. The friends, who had liked his company as a court favourite were not as anxious to be friend to a condemned prisoner.

Raleigh had known adventure in battle and on the high seas. He had been a leader with many friends. Now he could only commit himself to God. In his prison cell, he took pen and paper to write his last poem.

> *Even such is time which takes in trust*
> *Our youth, our joys, and all we have*
> *And pays us but with age and dust:*
> *Who in the dark and silent grave*
> *When we have wandered all our ways*
> *Shuts up the story of our days.*
> *And from the earth and grave and dust*
> *The Lord shall raise me up I trust.*

On the following morning, 29th October, 1618, Sir Walter Raleigh was led out and beheaded.

Others, too, have known what it was to be deserted by friends when they most needed them. Hear what St. Paul wrote:

Bible Reading: 2 Timothy 4: 11 & 16–18

St. Paul knew that, though friends had deserted him, God had been a friend who stood by him.

Almighty God our heavenly Father, we thank you for all the opportunities that are ours today. We do not know what the future may hold, nor what earthly friends we may have but, like your servant of old, may we know that you are ever with us to guide and to bless; through Jesus Christ our Lord. *Amen.**

Benediction No. 44

Making and losing friends (5)

King William II

Most people with no friends have only themselves to blame. The easiest way to lose friends is to be unkind, unjust, inconsiderate, dishonest, quarrelsome or bullying.

William Rufus, who became King of England in 1087 was such a man. Not satisfied with being King of England, he tried to take part of Normandy from his brother as well. He was unpopular with the barons, who found him a bully who could never keep his promises. He quarrelled with the Archbishop of Canterbury about Church lands, so that the Archbishop fled to France. Even the ordinary people had no time for such a bad ruler.

In the New Forest, there is a stone, on which the inscription reads as follows:

> *Here stood the oak-tree on which an arrow, shot by Sir Walter Tyrrel at a stag, glanced off and struck King William the Second, surnamed Rufus; of which stroke he instantly died, on 2nd August 1100.*

This is the official version of a story which can never be proved. It may have happened just like that, but there are those who believe that Tyrrel might just as easily have shot the King on purpose. Few people wanted to ask questions. The King was dead and there were few regrets. Tyrrel, fearing for his life, had fled to France, leaving the body where it lay to be discovered later that day.

The body was taken to Winchester and laid to rest in the cathedral. When, several years later, the cathedral tower collapsed, people said that it was proof that the King was not fit to have had a Christian burial.

Help us, O God, to so order our lives that we may do only that which is pleasing in the sight of our fellows and of you. Take from us all pride, envy, covetousness, hatred and all that would offend. Give us instead a spirit of love after the example of our Lord and Master Jesus Christ, in whose name we pray. *Amen.**

Closing prayer No. 1

Names and reputations (1)

Ivor Novello

How important is your name? Not very important you may think, but many a person has found his name to be a help or a hindrance, a name to be laughed at, a name to be respected or a name to be feared.

Many people in the entertainment world have changed their names, some finding success as soon as they have done so. As a singer, Jerry Dorsey never hit the highlights but as soon as he changed his name to Engelbert Humperdinck, he shot straight to the top. You will probably know of many others.

Nor is this something new. On 15th January, 1893, David Davies was born. Ask your parents or grandparents who he was and they will not be able to tell you. But speak of Ivor Novello, who was none other than David Davies, and they will remember some of the sixty or so popular songs which he wrote.

Writers often use names other than their own for a number of reasons. The late Poet Laureate, Cecil Day Lewis, also wrote detective stories under the name of Nicholas Blake; Mark Twain was really Samuel Langhorne Clemens; whilst George Eliot was none other than Mary Ann Evans, using a man's name because it was not considered right for a woman to write books in her day.

In Bible times, names were of the utmost importance and all had a meaning. God was thought so great that his name could never be spoken.

Listen to what St. Paul wrote about the name of Jesus.

Bible Reading: Philippians 2: 5–11

Your name may one day be honoured and respected or people may shudder when they hear it. But that depends upon you. Your name is what you make it.

O God our Father, help us to live uprightly after the example of our Lord Jesus Christ so that we may be recognized for our good works and respected by those around us; and to your Name be the honour and glory, now and for evermore. *Amen.**

Closing prayer No. 11

Names and reputations (2)

Amerigo Vespucci

Bible Reading: Genesis 28: 10–19a

Because Jacob dreamed about God, he called the place Bethel— 'house of God'. Many other places have been named by people for special reasons or named after people who discovered them. A glance at an atlas will reveal many countries, rivers, mountains, capes, bays, seas and towns, that have been named after people.

But there is only one man who has had a whole continent named after him. He was Amerigo Vespucci, who was born in Florence on 9th March, 1451.

How America came to be named after him is something of a mystery, because everyone knows that Christopher Columbus crossed the Atlantic before Vespucci. Some say that it was because Columbus landed on the islands, whilst Vespucci sailed along the coast of South America. Others think it may have been a mistake.

One thing is certain. A few years after his voyage, a map was published showing the New World that had been discovered. By the coast of South America was the name Amerigo—and America the whole continent became. Whether or not he deserved to have the continent named after him may be in doubt, but that he was a brave man to sail across unknown seas, no one will question.

Look around the neighbourhood in which you live and you will find streets, schools or blocks of flats named after people, many of them local people who have given their service to the neighbourhood. They may not be known far afield but their names will be remembered by those among whom they worked.

O God, our Father, we thank you for the town [village] in which we live and for all who have worked to make it what it is today. We thank you for our school and for all who have worked together to give it a name to be respected. Help us to build on the foundations that these have laid, so that we may make our school and our neighbourhood even better; for the sake of Jesus Christ our Lord. *Amen.**

Closing prayer No. 12

Names and reputations (3)

Kenneth Grahame

'There is nothing—absolutely nothing—half so much worth doing as simply messing about in boats.'

Some of you may immediately recognize this snatch of conversation from *The Wind in the Willows*, as Rat tried to explain to his new found friend, Mole, something of the wonder of boating on a bright sunny day.

Kenneth Grahame, who wrote the book, was born in Edinburgh on 3rd March, 1859, but moved to Berkshire at an early age after both his parents had died. Later he worked for the Bank of England, of which he was secretary for about ten years.

Two of his earliest books were *The Golden Age* and *Dream Days*, which were books for adults about children. Then came *The Wind in the Willows*, especially written for his own son, Alastair, who was affectionately known as 'Mouse'.

Perhaps it is not surprising that the characters in the book are animals, who behaved like people. There was Mole, filled with wonder at all he saw, and Rat, full of self-confidence. Then there was Toad, intelligent but boastful.

> '*The clever men at Oxford*
> *Know all there is to be knowed.*
> *But they none of them know one half as much*
> *As intelligent Mr. Toad.*'

These were pictures of people as Kenneth Grahame saw them,—pleasant, pompous, boastful, cheerful. How do other people see you? Remember that others judge us not by our looks but by our character.

Bible Reading: 1 Samuel 16: 1 and 4–7

O God, my Father, help me
To see myself as others see me,
To recognize those things in me which are unpleasant,
To correct any faults which I find,
And try to follow the example set by Jesus:
    This I ask in his name. *Amen.**

Closing prayer No. 21

Names and reputations (4)

It is natural to hope that others will always see the best in us, but are we always ready to see the best in other people?

Matthew sat at the gate of Capernaum collecting taxes. Nobody liked him. He was a traitor to his own people, the Jews, because the taxes he was collecting were for the Romans. To the Jewish leaders, Matthew was a sinner unfit to mix with decent people, But one man saw something more in Matthew. As Jesus passed by, he looked kindly on the tax collector and said, 'Follow me'.

Matthew did not wait to be asked a second time. And so Matthew the tax collector became Matthew the disciple—one of the twelve apostles.

Matthew was so overjoyed with his new friend that he called together other tax collectors so that they could have a feast. Let us read what happened.

Bible Reading: St. Matthew 9: 9–13

Notice how the Pharisees now thought badly of Jesus. If he mixed with sinners, they thought he could be no better himself.

Matthew made a note of this and of many other things that Jesus said and did. Later, these were included in the Gospel which now bears his name.

Nowadays, 21st September is the day that the Christian Church keeps as St. Matthew's day—a reminder of the man in whom Jesus saw the good that nobody else was able to see.

Do we look for the good in people? Or do we see only the bad?

O God our Father, forgive us when we think too much of ourselves and too little of others; when we are ready to find fault with others without noticing our own failings; when we look down on others because of what they are or do. Help us always to see the best in others, even those we find it difficult to like, for you are the Father of us all; through Jesus Christ our Lord. *Amen.**

Closing prayer No. 19

Names and reputations (5)

TRUSTWORTHY AND DEPENDABLE   *The Bank of England*

Once Jesus wanted to know what people were saying about him and who they thought he was. Our Bible reading tells what they said to Jesus and what he, in turn, said to Peter.

Bible Reading: St. Matthew 16: 13–18

One of the greatest reputations a person may have is to be regarded as 'firm as a rock', trustworthy and dependable. We feel much happier when dealing with people, businessmen and institutions that we know we can trust because we feel safe in doing so.

One such institution is the Bank of England, formed on 27th July, 1694. Today, below the great building in London, known as 'The Old Lady of Threadneedle Street', are the great vaults in which large amounts of money are kept quite safely.

In fact, when we want to say that something is quite safe, we say it is 'as safe as the Bank of England'. Because of this, we trust the pieces of paper which it issues.

Look at a one-pound note. The paper, the ink and the strip of metal are not worth anything. Its value lies in the promise—'Bank of England. I promise to pay the Bearer on Demand the sum of One Pound'. You know that you can always change your worthless piece of paper for coins because of this promise.

Likewise, we learn to trust in God, often described in the Bible as our Rock, because for hundreds of years people have trusted his promises and found them to be reliable.

O Lord, whose way is perfect, help us, we pray thee, always to trust in thy goodness; that, walking with thee and following thee in all simplicity, we may possess quiet and contented minds, and may cast all our care on thee, for thou carest for us; for the sake of Jesus Christ our Lord. *Amen.*

Christina G. Rossetti

Benediction No. 56

2 Everyday Things

This is a miscellany of fourteen themes on everyday matters

Animals	*Sport*	*Entertainment*
Music	*For our enjoyment*	*Our heritage*
Reminders	*Something worth saying*	*A listening ear*
Ships and travellers	*In the air*	*Stars and space*
Treasure	*Out of disaster*	

Again, some of the themes lend themselves to the use of additional material. No doubt some reference will be made in the *Animals* theme to the children's own pets. Is there, perhaps, a blind person with a guide dog known to the children? Music (1) might have some reference to the latest 'pop' charts. *Reminders* could begin with a reference to any local statues or memorials.

It might be helpful when music is the subject of the assembly if a work of the composer concerned is played as the children enter the assembly hall or as part of the talk.

Animals (1)

Guide Dogs

Many people like to have a pet around the house, probably a dog or cat, maybe a hamster or a budgie, though some prefer something a little unusual—a hedgehog, a snake, a monkey or a fox.

Pets are kept for a number of reasons. Children like to play with them; old people living alone like them for company; and many people think a house seems empty without a cat or dog.

Some cats earn their keep as mousers. Dogs prove useful as guard dogs, sheep dogs or police dogs. But probably the ones that most combine several purposes, as pets, companions and helpers are the guide dogs used by blind people. [*Attention could be drawn to any that are known to the children.*]

These guide dogs are carefully trained from their earliest days to obey commands. Then follows a long period at a training school, where they become used to wearing the special harness and are trained to stop at kerbs, walk round obstructions, and generally guide the person who is holding the handle on the harness.

The blind people have also to be trained in handling and looking after the dogs and there must be some time allowed for the dogs and their owners to get to know each other.

Then, at last, the blind people with their dogs are able to go home. The dogs will be the 'eyes' of these blind people for a number of years.

Unfortunately there are not enough guide dogs for all blind people, because the training costs a lot of money—several hundred pounds for each dog. Many people send gifts or raise money today so that more guide dogs can be trained.

Father we thank you for those animals and birds which we keep as pets, for the companionships formed and for the pleasure they give. We thank you for those which can work for people and especially the guide dogs for the blind. Help us and all people to be kind and considerate to animals and all your creatures; through Jesus Christ our Lord. *Amen.**

Closing prayer No. 33

Animals (2)

Many people have enjoyed friendships which they have made with animals and birds.

A little over a hundred years ago, a prisoner gazed through his prison window to where the sun gleamed in the clear blue waters of the Mediterranean Sea, caring nothing for the guard who was watching him closely lest he tried to escape. In fact he was showing no signs of escaping and seemed far more interested in the little bird which perched on his window-sill.

Each day he spoke to it, until the bird became very friendly. At last the guards became suspicious. Was he using the bird to send messages to his friends? They moved him to a different cell but the bird found him.

Still believing that the bird was carrying messages, they determined to catch and kill it but the prisoner was rescued by his friends before they could do so.

The prisoner was Giuseppe Mazzini, an Italian patriot, who was anxious to see his country become strong. As a boy he had been studious, fond of reading and very religious. As a man, he founded the 'Young Italy' movement, which aimed at making Italy one country.

Mazzini, however, made many enemies and was forced to spend much of his life in exile but he saw his dream come true in 1861, when Italy became a nation.

Mazzini returned to Italy disguised as a Dr. Brown and, as such, he died on 10th March, 1872, assured of his place in history. The bird that became his friend may still be seen in a museum in Milan.

The Bible tells how the prophet Elijah was once befriended by some birds.

Bible Reading: 1 Kings 17: 1–6

Almighty God, who created the world and all living things, we thank you for the friendship that can be formed between people and animals or birds. We thank you for the pets that share our homes and the wild creatures that come near us. Make us gentle and thoughtful, so that we may treat them kindly and so create happy friendships; for Jesus Christ's sake. *Amen.**

Closing prayer No. 30

Animals (3)

Many people have found comfort and help in a church and so has at least one animal. She was a stray cat, who liked to curl up in a pew in the church of St. Augustine and St. Faith in the shadow of St. Paul's Cathedral.

Try as he would, the verger could not keep her out, and so the Rector decided to let her stay. Often she sat quietly in a pew through a service. Soon she became the Rector's pet and was given the name Faith, after the church in which she lived. She moved into the church house where the Rector lived and there, in the summer of 1940, she gave birth to a black-and-white kitten.

One day in the September, Faith was very restless, wandering up and down, searching here and there. Then she took the kitten in her mouth and carried it down three flights of stairs to put it in a cubby-hole below. Four times the Rector carried the kitten back upstairs and four times Faith carried it down again, so the Rector cleared the cubby-hole to take the cat's basket.

Three nights later, on the night of 9th September, the Rector was away for the night. He returned the next day to find his house a smouldering ruin. The house had received a direct hit from a bomb, and had been blown to pieces and caught fire. Nothing was left.

Yet in the ruin, the Rector could see his little cat, crouching over her kitten, which she had protected through the horrors of that night.

For her courage, Faith was awarded medals by animal societies and was given a home in a safer place, where she lived contentedly to the age of fourteen.

Our Bible reading suggests that it is a good thing to seek protection from God.

Bible Reading: Psalm 121

O God, we know that there are many occasions when it is easier to run away than to remain where our duty lies. Give us courage and special strength when we need it and help us to remember that you are our refuge and strength and will preserve our going out and our coming in from this time forth, and even for evermore. *Amen.**

Benediction No. 50

Animals (4)

Robert Burns

There are many lessons to be learned from the animal world. The writer of the book of Proverbs urged lazy people to learn a lesson from the busy ants.

Bible Reading: Proverbs 6: 6–11

Jesus taught his disciples to learn from the birds which did not spend their lives in worrying as people do and yet found food.

Animals have been the subject of fine paintings or poems. One great poet was inspired to write a poem as he watched a tiny mouse.

The poet was Robert Burns, the great Scottish poet who lived over two hundred years ago and whose birthday, 25th January, 1759 is celebrated every year by Scotsmen all over the world. On that night Burns Night suppers are held at which the poems of Burns are recited. The highlight of the evening is the supper itself, when the haggis is brought in to the sound of the pipes, followed by the reciting of Burns' *Ode to a Haggis.* And what better way to round off an evening than by joining hands and singing *Auld Lang Syne*, the old song which Burns rewrote. Most of his poems are written in the Scottish dialect, which makes the reading of them difficult for those who are not Scots.

The last verse of his poem *To a Mouse* shows something of the uncertainties which he himself found in life.

> *Still thou art blest compared wi' me!*
> *The present only toucheth thee:*
> *But, och! I backward cast my e'e*
> *On prospects drear!*
> *An' forward, tho' I canna see,*
> *I guess an' fear!*

O God our Father, we thank you for the lessons that can be learned from the wild creatures who always appear to be busy about their daily activities and who do not seem to worry about the future. Help us not to waste today but to do all the things that we know must be done and trust you for those things we cannot see or understand, knowing that you care for us; through Jesus Christ our Lord. *Amen.**

Benediction No. 46

Animals (5)

The Last Great Auk

Most people are familiar with penguins, which are to be found in very large numbers in the cold southern part of the world. What is not commonly known is that they were given the name 'penguin' by the people who first saw them because they were similar to a commonly found bird in the northern part of the world, which was then sometimes called a penguin but whose real name was the Great Auk.

At one time, there were thousands upon thousands of these birds in northern Europe, Greenland, Canada, Alaska and northern islands. They were large, fat, flightless birds, pleasant to eat and only too easy to catch when on land. Fishermen looking for food would kill hundreds of them and load them on to their boats.

But the Great Auk only laid one egg a year and many of these were collected because they were tasty. Soon there were very few Great Auks left and they all lived on the island of Eldey, off Iceland. Museums were anxious to have a specimen of a Great Auk and would pay large sums of money for them. The Auks became fewer and fewer. On 4th June, 1844, three Icelandic fishermen went to Eldey. One found and killed a Great Auk: the second found and killed another; the third was unlucky for his companions had killed the last two Great Auks in the world.

Now there are Great Auks in museum showcases but no one will ever see a live one again.

Today there are many other kinds of animals and birds of which very few remain. Some are dying out because of changes in the country where they live; others have been hunted so ruthlessly that few remain.

Many animals are now protected by law or in special parks so that they have a chance of survival. It would be a pity if yet other animals and birds were to die out or be killed off as the Great Auk was.

Almighty God, who filled the world with so much that is beautiful, especially in the animal world; put into the hearts of people everywhere a desire to protect all wild life, so that it may remain to give pleasure to others in the years to come. *Amen.**

Closing prayer No. 20

Sport (1)

The Football Association

When the teams come out onto the green turf of Wembley for the F.A. Cup Final or when international matches are played before thousands of spectators, it is difficult to realize that the game of football began as a game which had no rules and in which anyone could join.

Hundreds of years ago on public holidays, village football matches were held. At each end of the village was a goal and anything which could be kicked served as a ball. Often people were hurt as the mob charged from one end of the village to the other in a match which lasted all day.

Gradually rules were introduced but they varied from place to place. This made it difficult for one team to play another. At Rugby School, for example, a boy once picked up the ball and ran with it—and that is how Rugby football began.

Because of the difficulties caused by differing rules, representatives of some clubs met to form an association of clubs which would all play to the same rules. On 26th October, 1863, the Football Association was formed. Some clubs, like Rugby Football clubs preferred their own brand of football but many agreed to play Association Football, or 'Soccer'. All soccer matches are played according to the rules of the F.A.

So, in life, it is necessary to have rules to live by and the wise people are those who are prepared to play the game of life according to the rules. Jesus once summed up the rules of the Christian life in a very simple way and his words are well worth remembering:

Bible Reading: St. Matthew 22: 35–40

O God, our Father, help us to remember that we cannot live only for ourselves but that we are a part of the community in which we live. Make us ready to live our lives according to the rules, so that we may be recognized as those who live and play fairly. Teach us also to listen to your commands, so that we may live the fuller life as taught by Jesus and press on to the goal with the help of our Captain, Jesus Christ. *Amen.**

Closing prayer No. 28

Sport (2)

Colin Cowdrey and Gary Sobers

As soon as the warm weather comes, cricketers turn out to play on county grounds or village greens. Some play just for the fun of it; others shine as batsmen or bowlers and may earn themselves a place in the England team to play in test matches.

One man, who might be said to have been born a cricketer was Colin Cowdrey. His father was so keen on cricket that he named his son Michael Colin Cowdrey, so that his initials were M.C.C., the same as those of the Marylebone Cricket Club, which governs English cricket.

Colin lived up to expectations. He played exceptionally well as a boy and became the youngest player ever to play at Lords. Later, he captained the Oxford University team. He made a record score in Australia and, in 1959 and again six years later, scored over 2,000 runs. In 1968, he became the first cricketer ever to play in one hundred test matches.

On 30th August, 1967, he was chosen to captain England on the tour of the West Indies. The captain of the West Indies team, Gary Sobers, was also one who had been brought up on cricket as a boy in Barbados. He became not only an expert with a bat but an accurate bowler. Someone once said, 'He is the nearest thing to a one-man cricket team we have ever seen'. He has scored many centuries in test matches and taken well over 100 wickets. In one match, in 1968, he scored 6 sixes in a single over.

Great cricketers such as these are a pleasure to watch as they play a good clean game—and one which has a reputation for fair play. In fact, when something is not as it ought to be, we have a saying that 'it really isn't cricket'.

O God our heavenly Father, help us
To work and play openly and honestly in all we do;
To be fair in our dealings with other people;
To be trustworthy in things both great and small;
To put everything into the things which we undertake.

Then, having been faithful in small things, make us faithful also in greater things; through Jesus Christ our Lord. *Amen.**

Benediction No. 40

Sport (3)

The Four-minute Mile

May 6th, 1954, was a warm, windy day. A little group of men who had met together on a running track at Oxford were pleased that the day was fine, but they wished the wind would drop. It could mean the difference between success and failure.

Their reason for being there was to do something which a few years before would have been considered impossible—to run a mile in less than four minutes. For some years people had been running a mile in just over four minutes—four minutes, eight seconds—four minutes, six seconds—four minutes, two seconds. But the mile in four minutes seemed just out of reach.

On this particular day, Roger Bannister was to make the attempt, paced by two of his friends, Chris Bracher and Chris Chataway. By five o'clock the wind was still blowing but shortly afterwards the flag began to flutter more gently. Bannister decided to try.

The first quarter of a mile was completed in less than a minute; at half a mile it was just under two minutes; but at three-quarters it was just over three minutes. The last lap must be done in 59 seconds. Bannister's feet pounded the track; his pace quickened to leave his friends behind; every ounce of energy was put into those last few yards.

There was cheering as he broke the tape. Then silence. 'Time', said the announcer, 'Three minutes, fifty-nine point four seconds'. But his voice was lost in the roar of applause. Bannister's hours of training had paid off. He was the first four-minute miler.

Here is what St. Paul wrote about an athlete's training and running—a lesson to remember for life itself if we are to make the most of our opportunities.

Bible Reading: 1 Corinthians 9: 24–27

O God our Father, we know that we cannot win every race nor expect to be first in all we do, but we can always do our best. Help us as we train for the race of life, to keep our bodies fit and our minds alert, so that we may give a good account of ourselves and do the very best we can; for Jesus Christ's sake. *Amen.**

Closing prayer No. 22

Sport (4)

Captain Webb

If you can swim, what is your ambition? To swim a length of the baths? To swim a mile? To swim the Channel? There are many people who would like to do that. At its narrowest part, between Dover in England and Cap Gris Nez in France, it is only about twenty-one miles—wide enough to make most people cross it by ship or plane, yet narrow enough to offer a challenge to the strongest.

As long ago as 1875, an American, Paul Boyton, swam from Cap Gris Nez wearing a special life-saving suit and taking nearly twenty-four hours for his crossing.

This, no doubt, inspired Captain Matthew Webb to make the attempt without any life-saving gear. He was a strong swimmer, having learned to swim when he was very young. He had also proved his stamina by swimming in an Atlantic gale to try to find a shipmate who had been washed overboard.

On 24th August, 1875, Captain Webb plunged into the water at Dover: on 25th August, twenty-one hours and forty-five minutes later, he stepped ashore at Cap Gris Nez, the first man to swim the Channel unaided. It is estimated that currents caused him to swim thirty-eight miles to make the twenty-one mile crossing.

Captain Webb had done what people regarded impossible and he became a national hero. Eight years later, he tried the even more difficult feat of swimming the river below the Niagara Falls but he was killed in the attempt.

Since Captain Webb's success over one hundred people have swum the Channel, the fastest taking less than half Webb's time. The challenge of the Channel remains.

Jesus spoke of the challenge of life—a challenge to choose the right way of the two that are open:

Bible Reading: St. Matthew 7: 13–14

O God, our Father, give us courage to face all the challenges of life. May we never be put off by difficulties or fear of failure, nor give in to the temptation to take the easy path. Grant us your help and inspiration so that we may be more than conquerors; after the example of our Lord and Master, Jesus Christ. *Amen.**

Closing prayer No. 13

Sport (5)

Universities Boat Race

Each year, crowds of people gather by the Thames to watch the Universities Boat Race, many of them sporting the dark blue rosettes of Oxford or the light blue of Cambridge.

The boat race was first suggested as long ago as 1829, when the rowers of Cambridge sent a challenge to those of Oxford to race them on the Thames during Easter vacation. In fact the race was held a little later, on 10th June, 1829.

The boats used were very heavy—nothing like the light 'eights' that are used today. The next race was held in 1836 and then at various intervals until 1856, when the race became an annual event. It was in 1845 that the present course from Putney to Mortlake was first used.

Both Universities have had their misfortunes. In 1959 the Cambridge boat sank beneath the crew, who were still rowing when their boat disappeared. In 1951, the Oxford boat sank. In 1877 the race ended in a dead heat.

The time taken for the boat race is very short; the record for the $4\frac{1}{2}$ miles being 17 minutes 50 seconds—but behind that time are months of training, with each crew man making himself as fit as he possibly can. The race takes every ounce of energy that can be found.

Perhaps the greatest reason for success is teamwork. This is a race in which no man can think only of himself. He must train himself so that he is as fit as he possibly can be but has also to train as a member of a team all of whom are pulling together for victory.

So, in life, some of our greatest successes are those which we achieve when we work closely with others as a team.

In the race of life, O Lord, give us wisdom. Help us to learn that we cannot live only for ourselves but that we need to work with and not against others, whether it be at home, at school, at work or at play, and that we have a responsibility to others and to you. Help us to keep our bodies fit and our minds alert so that we may live to your honour and glory. *Amen.**

Closing prayer No. 58

Entertainment (1)

Joseph Grimaldi

Most people like to be entertained from time to time, and in various ways because we are not all made the same. We enjoy some forms of entertainment because we find them exciting and others because they send a chill down our spines: we enjoy some because of the beautiful singing and dancing and we enjoy others because of mystery or magic: we enjoy things which make us laugh and we also enjoy some things which make us cry. You have probably heard someone say, 'That was a lovely film. I did enjoy it. I cried nearly all the way through it.'

Many children enjoy watching a Punch and Judy show—a show which was introduced into England from Europe over three hundred years ago and has remained popular ever since.

Over 150 years ago, one of the most popular forms of entertainment in London was a visit to Sadlers Wells to be entertained by a clown named Grimaldi. We might not think him as funny as people did then because our ideas of what is funny change but he certainly cheered up many people in his day. He died on 31st May, 1837.

Clowns of various kinds are still popular today, with their strange faces, hair which can be made to stand on end, baggy clothes and long shoes. There are also the famous clowns of the films, such as Laurel and Hardy and Charlie Chaplin. And, of course, we have our clowns, comics and comedians of the present day. No doubt we each have our own favourites.

There is much in life that has to be taken seriously and it is a good thing to have people like these who bring fun into our lives.

We thank you, O God
For all the opportunities of enjoying ourselves;
For all who work at entertaining;
For clowns and comedians who make us laugh;
For the sense of humour which you have given us.

Help us in our lives to be the cause of laughter rather than tears; for Jesus Christ's sake. *Amen.**

Benediction No. 46

Entertainment (2)

Dame Margot Fonteyn

Of all forms of entertainment, one of the most graceful and fascinating to watch is the ballet—a performance consisting entirely or almost entirely of dancing, yet having a story to tell. Some well-known ballets are *Swan Lake, The Sleeping Princess, Coppelia* and *Les Sylphides.*

Many little girls have fancied themselves as ballet dancers and have been thrilled to receive a pair of ballet shoes and the chance of ballet lessons. A few, who showed promise have been able to attend schools for ballet run by the famous ballet companies. One such girl, a certain Miss Peggy Hookham, who was born 18th May, 1919, joined the Sadlers Wells school in 1934. Her father was from Yorkshire and her mother was half Irish and half Brazilian. She herself was beautifully built for dancing and was very talented, with a natural response to the music and a determination to put everything she had into her work. For her dancing, she took the name Margot Fonteyn.

In 1939, she took the leading role—that of Aurora in *The Sleeping Princess*—and she never looked back. During the war years, her dancing with Robert Helpmann was responsible for a great rise in popularity of ballet in Britain. When the great ballerina Alicia Markova resigned, Margot Fonteyn became the prima ballerina of Sadlers Wells. She now has a world reputation as the greatest dancer of her time outside Russia. She was made President of the Royal Academy of Dancing in 1954 and, for her services in this kind of entertainment, she was awarded the C.B.E. in 1950 and the D.B.E. in 1956. Her dancing has brought pleasure to many thousands of people.

O God our Father, we thank you
For all that is lovely in music and movement;
For the enjoyment of ballet and all forms of dancing;
For talented dancers who dance for our pleasure.

Help us to appreciate all your blessings and to use such talents as we have to give pleasure to others; for the sake of Jesus Christ our Lord. *Amen.**

Benediction No. 47

Entertainment (3)

William Shakespeare

Had you lived a few hundred years ago, you would probably have had to make most of your own entertainment. You might have had fun on fair days and holidays; you might even have seen a travelling musician or minstrel; you might even have watched a group of Mummers or Strolling Players; but there were no theatres as we know them today to which you could go.

Theatres were built in London in the reign of Queen Elizabeth the First, about the time that a certain William Shakespeare was born in Stratford-on-Avon. Just when he was born we cannot be sure but it was probably St. George's Day, 23rd April, 1564. It was then the custom to christen babies when three days old and we know that John and Mary Shakespeare took him to the parish church on 26th April, 1564, and named him William.

He married at eighteen and went to London three years later. There he mixed with actors himself. However, his fame was not to be as an actor but as a playwright and poet. His plays, which are world famous, are still regularly performed today. They include *A Midsummer Night's Dream, Hamlet, Macbeth, The Merchant of Venice, Twelfth Night* and *Romeo and Juliet,* besides many, such as *Henry V,* which are stories of kings of England.

Shakespeare died on St. George's Day, 1616, at the age of fifty-two. Today a Shakespeare Memorial Theatre stands at Stratford-on-Avon and visitors are shown the house where he lived, but his greatest memorial is in the regular performance of his plays over three-and-a-half centuries after his death.

We thank you, O God, for those who through their lives and works have passed on something of value to those living in later years; we praise you for the wealth of literature, poetry and plays which have come down to us; make us aware of our heritage and teach us to appreciate all that we have: we ask it in Jesus Christ's Name. *Amen.**

Closing prayer No. 32

Entertainment (4)

The First Actress

Nowadays when we go to the theatre, we expect to see people made up to portray as accurately as possible the part which they play.

Sometimes, in comedies, people dress up in various ways to make people laugh. In winter many people enjoy pantomimes in which the 'principal boy' will almost certainly be a glamorous actress, whilst the 'dame' is likely to be a man.

Years ago, all women's parts were acted by men or boys. In the time when Shakespeare was writing his plays, it would have been considered most improper for a woman to act on the stage. Boys, whose voices had not yet broken, were almost always cast in women's roles.

No doubt many people were shocked on 8th December, 1660, when an actress first appeared on the stage in the role of Desdemona. Perhaps they shook their heads and muttered that they wondered what on earth the world was coming to.

But that was the year when King Charles II returned to Britain as King, when strict laws were brushed aside, and when the theatres were opened after having been closed for twenty years.

We do not know the name of this first actress, but there were many others who followed her example until it became the accepted thing for actresses to play women's parts on the stage.

Today is is difficult to imagine the theatre without actresses and we can only think that the theatre in the time of Shakespeare must surely have been the poorer without them.

We thank you, O Lord, for all that is offered for our entertainment and enjoyment; for actors and actresses of stage and screen; for television and radio to bring entertainment into our own homes; for singers and musicians, comedians and clowns, poets and playwrights; for all who give pleasure through their performance; praise be to you, O God. *Amen.**

Benediction No. 52

Entertainment (5)

John Logie Baird

Tonight millions of people will settle down in front of their television sets to be entertained by programmes of many kinds, most transmitted in Britain, but some perhaps relayed from other parts of the world.

Today television plays an important part in the lives of most people, giving entertainment, education, news and many things of interest. Not so long ago it was just a dream in the mind of one Scotsman, John Logie Baird.

He was born on 13th August, 1888 and lived at Helensburgh on the Firth of Clyde. As a young man, he worked at a power station and later in Trinidad. Back in Britain, he settled at Hastings, where he started to make his first television transmitter.

He had very little money and was compelled to use such odds and ends as he could lay hands on—bits and pieces of wood and string, an old biscuit tin, second-hand lenses and waste material. Yet with that he was able to transmit the first television picture from one side of his attic to the other.

Next he earned money demonstrating radio in a London shop and, with his takings, built a much better transmitter. Before long he was sending pictures for several hundred miles and, in 1928, he succeeded in sending a picture across the Atlantic Ocean.

So when next you sit in front of your screen, remember John Logie Baird who made it possible and others who have developed his ideas to give such things as colour television or who work today to bring you your entertainment.

O God our Father, we thank you for all those things which bring us enjoyment:
For books to read and for those who write them;
For music and for those who write or play it;
For radio and for those who prepare the programmes;
For television, the theatre and the cinema;
For work and the pleasures of doing it well;
For all that makes for richness in life;
    All praise be unto you, O Lord. *Amen.**

Benediction No. 49

Music (1)

Music plays an important part in the lives of most people, just as it has for thousands of years. We have already used music in our assembly; during the day we shall hear other kinds of music in our lessons, on the radio or the singing of other people.

Sometimes the music calls our attention to something we may know—the signature tune of our favourite television programme, the chimes of the ice-cream van, the jingle of the advertisement on television, or the music of church bells calling people to worship. Sometimes the music is provided for a particular purpose—a piano accompaniment for singing, a pop group or band for dancing, or for our enjoyment when we have time to relax. Sometimes we like to listen to the music of others: at other times we like to make our own with musical instruments or with our voices.

What kind of music do you like? No doubt there is some that you like and some that you cannot stand. It is equally certain that some people will dislike intensely the kind of music which you enjoy. That is one of the joys of music—there are so many kinds that we are almost certain to find something that we can enjoy. And for those who would like to make music themselves, there are instruments to suit all tastes, from organs to mouth organs and from violins to bongo drums.

In the Bible we are reminded that we can praise God with many kinds of instrument, with singing and with dancing.

Bible Reading: Psalm 150

We praise you, O Lord, as people have done throughout all ages. We thank you for the gift of music and for the ability to sing, for writers of tunes and makers of music, for instruments to play and for the ability to use them. For these and all your gifts, we praise you, God our Father; through Jesus Christ our Lord. *Amen.**

Closing prayer No. 6

Music (2)

Tchaikovsky

If you have ever tried to play the piano, you will know that it is not easy, especially while your hands are small. Some people, however, have learned to play at a very early age. One of them, the Russian composer Peter Tchaikovsky, who was born in 1840, had music lessons at the age of four and could play the piano quite well when he was six.

He became a clerk in the Ministry of Justice but his heart was not in the job. He wanted to spend his life making music and, as he had little money, he gave music lessons to make ends meet. Then in his middle thirties, his fortunes began to change. People began to recognize the greatness of his music and a wealthy widow, who admired his music offered him a yearly income so that he could compose more music without having to worry about money.

Most of his music was written to be played by an orchestra or by an orchestra and soloists—symphonies, concertos, operas and music for dancing. Among his best known works are *The Swan Lake, The Sleeping Princess, The Nutcracker Suite* and the *1812 Overture.*

Tchaikovsky visited many countries in order to perform his music and he was an immediate success.

Unfortunately, at the age of fifty-three, he drank some impure water, caught cholera, and died on 6th November, 1893. Today he is numbered among the great musicians who could hear in their minds the sounds made by many different kinds of instrument and blend them in such a way that the music, when played by all these instruments, gives a great amount of pleasure to those who hear it.

O God, our Heavenly Father, who filled the world with so many good things; we thank you for all that is lovely in music, in art and in literature, and for everything created for man's enjoyment. Make us conscious of all that is beautiful and help us to remember that such good gifts come from you. This we ask for Jesus Christ's sake. *Amen.**

Closing prayer No. 30

Music (2)   51

Music (3)

Richard Wagner

Wilhelm Richard Wagner was born at Leipzig, Germany, on 22nd
May, 1813. As a boy he learned to play the piano but, like many
boys, he was not keen on having to practise. He also took a great
interest in opera, which was hardly surprising, since his two older
sisters were both stage singers.

Wagner tried his hand at writing poems and, when only fourteen,
became very involved in a play which he had written. There were
no less than forty-two characters in it but he managed to kill them
all off before the last act, which could only be written by bringing
the characters back again as ghosts.

Wagner loved listening to other people's music and wondered
whether he could write music himself. Could he, perhaps, write
music for the play which he had written? At last he wrote an overture himself, only to find that people laughed at it when it was
performed because the music was not very good.

He was not put off, however, and tried again. He had to try
to put some feeling into his music. On a journey to London in very
rough seas he remembered an old legend about the Flying Dutchman who, for his sins, was sent to sail the seas for ever. He made
this story into an opera, which became a hit. He was made chief
conductor of the opera house at Dresden and he wrote more
operas.

After many ups and downs, Wagner died at Venice in 1883,
leaving behind many great pieces of music which are still enjoyed
throughout the world today.

We thank you, O God, for all the interesting things in life.
  For music and rhythm;
  For pictures and for plays;
  For wireless and for television;
  For things which make us laugh;
  For things which command our interest;
  For things which widen our knowledge;
    We thank you, O God. *Amen.*

                                                    Dr. William Barclay

Closing prayer No. 35

Music (4)

Henry Purcell

From very early times choirs were formed to sing the praises of God. We read of one in the Old Testament.

Bible Reading: 1 Chronicles 25:5b–7

About three hundred years ago, a well-known choir was that which sang before the King each Sunday in the Chapel Royal. In that choir was a boy named Henry Purcell—a boy whose talent for music was so great that when he was only twelve he was asked to write a special piece of music for the King's birthday.

When he was not singing, Henry played the harpsichord, the organ, and probably the violin and, when his voice broke so that he could no longer sing, he started copying music to be used in Westminster Abbey. Soon he was writing his own music for the church and the theatre. The Abbey organist was so impressed with young Henry that he resigned so that Purcell, then only twenty-one could take over. He played the organ in Westminster Abbey for two coronations and on other special occasions.

Purcell wrote music for the violin and the harpsichord; he composed many sacred songs and anthems; he wrote a number of songs, which are still frequently sung by choirs; and he composed special works for royal occasions. One of his last works was a special anthem for the funeral of Queen Mary II in 1695, the year in which he himself died on 21st November aged only thirty-seven.

Purcell, who is considered by many to be the greatest British composer, had great talent in music and used it very largely in the service of God.

Thank you, Father God
For all that is beautiful in the world around;
For the means of praising you with music and singing;
For all the talents which you have given.
  Help us always
To use all those talents for your glory;
To be ever grateful for all your blessings;
To praise you with our lips and in our lives;
  This we ask for Jesus Christ's sake. *Amen.**

Benediction No. 45

Music (4) 53

Music (5)

Imagine being given the sole right to print music and music paper in England. In no time at all you would be a millionaire because so much is printed.

It was not so about four hundred years ago, and two men who were given the sole right by Queen Elizabeth I had to go to the Queen again to ask if they could have some other money as well because they could not make enough for a living from printing music.

The two men were Thomas Tallis and William Byrd, the joint organists of the Chapel Royal and two of the greatest writers of Church music of their day. In fact two of Tallis's hymn tunes are frequently sung today.

We cannot be very sure about the details of the early life of Thomas Tallis because records were not kept then as they are today. He was probably born in Leicestershire about 1505 and later went to London to be educated in the Chapel Royal or in St. Paul's Cathedral.

In later years, Tallis held an important music post at Waltham Abbey before returning to the Chapel Royal. Queen Mary rewarded him for his music by allowing him the use of a manor house in Kent: Queen Elizabeth, as we have seen, gave him the right to print music and then a sum of money each year. During this time, he wrote not only music for choirs but also for strings, organ and other instruments. His last years were spent at Greenwich, where he died on 23rd November, 1585, having devoted much of his life to making music for the glory of God.

The psalmist of the Old Testament suggests that this is a very good thing to do.

Bible Reading: Psalm 92: 1–5

O God our Father, we bring to you our thanksgiving in word and song, praising you for all your blessings, and praying that we may be worthy of all that you have given us. Help us to show our thankfulness by using in your service the gifts which you have given us; through Jesus Christ our Lord. *Amen**

Benediction No. 43

For our enjoyment (1)

Most people enjoy receiving letters and many watch excitedly for the postman to see if he has anything to deliver.

Imagine living long ago when there was no postman and letters were few and far between. Getting a letter then would have been an important event.

Many of the important books of the New Testament are letters which St. Paul wrote to the churches. No doubt the people were pleased to receive them because they were helped by them and it was pleasant to hear from their great teacher. Here is a section of his letter to the Galatians, in which St. Paul tells how he wrote it himself.

Bible Reading: Galatians 6: 7–11

In those days few people could write and letters could only be sent if a messenger happened to be going in the right direction.

The idea of a postal service as we know it came from Sir Rowland Hill over a hundred years ago. In those days letters were carried by mail coaches and the high cost of the letter had to be paid by the person receiving it. Many poor people were disappointed because they could not pay for their letters. Sir Rowland Hill believed that letters could be carried to any part of the country for one penny, provided that the postage was paid in advance.

On 10th January, 1840, 'Penny Postage' began. Letters now cost more than a penny, but we have to remember that a penny then is about ten pence today, so postage is very cheap.

O Heavenly Father, in these days when we take so much for granted, help us to remember the everyday things which give us pleasure. We thank you especially for the means of getting in touch with friends and relatives throughout the world and for the joy that it brings. Help us also to know the great joy of keeping in touch with you all the days of our lives. *Amen.**

Closing prayer No. 25

For our enjoyment (2)

A GOOD BOOK   *Jules Verne*

Many people find much enjoyment in reading a good book. Today there are so many to choose from that it is not difficult to find one to our liking. It may be one about ordinary everyday things and people, or it may be something that we think could not possibly happen.

One author with a large imagination was Jules Verne, who was born at Nantes, in France, on 8th February, 1828. He went to study law in Paris but soon found himself writing short plays to be performed on the stage.

His great success, however, began when he wrote some strange traveller's tales of wonderful voyages and adventures. People enjoyed them, so he wrote more—stories of things which in his time seemed quite impossible but which do not seem so strange today. *Around the World in Eighty Days, A Journey to the Centre of the Earth, Twenty Thousand Leagues under the Sea* and *From the Earth to the Moon* are some of his best-known stories.

The man who dreamed about travelling in the air, under the sea and in space died in 1905, without seeing any of his dreams come true. Men then were only just learning how to make aeroplanes and submarines, but a journey to the moon was quite unthinkable for over half a century after his death.

Most of Jules Verne's books have been translated into English and are still enjoyed by those who like to read a good adventure story.

Almighty God, we thank you for all the good things which are ours to enjoy:

For tellers of stories and writers of books;

For those who have taught us to read and have provided books for our enjoyment;

For the greatest Book of all, in which we can learn about you.

Help us as we read to grow in knowledge, in wisdom and in love of yourself; for Jesus Christ's sake. *Amen.**

Closing prayer No. 8

For our enjoyment (3)

Franz Josef Haydn

Most people enjoy listening to music of one kind or another. Some like to sing or dance to it; some like to sit and listen to it; some like to play it themselves; and others like to write it.

Perhaps you would like to play an instrument yourself. When he was very small, young Franz Josef Haydn liked to pretend that he was a musician and, when his father sang or his brothers played their instruments, he amused himself by accompanying them on his 'violin'—two pieces of wood, which he pretended were his violin and bow.

When he was six, he became a choirboy in a church in a nearby town; at eight he sang in the cathedral at Vienna.

But young Franz Josef was disappointed. It was all very well teaching him to sing, but he wanted them to teach him to write music as well and this they did not do. So he took every piece of music paper he could and filled the lines with notes. If there were plenty of notes, then he thought it must be good music. He had a lot to learn but he put his mind to learning until he was able to compose some of the finest music.

He also liked his fun. One day he cut off the pigtail of another choirboy. That was the end of Haydn the choirboy: he was thrown out. This spirit of fun comes into one of his pieces of music. It is called the *Surprise Symphony*. After a period of quiet music, there is a sudden loud chord which makes people jump.

Haydn died on 31st May, 1809, leaving many great pieces of music. One well-known one is the hymn tune *Austria*, written by Haydn as a national anthem for his emperor.

Almighty God, we thank you for composers of fine music which gives us pleasure; for players of instruments whose skill can thrill us; and for so many kinds of music that we can all find something to enjoy. For these and all your blessings we praise your Name, O Lord. *Amen.**

Closing prayer No. 32

For our enjoyment (4)

Vasco Nunez de Balboa

Some of our greatest pleasures come with the discovery of something new, though it may have been known to others for a long time.

Christopher Columbus, for example, must have been extremely excited when he discovered America, even though other people, the Indians, knew a good deal about it already for it was their home.

After the time of Columbus, other Spanish ships sailed to the coast of central America and claimed parts of it in the name of the King of Spain. They made some interesting discoveries of cities and gold but a discovery of a different kind was made on 25th September, 1513.

As Vasco Nunez de Balboa, one of these explorers, was speaking to an Indian, he learned of a great land to the south where there was gold and beyond it was a great sea. Could this possibly be the great sea across which lay the spice islands which Columbus had tried to find?

With great excitement, he led his men southward, through marshes, over mountains and through dense forests, often attacked by Indians, until at last his guide led him up a high mountain. Leaving his men a little behind, Balboa went alone, to be the first European to see from America this great sea, which we now know as the Pacific Ocean.

Soon they had run down to the coast, found a couple of canoes and put to sea, the first Europeans to sail there. Balboa himself plunged in, sword in hand, and claimed the sea for Spain.

Father we thank you for the pleasure and the excitement of new discoveries; the discovery of new and interesting things in the world around us; the discovery that we are able to do something for the first time; and the discovery of yourself and your purpose for us. For all that is interesting or exciting, we praise your name O God. *Amen.**

Closing prayer No. 17

For our enjoyment (5)

Felix Mendelssohn Bartholdy

You might hardly think of work as something to be enjoyed. Yet there are few more miserable people than those with no work to do and few happier than those who enjoy their work.

Take, for example, the story of Felix Mendelssohn Bartholdy— better known simply as Mendelssohn, who died on 4th November, 1847.

His life story reads almost like a fairy tale, for he was blessed with greater gifts than most. His family were highly intelligent and big hearted people, who gave young Felix a fine start in life. Moreover he himself was intelligent, handsome and rich. He was able to speak several languages besides reading Latin and Greek.

But it is as a musician that he is chiefly remembered. He began playing the piano as a child and soon wrote music of his own. At fourteen, he wrote his first great symphony.

Mendelssohn loved to travel and some of his music was insipred by the places he visited. Scotland set the mood for *Fingal's Cave*; while Italy inspired his *Italian Symphony*.

Mendelssohn was a keen sportsman, dancer and horseman. He had a very happy life but died when he was only thirty-eight years old.

One reason for Mendelssohn's happy life was the ease with which he got on with others; another was his religion which meant a great deal to him; while yet another was his work. He once said, 'My work is a supreme pleasure'. In these three things lie the roots of successful living.

O God our Father;
Help us to live with others in such a way that they will enjoy our
    company;
Help us to find pleasure in our work so that we may do it well and
    know success;
Help us to know your presence and to find great joy in your service.
    This we ask for Jesus Christ's sake. *Amen.**

Closing prayer No. 5

Our heritage (1)

Edmund Spenser

We have many things to be thankful for, not the least being the books and poems and music which we can enjoy. What kind of poems do you like best? Humorous ones or descriptive ones? There are many different kinds. Perhaps you have a favourite poet whose poems you like very much. And, of course, the poems you like will not necessarily be the same ones that your friends like. Here is one small part of a poem from the Old Testament. You will find it different from the kind of poetry which you read today.

Bible Reading: Psalm 136: 1–9

You may enjoy listening to poetry or reading poetry, but have you tried writing it? If you have, you will realize what a tremendous effort is needed to write even a few lines. We sometimes wonder how a poet can sit and write page after page of verse.

Edmund Spenser, who lived in the time of the first Queen Elizabeth, was not content with a few pages, nor even one book for his great poem the *Fairie Queen*. He intended that there should be twelve volumes of it. In fact, only six had been written when Spenser died.

You would not enjoy his poetry and you would find it difficult to understand, but people of his day were most enthusiastic about his works and he was regarded as one of the greatest English poets, so much so, that after his death on 16th January, 1599, he was buried in Westminster Abbey, where many of our most famous poets are also buried.

At the beginning of this day, O Lord, we offer our thanks for your many blessings. Help us today to be diligent in our studies, careful in our work, and wise in our understanding, so that we may grow to enjoy all the good things which have been handed down to us by others and live profitable lives to the glory of your Name; through Jesus Christ our Lord. *Amen.**

Closing prayer No. 38

Our heritage (2)

MUSIC   *Franz Schubert*

Bible Reading: Psalm 33: 1–5

We often find people praising God for his goodness and we frequently find that music plays a part in their praise. For thousands of years people have enjoyed playing and listening to music; some have given their whole lives to the making of music.

Some years ago, a group of boys waited to see who would be lucky enough to be chosen to fill a vacancy in the royal music school in Vienna. They laughed as the curly-haired boy in spectacles, dressed in a coarse home-made suit walked past them to take his turn. But Franz Peter Schubert had the last laugh. He proved better than any and was offered the place.

It was a wonderful opportunity for him, especially as his parents were poor and had a large family. Often he was short of things he needed but he was never short of good friends who frequently helped him.

At school he played in the orchestra and he composed music himself. At home he played in a musical group with his family and friends.

Before long his works were being performed. Songs he wrote easily: music was a little more difficult as he had never been taught to write it. He wrote many songs, some short pieces of music, and some great symphonies. One, the *Unfinished Symphony* he put aside and never completed.

Schubert became ill and died on 19th November, 1828, when he was only thirty-one. In cash he left about £2.50 but he also left over 1,000 musical compositions which have made the world a much richer place.

There are many forms of riches which are more important than money.

Help us, O Lord, to make the world a better place because we have lived in it. Show us some way of helping other people and thus make their lives a little brighter. Help us to be cheerful, pleasant and easy to get on with. Show us how to use our talents and all our possessions unselfishly. So may we be true servants of yours today and all our days. *Amen.**

Closing prayer No. 12

Our heritage (3)

Richard Trevithick

In days when we take railways and complicated machinery for granted, and when we think more about jet engines, space travel, electronics and computers, it is difficult to imagine what it was like when these things did not exist. A century and a half ago, people were only just beginning to think about railways and we owe a great deal to these early pioneers of steam and transport.

One of these, Richard Trevithick, was born on 13th April, 1771 in Cornwall, where his father was an engineer in the mines. When Richard was about twenty-six, he took his father's place.

As an engineer, he was always looking for something better than the equipment he had already. He thought about the pumps which were being used and believed he could make a better one. So he set his hand to it and proved successful.

Then he had other thoughts. If steam could drive a machine which stood still, why not use it to drive a machine which would move along? He invented a locomotive which could pull carriages of people along the streets but it proved too costly to run.

He next invented a locomotive which could run on a tramway or railway. In 1808, he built a circular railway at Euston, in London, on which passengers were carried at the amazing speed of twelve or fifteen miles per hour.

Like many another inventor, he never received during his lifetime the recognition he deserved for his work, but we can look back now and say thank you for people such as Trevithick, whose ideas helped to develop the great machines which we know today.

We thank you, O Lord, for all the advantages of our present time, which so often we take for granted. We praise you for all the inventions of engineering and of other branches of science which are now a part of our way of life. Make us ready to count our blessings and to be thankful for these and all your gifts; for Jesus Christ's sake. *Amen.**

Closing prayer No. 26

Our heritage (4)

April 19th is still occasionally known as Primrose Day by members of the Conservative Party and their supporters, a reminder of a great leader of that party. He was Benjamin Disraeli, later known as the Earl of Beaconsfield.

Disraeli first entered Parliament in 1837, the year in which Queen Victoria ascended the throne. From the very beginning he caused a stir. When he stood to make his first speech, Members of Parliament laughed at him.

'Though I sit down now,' he declared, 'the time will come when you will hear me.'

And he was right. For many years, people in and out of Parliament, including the Queen herself, took notice of what Disraeli said. In 1868, he became Prime Minister: in 1876 he was made Earl of Beaconsfield. On 19th April, 1881, he died and Queen Victoria sent a wreath of primroses with a card on which she wrote 'His favourite flower' (meaning the favourite flower of her late husband, Prince Albert).

People who read the card thought it meant that primroses were Disraeli's favourite flower and so, on the anniversary of his death, those who admired him wore primroses in his memory.

Disraeli is especially remembered because he was Prime Minister at an important stage in history when Britain's influence was spreading in the world and when people all over the world regarded this country as Great Britain.

As a nation we still have much for which to be thankful but perhaps we need to remember these words from the Bible and pay more attention to God's teachings:

Bible Reading: Deuteronomy 4: 5–9

Almighty God, we praise and thank you for our native land and for all who have worked to make it great and free. Help us today to be unselfish and work for the common good so that our land may hold a respected position among the nations of the world. As you have blessed our people in past days, so bless us today, and to you be honour and glory for ever and ever. *Amen.**

Closing prayer No. 29

Our heritage (5)

St. Mark

April 25th is the day on which the Christian Church remembers St. Mark, who achieved fame as the writer of that account of the Gospel which bears his name.

Most of our information about him is found in the Bible. He was the son of a lady named Mary, who owned a house in Jerusalem, which became one of the meeting places for the disciples of Jesus. He was not, as some people mistakenly think, one of the twelve apostles, but there is no doubt that he knew them very well.

The Gospel story which he wrote is so clear that it would appear to be written by an eye witness of the events. Most people believe that St. Mark wrote down the stories that were told him by Peter and there is good reason for believing this.

At the same time, Mark undoubtedly saw and heard much for himself. He is believed to have been the young man who was seized by the soldiers in the Garden of Gethsemane but wriggled out of his cloak and ran home naked.

He also knew Paul well and accompanied him on his first journey but left to return to Jerusalem. Later, Paul wrote of him in his letters. Traditions tell that Mark became a bishop in Alexandria and was put to death but of this we cannot be sure.

Of one thing we can be sure. We owe a great deal of gratitude to St. Mark, who gave us such a clear picture of what Jesus said and did. Here is a small section of his book:

Bible Reading: St. Mark 3: 7–12 (or 19)

We should give thanks for all who gave us our Bible so that we can know God's ways.

O Lord our God, we praise and thank you for those who recorded the words and deeds of Jesus and so gave us the Gospel story. May we never forget your word but try to understand what the Bible can tell us today. Help us to heed all your words, so that we may follow in the footsteps of Jesus and ever walk in your holy ways; through Jesus Christ our Lord. *Amen.**

Closing prayer No. 20

Reminders (1)

HE DID HIS DUTY   *Lord Nelson*

Most cities and towns, and even some villages, have their memorials to famous men, to serve as a reminder of all that they did for their fellows.

Some, who have done much for their country are honoured in many places. There are monuments to Nelson, for example, in many places, though none so grand as Nelson's column and Trafalgar Square, in London. This was planned in memory of one who had given a great deal, even his life, to keep Britain free from the French Emperor Napoleon.

Nelson fought in several battles, the greatest being the Battle of Trafalgar on 21st October, 1805. The combined French and Spanish fleets numbered thirty-four ships: Nelson had twenty-seven.

Nelson ordered his famous signal to be hoisted—*England expects that every man will do his duty*. It was a fierce, bloody battle with both sides firing broadsides at close quarters and hand-to-hand fighting on the decks. As he stood on the deck of the *Victory*, Nelson was struck by a sniper's bullet and mortally wounded. He was carried below, where, after some time, he died. Nelson's last words were 'Thank God I have done my duty'.

On 9th January, 1806, his funeral took place and his body was laid to rest among the great and the famous in the crypt of St. Paul's Cathedral. The building of Trafalgar Square was only one of many ways which people found in which to honour their hero, who had died as he did his duty.

Help us, O God, to recognize our responsibilities and to do our duty. Help us to remember that we cannot please ourselves in everything we do, for we have duties toward our family, our friends, our neighbours, our school, and to you. Above all, teach us that we have a responsibility toward ourselves, to make our lives all that they can be and ought to be for the benefit of ourselves, the happiness of others and the glory of your Name; through Jesus Christ our Lord. *Amen.**

Closing prayer No. 9

Reminders (2)

Reminders (1)

HE ENCOURAGED OTHERS   *Rev. George Walker*

High above the city of Londonderry, in Northern Ireland, stands a huge column on top of which is a statue of Rev. George Walker, who gained fame for himself when the city was besieged in 1689.

In the previous year, James II had been exiled from Britain and took refuge in France. From there he thought to regain his crown by invading first Ireland, then Scotland and ultimately England.

Those who were faithful to the cause of the new English King, William III, fled to the north of Ireland and took refuge in the towns of Enniskillen and Londonderry.

James II marched to Londonderry with his armies, expecting to be allowed in by the governor, who was prepared to open the gates. The people, however, had other ideas and the governor was forced to flee. Then, encouraged by the Reverend George Walker, the citizens of Londonderry defied the King.

On 20th April, 1689, the King's armies surrounded the city, placed a barrier across the river, and vowed to starve the people of Londonderry into surrender. How the citizens held out it is difficult to tell. The walls were not very strong; the supplies of ammunition were low; and the people were soon starving.

The city was relieved at last on 30th July, after several thousand had died. The others had only made their heroic stand because of the continual encouragement of George Walker.

This story from the Old Testament tells of a siege and how Elisha encouraged the people.

Bible Reading: 2 Kings 6: 24–5 and 7, 1–2

O Lord our God, you know how often we find ourselves surrounded by the forces of evil that are set against us. Encourage us, we pray, through the words and example of your faithful servants, so that we may fight our battles bravely and live our lives courageously; in the Name and for the sake of Jesus Christ our Lord. *Amen.**

Benediction No. 42

Reminders (3)

                          Hans Christian Andersen

One thing that most visitors to Copenhagen wish to see is the statue of the Little Mermaid. Another is the actual memorial to Hans Christian Andersen, one of the greatest tellers of tales and one of the best loved.

Many people are surprised to learn that Andersen not only wrote fairy tales but was also a novelist, playwright and poet.

Andersen, who was born in 1805, once said 'life is the most wonderful fairy tale of all' and for him this was really true. His father was a shoemaker with very little money, but he was also a dreamer and told young Hans many stories. His mother, a washerwoman, was very superstitious but she gave Hans much of the Danish folk-lore that he later wove into his stories.

It was just as well that Hans Andersen learned as a boy how to make a little money go a long way, for once he took to writing there were times when he was poor and very hungry.

Hans Anderson was a big awkward man, but a very loveable one. Many of his stories are like parables with hidden meanings. Often they reflect something of the life of Andersen himself. He was probably thinking of himself, for example, in the story of *The Ugly Duckling*.

Andersen died on 28th July, 1875, leaving behind him a large number of fairy tales, which are enjoyed today not only in his native Denmark but by children of many lands, who have the stories translated into their own language.

O God our Father, we thank you for tellers of tales and writers of books, who have given us so much that we can enjoy. We thank you for the enjoyment of reading a good book. Help us to improve our reading so that we may enjoy even more; for Jesus Christ's sake. *Amen.**

Closing prayer No. 17

Reminders (4)

The Pilgrim Fathers

Bible Reading: 1 Chronicles 16: 23–31

From the earliest times people have wanted to worship God and, because people are different, they have found different ways in which to worship. Today we find many kinds of church and people choose the one which they prefer. Many people would resent being told that they must worship in a particular way.

Outside the city wall of Southampton, overlooking the river, is a monument to some people who sailed from Southampton on 5th August, 1620, to find a new home where they could worship as they pleased. They were known as the Pilgrim Fathers and their ship was the *Mayflower*. They had with them a smaller ship, the *Speedwell*, but this began to leak and had to be left at Plymouth. After a stormy and most uncomfortable voyage, they arrived in America on 16th December.

One of their leaders, William Bradford, wrote in his diary:

'Being thus arrived in a good harbour and brought safe to land, they fell upon their knees and blessed the God of Heaven, who had brought them over the vast and furious ocean, and delivered them from all the perils and miseries thereof . . .'

Before them lay the difficulties of making a new home in a barren land in the depths of winter, but it was a free land, where they could worship as they pleased and it was for this reason that they had travelled so far. Moreover, they had great faith that God would care for them in this new land.

Few people may have seen the memorial at Southampton, but millions have read of their brave adventure in the pages of history.

Almighty God, who in your wisdom gave us freedom of thought and action, guide our thoughts so that we may decide what are the right things to do in life. Then, when we have decided, give us courage to remain true to ourselves and to you, to whom be all praise and glory, world without end. *Amen.**

Closing prayer No. 18

Reminders (5)

Some of the finest buildings are those which have been built for the glory of God—cathedrals, temples and other places of worship. This Bible reading tells how David instructed Solomon to build a temple at Jerusalem.

Bible Reading: 1 Chronicles 22: 11–16

Christopher Wren was also commissioned to build a house of God. Originally it had been to improve the old St. Paul's Cathedral in London, but this was burned down in the Great Fire of London. Now Wren could plan an entirely new cathedral.

Day by day he watched it grow as stone masons, artists, wood-carvers and carpenters all put their skill into the building of this great cathedral. The last stone was laid some thirty-five years after the building had begun.

Meanwhile, Wren had designed no less than fifty other churches in the City of London, beside hospitals and other great buildings.

But St. Paul's was his masterpiece and he made frequent visits to it from his home at Hampton Court. It was after one of these visits, at the age of 91, that he died on 25th February, 1723.

Where better to be buried than in the crypt of St. Paul's! Many a famous man has been buried here and memorials have been placed there to others—Nelson, Wellington and Scott, to name but a few.

But none has a greater memorial than Wren, for the words in Latin over his grave, are translated *Reader, if you seek a monument, look about you.*

O God, we thank you for everything of beauty which has been created by those with skill in art or craft. We remember that many have used their skill for your glory and we humbly pray that we may dedicate such gifts as we possess to your service for Jesus Christ's sake. *Amen.**

Closing prayer No. 34

Reminders (5)   69

Something worth saying (1)

Samuel Plimsoll

There are times when people feel so strongly about something that nothing will keep them quiet. Sometimes there is anger in the tone of the speaker. We read what Jesus said when he went into the temple.

Bible Reading: St. Mark 11: 15–18

Samuel Plimsoll was angry when he rose to his feet in the House of Commons on 22nd July, 1875. 'Villains!' he shouted at the other Members of Parliament. Then he shook his fist at the Speaker before being ordered from the House of Commons until he had apologized.

The reason for his anger was that the Members of Parliament had just voted against something for which he had been working for a long time. Plimsoll was very unhappy about the conditions under which many sailors had to go to sea. Some ships then were known as 'coffin ships'. They were not fit to put to sea and would almost certainly sink in bad weather. The risk was increased because they were overloaded and their cargoes badly stowed.

The owners of these ships did not mind. The ships were insured for large sums of money. If the sailors went down with them, that was just too bad. Plimsoll was determined to put a stop to this.

When people heard that he had been angry, many felt that he had good reason to be. In the following year he was successful. Ships had to be inspected for seaworthiness and have a load-line painted on the side to prevent overloading.

Next time you see a load-line on a ship, remember it is a sign of victory for all that Plimsoll fought for.

We thank you, O Lord our God
For those who sail the seas to bring us things we need;
For all whose work has made life at sea much pleasanter;
For all who are concerned with the safety of sailors.

Bless the men of the merchant navy and fishing fleets and bring them in safety through stormy seas to enjoy the rewards of their labours; through Jesus Christ our Lord. *Amen.**

Closing prayer No. 19

Something worth saying (2)

St. Hugh of Lincoln

It is not easy to speak out to someone with great power such as a king, but there are times when it must be done, as Elijah knew.

Bible Readings: 1 Kings 18: 7–8 and 16–18

Many years later, in the reign of King Henry II, there lived a monk named Hugh of Avalon, who had a reputation for fair play and was particularly capable when dealing with awkward people. Hugh knew his responsibilities and was not afraid to speak his mind even to the King.

Henry II liked this outspoken monk, who had refused to take charge of a monastery in Somerset until the last penny had been paid to those who lost land when the monastery was built. Later, Hugh left the monastery to become Bishop of Lincoln, where he began building the cathedral which still graces the city today.

On one occasion, Hugh supported the common people against one of the King's cruel foresters. The King at once sent for him, then pretended to ignore him. Instead he began to sew a torn glove. After a brief silence, Hugh remarked, 'Just like your relatives in France!'

The King could have been very angry at this reference to his humble French relatives on his grandmother's side of the family, but he could not be angry with Hugh. The quarrel was over.

Hugh, loved by rich and poor alike, died in London late on 16th November, 1200, and he was buried in Lincoln Cathedral.

Today, O God, make me
Brave enough to face the things of which I am afraid;
Strong enough to overcome the temptations which try to make me do
   the wrong thing and not to do the right thing;
Persevering enough to finish every task that is given me to do;
Kind enough always to be ready to help others;
Obedient enough to obey your voice, whenever you speak to me
   through my conscience.
Help me to live in purity; to speak in truth; to act in love; all
   through today. This I ask for Jesus' sake. *Amen.*

                                          Dr. William Barclay

Closing prayer No. 24

Something worth saying (3)

SPEAKING PERSUASIVELY   *W. E. Gladstone*

The highest position to which one can rise in Britain is that of Prime Minister, the person with the great responsibility of leading the government of the country and making very important decisions.

Some Members of Parliament never hope to be Prime Minister because it is such a responsible job. Some find the responsibility so great that one term of office is enough. Yet, on 18th August, 1892, William Ewart Gladstone, a great statesman of last century, became Prime Minister for the fourth time. And, strange though it may seem, as a young man, Gladstone had no particular wish to enter Parliament at all. He wanted to become a clergyman. It was his father's wish that he should enter Parliament and he agreed to do so to please his father.

In Parliament, there were some who held the same views as he did and there were others who disagreed with him but they all recognized that Gladstone was a great speaker, who was able to persuade many by the words he used and the way he used them. He also had a personality which was admired by those on both sides of the House of Commons.

For his last few years, Gladstone was affectionately known as the Grand Old Man and when he died, at the age of eighty-eight, he was buried in Westminster Abbey.

In the Acts of the Apostles, we read of another great speaker who was able to persuade others with his sensible speaking. He was a Pharisee named Gamaliel, whose wise words calmed down some angry Pharisees:

Bible Reading: Acts 5: 34–40

O God, Almighty Father, King of Kings and Lord of Lords, grant that the hearts and minds of all who go out as leaders before us, the statesmen, the judges, the men of learning and the men of wealth, may be so filled with the love of thy laws, and of that which is righteous and life-giving that they may be worthy stewards of thy good and perfect gifts, through Jesus Christ our Lord. *Amen.*

Knights of the Garter (14th Century)

Closing prayer No. 2

Something worth saying (4)

St. John Chrysostom

Bible Reading: St. Mark 4: 30–34

When Jesus taught the people about God, he often did so by a parable. They could follow better the things which he had to say by listening to a story. Jesus was never without hearers, for many loved to listen to him.

Nearly four hundred years later, a Christian by the name of John also tried to teach people about God. He, too, knew that it was no use teaching unless the people could understand him. So he spoke in such a way that those who listened, mostly very ordinary people, could understand.

In Antioch, his fame as a preacher spread abroad, so much that he was known as John Chrysostom, which means John 'Golden-mouth'. The crowds who came to hear him were so great, and the people so carried away by his words, that he had to warn his listeners to leave their purses at home. Pickpockets were finding it all too easy to take the purses as the people listened.

After twelve years in Antioch, John Chrysostom was made Bishop of Constantinople. Unfortunately, there were those who did not like the things he said. Perhaps it was not very tactful to speak against the Emperor's wife, but John said what he thought ought to be said. As a result of this and because of words he spoke against other important people, he was sent into exile, where he died.

Each year, on 27th January, the Christian Church honours St. John Chrysostom, the learned and skilful speaker, who was not afraid to say what he thought.

A prayer of St. John Chrysostom:

Almighty God, who hast given us grace at this time with one accord to make our common supplications unto thee; and dost promise that when two or three are gathered together in thy Name, thou wilt grant their requests: fulfil now, O Lord, the desires and petitions of thy servants, as may be most expedient for them; grant-ing us in this world knowledge of thy truth, and in the world to come life everlasting. *Amen.*

Closing prayer No. 11

Something worth saying (5)

John Wyclif

Bible Reading: St. Luke 4: 16–21

In this passage from the Bible, Jesus makes it clear that one of his important tasks was to preach the Gospel, or to tell all people the good news about God.

The Christian Church has always believed in preaching. The last command Jesus gave his disciples was to go into all the world and preach the Gospel. This was especially important for people who were unable to read things for themselves.

A few hundred years ago in England, the only Bibles were written in Latin and church services were held in Latin. People could 'see' the stories in wall paintings and stained glass and have them explained by the priest but John Wyclif believed that people should be able to hear and understand the actual words of the Bible. With the help of a friend, Nicholas of Hereford, he began to translate the Bible into English. Then he gathered together a group of preachers, known as Lollards, who would tell the Bible stories to ordinary folk, wherever they might be. Each preacher made his own copy of Wyclif's translation.

Soon Wyclif was in trouble. He had enemies who did not want his work to continue. Many of his preachers were put to death as was his friend Nicholas of Hereford. But Wyclif was more fortunate and was allowed to live quietly in the village of Lutterworth until he died on 31st December, 1384.

Wyclif had started something. People who listened to his preachers wanted Bibles they could read. Nowadays, when most people have Bibles of their own, preachers still have the important job of helping them to understand what they are reading.

Almighty God, our Heavenly Father, who hast shown us thyself through the Holy Scriptures; help us to read, to learn, to understand and to accept the guidance of others, that we may become true children of our Father in heaven; through Jesus Christ our Lord. *Amen.**

Closing prayer No. 38

A listening ear (1)

THE BLESSINGS OF HEARING   *Ludwig van Beethoven*

In the Bible we read how, after a busy time, Jesus went away to be quiet with God.

Bible Reading: St. Mark 1: 32–36

It is pleasant sometimes to forget the noise of everyday and to spend a while in silence. But even as we do so, we realize that it is not completely silent. We hear the ticking of a clock, footsteps on the path outside or the song of a bird. [Listen now (about 15 seconds) What did you hear?]

Often the silence is broken by pleasant sounds like music or the voice of someone we know. Silence makes a pleasant change from noise but few people would choose to live in complete silence without ever hearing a sound. Yet that is what it is like for a person who is completely deaf.

It is even more tragic when the person who is deaf is one for whom sounds have meant a great deal, and particularly a great musician, whose music has charmed the ear of millions of people. Such a one was Ludwig van Beethoven, who became so deaf that he never heard some of the great music which he composed.

Beethoven, who was born in Bonn, Germany, came from a musical family. When he was twenty-two he went to Vienna to study and there he spent most of his remaining days, playing, teaching and composing music. He watched his music being played but could not hear a note. He could, however, tell what it sounded like by looking at the music, just as you know the sounds of words you read in a book without having to hear them spoken. Beethoven died in Vienna on 26th March, 1827.

Father we thank you for the gift of hearing and for all the pleasant sounds of life; for the voices of family and friends; for the many sounds in the world of nature; for music, singing and everyday sounds. We pray for those who cannot hear and ask that we, who are blessed with hearing, may have patience with those who are not; for Jesus Christ's sake. *Amen.**

Closing prayer No. 25

A listening ear (2)

On the evening of 14th November, 1922, an announcer spoke into a microphone:

'Hallo! Hallo! . . . 2LO calling . . . 2LO calling
. . . This is the British Broadcasting Company . . .
2LO . . . Stand by for one minute please . . .'

This was the first regular broadcast of the British Broadcasting Company (later to be the British Broadcasting Corporation) and people in many places listened to the broadcast on their simple receiving sets.

Many of these sets were home-made. They consisted of a cardboard cylinder with wire round it. On one end of the wire was a piece of mineral, known as the 'crystal': on the other, a thin piece of wire, known as the 'cat's whisker', rested on the crystal. An old tobacco tin for a tuning condenser, a piece of wire for an aerial and another for an earth, and a pair of head-phones completed the set. Everytime the cat's whisker moved the programme was lost. The reception was poor, but how exciting it was to hear someone miles away.

What a long way we have come since then. Think what an important part broadcasting plays in our lives. We now have perfect transmissions and accurate receivers, some of which are small enough to carry in our pockets. The sounds are all around us. To get a good reception, all we have to do is ensure that we are tuned in correctly on the right wave band to the right station.

God is also ever present. To be in touch with him we also have to tune in. Listen to the words of Isaiah.

Bible Reading: Isaiah 55: 6–8

Isaiah was not suggesting that people should only call on God when in trouble as so many people do, but rather to keep in touch with him always.

O Lord our God, we thank you for this opportunity to meet in your presence. We know that you are waiting to speak to us and that you are always there, but we often fail to receive the message. Teach us how to tune in to you so that we may know your will; then help us to do it; for Jesus Christ's sake. *Amen.**

Closing prayer No. 8

A listening ear (3)

Harriet Beecher Stowe

It is one thing to listen—quite another thing to do something about what we hear.

Bible Reading: James 1: 22–25

Over a hundred years ago, the southern states of the United States of America were slave states, in which thousands of negroes were forced to work long hours on the plantations and were brutally treated. Families were split up, slave children were sold and men were often beaten until they died.

In the northern part of the U.S.A. people heard about this cruelty and thought it should be stopped. On 14th June, 1812, Harriet Beecher was born among those who hated slavery.

But it was after she married and went to live in Ohio that Mrs. Harriet Beecher Stowe saw at first hand some of the cruelties of slavery. Ohio was a free state but neighbouring Kentucky was a slave state. Mrs. Stowe heard horrifying stories from slaves who had escaped.

What could she do? One day, whilst sitting in church, she felt that she must write about slavery. The result was *Uncle Tom's Cabin*, first published as a weekly serial, then as a book which has been translated into more than twenty languages.

It was a book which brought the evils of slavery to the notice of many people so that they too realized that something must be done to stop it.

Mrs. Stowe would take no credit for writing it. 'I the author of *Uncle Tom's Cabin*?' she would say. 'No, the Lord himself wrote it. To him alone be the praise.'

But when, in 1865, all slaves were freed by law, many realized how much was owed to Mrs. Harriet Beecher Stowe, who heard and saw, then did something about it.

Almighty God, who through the years often used your servants to fight evil wherever it appeared; help us to shun evil and do good, to fight against all that causes distress, and to seek always to do your will. This we ask in the Name of him who taught us to love our neighbours as ourselves, Jesus Christ our Lord. *Amen.**

Closing prayer No. 16

A listening ear (4)

LISTENING TO GOD   *Leslie Thexton*

Bible Reading: 1 Samuel 3: 1–10

This story tells how the boy Samuel heard God speaking to him. God speaks to people in different ways but sometimes just as clearly as he did to Samuel.

One day in 1927, Leslie Thexton was walking home from the station after a busy day in London, thinking of nothing in particular. Suddenly it seemed as though a voice spoke to him, 'Leslie, you are wanted to become a missionary'. It was so real that he turned to see who was speaking to him but no one was there.

He had never thought of being a missionary and he did not want to think of it then. He had just qualified as a cutter in the family tailoring business and had a good career in front of him. So he went home and told no one about it.

About four months later, exactly the same thing happened. This time he was so disturbed that he spoke to his minister about it. He was told that the only way of testing whether this was God speaking to him was to put it to the test and offer to be a missionary. This meant training as a Methodist Local Preacher and then attending college to become a minister. The thought terrified him but he did it. In 1936 he went to China as a missionary and remained there until 1949 when all missionaries were forced to leave. Back in England, he found other work to be done as a minister in the Methodist Church.

Some years later he wrote, 'I still cannot understand the "why" or the "how" of it but shall always be glad and grateful for all that has followed from it'.

O God our Father, we never know how you will speak to us but we do know that you are able to speak to people in many different ways so that they know what you want them to do. Help us always to listen for what you have to say to us: then make us bold to do your will; in the Name of Jesus Christ our Lord. *Amen.**

Closing prayer No. 25

A listening ear (5)

Wilfred Grenfell

Bible Reading: Amos 7: 12–15

Amos did not think of himself as a prophet. He was a humble herdsman until God called him.

Similarly, Wilfred Grenfell, who was born on 28th February, 1867, never saw himself as a missionary. He was always ready for adventure. He loved the sea and was never more thrilled than when he sailed a small boat in a high wind. But he had little time for religion until he suddenly realized that God wanted him. It happened like this.

As a medical student at London Hospital, he was attracted one night to a large tent in which a religious meeting was being held. He went out of curiosity. Something that night made him think. The next night he went again and pledged himself to be a follower of Jesus Christ.

When his examinations were finished, Grenfell learned that a young doctor was needed by the Mission to Deep Sea Fishermen to work in the North Sea. He offered his services. Here was a chance to be a doctor at sea *and* a missionary for Jesus Christ.

Three years later, he left for the great fishing grounds off the coast of Labrador. He helped the fishermen at sea; he worked amongst the Eskimos; he found adventure in icy waters and on sledge journeys across the snow.

In 1906 he built a children's home and, in 1927 a fine hospital. Grenfell died in 1940 but he will long be remembered in Labrador, where he served God and his fellows faithfully for half a century.

We remember before you, O Lord, all who sail the seas and do business across the waters. Keep them from the dangers of the sea and bring them to a safe harbour. Bless the work of the Mission to Deep Sea Fishermen, the Missions to Seamen and all who minister to seafarers, that their work may prosper in the service that is offered in your Name; through Christ our Lord. *Amen.**

Benediction No. 48

Ships and travellers (1)

The Queen Liners

The rain fell in torrents on 26th September, 1934, but about 200,000 people turned out to welcome King George V and Queen Mary to Clydebank.

This was the day they had awaited for several years. Early in 1931, they had begun building the giant luxury liner, which they knew as No. 534. But times were difficult and there was little money about. At the end of 1931 the work had stopped. For twenty-eight months the great ship lay still. The noise of the riveters was hushed. At last work began again and the exciting moment arrived when No. 534 was to be launched. Many tried to guess what she would be called.

The King and Queen mounted the platform and the Queen named the ship—*Queen Mary*. A thunderous roar rose from the crowd as the giant liner—the largest in the world at that time—slid slowly into the water.

Four years later, almost to the day, on 27th September, 1938, the other giant, *Queen Elizabeth* was launched from the same yard.

Another nineteen years passed and 20th September 1967 marked the launching of the new Cunard super liner, *Queen Elizabeth 2*, just as the *Queen Mary* was making her last Atlantic voyage to New York. The grand old ship was 'retiring' after $31\frac{1}{2}$ years' service. Once the *Queen Mary* was the last word in ships but times and fashions change.

The Bible reminds us that although other things may change, God always remains the same.

Bible Reading: Psalm 102: 24–27

Almighty God, we praise you because you are always the same and through the years you have helped those who have called upon you. We know that you do not change with the passing years and we pray that you will help us just as you have helped people of the past. Help us to know you, to trust you and to depend upon you for all our needs; for Jesus Christ's sake. *Amen.**

Benediction No. 45

Ships and travellers (2)

Virginia Settlers

The disciples of Jesus were only sailing across the Sea of Galilee but even there they found trouble.

Bible Reading: St. Mark 4: 35–41

Most people try to find a ship that will stand up to any storms it may come across. If you were sailing to America, you might choose to travel on a luxury liner, or at least one which seemed large enough to battle with stormy seas.

If you had lived a few hundred years ago, you would have had very little choice. There were no large ships. When, on 19th December, 1606, over a hundred people set sail for America, they did so on three tiny ships, the *Susan Constant* (100 tons), the *Godspeed* (40 tons) and the *Discovery* (20 tons), no bigger than small fishing boats that we may see on holiday. They were setting out to form the first British colony in America, which was to be called Virginia.

They were brave people to set out in ships of that size to face the mighty Atlantic Ocean, and how often they wished they had never sailed we shall never know. For about six weeks they were held up by bad weather in the English Channel, then came the long Atlantic crossing, and a terrible storm in which the little ships lost touch with each other.

Then when the voyagers did land in America, they faced a storm of arrows from Indians who did not wish to have strangers in their land.

They landed and formed their colony because they were people with stout hearts, plenty of courage and a belief that God would be their helper.

O God our Father, as we set out on life's adventure, give us courage to face the unknown future. In the storms of life, help us to remember how Christ stilled the storm and gave peace to his disciples. Give us faith to believe that you can help and strengthen us too, and grant us your peace; through Jesus Christ our Lord. *Amen.**

Benediction No. 48

Ships and travellers (3)

Captain Phillip

Most people make journeys across the sea because they want to but, about two hundred years ago, some people embarked on a voyage that was to make history and they had no wish to go.

They were convicts—people who had been put in prison for what we would consider today to be minor offences—but because the prisons were so full, they were being sent on a voyage half-way round the world to Australia, which had been claimed for Britain by Captain Cook a few years earlier.

Captain Phillip was chosen to command the eleven ships which sailed in May 1787, carrying 750 prisoners, with soldiers to guard them, to the great island of Australia in which no white man lived.

Nine months later, on 26th January, 1788, the ships dropped anchor in Sydney Cove, which became the new home of 1,030 men, women and children, 7 horses, 7 cows and bulls, 29 sheep, 74 pigs, 4 goats and 5 rabbits.

The difficulties of starting the new colony were many but Captain Phillip wrote, 'I do not doubt but that this country will prove the most valuable acquisition that Great Britain ever made.'

Times have changed. Instead of 29 sheep, Australia has over 150 million; instead of 7 cattle there are 17 million. No longer is it a British colony with a thousand people, most of them convicts, but a great free nation of millions of people from many countries, many of whom have chosen it as their home and all of whom look upon 26th January as the anniversary of the founding of their country.

Almighty God, we praise you for the knowledge that little things can often accomplish a great deal. As we remember how great nations have come into being because a few people faced incredible hardships and unexpected dangers, we remember also how your kingdom on earth has grown and praise you for all who have worked to make it possible. Accept our service, humble as it may be and use it for the benefit of future generations and the glory of your Name. *Amen.**

Closing prayer No. 14

Ships and travellers (4)

BENEATH THE NORTH POLE   *U.S.S. Nautilus*

When man had made all the voyages on the sea that could be made, he had one more still to make—a journey under the water to the North Pole. A voyage like this is possible because the North Pole is not on land but in the centre of a huge floating mass of ice with water beneath it.

The first attempt to reach the North Pole by submarine was made in 1931 in an old submarine, renamed *Nautilus* after the submarine in Jules Verne's book, *Twenty Thousand Leagues under the Sea*. This attempt by Sir Hubert Wilkins was a failure.

It was fitting that the first submarine to make the voyage under the Pole was also named *Nautilus*, this time an atomic powered submarine of the United States Navy, capable of travelling 60,000 miles without refuelling and having every comfort for the crew.

Nautilus sailed northwards from the Pacific Ocean. On 3rd August, 1958, Captain Anderson spoke to the crew: 'All hands—this is the Captain speaking ... The distance to the Pole is now precisely four tenths of a mile. As we approach, let us pause in silence dedicated with our thanks for the blessings that have been ours during this remarkable voyage—our prayers for lasting world peace.' After a short pause in silence, the captain began the countdown and *Nautilus* reached the Pole at 12.15., then completed her journey into the Atlantic Ocean.

Shortly afterwards another U.S. submarine, the *Skate*, actually broke through the ice to surface at the North Pole.

We thank you, O God, for the thrill of adventure and the joy of success. Our adventures in life may never make history but we pray that we may pursue them with courage and determination and find our reward in a job well done. Then, in our moments of success, make us to remember all that you have done to help us and give us thankful hearts. Hear our prayer through Christ our Lord. *Amen.**

Closing prayer No. 34

Ships and travellers (5)

St. Christopher and St. James

Some people would not dream of travelling very far without their 'St. Christopher'—a medallion bearing a picture of St. Christopher carrying Christ on his shoulders.

Various legends are told about St. Christopher, especially one which tells how he carried Christ across some water, but we know very little about him. He is, however, the patron saint of travellers and his day is 25th July.

The same day, 25th July is shared by another saint, who is said to have travelled himself and has certainly been the cause of many other people travelling. He is St. James, the brother of St. John, one of the fishermen whom Jesus called to be his disciples.

St. James is remembered as the patron saint of Spain, where he is known as Santiago. In Britain he is called St. James the Great. Legends tell how he made an early journey to Spain as a missionary. This must have been very early in the history of the Church because James was put to death by King Herod Agrippa to please the Jewish leaders.

A shrine was built to St. James in Santiago de Compostella and this became one of the most important shrines to be visited by pilgrims in the Middle Ages. Thousands of people went to Spain to visit it and, to prove they had been there, they wore a shell in their hats. In early paintings and stained-glass windows, St. James is shown with his shell.

Today people go on many journeys, by land, sea or in the air. Some may carry their St. Christopher with them but many more pray to God for their safe journey.

Almighty God, our loving heavenly Father, we ask your care and protection for all who must travel this day by land, by sea or in the air. Grant them comfort on their journeys and a safe arrival at their destinations. Bless us on our daily journeys and help us to be watchful and alert to all dangers that could harm us. This we ask for Jesus Christ's sake. *Amen.**

Benediction No. 45

In the air (1)

R 101 Disaster

For hundreds of years, people wished they could fly or had dreamed of so doing but it seemed to be impossible.

Bible Reading: Psalm 55: 1–6

After many unsuccessful attempts, in 1783 the first man to fly did so in a balloon filled with hot air. (You may have seen hot-air balloons at fêtes nowadays.) But balloons were carried by the wind and could not be steered. After the round balloon came a sausage-shaped balloon filled with gas and driven by an engine. It was the first airship which could be made to go where the pilot wished.

Airships were developed by the German Count von Zeppelin, who used his airships, or Zeppelins, to drop small bombs on England during the First World War. After the war had ended, these lighter-than-air craft were developed for carrying passengers.

Britain built several, the finest being the *R 101*. The great silver balloon with its carriages slung underneath made a fine sight as it flew over London. Only a short time afterwards, on 5th October, 1930, the *R 101* crashed into a hillside at Beauvais, France, burst into flames and killed all the passengers.

Britain stopped building airships: so did America after two of hers crashed. The airship had been quite a good idea but it had not worked—but then there have been many unsuccessful experiments in the course of progress.

But maybe there is hope for the airship yet. Some airships have been built and filled with a gas which does not burst into flames and people are talking of large safe cargo carrying airships.

O God, give us courage—courage to make experiments, and not to be afraid of making mistakes; courage to get up when we are down; courage to work with all our might for the coming of thy kingdom on earth; through Jesus Christ our Lord. *Amen.*

Source not known

Closing prayer No. 22

In the air (2)

The Wright Brothers

It was a cold windy morning for working on the sand dunes of Kitty Hawk, North Carolina, but Orville and Wilbur Wright had more to think about than the weather. They were putting the finishing touches to a strange looking machine in which they hoped to make history.

For hundreds of years people had dreamed of flying and had tried many ways of doing so. They had made wings and had jumped from high buildings only to crash headlong to the ground. They had travelled high into the air in balloons which they could not control. They had glided from high hills but their flights had been short. They had built machines with engines but they failed to leave the ground.

Now Orville and Wilbur Wright were ready. Their aeroplane, known as the *Flyer* looked something like a large kite. It had two huge wings and a small body framework. It was powered by a small twelve horse-power petrol engine with a tank containing a third of a gallon of petrol.

The *Flyer* was turned to face the wind; Orville took his place at the controls; and the rope holding the machine was cast off. With a roar of its engine, the *Flyer* lurched forward and left the ground. Twelve seconds later it was down again, having travelled one hundred and twenty feet.

On that day, 17th December, 1903, Orville Wright made history as the first man to fly a machine that was heavier than air. It was a milestone in the history of the world.

O God our Father, there are times when we try to do something which seems almost impossible, but we pray that we may have strength and courage to try until we succeed. Help us to remember that each difficulty overcome will not only give us joy and satisfaction but will make us more fit for a full life; through Jesus Christ our Lord. *Amen.**

Closing prayer No. 26

In the air (3)

Amy Johnson

It frequently pays not to be put off by what people say. One woman in the Bible found this to be true:

Bible Reading: St. Mark 7: 24–30

In much more recent times, a young woman named Amy Johnson became fascinated by aeroplanes and thought how wonderful it would be if she could fly one. That was in 1928 when flying was still a new hobby and quite an adventurous one at that. Men who wished would join flying clubs and practise at week-ends.

For a woman to fly was unheard of and, when Amy approached a flying club and asked to join, the members laughed. Whatever made a woman think she could fly!

Amy was bitterly disappointed at their attitude but she refused to be put off. She showed herself so keen that eventually she was allowed to join. How amazed those men were to discover that she could not only learn to fly but that she could pass the test as a ground engineer too and maintain the machines.

In 1930 came her great adventure. On 5th May, she left Croydon in Surrey, in a tiny Moth aeroplane and flew it single-handed to Australia—a perilous journey which took nineteen days to complete.

On that flight and on others she broke world records. Amy became known to many people because of her courage and determination. Then she married an airman, Jim Mollison, with whom she broke more records. Amy lived for flying—and died flying too, when her plane crashed into the Thames estuary on 5th January, 1941.

Almighty God, who gave us a spirit of adventure, help us to take hold of our opportunities and make the most of life; give us courage to tackle what may seem impossible without the fear of failure; and above all, help us to learn, as thousands before us have learned, that the greatest adventure of all is in your service, after the example of Jesus Christ our Lord. *Amen.**

Closing prayer No. 23

In the air (4)

A DREAM COME TRUE   *Frank Whittle*

Sometimes dreams come true and sometimes they do not. Often when they do it is because the dreamer has worked hard to make it so. Some of the world's greatest inventions have come as a result of people working away at dreams which others have regarded as foolish.

Frank Whittle was a dreamer. His particular dream was of an aeroplane which could fly without needing a propellor. The idea came to him when he was at the Royal Air Force College at Cranwell in 1923 and he was determined that his dream should become a reality.

In later years as a flying instructor he took part in air displays but frequently thought about his new type of engine. At last he had the opportunity to work at his plans in a workshop in Rugby in 1936. Three years later he convinced the Air Ministry that he was working on the right lines. A new plane had to be built to carry his engine.

So, on 8th April, 1941, an experimental plane taxied onto the runway and took off. It was the first jet-propelled flight and the fulfilment of Frank Whittle's dreams after eighteen years. Today, giant jet air liners and fighters, which fly faster than the speed of sound, are a tribute to the man who invented the engine and was knighted for doing so, Sir Frank Whittle.

Most people have their dreams of what might be. For many they remain just dreams because people wait for miracles to happen instead of working hard to make their dreams come true.

O God, our Father, we thank you that through the years men have had their dreams and visions of a better world and have seen some way of doing something about it. Inspire us today by showing us what we might become or what we can do, then give us strength and patience to work to that end; for your glory and for the sake of Jesus Christ our Lord. *Amen.**

Benediction No. 49

In the air (5)

Nowadays for many people flying is no longer an adventure but a part of life. It is possible to take a plane for holidays or for business purposes to almost any part of Britain or, for that matter, almost any part of the world.

If you have flown, you will realize that you may not land very close to where you are finally going because airports must be built some way outside town. Flying to London, for example, you may land at any one of a number of airports around London or at the main London Airport of Heathrow, which is some miles west of the city.

Heathrow is one of the largest and busiest airports in the world. It was built just after the Second World War to replace Croydon as London's airport and was opened on 25th March, 1948. The planners thought that as London was one of the chief cities in the world it should have a very large airport. They also knew that planes would get larger and there was room at Heathrow to accommodate the largest of them. At the time, London Airport must have seemed huge but we know today that it is not big enough. So many people fly in and out of London that other airports must be used as well.

One of the lessons that we have to learn in life is not to be content with little things but to aim as high as we can, thinking not just of the present but of what might happen in the future too. And of all things the most important is to aim high in becoming all that God would have us to be.

Bible Reading: Philippians 3: 12b–14

O God our Father, help us to think big so that we may see the world as your kingdom and you as ruler over all. May we aim for what is right and true and honourable, taking as our example our Lord Jesus Christ, to whom with you and the Holy Spirit be all honour and glory now and forever. *Amen.* *

Closing prayer No. 13

Stars and space (1)

Discovery of Pluto

Have you ever tried to count the stars? If so, you have probably given up in despair. There are 100,000 million of them, and each one is a sun like our own.

Around these suns there may be planets like those which travel around our own sun, of which Earth is only one. Some of these planets have been known for a long time but it was only in 1930, on 13th March, that the announcement was made that the planet Pluto had been discovered.

Many of the stars are much more powerful than our sun but they look so small because they are so far away. Even the sun, which gives us heat and light, is about 93 million miles away and the light which leaves the sun takes just over eight minutes to reach us.

This is how distances are measured in the universe. Stars are said to be so many light years away. Light travels about 186,000 miles per second. In a year, it travels $186,000 \times 60 \times 60 \times 24 \times 365$—nearly six million million miles. And the nearest star is about four and a half light years away.

Take a look at the Pole Star on a clear night. What you are really seeing is light which left it about 680 years ago. The light of some stars which can be seen without using a telescope has been travelling for over two thousand years—since before the time when Jesus was on earth.

It is small wonder that the psalmist looked at the stars and asked, 'What is man that thou art mindful of him?' And the psalmist did not know half of it!

Bible Reading: Psalm 8

Almighty God, Creator of all we can see and of things which we cannot see, we praise you for all the wonders of the universe. Above all we thank you for sending your Son to show us that you are not only the great Creator but the Father of us all. Help us to recognize your greatness, to know your love and to be mindful of your presence; through Jesus Christ our Lord. *Amen.**

Benediction No. 40

Stars and space (2)

Copernicus

No matter how hard you try, you cannot feel the earth moving. Moreover, at various times of the day and night, the sun and moon are seen in different positions. If you knew no better, you would think that the earth stood still and the sun, moon and stars moved around it.

This was just what early people believed. Their pictures of the world showed it to be flat, with a bowl over it for the sky. Sun, moon and stars moved across the surface of this bowl.

The first chapter of the Bible, in the book of Genesis tells, in picture language, how God created the world, the sun and the moon, but it tells nothing of their movements. This is what it tells.

Bible Reading: Genesis 1: 14–18

So men set out to discover for themselves. One of the greatest of these was Nicolaus Copernicus, who was born in Poland on 19th February, 1473. He studied medicine and theology in Poland, then taught mathematics and astronomy in Rome.

The more Copernicus studied the stars, the more he realized that old ideas were wrong. He believed that the earth moved round the sun, that the earth might possibly spin round as it moved, and that the stars were further away than people had believed.

Copernicus had taken a tremendous step forward but not without a great deal of opposition, even from Church leaders, who said that he had no right to say such things.

But Copernicus was merely revealing the truth, which had remained hidden for so long.

Almighty God, who put it within the reach of man to discover the great truths about the universe, of which our world is but a tiny part; help us to discover more about your creation, so that our hearts and voices may be filled with wonder and praise now and for evermore. *Amen.**

Closing prayer No. 20

Stars and space (3)

Greenwich Observatory

In the Bible we read of various people who studied the stars, some of the best-known being those who followed the star to Bethlehem.

In those days they had to rely upon what they could see with the naked eye, for they had no telescope to help them. Yet people in Greece and Egypt, in Babylon and Baghdad, learned remarkable things about the universe.

Many years later came the telescope, invented in Holland, improved by Galileo, and found very useful for studying stars. But to study the stars accurately, astronomers needed a place in which their telescopes could be fixed and their instruments kept. A place like this, from which stars could be observed was called an observatory.

In the reign of King Charles II of England one man was particularly anxious to find out about stars, times, distances and how the heavenly bodies could be used in navigation. He was John Flamsteed, who was given by the King the position which we now know as Astronomer Royal. Moreover, he was given a fine new observatory at Greenwich, which was founded on 10th August, 1675.

Before long, Greenwich Observatory became the place from which time and distances were measured. Times throughout the world are based on Greenwich Mean Time and distances are measured east or west of the Meridian of Greenwich.

Today, with radio telescopes, men can probe even deeper into the universe. The more they discover, the more wonderful it all seems.

Isaiah draws a lesson from the universe and points out that the God who created it all is the God who gives strength to those who trust him.

Bible Reading: Isaiah 40: 25–28 (or 31)

Almighty God, Creator of heaven and earth and all that is within them, we praise you for the wonders of your creation but also for the strength received from you from day to day. Make us aware of your power and ready to trust you; through Jesus Christ our Lord. *Amen.**

Benediction No. 50

Stars and space (4)

Yuri Gagarin

April 12th, 1961 was described by the Russian leader Khrushchev as 'a landmark in the history of mankind' for it was on that day that Yuri Gagarin became the first man to orbit the earth in space.

This had been the dream of people for many years and space travel had been the subject of many science fiction books and comics. It was not until the Germans developed rockets during the 1939–45 war that it even came within the realms of possibility.

Once the war ended, both America and Russia entered upon great research programmes of space travel. Rockets hurtled into space; animals were sent up and recovered; a Russian Sputnik was put into orbit; and the way was opened for human space flights.

Yuri Gagarin was one of many who were trained to be astronauts. He was born in 1934, lost his home during the war, studied near Moscow, joined a flying club and was accepted as a pilot in the Russian Air Force. He showed tremendous will-power and per-severance in his training and this led to his being selected for training as an astronaut.

There were medical examinations, tests under 'space conditions' and practices in parachuting. At last he found himself hurtling round the earth at 17,500 miles per hour, completely weightless, with food, pencils and other things hanging in the air in front of him. The world was thrilled when after such an amazing journey he landed safely.

Of course, there have been much more spectacular achievements since then but this was the first and April 12th is celebrated in Russia as 'Cosmonauts' Day'.

Almighty God, we praise you because you have given men active minds with which to discover the wonders which have existed in the universe since the beginning of time. Grant that all scientific discoveries, whether on earth or in space may be put to useful purposes for the benefit of all mankind and the glory of your holy Name. *Amen.**

Closing prayer No. 10

Stars and space (5)

'Apollo 8' Astronauts

People have often stood looking at the moon, but very few have had the opportunity to look at the earth from the moon. The first to do so were three American astronauts in the spaceship 'Apollo 8', which blasted off in December 1968, carrying the three, Frank Borman, Jim Lovell and Bill Anders on a 480,000 mile journey round the moon and back.

On the second day of their journey, 22nd December, they sent back the first television pictures, when they were half-way to the moon. On the following day, millions of people in many countries were able to sit at home and watch on television pictures of the earth taken at a distance of about 200,000 miles. It shone brightly reflecting the light of the sun.

The astronauts were excited and kept referring to it as 'the good earth'. Then, on Christmas Eve, as they orbited the moon, the three read from the first chapter of the book of Genesis, reading these verses in turn.

Bible Reading: Genesis 1: 1–10

They concluded, 'and from the crew of Apollo 8 we pause with good night, good luck, merry Christmas, and God bless all of you on the good earth'.

If we keep our eyes open, we too can appreciate the wonders of the world in which we live. At Christmas time, we especially remember that God, who created the world and saw that it was good, sent Jesus Christ to teach us to know him not just as the great Creator but as our Father.

Almighty God, our heavenly Father, we praise you for the wonders of your creation and for the good earth on which we live. Even more we praise you because you sent your Son, Jesus Christ, to be the saviour of mankind. Teach us to follow his example that we may live as true children in our Father's world and know the peace that comes to all who believe; through the same Jesus Christ our Lord. *Amen.**

Benediction No. 53

Treasure (1)

Many stories are told of buried treasure, but there are few people who succeed in finding any. One who did was an Englishman, Howard Carter, who discovered the entrance to a tomb in the Valley of the Kings, in Egypt. He hardly dared to hope that it might contain treasure, for most of the tombs had been looted years before and their treasures removed. This one was underground.

Imagine his pleasure when he discovered a room containing furniture, statues, chests, vases and other articles of value. Beyond was a sealed door, guarded by two statues of the King, whose name was Tutankhamun. After months of work, this door was opened on 16th February, 1923.

Inside was a burial shrine, a huge box, the size of a room, made of wood and covered with gold. There were three more of these shrines, one inside the other and all covered with gold. The innermost one contained a coffin inside which were three mummy cases, one inside the other, the smallest being of pure gold and weighing nine hundred pounds. Inside this was the mummified body of the boy king, with all his jewels, where he had been placed 3,270 years before.

In the tomb were things the young King might need: grains of wheat, clothing, daggers and a host of other things worth a great fortune.

But Tutankhamun was dead and his treasure was left behind. No matter how much we may have, we cannot take it with us and we do well to remember the words of Jesus about building up treasures in Heaven rather than upon the earth.

Bible Reading: St. Matthew 6: 19–21

O God our Father, teach us in life always to put first things first. Help us to look for those things which bring greater joy than riches and, by serving others and you to build up for ourselves treasures in heaven; through Jesus Christ our Lord. *Amen.**

Closing prayer No. 38

Treasure (2)

Andrew Carnegie

Our Bible reading today tells what Jesus said to a very rich man.

Bible Reading: St. Mark 10: 17–22

What would you consider to be a large amount of money? Most people would think that £100 is a lot, £1,000 a fortune and £1,000,000 a figure too large to mean anything at all. Yet, on 11th August, 1919, a man died who, during his lifetime had given away something like £70,000,000.

Even more strange is the fact that he was the son of a poor Scottish weaver, who once had such a hard time that he packed his belongings and went with his family to America. There, at the age of thirteen, young Andrew Carnegie worked in a factory for eleven hours a day to earn about five shillings a week.

But Andrew was no ordinary young man. He became in turn a telegraph clerk, office manager, secretary and superintendent. During the American Civil War, he was second in command of all railways and telegraphs in the Northern states.

By the time he was fifty-three, Andrew Carnegie had used his money to buy steel works, coalfields, ironfields, hundreds of miles of railways and a line of steamships. In 1901, the United States Steel Corporation bought all he owned for one hundred million pounds.

Carnegie, who had made a fortune, now decided to give it away. By the time he died, at the age of eighty-four, Carnegie had given away to libraries, universities and others about three-quarters of his vast fortune.

O God our Father, help us to remember that, though we may not have our millions, we all have something we can give to others. Keep us from selfishness and greed and fill our hearts with kindliness and love. Accept what we can offer to others in your name and for your glory so that we may build up treasures in Heaven and inherit eternal life; through Jesus Christ our Lord. *Amen.**

Closing prayer No. 35

Treasure (3)

THINGS TO TREASURE   *Michael Faraday*

What kind of things do you treasure? No doubt you have some things at home which mean a lot to you but which have no real value, a letter perhaps or a photograph. Although they have little value, you would be sorry to lose them. Here is a story from the Bible about a woman who lost and found one of her treasures.

Bible Reading: St. Luke 15: 8–10

You might hardly imagine that a ticket to attend a lecture could be regarded as something to be treasured but, if you had been Michael Faraday you, too, might have jumped at the opportunity to go to hear the famous scientist Sir Humphry Davy.

Faraday was born on 22nd September, 1791. There was precious little money in his home and young Michael was pleased to find a job as errand boy to a bookseller. It was hard work but the money was useful. It was while working as a bookbinder that a customer offered him the ticket to attend the lectures.

After hearing Sir Humphry Davy speak, Faraday was determined to become a scientist too. He wrote to Sir Humphry to ask for a job and was delighted when the answer was 'Yes'.

After many experiments with electricity, Faraday was successful in building the first dynamo to make electricity.

Think for a moment of all the things for which electricity is used—lights, trains, machinery, telephones, television, and a host of other things—and you will realize how much we owe to Michael Faraday . . . and that ticket.

We praise you, O God, for all those things such as prizes or photographs or presents which we can treasure and for the enjoyment which they give us. We thank you too for the many treasures which so often we take for granted—the discoveries and inventions such as cars, television, transistor radios or washing machines, which mean so much to us in our daily life. Make us mindful of all our blessings and give us thankful hearts; now and for evermore. *Amen.**

Closing prayer No. 32

Treasure (4)

A BIBLE TO TREASURE   *Mary Jones*

Jesus told two short parables about treasures.

Bible Reading: St. Matthew 13: 44–46

Some of our greatest treasures are those for which we have had to make a great effort or sacrifice.

Mary Jones, who was born in a little Welsh village on 1st December, 1784, loved to hear the stories her father told, especially those from the Bible.

'If only I could read them for myself,' she used to say. But she could not read and there were few books printed in Welsh. By the time she was eight, Mary Jones had one ambition, to have a Welsh Bible of her own.

Mrs. Evans, who owned the only Bible in the district offered to let Mary read it if she could learn to read. So she went to school, learned to read, and became more determined than ever to have a Bible of her own.

Every penny and halfpenny was saved until, when she was sixteen, she learned that a Mr. Charles had a few Welsh Bibles to sell.

Over the hills she trudged, carrying the money she had saved and, the next morning, told her story to Mr. Charles. 'I had a few,' he said, 'but they are all sold and no more are being printed.'

Mary wept bitterly. All her years of saving had been in vain. Mr. Charles, however, did manage to find her one and that day the happiest girl in Wales carried her precious treasure home.

Mr. Charles sat down and wrote her story, pleading that Bibles should be printed for all to read. The result was the formation in 1804 of the British and Foreign Bible Society, which has now printed Bibles in over a thousand languages. One of its greatest treasures is that Bible, once owned by Mary Jones.

We thank you, God our Father, for the Bible in which we learn of you and for those who translated it into our own language. Bless those who translate into other tongues today: may their work be rewarded as people throughout the world learn of your love. *Amen.**

Closing prayer No. 33

Treasure (5)

One of the best things to do with treasure is to give it away. This may seem strange but it is true. The happiest people are not those who keep everything for themselves but those who use it to bring happiness to others. You may feel that you have very little to give to others. Listen to the story of someone who had very little indeed.

Bible Reading: St. Mark 12: 41–44

Our gifts may sometimes seem very small compared with those that others give, but there is no one who has nothing to give.

Christina Rossetti, who was born on 5th December, 1830, is considered by many people to be one of the greatest English poetesses. She wrote many simple poems about ordinary, everyday things. Perhaps you can find some for yourself. She also wrote hymns and carols. In one of them, *In the bleak midwinter,* she asks the question:

> *What can I give Him,*
> *Poor as I am?*
> *If I were a shepherd,*
> *I would bring a lamb;*
> *If I were a wise man,*
> *I would do my part;*
> *Yet what I can I give him—*
> *Give my heart.*

Christina Rossetti knew the secret of true living. She gave her greatest possession—herself—to God and discovered him to be someone to whom she could speak in prayer and who could help her day by day. There is no greater treasure than this.

A prayer of Christina Rossetti:

O Lord, whose way is perfect, help us, we pray thee, always to trust in thy goodness; that, walking with thee and following thee in all simplicity, we may possess quiet and contented minds, and may cast all our care on thee, for thou carest for us; for the sake of Jesus Christ our Lord. *Amen.*

Closing prayer No. 23

Treasure (5)   99

Out of disaster (1)

THE EARTH MELTED . . . *Krakatoa*

Bible Reading: Psalm 46: 1–7

It may seem strange to think about the earth melting or the mountains being carried into the midst of the sea but that was what did happen on 27th August, 1883.

The British tea-clipper *Kaisow* anchored off the little town of Anjer, on the coast of Sumatra to obtain fresh water and stores but the boat which usually met visiting ships was nowhere to be seen.

The captain lowered his own boat and went ashore, where he discovered that the volcano on the island of Krakatoa was erupting and the people of Anjer had fled to high ground in case a great wave hit the town. The captain went straight back to his ship and ordered full sail to be set so that he could try to escape.

As the ship passed Krakatoa, fire could be seen belching from the top of the mountain as molten lava poured down the sides into the hissing, boiling sea.

There were rumblings and great waves as the *Kaisow* reached the safety of the Indian Ocean just before a gigantic explosion blew most of the island of Krakatoa to pieces. The explosion was so loud that it could be heard nearly three thousand miles away and the giant wave that followed it swept across the islands, killing many thousands of people.

From time to time we hear of other natural disasters, earthquakes, volcanoes, floods and hurricanes, which destroy life and property. When we do, we might remember that there are always others less fortunate than ourselves and that we have much for which to be thankful.

We thank you, God our Father
For the shelter and comfort of our homes;
For the love and companionship of family and friends;
And for all the blessings which we take for granted.

Hear our prayer for all who are less fortunate than we are and bless all who work to help them; through Jesus Christ our Lord. *Amen.**

Closing prayer No. 15

Out of disaster (2)

Every now and then floods come to one area of the country or another because of melting snow, heavy rain or extra high tides. When they do, there is always hardship and heartbreak for people whose homes are affected.

One very picturesque and popular holiday resort is the little village of Lynmouth, lying in North Devon at the foot of Exmoor, with its river tumbling over rocks on its way to the sea.

But, in 1952, at the height of the holiday season, August 16th was a day of reckoning, of trying to count up the damage to life and property caused by a disaster which had hit the village during the night.

On the previous day, it had rained for hour after hour until, about 8.30 in the evening, there was a cloudburst. Exmoor was flooded; the little streams which drain it burst their banks; and Lynmouth's river could not cope with all the extra water. During the night it was as though a giant wave swept through the village, carrying with it trees, houses, livestock and huge boulders torn from the hillsides.

The morning light revealed a scene of horror. 93 buildings were destroyed or badly damaged, 28 bridges destroyed, and 31 people lost their lives.

But it was not the end. Out of the rubble, Lynmouth grew again to be a holiday-makers' paradise. But it was different. Lynmouth was built with a wider river course so that no similar disaster could occur.

When Lynmouth first grew, no one imagined anything like this would happen. Listen to what Jesus had to say about making wise preparations for life:

Bible Reading: St. Matthew 7: 24–27

Help us, O God our Father, to place our trust in you and so build our lives on a firm foundation. We know that we shall face the storms in life but we pray that when they come we may have strength to rise above them and find enrichment of life in your strength; through Jesus Christ our Lord. *Amen.**

Benediction No. 48

Out of disaster (2)   101

Out of disaster (3)

Tay Bridge Disaster

Bible Reading: Proverbs 16: 16–20

The new railway bridge over the Firth of Tay was a fine piece of engineering. When opened in 1878, it was the longest bridge over water. Its builders had every reason to feel proud of it as the trains rumbled across it to Dundee and the North of Scotland.

Their pride was short-lived. On 28th December, 1879, a violent storm swept along the Firth of Tay, with winds so strong that people could scarcely keep their feet. Many an anxious eye was cast toward the bridge.

In the darkness a few people gathered to watch the mail train begin its journey south. The glow of the engine moved from them. Then a streak of fire plunged into the waters of the Tay. The observers were horrified as they realized that the engine with the mail coaches and seventy-five people on board had disappeared under the water.

Two men braved the storm to investigate, crawling along the bridge until they came to a half-mile gap, where the section of bridge had been carried away. The bridge that had been the pride of its builders was a useless ruin.

But that was not the end of the story for, having learned from their mistakes, men built again, so that a fine new bridge was opened in 1887, alongside the foundations of the old.

There are times when we may become a little too proud of our achievements and, as our Bible reading suggested, pride is often followed by a fall. That, however, is not the end, for the wisdom we gain enables us to make a fresh start with more chance of success.

O God our Father, forgive us when we become too proud of ourselves or of our achievements; strengthen us so that we can withstand the storms of life; and if in our weakness we fall, give us courage to begin again; through Jesus Christ our Lord. *Amen.**

Closing prayer No. 27

Out of disaster (4)

The 'Titanic'

A violent storm sprang up as Paul was travelling toward Rome. Here is the end of the story.

Bible Reading: Acts 27: 37-44

In those long ago days, shipwrecks were common. But when the *Titanic* was built just over half a century ago, her builders claimed that she was unsinkable. She had a double bottom and many water-tight compartments.

Suddenly, on the night of 14th April, 1912, the *Titanic* shuddered and there was a grinding noise as she struck an iceberg, which tore a long gash in her hull. Quickly she filled with water and it was clear that she could not stay afloat for long.

Boats were lowered, filled with women and children and then rowed clear of the ship. But there were not enough. Those who thought the *Titanic* unsinkable had seen no reason to provide many lifeboats.

On deck the ship's band played hymns as passengers scrambled over the side or threw themselves into the water to grasp at anything that could keep them afloat. Just after midnight, in the early minutes of 15th April, the *Titanic* slid beneath the ocean. Two thirds of her 2,200 passengers were lost in what was the worst ever disaster at sea, except in war.

But there is always something to be learned and good can even come out of a disaster. From this, people learned to keep a much closer watch on icebergs. They also learned that, no matter how fine a ship might be, she must carry enough life-saving gear for all on board. Because of the *Titanic*, travel by sea is now much safer than it was.

Almighty God, ruler of the winds and the waves, take into your care and keeping the men of the merchant navy, the fishing fleets and all who are at the mercy of the seas. In times of difficulty or danger, grant them your strength. [At this time we remember especially . . .] Bless too the families which they leave on shore and grant unto them your comfort and peace; through Jesus Christ our Lord. *Amen.**

Closing prayer No. 10

Out of disaster (5)

Coventry Cathedral

On the night of 14th November, 1940, the city of Coventry suffered the longest air-raid made on any British city during the whole war.

As high explosive bombs fell in many parts of the city, other parts were destroyed by fire bombs, and among these was the beautiful cathedral of St. Michael. Fire swept through the building, burning the roof, the ceiling, the pews and the screen, leaving only the stone walls standing—an empty shell.

The following day it was decided that the cathedral should be rebuilt, but sixteen years were to pass before the first stone was laid. Meanwhile, the debris was cleared from the ruins and Coventry had an 'open air cathedral'.

From the ruins were taken two charred beams from the old roof. These were bound with wire into a cross and set up in an old dustbin of sand at the eastern end of the ruins.

The new cathedral was to be nothing like the old. Built to a modern design, with ultra-modern works of art, craftsmanship and tapestry, it was a cathedral that fitted the modern age. It was consecrated to the glory of God on 25th May, 1962.

The new cathedral has attracted visitors from many parts of the world, who have come to admire and to pray in the modern building.

But many of these are also greatly moved by the ruins of the old cathedral, open to the sky, with the charred cross set on a simple stone altar and the two words inscribed on the altar,
FATHER FORGIVE.

Father forgive us
When we are selfish in thought and deed;
When we try to force others to do things our way;
When we fail to live at peace with one another.
Because the world is filled with hatred and violence;
Because we do not have your love in our hearts;
Father forgive; and grant us your peace. *Amen.**

Closing prayer No. 9

---

3 Through the Year

The seven themes in this section are best taken at the appropriate season of the year.

A guiding light	To begin the term in January
Out in the cold	A cold spell in January–March
Springtime	Around 1st May
Summer	Late June
Autumn	End of September
Ordinary and extraordinary	End of October, beginning of November
Christmas tide	Last week before Christmas holiday

As some of these are related to specific days, it may be helpful to change the order within the theme so that stories fall on the correct days. If Midsummer Day, for example, falls on a Wednesday, it would be better to take it as third in the series instead of first. Perhaps topics could be alternated with those of other themes so that the Longest Day and Beltane could also fall on appropriate dates. This is perhaps even more important in the *Ordinary and Extraordinary* theme.

While working through the year, it could also be useful to keep in mind *The Christian Calendar* (pp. 150–5) and *International Days* (pp. 184–6).

A guiding light (1)

The Romans had a god, Janus, who is pictured as having two faces, one looking forward and one looking back. From this god, January took its name.

New Year is always a time of looking back and forward. We look back with many happy memories and we are thankful for all that gave joy. We also look back on things which are best forgotten— those which would have been better left undone. But we cannot change what has happened. We can only try not to repeat our mistakes in the New Year. That is why people make New Year resolutions.

Many have learned that the best resolution of all is to place our trust in God for the guidance and help we need. Many have found encouragement in the words of M. L. Haskins:

> *And I said to the man who stood at the gate of the year: 'Give me a light that I may tread safely into the unknown!'*
> *And he replied:*
> *'Go out into the darkness and put thine hand into the Hand of God. That shall be to thee better than light and safer than a known way.'*
> *So I went forth and finding the Hand of God trod gladly into the night.*

Now let us read how God promised to guide Joshua as he stepped forward into the unknown.

Bible Reading: Joshua 1: 1–9

O God our Father, another year has gone and we look back with pleasure on many things. Thank you for all that has given us enjoyment and for all that has helped us to grow wiser and stronger. If we have displeased you, forgive us, and let your light guide us in the coming days so that we may do what is your will and make the year ahead one of blessing to us and to others for Jesus Christ's sake. *Amen.**

Benediction No. 54

A guiding light (2)

William Chatterton Dix, a Bristol insurance agent, lay in bed ill. It was Sunday, 6th January, 1860 and, as he was unable to go to church, he decided to read the Bible in bed, and particularly the passage that he knew would be read in church that day.

January 6th is known as Epiphany—the day on which the Church remembers the arrival of the wise men to present their gifts to the infant Jesus. This is what he read:

Bible Reading: St. Matthew 2: 1–12

As he read, Dix thought about the story, which struck him more vividly than it had done before. He realized that, just as the wise men travelled to find Jesus and then worshipped him, offering their costly gifts, so too must we. Before the night was out, he had written his great hymn:

> *As with gladness men of old*
> *Did the guiding star behold,*
> *As with joy they hailed its light,*
> *Leading onward, beaming bright;*
> *So, most gracious Lord, may we*
> *Evermore be led to thee.*

Dix wrote many other hymns too, including *Allelujah, sing to Jesus* and some written for particular seasons of the Christian year but *As with gladness* is the best known.

Today we are invited to seek Jesus, worship him and offer our gifts for his use.

Almighty God, by whose guidance the wise men of old were led to present their gifts to Jesus, help us to bring such gifts as we have and lay them before you, knowing that as we do we shall find blessing not only for ourselves but for others too. Help us to use all that we have wisely and for your glory; through Jesus Christ our Lord. *Amen.**

Benediction No. 47

A guiding light (3)

Henry Winstanley

Henry Winstanley loved playing practical jokes and his house was full of gadgets, such as chairs with movable arms to imprison anyone who sat in them. He liked to think of himself as an engineer and, in 1696, decided to build a lighthouse on the treacherous Eddystone Rocks near Plymouth.

On one rock, he built a stone pillar, twelve feet high and fourteen feet across. To this he bolted a wooden framework, eighty feet high.

It was the weirdest looking lighthouse imaginable, with balconies, cranes, a chimney and many elaborate decorations. Placards around the outside told in large letters who had been responsible for placing it there and carried such slogans as *Glory be to God*. At the top, the light given by a cluster of candles shone through a glass lantern.

But as the sea pounded it, the structure shook alarmingly. Winstanley added strength but it was in vain. On 26th November, 1703, a great storm swept the lighthouse and its builder off the rock. The lighthouse was wrecked and Henry Winstanley was never seen again.

But his efforts had not been wasted. Future lighthouse builders learned from his mistakes. Many seamen have cause to thank Winstanley and others like him for the lights which guide them to safety.

We recall how Jesus, the Light of the World, commanded his followers to let their lights shine to guide others on a safe pathway.

Bible Reading: St. Matthew 5: 14–16

Almighty God, who sent your Son, the Light of the World, to guide us through the troubled waters of this life, help us to follow his guiding light so that we may steer a true course all our days and come at last to your heavenly harbour; through Jesus Christ our Lord. *Amen.**

Benediction No. 51

A guiding light (4)

Henry Fawcett

On 3rd May, 1879, Henry Fawcett became the Postmaster-General of Britain, responsible for all the work of the Post Office and the thousands of people who worked in it. This in itself may not seem very important for there have been many men to hold this high office in Parliament. But Henry Fawcett was blind.

Very early in life he had realized that laws could be very hard on poor people and his one ambition had been to enter Parliament to help make better laws.

One September morning, Henry and his father took their guns to shoot partridge. Suddenly one flew up. Henry's father raised his gun and fired, without realizing that his son was just in front of him. Some pieces of shot went into Henry's eyes and blinded him. At twenty-five he knew he would never see again.

Many people would have given up, but not Henry. He was as determined as ever to enter Parliament and he began at once to make the changes in his life which blindness made necessary. Then, in 1863, he stood for Parliament but was defeated. Who wanted a Member of Parliament who could not see what he was doing?

At his third attempt he was successful and took his seat in the House of Commons, where he soon made a deep impression. Throughout his life he continued to speak up for those in need, to show kindness, sympathy and patience, and all this without complaining about his own problems. Moreover he was an inspiration to others who, like him, were blind.

O Lord our God, as we look around us and see all the beauty of the world in which we live, help us to remember those who cannot see but must spend their lives in darkness. Hear our prayers for these and all who are in need, and make us ready to count our blessings; for Jesus Christ's sake. *Amen.**

Closing prayer No. 15

A guiding light (5)

Are there any Christmas decorations in your home that have not yet been taken down? Nowadays we usually have them down by twelfth night, 6th January.

In the past, when people decorated their homes with greenery, they made quite certain that not a leaf nor a twig remained in the house on 2nd February. People then were so superstitious that they believed evil goblins would enter any house where the decorations remained and bring misfortune to the lazy housewife.

Churches were also cleared out to make room for the candles which would be lit on this day, known as Candlemas.

Candlemas means the Festival or Feast of Candles and it comes forty days after Christmas. The candles are lit to remind people of Jesus, who said that he was the Light of the World.

The custom of the Jews was that a mother would take her first-born son to present him to God on the fortieth day after his birth, and it was on this day that Jesus was taken to the temple at Jerusalem.

Here, from the Gospel according to St. Luke, is the story of what happened in the temple.

Bible Reading: St. Luke 2: 25–33

In later years, when he began his teaching, Jesus showed how he was a guiding light to show the way to God and to lighten the hearts of all who believed in him.

A prayer of the Eighth Century from the Gelasian Sacramentary:

O thou, who art the light of the minds that know thee, the life of the souls that love thee, and the strength of the wills that serve thee, help us so to know thee that we may truly love thee, so to love thee that we may fully serve thee, whom to serve is perfect freedom; through Jesus Christ our Lord. *Amen.*

Closing prayer No. 29

Out in the cold (1)

Frost Fair on the Thames

Each season of the year brings a different kind of weather. Here is a reading from the Old Testament.

Bible Reading: Job 37: 5–10

This is the season when we expect the icy winds to blow and snow to fall; when icicles hang from gutters and pipes; and when we awaken to find that Jack Frost has drawn his pictures on our window panes.

Sometimes we long for warmer days; at others we enjoy the freshness of the frosty air. Had you been living in London in 1740, you would probably have spent much of January playing games or enjoying the fun of the fair on the River Thames, for the weather was so cold that the river was frozen solid above London Bridge.

This happened whenever there was a hard frost, because the old London Bridge prevented the flow of water. The last time it froze was in 1814, a few years before the old bridge was taken down.

When the river froze a Frost Fair was held and London went gay until the thaw came. Popular sports were arranged on the ice; stalls were set up on the ice for the sale of food, drink and other commodities; and great fun was had by all. Some of the Frost Fairs lasted for several weeks.

London has changed since then and it is difficult to imagine the river freezing. The freezing of smaller rivers and lakes may not seem quite as exciting and fairs are not held on them, but there is still plenty of fun to be had when winter covers the scene with snow and ice.

We thank you, God our Father, for all the joys of winter:
For fresh frosty winds, which make our faces glow;
For fun we can have on the snow and on the ice;
For snowmen and sledges, skating and slides;
For hot drinks, roast chestnuts and blazing fires;
For cosy warm beds to snuggle into at night.

Help us to show our thanks by bringing comfort and help to those for whom winter brings hardship; for Jesus Christ's sake. *Amen.**

Benediction No. 56

Out in the cold (2)

NOT MUCH FUN . . .   *'Worst journey in the world'*

In winter, when the temperature drops below zero, we wrap ourselves up to keep out the cold. Seldom are there more than a few degrees of frost and it is difficult for us to imagine what extreme cold is like.

Between June and August, 1911, three men undertook what has been described as 'The Worst Journey in the World'. The three were members of Captain Scott's Antarctic expedition, Doctor Wilson, Lieutenant Bowers and Mr. Cherry-Garrard.

The three had gone, in the middle of the Antarctic winter, to find out how the Emperor penguins nested. Captain Scott wrote of their journey, which took place entirely in darkness, as follows (Remember that Scott used the Farenheit scale, not the Centigrade one.)

'. . . the temperature had been falling, and now for more than a week the thermometer fell below $-60°$. On one night the minimum showed $-71°$, and on the next $-77°$, $109°$ of frost. Although in this truly fearful cold the air was comparatively still, every now and again little puffs of wind came eddying across the snow plain with blighting effect. No civilised being has ever encountered such conditions before with only a tent of thin canvas to rely on for shelter . . .'

The cold was almost unbearable; their fingers blistered with frostbite; and their faces became encased in a sheet of ice. When they returned, Scott wrote; 'They looked more weather-worn than anyone I have yet seen'.

No, it was not much fun: it was the action of men of great courage, who went out in the cause of science to increase our knowledge of the world and did so in the most appalling conditions.

We thank you, God our Father, for all who have found out facts about our world so that our knowledge might be the greater. We remember especially those who have taken their lives into their hands in order to do this. Help us to remember that everything worthwhile demands some sacrifice and that nothing can be achieved without endeavour. Make us live courageously all our days; through Jesus Christ our Lord. *Amen.**

Closing prayer No. 37

Out in the cold (3)

February 15th, 1874, was the birthday of that great explorer Ernest Shackleton, whose name will always be remembered in connexion with bold adventures in the ice wastes of Antarctica.

With Scott, in 1901, he had his first adventure, but was taken ill and had to be sent home. Then, a few years later, in 1907, he was off again, determined to reach the South Pole. When only 97 miles from his goal, he had to give up owing to shortage of food, but he made such a valiant effort that he was given a knighthood, becoming Sir Ernest Shackleton.

His third journey, made after others had reached the Pole, almost ended in disaster when his ship was crushed in the ice.

With five companions, he set out in a small boat to find help to rescue the other twenty-two men. The five crossed 800 miles of icy seas in an open boat to South Georgia, where three of them had to cross the island to reach help. Shackleton wrote:

'When I look back I have no doubt that Providence guided us not only across the snowfields but across the storm-white sea. I know that during that long and raking march of thirty-six hours over the unnamed mountains and glaciers of South Georgia it seemed to me often that we were four, not three. I said nothing to my companions; but afterwards Worsley said to me, "Boss, I'd a curious feeling on that march that there was another person with us".'

Bible Reading: Psalm 23

O God, who gave us a spirit of adventure, we thank you that we have our difficulties to face, for it is in facing them that we find our true manhood. As we face the adventures of life, we pray that we may be conscious of your abiding presence, so that, in difficulty or danger we may know that we need never walk alone. Guide us and strengthen us; for Jesus Christ's sake. *Amen.**

Closing prayer No. 36

Out in the cold (4)

SUCCESS IN THE ICY NORTH   *Robert Peary*

On a very hot day in the summer of 1908, thousands of people gathered along the New York waterfront in order to watch the little ship *Roosevelt* leave. As she did so, there arose a mighty roar of cheering from the crowd and a salute was fired from the gun on the President's yacht. On board the *Roosevelt* was Robert Peary, the American explorer. His thoughts were not on the hot summer weather but on the cold of the Arctic. He hoped to be the first man to reach the North Pole.

For hundreds of years, men had made their way northwards but none had reached the Pole. Peary himself had taken part in many polar expeditions and, only three years before had been forced to give up when almost at his goal owing to lack of food.

Soon he was steaming northwards through icy seas. 'Imagine,' he wrote, 'about three hundred and fifty miles of almost solid ice, ice of all shapes and sizes, mountainous ice, flat ice, ragged and tortured ice; then imagine a little black ship, solid, sturdy, compact, strong, and resistant and on this ship are sixty-nine human beings. . . .'

Of the large party which left for the Pole, one group after another returned until only Peary, his servant Henson, and four Eskimos were left to make the final dash to the North Pole, which they reached on 6th April, 1909.

It was a very happy Peary, who wrote, 'The Pole at last! The prize of three centuries! My dream and goal for twenty years. Mine at last! I cannot bring myself to realise it.'

O Lord our God, grant us to know what we should do with our lives, so that we may have a goal to aim for. Then give us, we pray, patience to work for it, courage in our failures and joy when we reach our goal. In this way, may we ourselves find satisfaction in life and give glory to you; through Jesus Christ our Lord. *Amen.**

Closing prayer No. 5

Out in the cold (5)

Out in the gold (4)

A LOVE OF ICE AND SNOW   *Roald Amundsen*

When the cold weather comes, there are many who long for the warmth of summer but there are also those who love the ice and snow. One of these, Roald Amundsen, is counted among the greatest of polar explorers.

Born in Norway in 1872, he was determined from a very early age to become a polar explorer. When the opportunity came, he travelled to Antarctica as mate in a Belgian ship. Then, in his own forty-seven ton fishing boat, he sailed to the Arctic and right round the north of America to the Pacific Ocean.

He then planned to drift across the North Pole in a larger ship, the *Fram* and become the first man to reach the North Pole but, even as he planned, he learned that the American explorer Peary had already reached it. He carried on with his plans for exploration, keeping a secret from most people his intention to travel south instead and be first at the South Pole. From his base camp in Antarctica, he made a splendid dash for the Pole, to reach it before his British rival, Captain Scott.

On 14th December, 1911, he thought he had reached the Pole but, after taking observations of the sun, he realized that he had five and a half miles still to go, so, on 16th December, he moved his tent to the Pole. He then turned his attention to the Arctic again, this time travelling over the North Pole in an airship. He retired from exploring only to fly to the rescue of the Italian explorer Nobile. Amundsen was never seen again.

Shortly before, he had said, 'If you only knew how splendid it is up there! That's where I want to die; and I wish only that death will come to me chivalrously, will overtake me in the fulfilment of a high mission, quickly, without suffering.' He had his wish.

O God our Father, help us to appreciate the beauties of our world. In winter days help us to see your handiwork in the frost, the ice and the snow. We thank you for these but also for the warmth of our homes and for health to withstand the cold. Bless those with poor health and little warmth, for whom the winter brings hardship. We ask these things for Jesus Christ's sake. *Amen.**

Benediction No. 53

Springtime (1)

Jethro Tull

Spring is the time of year when much of the seed is planted. Listen to the parable Jesus told about the sower.

Bible Reading: St. Matthew 13: 1–9

This method of broadcasting the seed far and wide was commonly used for many hundreds of years and is still seen in some lands today.

But what a hit-and-miss way of sowing seed, thought Jethro Tull. Surely there must be a better way of sowing seed so that it was planted in straight rows and all went into the good ground.

It was while he was sitting in church that Jethro had a brilliant idea. In front of him was the organ with its rows of pipes. Beneath each pipe was a stop, which closed a small hole. As the key was pressed, the stop opened and allowed one note to come out.

Soon Jethro Tull was busy making his own machine, which he called a seed drill. It was like a box filled with seed and had several pipes leading from it to the ground. As the drill was pulled, the seed dropped through the pipes to be planted in straight rows.

Tull, who died on 21st February, 1741, was one of the pioneers of modern farming methods. Today you may often see a farmer ploughing the fields but in this country you will rarely see him 'scatter the good seed on the land'. His work is made much easier with modern machinery.

O God, giver of the seed, the rain, the sun and the harvest, we thank you for all who have learned to obtain better harvests from the land, in the orchard, from the desert, or from the sea. Bless all who work for better harvests where modern methods are unknown and people starve. May those who have money and knowledge help those who have not; in the name of Jesus Christ. *Amen.**

Closing prayer No. 31

Springtime (2)

FLOWERS OF SPRING   *William Wordsworth*

One of the pleasures of spring is the beauty of spring flowers. Snowdrops, crocuses, daffodils, hyacinths, tulips and others have all pushed their way through the snow and the frozen earth to give their own touch of colour to the world.

Those who live in town can admire the flowers planted in gardens: country dwellers may find the wild bluebells or daffodils which are a fine sight to behold. It was the sight of a host of these daffodils which inspired the poet Wordsworth to write his famous poem, which begins:

> *I wandered lonely as a cloud*
> *That floats on high o'er vales and hills,*
> *When all at once I saw a crowd,*
> *A host, of golden daffodils;*
> *Beside the lake, beneath the trees,*
> *Fluttering and dancing in the breeze.*

William Wordsworth, who was one of the great English poets, was born at Cockermouth, Cumberland on 7th April, 1770. He was orphaned as a boy and he lived with his sister in various parts of the country before settling in the English Lake District not far from his birthplace. In 1843, when he was seventy-four, Wordsworth was appointed Poet Laureate, the poet chosen to write poetry for the King or Queen.

Wordsworth died in 1850 and was buried at Grasmere, near the spot where he had been inspired by the daffodils and had become aware of the beauty of nature that was to be seen all around him.

Loving Father, we praise thee for the wonderful things which thou hast given to us:

For the beautiful sun, for the rain which makes things grow, for the woods and the fields, for the sea and the sky, for the flowers and the birds, and for all thy gifts to us.

Everything around us rejoices: Make us also to rejoice and give us thankful hearts. *Amen.*

Prayers and Hymns for Little Children

Closing prayer No. 30

Springtime (3)

Bible Reading: Song of Solomon 2: 10–13

For centuries people have celebrated May Day as one of the happiest carefree days of the year. The customs associated with it went back to the time of the Druids and beyond; they were added to by the Romans in honour of Flora, the goddess of flowers; and they all added up to make a very gay holiday.

May Day began early in the morning, for young people would go out before sunrise in order to gather flowers and greenery for decoration. The girls would make a special point of washing their faces in the dew of early morning, since this was supposed to make them beautiful.

The celebrations included decorating the doorways with flowers, and processions of children through the streets. On the village green a tall maypole was set up and people danced around this holding the gaily coloured ribbons. Nearby in a leafy bower was the May Queen—and what an honour it was to be chosen. Lord Tennyson wrote:

> *You must wake and call me early, call me early,*
> *   mother dear;*
> *Tomorrow 'ill be the happiest time of all the glad*
> *   New-year;*
> *Of all the glad New-year, mother, the maddest*
> *   merriest day;*
> *For I'm to be Queen o' the May, mother, I'm to be*
> *   Queen o' the May.*

Today May Day customs, like many other old customs, are seldom kept. The carefree holiday at the beginning of May has given way to the Spring Bank Holiday later in the month.

We praise you, O Lord, for this happy time of the year, when bud and blossom, blue sky and sunshine, the song of birds and the scent of flowers all remind us of your great love and goodness. As the world of nature echoes your praise, may we join with the whole of creation to praise your holy Name. *Amen.**

Closing prayer No. 35

Springtime (4)

A FESTIVE OCCASION *Cornish 'Flora Day'*

Bible Reading: Psalm 149: 1–4

In the psalm, people were invited to show their thankfulness to God in music and dancing. At Helston, in Cornwall, people do just that each year on May 8th, which is known as 'Flora Day'.

A legend tells that centuries ago a fiery dragon appeared over the town and dropped a huge stone, which fell harmlessly clear of the houses. The people were so thankful for their wonderful deliverance that they began dancing in the streets and into the houses.

Today, 'Flora Day' is celebrated as a public holiday and people arrive in Helston to enjoy the fun. Perhaps you know the song *The Cornish Floral Dance.*

Early in the morning, the bells of the church ring out and the people gather flowers to make garlands. Then, at seven in the morning, the Furry Dance begins in the streets to music played by the town band. The children have their own dance at 10 a.m. and at noon there is a dance for adults.

At 5 p.m. there is another adult dance, when people remember their former custom and dance through the houses, in at the front door and out at the back.

Later in the evening there are more celebrations when old and young parade the streets singing:

> *Summer is come-O*
> *And winter is gone-O.*

Similar festivities are also held in other parts of the country in May as a reminder that winter days are behind and summer not far away.

Father we thank you for the glory of the springtime; for the green of the field, wood and garden; for the blue sky and sea; and for the multitude of colours as the world of nature breaks into blossom. Help us to behold your glory and give thanks; for Jesus Christ's sake. *Amen.**

Closing prayer No. 38

Springtime (5)

Robert Louis Stevenson

Take a good look around you at all the good things which the world contains and you will probably see the truth of the lines written by Robert Louis Stevenson:

> *The world is so full of a number of things,*
> *I'm sure we should all be as happy as kings.*

Robert Louis Stevenson was a man who might have been an engineer like his grandfather and his father had it not been for his health. Instead he gave us not only poems in a *Child's Garden of Verses* but exciting books such as *Treasure Island, Kidnapped* and *Dr. Jekyll and Mr. Hyde.*

Stevenson tried many places in order to find a climate that was suitable for his health, eventually settling at Apia on the island of Samoa in the Pacific Ocean.

On Apia he was much loved and respected by those who lived there. Often, in the evening, they would walk along the road which they built from the village to his house to listen to the stories which he told. They called him 'Tusitala'—the Teller of Tales—and the road was known as 'The road of the loving heart'.

When he died on 3rd December, 1894, he was buried near this very road. Stevenson had suffered much in health, but he was a happy man with a strong faith in God, ever ready to give God the glory for the world and all that is in it, as the psalmist also did in these words:

Bible Reading: Psalm 100

A prayer of Robert Louis Stevenson:

The day returns and brings us the petty round of irritating concerns and duties. Help us to play the man; help us to perform them with laughter and kind faces, let cheerfulness abound with industry. Give us to go blithely on our business this day, bring us to our resting beds weary and content and undishonoured, and grant us in the end the gift of sleep. *Amen.*

Closing prayer No. 39

Summer (1)

Midsummer Day, 24th June, is also the Feast Day of the Nativity of John the Baptist—a day which, once upon a time, was kept in a similar manner to Christmas, with decorations, feasting and merrymaking.

No doubt these celebrations dated back long before the time of John the Baptist and were connected with the worship of the sun during the period 21st to 24th June. The eve of St. John was an evening of superstition. Bonfires were lit and people danced round them, hoping to keep evil spirits from their crops. Certain plants were gathered which were supposed to keep evil things at bay. Young women believed that by various means they might discover who they were to marry. Many stayed up until well after midnight.

And if they were tired the next day, what matter? Midsummer Day was a holiday, with fairs, shows, contests and sports to be enjoyed. Today it is kept as any other day without the merrymaking.

As feast day of John the Baptist, it is a little unusual. Most feast days commemorate the death of the saint. St. John's Day commemorates his birth, six months before the birth of Jesus.

Perhaps this is because the circumstances of his birth were unusual and because it is often associated with the birth of Jesus, for John was the herald who paved the way for Jesus later in his life.

Bible Reading: St. Mark 1: 1–8

Today we remember John the Baptist as the prophet who was not afraid to say what he believed and was eventually put to death because he did so.

Help us to remember, O God, that all we have is a gift from you, to be used in your service and for the benefit of others. Make us clear in our thinking, wise in our doing, and bold in our speaking, never fearing to speak what we believe but trusting you for all our needs and knowing that you will strengthen us; through Jesus Christ our Lord. *Amen.**

Closing prayer No. 20

Summer (2)

The longest day of the year is 21st June when, early in the morning, people gather before dawn to see the sun rise at Stonehenge, on Salisbury Plain.

They stand where people stood nearly four thousand years ago, when Stonehenge was first built. In those days many people worshipped such things as the sun and the moon, which they regarded as gods. In the Bible, the prophet Ezekiel warns against worship of the sun instead of God.

Bible Reading: Ezekiel 8: 1 and 16–18

It was only natural that sun worshippers would make much of the day when the sun was seen for the longest time, and not only at Stonehenge but elsewhere by the Druids and ancient peoples of Scotland and Ireland.

Sometimes the worship of the sun was linked with the worship of fire and 21st June was kept in Ireland as Beltane, the day on which all fires had to be extinguished. Then the Beltane fire was lit on top of a hill and other fires were lit from the Beltane fire.

Beltane Day in Scotland was like a May Day celebration. As time passed, people ceased to worship the sun or fire but, for hundreds of years, Beltane proved to be a good opportunity for having a bonfire.

We know, of course, that the sun is not a god but a part of our universe. We look further than the sun and worship the God who created these things as well as the world in which we live.

Almighty God, Creator of all things, we praise you for all that tells of your greatness and your love. Help us to see in the world around us and in the heavens above all the wonders of your creation, and then praise you, the God of Creation whom we can also call our Father; through Jesus Christ your Son, our Lord. *Amen.**

Benediction No. 52

Summer (3)

July 5th is Old Midsummer Day, the day on which summer celebrations used to be held. It is also the day on which an interesting ceremony takes place on the Isle of Man.

The Isle of Man has its own government, which makes laws for the island. The Manx Parliament consists of two houses, the House of Keys, like the House of Commons, and the Legislative Council, like the House of Lords. Bills passed by both Houses have to be sent to the Queen before they become law.

When both Houses meet together, they are said to be assembled 'in Tynwald'.

July 5th is known as Tynwald Day and, each year, the people gather round Tynwald Hill at St. John's, to hear read out all the laws which have been passed during the previous twelve months.

For eleven hundred years or so, the rulers of Man have met on this hill to give their commands, demand duties or settle grievances. Today it is the Lieutenant-Governor, on behalf of the Queen, who takes the seat of honour.

He will firstly have been to church to offer prayers. Then he walks in procession from the church, between an avenue of flag-poles, to the hill, where he sits on a chair facing the church, with the sword of state resting on a table before him. Beside him sits the Bishop and around him, on lower tiers, the Council and the Keys.

The people, assembled round the hill, then hear the laws read in English and Manx, in this colourful ceremony that has roots in the past.

We remember before you, O Lord, those who have been chosen to rule our land or any part of it, and ask that they may have wisdom and sound judgement. May they govern in your faith and fear, seeking righteousness and justice, and setting aside all that is unworthy, so that in all things your will may be done; for the sake of Jesus Christ our Lord. *Amen.**

Closing prayer No. 57

Summer (4)

H. W. Longfellow

If we wander by the sea on summer days, we know that sometimes the tide will be in and sometimes it will be out. If we build our sandcastles on the wet sand we can be sure they will disappear within a few hours. No matter what else may change, the rising and falling of the tide never does. Nor can we hold it back a while to suit our wishes. An old proverb states, *Time and tide wait for no man.*

Henry Wadsworth Longfellow, who was born in the U.S.A. on 27th February, 1807, wrote such well-known poems as *Hiawatha* and *The Windmill*. Listen to part of another poem he wrote called *The Tide Rises, the Tide Falls*.

> *The tide rises, the tide falls,*
> *The twilight darkens, the curlew calls;*
> *Along the sea-sands damp and brown*
> *The traveller hastens towards the town.*
> *And the tide rises, the tide falls.*
>
> *Darkness settles on roofs and walls,*
> *But the sea, the sea in the darkness calls;*
> *The little waves, with their soft white hands,*
> *Efface the footprints in the sands.*
> *And the tide rises, the tide falls.*

Perhaps this serves as a timely reminder that people come and go and changes frequently occur but, as the tide rises and falls regularly without fail, so the things of God are changeless and completely dependable.

Bible Reading: Psalm 145: 1–3 and 8–13

We praise you, O God, that you do not change but that we can turn to you, just as people have done for thousands of years, and be sure of your help and guidance. Teach us to say as the psalmist of old, 'the Lord is good; his mercy is everlasting and his truth endureth to all generations'. *Amen.**

Benediction No. 42

Summer (5)

The countryside in summer is a hive of activity as people begin to gather in the crops which have been tended during the year. The sound of birds and bees mingle with the clatter of machinery, while here and there wafts the smell of new mown hay.

For hundreds of years hay has been grown as food for animals and it used to be the custom for people to keep their animals out of the meadows until the hay had been harvested. These lands were known as Lammas Lands, because they could not be used before Lammas, 1st August, which was an important day throughout Britain.

The name Lammas, probably came from a Saxon word, Hlafmass, meaning Loaf-Mass, because it was the custom to make loaves from the first corn to be cut and to present these to the church as a thanksgiving to God. It was also the day, hundreds of years ago, when people were expected to bring money known as Peter's Pence, to the priests so that they could send it to the Pope in Rome.

Of course, the day was also a holiday, when no work was done other than feeding the animals and when there were all manner of amusements, fairs and strange customs, some of which were particularly rowdy.

The customs and amusements associated with Lammas and other holy days now belong to the past, but the work on the land continues. For country people, the warm summer days are welcomed for the harvesting of the crops. For the townsfolk, they sometimes provide the opportunity for getting out into the pure air and enjoying the sights and sounds which the countryside has to offer.

During this season of summer, O God, we praise you for all the blessings that are ours to enjoy;
    For blue sky, green fields and warm sunshine;
    For outings, holidays and amusements;
    For health and strength and happiness;
    For these and all your blessings, we praise your Name, O God. *Amen.**

Benediction No. 14

Autumn (1)

Most people find early autumn an attractive time of year. Often there is a spell of warm sunshine shortly after we have returned to school after the summer holidays and we wish it were possible to be out in the country instead of in school. Had you lived in England several hundred years ago, one day on which you would almost certainly have gone out into the countryside to look for nuts was September 14th.

The reason was that September 14th is known as Holy Rood Day. A rood is another name for a cross, especially the kind of cross on which there is a figure of Christ.

A legend tells how, long ago in the A.D. Fourth Century, St. Helena found a cross on which it was supposed that Jesus had been crucified and September 14th came to be the day on which the finding of the cross was celebrated. Because it was a holy day, children were not expected to do lessons or any other kind of work.

As for the nuts, it just happened that there were plenty of nuts in autumn for them to find and it became the custom to go nutting on Holy Rood Day.

For that matter, there are many other interesting things to be found in autumn if we like to keep our eyes open. Flowers and fruits, leaves of many colours, ripening corn—just a few of the things that remind us of the goodness of God. Listen to the words of the psalmist:

Bible Reading: Psalm 65: 1–2 and 9–13

O God our Father, help us to see beauty in the world around us; the fruits and berries of woodland and hedgerow; the fruit of the orchard and the fields of golden corn; the beautiful colours of trees and falling leaves; and the glow of autumn sunshine after misty mornings. For these and all your blessings we praise your Name, O God. *Amen.**

Benediction No. 44

Autumn (2)

September 29th is Michaelmas Day—a day which, through the centuries, has been celebrated by people in many different ways.

In the Middle Ages, it used to be the custom to hold large fairs in some parts of the country. By Michaelmas the harvest was in, so some people had things to sell and others had money to buy them. To some of these fairs came people from many parts of Europe with their wares.

There was also lots of fun to be had at the fairs and good entertainment. Where there was no fair, the people found other ways of amusing themselves. It was the custom then, and still is in some places, to eat goose on Michaelmas Day, for an old rhyme said:

> *Whoso eats goose on Michaelmas Day*
> *Shall never lack money his debts to pay.*

Having money was important for many people because Michaelmas is one of the Quarter Days on which rent has to be paid for land.

Michaelmas, of course, means the Feast of St. Michael, and we might wonder who he was. He was not a man, as most of the saints were, but an angel who is mentioned in the Bible.

In the Book of the Revelation, for example, we read of a vision of Michael and his angels defeating the forces of evil. Consequently, St. Michael and his angels came to be regarded as the protectors of the Christians, and many churches, including Coventry Cathedral have been dedicated to St. Michael.

The psalmist tells how God watches over his own.

Bible Reading: Psalm 145: 14–21

Lord Jesus Christ, Keeper and Preserver of all things, let thy right hand guard us by day and by night, when we sit at home, and when we walk abroad, when we lie down and when we rise up, that we may be kept from all evil, and have mercy upon us sinners. *Amen.*

St. Nerses of Clajes (Fourth Century)

Benediction No. 56

Autumn (3)

Corn Laws

When we pray 'Give us this day our daily bread', we probably think of many other things as well, for life would seem very dull if bread were all we had to eat.

Yet, for hundreds and hundreds of years, bread has been the most important food for people of many lands and people are always anxious to make sure that there are plentiful supplies of flour for making it.

In the early years of the last century, when Napoleon wanted to be master of the world, he thought he could begin to crush Britain by cutting off food supplies. British farmers began growing more wheat on their land to make up for the lost supplies from overseas.

In 1815, when Napoleon was defeated, the British government wanted to make sure that the farmers could still sell their wheat for a good price. On 17th February, 1815, the Corn Laws were passed, which forbade the buying of corn from overseas unless the price of British corn dropped below a certain price.

But because the price of corn was high, the price of bread was also high. Many poor people starved because they could not afford to buy bread.

Today there are people starving in many lands, not only because of the price of corn but because the harvests have not grown.

An Old Testament law ensured that some corn was left in the corners of the fields to feed the poor.

Bible Reading: Leviticus 19: 9–10

Today, as we thank God for our daily food, we also remember others who will starve unless people who have plenty will give something to help them.

O God our Father, as we thank you for our daily food we remember those in other lands who have little to eat and we pray that ways may be found to provide them with food. Bless those who give money, or dig wells, or supply machinery, who research for better crops or who feed the starving, until the day when all people shall have enough food; through Jesus Christ. *Amen.**

Closing prayer No. 22

Autumn (4)

R. S. Hawker

In the summer months, many people travel south and west to enjoy their holidays in the West Country. Sandy beaches, washed by great Atlantic rollers, are ideal for swimming, surfing and sunbathing, while quaint little fishing villages and rocky coves provide opportunities to explore or relax.

Yet those same waves and rocks, which give pleasure in the sun, can bring disaster at other seasons. Many a fine ship has been wrecked on the Lizard, near Lands End, or elsewhere on the unfriendly rocky coast.

In the days gone by, these were the haunts of smugglers and wreckers. It was not unknown for people to light false beacons so that sailors, thinking themselves to be on a safe course, would find their ships being dashed to pieces on the rocks and their cargoes looted by wreckers.

Robert Stephen Hawker found this happening when he became Vicar of Morwenstow in 1834. He soon made friends with his parishioners, who found him always ready to help them, to give them even the coat from his back or the food from his own larder.

Hawker was a man who saw beauty around him and he sought to draw the attention of the villagers to this instead of their other activities. He is believed to have started the custom of holding Harvest Thanksgiving services, with people bringing a gift to church, much as the people of Old Testament times did.

Bible Reading: Deuteronomy 26: 1–4

Hawker, who also wrote poetry, left Morwenstow a much pleasanter place than he found it, when he died on 15th August, 1875, having been its vicar for forty-one years.

Almighty God, Creator of heaven and earth and all that is in them; we praise you for the beauty around us; for sunshine, clear skies and golden sunsets; for flowers and all your creatures; for ripe fruits and fields of golden corn; for hills and streams and open spaces. We praise you too for eyes to see, for ears to hear and for full stomachs. Help us to share your gifts with others; for Jesus Christ's sake. *Amen.**

Closing prayer No. 19

Autumn (5)

'COME, YE THANKFUL PEOPLE . . .' *Dean Henry Alford*

Some people find difficulty in doing anything well: others seem to be successful at anything they put their hand to. One of the latter was Henry Alford, who was born in London on 7th October, 1810.

He began writing when he was only six and, when he was sixteen he declared his intention to give his talents to God. 'Henceforth', he wrote, 'to become his, and to do his work as far as in me lies.'

In the years that followed, he became known as a poet, hymnwriter, scholar, Bible translator, preacher, lecturer, author, musician and painter. When he was forty-seven, he became Dean of Canterbury Cathedral, with the responsibility of running the day to day affairs of the cathedral.

Some of his hymns were especially written as processional hymns, to be sung as the choir walked round the cathedral. It was a long way, and so the hymns too were quite long.

But his best-known hymn was written to be sung at harvest festivals, which were then becoming popular and, from that day to this, people have sung with enthusiasm 'Come, ye thankful people, come', which is now one of the best-known harvest hymns.

It is fitting that we should remember to thank God for the harvest and, at the same time pray that God may gather in his harvest of people from the whole world. This hymn provides us with the words for doing both.

This is what Jesus had to say about the harvests.

Bible Reading: St. John 4: 31–36

A prayer of Henry Alford:

O God, who hast commanded us to be perfect, as thou our Father in heaven art perfect; put into our hearts, we pray thee, a continual desire to obey thy holy will. Teach us day by day what thou wouldst have us to do, and give us grace and power to fulfil the same. May we never from love of ease decline the path which thou pointest out, nor, for fear of shame, turn away from it; for the sake of Christ Jesus our Lord. *Amen.*

Closing prayer No. 12

Ordinary and extraordinary (1)

Hallowe'en—October 31st

There is an old Scottish prayer which says:

> '*From ghoulies and ghosties and long leggety beasties*
> *And things that go bump in the night,*
> *Good Lord, deliver us.*'

Tonight would be as good a night as any to offer such a prayer, for tonight is Hallowe'en, the night on which people used to believe that witches, wizards, warlocks, hobgoblins and all manner of evil spirits had special powers.

One reason is that tomorrow is All Saints' Day, or All Hallows and it was thought that the evil spirits made the most of Hallowe'en because they would not dare to be about on All Saints' Day.

Hallowe'en was always an occasion for amusements and apples and nuts played an important part in these.

But for many, Hallowe'en was a time for fear and all sorts of things were done to try to break the spells of evil spirits. Farmers would light bonfires in the farmyard to keep the evil from their cattle and horses. Others would march round their fields with torches, believing that this would protect their crops in the following year.

Back in Bible times, people used to believe that evil spirits were much to be feared.

Bible Reading: St. Luke 10: 17–20

Nowadays few people live in fear of evil spirits. Our prayer today is not for deliverance from ghoulies and ghosties and long leggety beasties, but one of thankfulness to God that we have no need to live in fear of such things.

We thank you, O God, that, through trust in you, we can be free from superstition and fear. We remember before you the people of many lands, who still live in dread of the power of evil spirits. O God, let your light so shine in the world that all men may know you, and knowing you love you, and loving you find freedom from all their fears; through Jesus Christ our Lord. *Amen.**

Closing prayer No. 4

Ordinary and extraordinary (2)

For hundreds of years, November 1st has been kept as All Saints' Day or All Hallows, a somewhat quiet day after the excitement and bonfires of Hallowe'en.

It has always been kept as a special day in the Church on which many great Christians are remembered. During the year, many days are set aside as feast days of particular saints. In fact almost every day of the year is the feast day of one or more saints, about some of whom we know very little except their names and why they were called saints.

We cannot even tell how many people have been called saints. The Roman Catholic Church lists about 4,500 but there are many others besides. So 1st November is kept as All Saints' Day—a day upon which all saints can be remembered, whether they have their own special day or not.

Of course, there are many people who might be regarded as saints apart from those who are called saints. The saints whose days we keep are those who have been 'canonized' by the church. That means that their names were put on the list of recognized saints. They were called saints because they had given all they had to God.

True saints are those who have been ready to do as Jesus did and to follow in his footsteps, sometimes at great cost to themselves.

Bible Reading: St. John 14: 12–15

A saint cannot be made. St. Paul once wrote, 'I live: yet not I, but Christ liveth in me'. A saint is one who is like Christ in his ways because he has Christ in his heart.

We thank you, God our Father, for the saints of all ages who discovered what your will for them was and were then prepared to do it. Help us to follow their example so that we may learn of you and walk for ever in your holy ways after the example of Jesus Christ our Lord. *Amen.**

Closing prayer No. 2

Ordinary and extraordinary (3)

Abraham Lincoln, one time President of the United States of America, is said to have remarked, 'The Lord prefers common-looking people. That is the reason he makes so many of them.'

When you come to think of it, there are far more ordinary-looking people than there are beautiful ones or ugly ones. There are far more ordinary people than there have been saints or particularly bad people.

Yesterday (November 1st) was All Saints' Day, when the Church remembered all the saints; today (November 2nd) is All Souls' Day, when the Church remembers those who have never been counted as saints—the millions of people of every land who have died.

Many years ago, it was thought that the souls of those who had died would like the chance to eat some earthly food again. So, on the evening before All Souls' Day, a meal was laid and the door left open overnight so that the food could be eaten.

Those who were poor and wished to set a meal would beg for food. They were given buns known as 'soul-cakes'. These were eaten by the poor themselves.

When November 2nd dawned, the church bells began to toll, and continued to do so all day, as prayers were offered for the souls of those who had died.

The names of some people will never be forgotten: today we think not of these but of the millions of ordinary people forgotten by us but remembered by God.

Bible Reading: St. Luke 12: 6–9

We remember before you, O Lord, the millions of ordinary folk who have trodden this earth before us, especially those who have tried to live good lives after the example that Jesus set. May we follow their example so that by believing in your Name and heeding your commands we may one day hear you say to us, 'Well done, good and faithful servant'; through Jesus Christ our Lord. *Amen.**

Closing prayer No. 28

Ordinary and extraordinary (4)

Yeomen of the Guard

Bible Reading: Ecclesiastes 3: 1–8

Times change, but every now and then we have a glimpse of the past which reminds us of times very different from our own.

No visit to London is complete without seeing a 'Beefeater' at the Tower of London. He may be dressed in a uniform of navy-blue and red, or he may be resplendent in his dress uniform of red and gold.

His uniform may appear old-fashioned, but then, of course, he is a member of the oldest professional military body in England, the Yeomen of the Guard.

When Henry VII became King of England he decided to have his own bodyguard, which was no doubt a very wise decision in those troubled times. This bodyguard of fifty men, the original Yeomen of the Guard, began their duties on the day that the King was crowned, 30th October, 1485.

There are now one hundred in their ranks. Beside their duties at the Tower of London—their correct title being the Yeomen Warders of the Tower—the 'Beefeaters' undertake only ceremonial duties as the bodyguards of the sovereign. They are usually on duty on state occasions.

Each autumn they have another duty to perform. Before the Queen goes to the State Opening of Parliament, they search the cellars even as they have done since Guy Fawkes tried to blow up the Houses of Parliament.

In these days, when the Queen's bodyguard is more likely to consist of plain-clothes detectives, it is pleasant sometimes to reflect on bygone days and then be thankful for the way of life that we know today.

Grant to us, Lord, we pray thee, day by day the joy of true living, that we who seek thy service may find thy peace and grow into the likeness of thy Son, Jesus Christ our Lord. *Amen.*

Prayers in use at Uppingham School

Benediction No. 55

Ordinary and extraordinary (5)

The Lord Mayor's Show

For hundreds of years, November 9th was kept in London as Lord Mayor's Show day, when the new Lord Mayor began his term of office.

This office is a very old one, going back nearly nine hundred years to the time when the merchants of London were given the privilege of electing their own mayor, or chief magistrate, in return for paying a sum of money to the King. Some years later, the holder of the office became known as the Lord Mayor.

One of the principal features of the Show is the long procession of military bands and colourful tableaux on lorries, together with other interesting or amusing people and vehicles. Large numbers of Londoners have turned out to see the procession, which has stopped all traffic. Nowadays, to avoid this, the Lord Mayor's show is held on a Saturday.

On this day, the Lord Mayor takes office in the Guildhall. Then he proceeds in his gilded coach, escorted by his special bodyguard of pikemen, to Temple Bar on the boundary of the City of London, to receive the Queen's approval of his election. The procession then returns to the centre of the city.

For the Lord Mayor it is a very important occasion, for he becomes the most important citizen of London. Other cities also have their Lord Mayor: towns and boroughs have a mayor. All of these have been chosen because of the great service they have given over a period of many years to the area of which they become 'first citizen'.

Let us hear how St. Paul told Timothy to pray for those in authority.

Bible Reading: 1 Timothy 2: 1–3

Almighty God, we ask your guidance for all who have authority in our towns and cities, so that they may use their office wisely for the benefit of all citizens. Grant unto them wisdom as they govern, strength for all their tasks, and a true vision as they plan for the future. May all they say or do be for the good of your people and the glory of your name. *Amen.**

Benediction No. 44

Christmas tide (1)

Long before Christmas people begin to make their preparations. Shop windows are attractively set with gifts and decorations; coloured lights adorn the streets of some large cities; and decorated Christmas trees appear in town and village.

Christmas is celebrated in many different ways all over the world and each country has its own special customs and festivities.

In Sweden, for example, the people begin their Christmas season as they celebrate St. Lucy's Day on 13th December. In Sweden she is called St. Lucia.

We know very little about St. Lucy, except that she was put to death as a Christian at Syracuse in Sicily in the A.D. Fourth Century, and that 13th December was set aside as her feast day.

As is the case with many of the saints, there are several legends told about her, which may or may not be true, suggesting that somehow she lost the sight of her eyes and that God gave her her sight again. For that reason, her help was often sought for people who had diseases of the eyes. On the other hand, it may just be that her name means 'light' and the eyes are the way of letting light into the body.

St. Lucia's Day in Sweden is a festival of light. Pretty girls dress themselves as St. Lucia and wear crowns of lighted candles. Then they go from house to house with trays of coffee and sweet cakes.

In the dark northern winter nights, the lights of St. Lucia's Day make a pleasant beginning to the Christmas celebrations, the most popular holiday of all, when we remember the birth of Jesus, who came to be the Light of the World.

Bible Reading: St. John 1: 1–14

Shine upon us, O God, as the sun that shines in the sky, giving us light to see the right way through life and the warmth of your love to set our hearts aglow, so that we may become more truly your children; through Jesus Christ our Lord. *Amen.**

Benediction No. 51

Christmas tide (2)

St. Nicholas

One of the best-known figures at Christmas time is St. Nicholas, or he may be called Santa Claus or Father Christmas. Children in many parts of the world will be writing letters to him in the hope that he will fill their stockings with good things.

The original St. Nicholas, whom the Christian Church remembers on 6th December, was Bishop of Myra in Asia Minor about sixteen hundred years ago.

One story told of St. Nicholas is that there lived in his town a poor man with three daughters, none of whom could marry because they did not have the money for a dowry—a sum of money paid to a husband at the time of marriage. One night St. Nicholas went quietly to the house and dropped a bag of gold through the window. Then he slipped away so that no one would see him. The next morning, the eldest girl was delighted. Now she could marry.

Another night visit with a purse of gold brought happiness to the second daughter. But now the father was on his guard. If a third bag of gold came for the other daughter, he would be there to see who had been so kind. So when St. Nicholas came the third time, the secret was out.

It is small wonder that many children will be hoping, not for a bag of gold, but for a present they would dearly like to have. No doubt this Christmas St. Nicholas will bring joy to many as he has done through the centuries. No doubt many too will remember that the giving of Christmas gifts began when God gave his Son to the world.

Bible Reading: St. John 3: 16–19

O Lord Jesus Christ, who by your example taught men to be kind to one another and generous to those in need; bless all who seek to bring cheer to the hearts of others during the coming days; let your spirit of goodwill be abroad in the world; and help us to remember that it is more blessed to give than to receive; for the sake of Jesus Christ our Lord, to whom be the praise and glory for ever. *Amen.**

Benediction No. 49

Christmas tide (3)

Charles Wesley

Charles Wesley, who was born on 18th December, 1707, was the eighteenth child of the rector of Epworth in Lincolnshire and a young brother of John Wesley, who founded the Methodist movement.

Charles Wesley's fame lies in the writing of hymns. He seemed to be able to write a hymn on almost any subject at any time. During his lifetime, he is believed to have written about 6,500 hymns, many of them among the finest we have. They include *Jesu lover of my soul, Love divine all loves excelling* and *Rejoice, the Lord is king.*

Charles Wesley also wrote a hymn which he entitled *A hymn for Christmas Day.* It began *Hark how all the welkin rings* and it was included in the Church of England Book of Common Prayer by mistake. The Wesleys were not then popular in the Church of England and the hymns which Charles had written were frowned upon. The printer who slipped it in did not know that.

However the hymn proved popular and was sung at Christmas time for many years. Then, one day, a singer fitted the words to a tune which had been written by Mendelssohn, changed the first line and the hymn rocketed to become a firm favourite, sung wherever Christmas music is sung:

> *Hark! the herald-angels sing*
> *Glory to the new-born King.*

It is one of the many lovely carols which we sing at Christmas time in praise of God for sending his Son, Jesus Christ into the world.

Now let us hear in the words of the prophet Isaiah one of the promises made concerning Jesus.

Bible Reading: Isaiah 9: 2 and 6–7

O God, our Father, we would join with the angels to praise you for your great and wonderful gift to the world. As we remember the birth of Jesus, fill our hearts with gladness and the spirit of goodwill, so that we may praise you both in word and deed; and to you be the glory for ever and ever. *Amen.**

Benediction No. 43

Christmas tide (4)

Christmas tide (4)

CHRISTMAS EVE   *Joseph Mohr*

Bible Reading: St. Luke 2: 8–16

It was the night before Christmas 1818 in the little village of Oberndorf, Austria. Joseph Mohr, the vicar, had just read this passage when a few verses inspired by the reading came into his mind. It would be pleasant, he thought, if they could be used at the Christmas Eve service, so he called on the organist and handed him the verses.

Franz Gruber, the organist, thereupon composed a tune to which the verses could be sung and that was how one of the greatest Christmas hymns—*Silent Night*—was created.

That evening the organ broke down but, not to be outdone, the vicar and organist sang the hymn as a duet.

There the story might have ended had it not been for the organ. When the instrument had been repaired, the organist sat down to test it and played the tune composed by Gruber. He liked it and asked for a copy which he took back to his home town. There a ladies' choir added it to their repertoire and it was included when they sang in other towns as well.

Gradually it became known by more and more people and it increased in popularity until today it must surely be the most frequently sung Christmas hymn. Moreover it is sung, not only in the language in which it was written, but it has been translated into others too, so that, all over the world, people are united at Christmas in singing *Silent Night* in their own language.

O Lord our God, help us we pray, in the bustle of today, to draw aside and think of your great gift to us, your son Jesus Christ, who was born to help us to know more of your love. Then, in the quietness, may we too hear your words of peace to men of goodwill. Help us to do what we can to extend your kingdom of peace now and always; through Jesus Christ our Lord. *Amen.**

Closing prayer No. 7

Christmas tide (5)

> *Good King Wenceslas looked out*
> *On the feast of Stephen ...*

We all know from the song how his heart, full of the Christmas spirit, led him to go out and help the poor man whom he saw in the snow.

The day was 26th December, the Feast of Stephen being the day on which the Christian Church remembers St. Stephen, the first man to be killed because of his faith in Jesus Christ.

In those early days of the Christian Church, much help was given wherever possible to those who were in need but the Bible tells how one group felt neglected and how the apostles did something about it.

Bible Reading: Acts 6: 1–(4 and) 7

Of the seven men whom they chose, Stephen was described as a 'man full of faith and of the Holy Ghost'.

Soon, Stephen had made his mark by doing great wonders and miracles among the people. But he also made certain enemies, who were determined to stop him. Some of these persuaded the council that Stephen had been speaking blasphemous words against God.

So Stephen was taken before the council to answer the charges that had been made. The Bible tells that 'all who sat in the council saw his face as it had been the face of an angel'. They asked him, 'Are these things right that we hear?'

Stephen was so outspoken in his reply, that he was cast out of the city and stoned, praying with his last breath, 'Lord lay not this sin to their charge.'

O God our Father, at this season when our hearts are filled with the spirit of Christmas and we thank you for Jesus, help us remember also that he was rejected and crucified. Forgive us when sometimes we turn away from you. Fill our hearts with the spirit of our Lord Jesus Christ so that we may try to do your will. Help us, for Jesus Christ's sake. *Amen.**

Closing prayer No. 8

4 The Christian Church

This section of six themes is particularly related to the Christian Church and to worship.

The Christian Church	*The Christian calendar*
The Bible	*Prayer*
Hymns we enjoy	*Thank you for these*

Each is of five topics with the exception of *The Christian Calendar*, which has six. This particular theme should be regarded rather as a series of topics normally to be taken appropriately through the year as near as possible to the festival:

Advent	begins 4th Sunday before Christmas
Christmas	25th December
Epiphany	6th January
Holy Week	Week leading up to Easter
Good Friday	Friday of Holy Week
Easter	Date variable (consult diary)
The Ascension	Thursday, 40 days after Easter
Whitsun	Seven weeks after Easter

Perhaps appropriate hymns could be sung on the days when *Hymns we enjoy* are used—either the hymns in question or others by the same hymn writer.

The theme *Thank you for these* may not obviously come into this section but has been included as a general theme of thanksgiving to God for everyday things—which is an essential aspect of Christian worship.

The Christian Church (1)

St. Ninian

For hundreds of years, the Christian Church has played an important part in the lives of the people of Britain. Great cathedrals and churches rise above cities and towns, while even the humblest village may boast its parish church and maybe a chapel too.

But what is a church? In one respect it is a building in which people worship God, but it is also the name given to the group of people who worship there. The Christian Church is not a building but a large body of people. In the Acts of the Apostles we can read of the very early Christian Church.

Bible Reading: Acts of the Apostles 2: 41–47

These people spread Christianity far and wide starting small communities or churches wherever they went. Here and there in Britain, we find traces of early Christian worship. On the Isle of Whithorn, in SW. Scotland, for example, can be seen the remains of a chapel built by St. Ninian, a missionary whose work was to teach the Picts about Jesus Christ.

We cannot be sure how long he worked there, nor how far he travelled but Whithorn became an important Christian centre for hundreds of years.

St. Ninian died about A.D. 436, and he is remembered on 16th September by the church. He is also remembered at Whithorn, where many of the relics of his time may be seen in the priory.

But perhaps Ninian, and other great Christian teachers who worked before or after him in other parts of Britain would feel that their greatest memorial is a land filled with churches and chapels for the worship of God.

Almighty God, our heavenly Father, by whose Son men were commanded to go forth and preach the Gospel, we thank you for those who have answered your call and especially those who brought your word to our land. May we show our thanks in our remembrance of you and in our readiness to do your will; through Jesus Christ our Lord. *Amen.**

Closing prayer No. 17

The Christian Church (2)

St. Paul's Cathedral

For over thirteen and a half centuries, there has been a cathedral, bearing the name of St. Paul, on Ludgate Hill in the City of London.

The first St. Paul's was a wooden church, burned down after only a few years. The next was a stone building, destroyed by the Vikings. Then came another Saxon building, burned down in 1087, after which the great cathedral, known as 'Old St. Paul's' was begun. This was destroyed during the Great Fire of London, and the present one was built.

Being the cathedral of the City of London, St. Paul's has seen many great occasions. Here some of the greatest people in the land have been brought so that the nation could mourn their death—Lord Nelson, the Duke of Wellington, Sir Winston Churchill and others.

Here kings and queens have gathered in order to offer thanks to God for special mercies or blessings. It was here, on 27th November, 1588, that Queen Elizabeth the First attended a special thanksgiving service for England's victory over the Spanish Armada.

The Queen travelled to the cathedral in a kind of chariot drawn by four white horses, amid a sounding of trumpets, to find the cathedral decorated with ensigns captured from the enemy ships.

Thus the Queen and her subjects offered thanks to God for his mercies—a simple thing to do, but one which is all too often forgotten.

Bible Reading: Psalm 95: 1–7a

Almighty God, we praise and thank you for all your great and wonderful works. We try to count the blessings received from you and find ourselves quite unable to do so. O God, help us to recognize your blessings and give us thankful hearts, that we may be more ready to serve you with our whole being; through Jesus Christ our Lord. *Amen.**

Closing prayer No. 34

The Christian Church (3)

Even in the early days of the Church, differences of opinion arose. Paul had to write to the Church at Corinth to remind them that there was only one Church of Jesus Christ.

Bible Reading: 1 Corinthians 1: 10–15

A few hundred years ago, the Church became really divided. In fact, when King Edward VI of England died on 6th July, 1553, at the age of sixteen, some people were very sad but others were secretly pleased. It was not that they wished to see the King die young, but they were concerned about their religion.

The young King's father, Henry VIII, had said that the Church in England would no longer recognize the Pope as leader. This pleased some but made others angry. Those who wanted the Pope were Roman Catholics. Those who did not were known as Protestants. Edward VI's reign saw even more changes, such as printing prayer books in English instead of Latin. This pleased the Protestants but not the Roman Catholics.

When the King became ill the Protestants were sad and the Roman Catholics pleased, for the next ruler would be Mary, who was a Roman Catholic. For many years there was much bad feeling and dreadful things were done by both groups.

That was over four hundred years ago and feelings aroused then are still remembered, but we can thank God that there are many Christian people today who are ready to try to understand the views of those with whom they cannot see eye to eye.

Let us pray for the Churches throughout the world, for their truth, unity, and stability; that in all, charity may flourish, and truth may live. For our own Church, that what is lacking in it may be supplied, and what is unsound corrected; for the sake of Jesus Christ, our only Lord and Saviour. *Amen.*

Bishop Lancelot Andrewes

Closing prayer No. 21

The Christian Church (4)

World Council of Churches

How many churches or chapels do you know near your home? If you have looked at the notice-boards, you will realize that there are many different kinds. There is certain to be an Anglican Church—the Church of England. There may also be Roman Catholic, Methodist, Baptist, United Reformed or other Churches too.

There are so many different denominations because, through the years, one group after another broke away from the original Church, mainly because some people thought that one belief or another was most important, whilst others did not agree. Although all these Churches worshipped the same God, there was often bad feeling between them. In recent years, they have learned the wisdom of working together, in the spirit of the words of St. Paul.

Bible Reading: Ephesians 4: 1–6

One organization through which this is done is the World Council of Churches, which was formed on 23rd August, 1948. It is described as 'a fellowship of Churches, which accept Jesus Christ our Lord as God and Saviour'. Over two hundred Churches, from all parts of the world are members.

The World Council of Churches meets roughly every five years to discuss matters of concern to all the Christian Churches—ways of helping one another and those in need, and seeking a united answer to some of the problems of today's world.

Hear our prayers for your Church, O God:

Grant that all who call themselves by the name of Christian may work together in unity and love:

Grant that the branches of the Church may set aside any differences and seek only what is your will:

Grant that the World Council of Churches and all its activities may receive your blessing.

So may your Kingdom grow and your Name be glorified; through Jesus Christ our Lord. *Amen.**

Benediction No. 53

The Christian Church (5)

A CHURCH THAT CARES   *Charles Haddon Spurgeon*

Bible Reading: 1 Thessalonians 5: 14–18

These words of St. Paul remind us that the duty of the Christian Church is not only to worship God but to care for those in need.

One who tried to do this was Charles Haddon Spurgeon, who was born at Kelvedon, Essex, on 19th June, 1834.

When quite young, he decided that his life would be spent in the service of Christ. As a teenager, he became pastor of a little country Baptist church, but he was not to stay there for long. At the age of twenty, he moved to a church in Southwark, London.

Now, if there was one thing that Spurgeon could do, it was preach—and people soon came to know about him. Before long, the chapel was not large enough to contain all those who wanted to hear him, so a hall was hired instead. Then a new church, the Metropolitan Tabernacle was built and Spurgeon preached regularly to congregations of many thousands of people.

His sermons were taken down in shorthand and printed; they were also translated into other languages. He founded a college, an orphanage, a book organization, alms houses, schools and other organizations. He also wrote over a hundred books.

Yet, for all this, he thought much of other people and he loved to surprise the old or the sick by calling at their homes and giving them a few pounds to help them over a difficult period. Spurgeon was a man who put his preaching into practice. He knew that the Christian Church must be a caring Church.

Almighty God, help us to remember the words of the prophet Micah, that you require us to do justly, to love mercy, and to walk humbly with you. May we uphold what we know to be right and love our neighbours, and as we do so may we know in our hearts that we walk with you; through Christ our Lord. *Amen.**

Closing prayer No. 6

The Christian calendar (1)

The Christian calendar begins with the season of Advent. The first day of Advent is Advent Sunday, which is the fourth Sunday before Christmas.

The word Advent means 'coming' or 'arrival' and the season of Advent is one in which Christian people prepare themselves for Christmas, when Jesus came into the world.

In other words, Advent is a time of looking forward to something very happy. Most of us have our times of looking forward, to birthdays, holidays or special occasions. Sometimes this time of waiting seems to go so slowly and we long for the day to come that we have been looking forward to.

The Jewish people of Old Testament times were also longing for something to happen. They had been promised that one day a Messiah would come who would make life so much better for them. They believed he would overthrow their enemies. Here are some of the things which Isaiah the prophet spoke about the Messiah:

Bible Reading: Isaiah 11: 1–5

Christian people believe that Jesus came as the Messiah, not to deliver them from earthly enemies but to save them from their sin and selfishness and to show what God can really mean to people as God and Father of us all. So Advent is a time to prepare ourselves to receive Jesus at Christmas.

But it is more than that, for Jesus told his disciples that one day he would come again. Advent is therefore a time to remember how Jesus came and also how he promised to come again.

We praise you, God our Father, for sending Jesus Christ into the world to be the saviour of mankind. At this happy season of the year we rejoice at his coming and we remember his words that he would come again. Make us ready to receive him and willing to work for the day when people throughout the world shall worship him as King of Kings. *Amen.**

Closing prayer No. 19

The Christian calendar (2)

The first festival in the Christian year is Christmas, the day on which we remember the coming of Jesus into the world. In many countries, Christmas is traditionally kept on 25th December, though there is nothing to suggest that Jesus was born on this day. In fact his birth was probably much earlier in the year but the early Christians found it convenient to celebrate Christmas on a day which was already a holiday.

The stories surrounding the birth of Jesus are all found in the Gospels, some in St. Luke and some in St. Matthew. Those in St. Luke tell how Jesus was promised to Mary and of the circumstances surrounding his birth. They tell how Mary and Joseph had to go to Bethlehem for a census and how Jesus was born in a stable because there was no room in the inn.

Bible Reading: St. Luke 2: 1–20

In St. Matthew we read how a promise of a son was given to Joseph and how, later on, wise men from the east brought gifts, possibly about two years after Jesus was born. Although this story is remembered at Christmas, it is also commemorated on Epiphany, 6th January.

Whatever we may know or may not know about the birth of Jesus, Christmas remains a season of goodwill when, for a time, people think a little more kindly and try to bring a little cheer into the world.

For Christian people it is a special reminder that God showed himself to the world in Jesus Christ—a story which only began at Christmas and continued during his ministry of teaching.

We thank you, God our Father, for the wonder of the story of the first Christmas, of the journey to Bethlehem, the birth of the Baby for whom there was no room in the inn, the wonder of the shepherds, and the adoration of the wise men. Help us to make room for Christ in our hearts, and to offer to him the best gifts we have in thankfulness for all he gave for us. We ask it in his Name. *Amen.**

Closing prayer No. 12

The Christian calendar (3)

The week leading up to Easter is known as Holy Week. It begins with Palm Sunday, the day on which we recall how Jesus rode into Jerusalem on an ass, while the disciples cast clothing onto the ground for the ass to walk upon, and the people shouted with a loud voice, 'Hosanna to the Son of David: Blessed is he that cometh in the name of the Lord: Hosanna in the highest.'

As Jesus rode into the city, people asked, 'Who is this?' and they were told that he was the prophet from Galilee. The people thought that here was the one who would now lead them into battle and fight off the Roman overlords.

For Jesus, however, it was not a moment of triumph, but one of sadness, for he knew that the people who were shouting so loudly were wanting a ruler—but not one who had come to teach them a new way of life as he had. He had already wept as he looked at the city and realized all that the people could have become if only they had accepted his words.

After the procession reached the city, the religious leaders, the Scribes and the Pharisees, were angry. 'Tell these people to be quiet,' they told Jesus. They were furious when Jesus went into the temple and cast out those who were changing money or selling animals for sacrifice. They were more angry when Jesus taught the people openly in the city. Something had to be done.

During those days, they laid their plans and found unexpected help from one of the disciples, Judas Iscariot, so that they could take Jesus by night to be tried and crucified.

Bible Reading: St. Matthew 26: 1–5 and 14–16

Almighty God, help us to remember how your Son, our Lord and Saviour Jesus Christ was welcomed as a king by those who soon shouted for him to be crucified. Help us to accept him as king of our lives and to remain true to him forever, ignoring those who would laugh at us or ridicule us and standing firm on the side of righteousness; through Jesus Christ our Lord. *Amen.**

Closing prayer No. 11

The Christian calendar (4)

In the very early hours of the morning, Jesus Christ stood before Pontius Pilate, the Roman governor, accused by the Jewish leaders, who wished to see him put to death.

Pilate, who could find no fault in Jesus, offered to release him, but the people in the courtyard cried out for him to be crucified. Pilate, at last, gave in to them and allowed Jesus to be delivered into the hands of the soldiers to be crucified.

Finally, he was scourged with a cruel whip, then mocked by the soldiers, who plaited a crown of thorns and put it on his head, dressed him in a scarlet robe, spat on him, beat him and eventually led him to his death.

Carrying his cross, he was taken by the soldiers through the streets toward the hill called Calvary. Weakened by the ill-treatment, he stumbled and a man in the crowd was compelled to carry the cross for him.

On Calvary, or Golgotha—'the place of a skull'—he was nailed to the cross and left to die in agony, while the soldiers divided his clothes between them and the Jews hurled insults at him. On either side was crucified a common thief.

Bible Reading: St. Mark 15: 25–39

It was nine in the morning when Jesus was crucified: it was three in the afternoon when he died. Almost his last words from the cross were a prayer for forgiveness for those who had crucified him.

His body was taken from the cross, bound in linen cloths and laid in a tomb which was sealed by a huge stone.

O God, our Father, who loved the world so much that you gave your only begotten son; help us to know that through his death on the cross we are saved from our sin and our selfishness. May we show our love for you by seeking to keep your commandments; and may we be ready to give all that we have to him who gave all he had for us; Jesus Christ our Lord. *Amen*

Closing prayer No. 21

The Christian calendar (5)

A little group of men and women had met together, wondering what to do. Jesus, their leader, in whom they had placed their trust, was dead and sealed in a tomb. Some of the women decided that, as the Sabbath was over, they would go to the tomb to pay their last respects.

Imagine their surprise to discover that the huge stone was rolled away; the linen clothes were lying just where the body had been; but of Jesus there was no sign. Instead they saw two angels.

'Why are you looking for the living among the dead?' they asked. 'He is not here, but is risen, as he told you in Galilee.'

The women did not know what to think. They ran back and told the disciples, who did not believe them until they had seen the empty tomb for themselves.

Mary Magdalene remained behind, weeping in the garden. Seeing someone whom she thought to be the gardener, she asked where the body had been taken. Jesus, for it was he, just spoke her name and then she recognized him.

That night the disciples were in the upper room when Jesus came to them and spoke with them.

Here is one of the Bible stories, which tells how Jesus came to his disciples.

Bible Reading: St. Luke 24: 36–43

Jesus also appeared to others on that day and on days that followed. So, the day that had begun in despair was turned into something more wonderful than ever they could have imagined and Christian people still shout for joy: 'Christ is risen, Hallelujah! (Praise the Lord!)'.

At this Easter time, O Lord, help us to remember that Christ is not just a figure in a story book but one who lives today in the hearts of all that love him. Help us to understand that it is through his death and rising again that we learn of your love for us. Help us to find Christ for ourselves and know the true joy of Easter in the presence of the living Lord, to whom be praise and glory for ever and ever. *Amen.**

Closing prayer No. 36

The Christian calendar (6)

During the period of forty days after Easter, Jesus appeared to his disciples on a number of occasions, sometimes to individuals and sometimes to groups. On some of these they were reminded that they were to continue the work that Jesus had started.

The last of these appearances was on the Mount of Olives near Jerusalem. We can read what happened then in the opening verses of the Acts of the Apostles.

Bible Reading: Acts 1: 1–11

This took place on the fortieth day after Easter—the day which we still celebrate as Ascension Day.

The disciples then had to wait. They were told to do nothing until the Holy Spirit came to them to give them power for their work: then they could preach the Gospel to the ends of the earth. So they waited in an upper room, spending much of their time in prayer.

Shortly afterwards came the Jewish festival, Pentecost, and it was on this day that the disciples suddenly found that the power of God was in them. Being filled with the Holy Spirit, they left the room where they had hidden themselves away and went into the heart of the city, where they amazed people with their preaching. Peter made a very strongly worded speech which led to the addition of about three thousand people to the Christian Church.

The Pharisees had been pleased to see Jesus out of their way: now they realized that his followers had to be reckoned with. In those days, and in the centuries since then, Christian people have found strength and inspiration for their work through the Holy Spirit and the Church has steadily spread throughout the world.

Grant unto us, O God our Father
The power of the Holy Spirit to strengthen us;
The guidance of the Holy Spirit through our conscience;
And the inspiration of the Holy Spirit so that we know your will;
    Through Jesus Christ our Lord. *Amen.**

Closing prayer No. 27

The Bible (1)

Those who wish to study any subject usually make good use of a library, where they can find books to give them the information they need. Those who wish to learn about God also have special books from which they can learn. Christian people find their help in the Bible.

The Bible has often been described as a library of books. It is not just one book but many—sixty-six in all—and they are so arranged that people can find them easily. In the first place, the Bible is divided into two parts—the Old Testament and the New Testament. The books of the Old Testament were the Holy Scriptures of the Jewish people and they are arranged so that the books of laws come first, then other history books, then books of poetry and finally the books of the prophets. There are thirty-nine books in the Old Testament.

The books of the New Testament tell the Gospel story about Jesus and his teachings. There is also the book of the Acts of the Apostles, telling how the Church grew, some letters written by Paul and others and a book called The Revelation. There are twenty-seven books in the New Testament.

From all of these we can learn what God is like and what he would have us do. The Bible, therefore, is not just a book to be read but a book to be studied. Many people like to set aside a time every day when they can study their Bibles and so try to become better Christians. Lots of people buy daily notes to read with their Bibles so that as they read each passage from the Bible they can also have some help in understanding it.

St. Paul knew the value of studying the scriptures and this is what he wrote to Timothy:

Bible Reading: 2 Timothy 3: 14–17

We praise you, O God, for teaching us your laws for life through the words of the Holy Scriptures. Guide us by your Holy Spirit as we read so that we may understand your will, walk in your ways, and grow in the knowledge of our Lord Jesus Christ. *Amen.**

Benediction No. 42

The Bible (2)

Psalm 119 is a very long one and it gives many reminders of the value of knowing God's word and of obeying His commands. This is how it begins:

Bible Reading: Psalm 119: 1–7

Now the Bible was not written all in the same language. The Jewish scriptures, which became the Old Testament, were written in Hebrew: the language of the New Testament was Greek. But in the early days of the Church, Christian leaders settled in Rome where, even today, the Pope, the head of the Roman Catholic Church, lives. Because Latin was the language of Rome, Latin became the language used by the church, and it was important that there should be a reliable version of the Bible in Latin.

The task of preparing this was given to one of the greatest Bible scholars of early times, Eusebius Hieronymus, better known today as St. Jerome, whose feast day is 30th September. It was a tremendous task and it took St. Jerome about twenty-one years to complete it. Most of the work was done in Bethlehem, where St. Jerome and his companions opened a school for local children and a resting-place for weary travellers.

St. Jerome's work was so well done that for hundreds of years it was regarded as the only worthwhile translation of the Bible. It was called the Vulgate—a name from the same source as vulgar, meaning common—because it was in common use. Most people who wanted a Bible in their own language used Jerome's Vulgate instead of translating themselves from the original documents.

For all who were inspired by your Holy Spirit to write the Holy Scriptures;

For all who translated the Scriptures faithfully into other languages;

For all who laboured, in face of death or danger to give us a Bible in our own language;

For all whose knowledge helps us to understand your Word today;

Praise be to you, O God. *Amen.**

Benediction No. 48

The Bible (2)   157

The Bible (3)

AN ENGLISH BIBLE   *William Tyndale*

Five hundred years ago, few people were able to read the Bible for themselves, for all Bibles were printed in Latin. Although the Pope was against having Bibles printed in other languages, there were some, such as William Tyndale, who did not agree. How could people learn of God if they had no Bible to learn from?

Once, when Tyndale was arguing with a learned man, he said, 'If God spare my life, ere many years I will cause a boy who drives the plough to know more of the Scriptures than you do.'

Tyndale resolved to use his talents to translate the Bible into English, but this was easier said than done. Where was he to do it? If he did it anywhere in England there was a chance that his work would be destroyed, so he decided to leave home and work in Europe. When his work was completed, he took it to Cologne to be printed but he had to leave hastily after a drunken printer had betrayed his secret.

At last the New Testament was printed but then it had to be smuggled into England, hidden in barrels or sacks of flour. If copies fell into the hands of the Bishop of London, they were immediately burned.

Then, after a number of years, Tyndale was betrayed once more and imprisoned. On 6th October, 1536, he was strangled and his body burned. His last prayer was, 'Lord, open the King of England's eyes'. His prayer was answered. Within two years the King did have a change of outlook and copies of the Bible in English were then produced in England for anyone who could read.

O Lord our God, we thank you for the privilege of being able to read the Bible for ourselves in our own language and we thank you for all who made it possible for us to do so. Hear us as we pray for the work of Bible Societies and others who are printing Bibles today so that people of other lands may also be able to read for themselves and learn your perfect way of life; through Jesus Christ our Lord. *Amen.**

Closing prayer No. 8

The Bible (4)

Lancelot Andrewes

Bible Reading: Psalm 119: 97–104

Lancelot Andrewes died on 27th September, 1626. His name may not be familiar to many people, but part of his work is known throughout the world.

Lancelot was born in London, in 1555, the son of a merchant who expected him to follow in his father's footsteps. Lancelot did so well at school, however, that his father was persuaded to allow him to go to a good school and to university so that he could make good use of his talents.

At Cambridge, he decided to become a clergyman. After holding a number of positions, he was appointed Dean of Westminster, and chaplain to Queen Elizabeth I: later, he was a favourite of King James I. In 1605 he became Bishop of Chichester; in 1609, Bishop of Ely; and in 1619, Bishop of Winchester. He was a great preacher, writer and compiler of prayers.

At that time, more people were demanding a Bible they could read. Although there had been several translations from Latin into English, it was agreed, in 1607, that a new translation should be made.

Fifty-four scholars were appointed to make this translation and, at the head of the list, was Bishop Lancelot Andrewes. The new Bible, published in 1611, was the one authorized by King James, and has become known as the Authorized Version.

In recent years there have been several translations into more modern English but in spite of this, the Authorized Version is still the one which is most widely used today. Next time you read from it, you might give a thought to Bishop Andrewes and his team of scholars who made it possible.

A prayer of Bishop Lancelot Andrewes:

O thou who didst command thy Apostles to go into all the world, and to preach the Gospel to every creature; let thy Name be great among the Gentiles from the rising up of the sun unto the going down of the same. *Amen.*

Closing prayer No. 13

The Bible (5)

The 'Bounty' Mutineers

Bible Reading: Psalm 119: 105–112

'Thy Word is a lamp to guide my feet . . .' There are many people who have learned a better way of life when they have turned to their Bibles.

Take, for example, the story of some mutineers, in the days, two hundred years ago, when conditions at sea were dreadful. Not only were the food and accommodation bad, but some captains were harsh and brutal—one of them being Captain Bligh of H.M.S. *Bounty*.

For two years he had ill-treated and half-starved his crew and now, after two years in the Pacific, they were about to sail for home. Shortly after leaving Tahiti, most of the crew, led by Fletcher Christian, broke into the arms store, seized weapons and ammunition, then overpowered the Captain and his supporters on 28th April, 1789.

At first they thought to leave the ship themselves but they decided instead to turn Captain Bligh and the loyal few adrift in a small boat with a supply of provisions. Then the *Bounty* returned to Tahiti, where some decided to stay.

Fletcher Christian, however, with eight other crew members, six men from Tahiti, nine women and one girl, sailed the *Bounty* until they reached Pitcairn Island, which they made their home.

All traces of the ship were destroyed. At first all went well but then there were fights and murders. One day they found a Bible in the ship's stores and read from it. They resolved to change their ways and to live according to the words in the Bible.

When, at last, a ship called at the island, it found a happy group of people—changed by the discovery of a Bible.

O God, we thank you for showing us yourself through the words of scripture and by the example of your Son, Jesus Christ: help us to know and to understand what is your perfect will, so that we may live in love and at peace with our neighbours, and so bring joy wherever we go; to the glory of your holy Name. *Amen.**

Benediction No. 53 (taken from the Bible)

Prayer (1)

From earliest times, people have believed that they can be helped by praying to God. The disciples asked Jesus how to pray and he taught them.

Bible Reading: St. Luke 11: 1–4

Five hundred years later, a young man named Benedict became disgusted with the kind of life lived by many people in Rome so he went some miles away into the open country, where he lived in a cave. There he spent much time in prayer and learned the importance of speaking and listening to God.

Later, some monks who knew Benedict to be a very religious man asked him to be their leader. He agreed to do so and made strict laws for them to keep.

During the years that followed, he organized twelve small groups of monks before beginning his greatest work, which was to found the great monastery at Monte Cassino. There, for fourteen years, the monks led a life in which prayer played an important part.

Benedict believed in strict discipline but he was very mindful of the needs of others and he was very kind, sensible and thoughtful. Just before his death, when he realized that the end was near, he was carried into the chapel where he died. But his work went on and greatly influenced the Christian Church, for his rules were accepted by groups of monks for about six hundred years and still by many today. St. Benedict is remembered each year on March 21st. His monastery at Monte Cassino was destroyed during the Second World War but was later rebuilt.

A prayer of St. Benedict (written nearly 1500 years ago):

O gracious and Holy Father, give us wisdom to perceive thee; intelligence to understand thee; diligence to seek thee; patience to wait for thee; eyes to behold thee; a heart to meditate upon thee; and a life to proclaim thee; through the power of the spirit of Jesus Christ our Lord. *Amen.*

Benediction No. 40

Prayer (2)

Mohammed

Some of our most important prayers are the ones we pray when we are on our own. Jesus taught his disciples to pray in the quiet of their rooms.

Bible Reading: St. Matthew 6: 5–8

In olden times, people would sometimes pray in the wilderness or in a cave. One who did so changed the whole history of the world. He was a poor orphan named Mohammed. He liked to think about God, whom he called Allah and sometimes stayed in a cave near Mecca to discover what was Allah's will.

At the age of about forty, he announced that he was Allah's prophet. His religion he called Islam—a complete obedience to God's will. During the next twenty-three years his words were collected to form a book called the *Koran*, which is the 'Bible' of the Muslim people.

Mohammed had many followers but also enemies who sought his life. To escape from them, he left Mecca for Medina and it is from the date of his flight, 16th July, 622, that the Muslim calendar begins.

It was not very long before the Muslim faith spread to many parts of Asia and Africa, where many people are Muslims to this day.

Five duties are expected of all Muslims; to declare the greatness of Allah, to worship five times a day, to give alms for the needy, to fast during the month called Ramadan and to make a pilgrimage to Mecca. They believe in the one God, who is the same God worshipped by Christians and Jews, but they do not regard Jesus as God's Son, rather as a prophet of God. Today, many millions of people consider Mohammed to be God's greatest prophet.

A prayer of Mohammed:

O Lord, grant us to love thee; grant that we may love those that love thee; grant that we may do the deeds that win thy love. Make the love of thee to be dearer to us than ourselves, our families, than wealth, and even than cool water. *Amen.*

Closing prayer No. 31

Prayer (3)

PRAYER BEFORE A MISSION *Vasco da Gama*

One thing we learn from the life of Jesus is that he always prayed before doing anything important.

Bible Reading: St. Luke 6: 12–18

Nearly five hundred years ago, a group of Portuguese seamen gathered in a small chapel near Lisbon and spent the night in prayer, kneeling on the cold stone floor. They felt the need for the blessing of God, for they were about to embark on a dangerous mission from which they might never return.

On the following morning, Saturday 8th July, 1497, they boarded four small ships and set sail. Their job was to sail round Africa to India and see whether it was possible to trade with that country. It was a voyage that the Portuguese had long hoped might be possible. Now Vasco da Gama hoped to trade his cargo for spices, silks, muslins and gems.

It was a perilous voyage. They were beset by fog, storms and currents which swept them from their course. Some native people attacked them when they landed; others refused them fresh water and some tried to wreck their ships. At last, after ten months, they reached India and traded their goods. The return journey took longer and many died before reaching home.

On the whole, the voyage was a success. Da Gama had done what he set out to do and to show his gratitude, the King built a great monastery on the site of the chapel where they had prayed for God's blessing before leaving.

It is a good thing to pray for God's help but it is also important to remember to give thanks for it.

O God our Father, as we embark on another day's journey, we gather before you in prayer. We ask you to be our guide and helper throughout its hours; to strengthen us in times of weakness or temptation; to keep us from harm and danger; and to bring us to the close of the day with thankful hearts for all your mercies; through Jesus Christ our Lord. *Amen.**

Closing prayer No. 7

Prayer (3)   163

Prayer (4)

Thomas Barnardo was born in Dublin in 1845 and left home in 1866 to study medicine at the London Hospital. While a student there, he took a great interest in the poor people of the East End of London.

One night, after talking to a boy dressed in rags, he said to him, 'Run along home now'.

'Ain't got no 'ome,' was the reply.

Barnardo could hardly believe his ears, but soon discovered that it was true. This was just one of many boys who slept in sheds, under barrows, or in any other place where there was shelter. They had no homes.

Barnardo decided to do something about it. But how? He was far from being a rich man and he did not know where the money might come from. But he did have faith in God and he did remember the words of Jesus:

Bible Reading: St. Matthew 7: 7–11

If he prayed for God's help in this work, he was sure his prayers would be answered. He took a large house in Stepney, which he said would have an 'ever open door'. Each night he prayed about his work: each morning post brought letters with gifts of money from people who wanted to help his work.

His one home grew into many. There were homes for boys, for girls, and for unwanted babies. One baby was even sent to him in a box. There was a welcome for the cripple and the outcast.

Dr. Barnardo died on 19th September, 1905, but his work continues to this day, helping the homeless to find happiness.

Almighty God, we commend into your fatherly care and goodness, all who work to help homeless children today—Dr. Barnardo's Homes, the National Children's Home, and many others. May their doors never be closed for want of money; and may their work be blessed. We ask it in the name and for the sake of him who blessed the children, Jesus Christ our Lord. *Amen.**

Closing prayer No. 14

Prayer (5)

On 11th February, 1858, Marie-Bernarde Soubirous, the fourteen-year-old daughter of a poor miller of Lourdes, in France, had a strange experience. Bernadette, as she was called, had gone to collect firewood outside the town.

Startled by a noise, she looked up to see standing in a cave a beautiful young woman dressed in white and having a long white veil. Bernadette was so sure she had come from heaven that she knelt to say a prayer. She became quite sure that she was speaking to the Virgin Mary, the Mother of Jesus.

During the next few months, Bernadette saw her lady eighteen times but, though others were with her, none could claim to see her. On one of these visits, the lady pointed to the ground. When Bernadette scratched where her finger pointed, a spring of water began to flow, which still flows to this day.

Bernadette became a nun and gave her short life to helping the sick. In later years, a statue of the Virgin Mary was erected in the cave and today millions of people go to Lourdes every year to pray.

Thousands of these are sick people, who bathe in the water and occasionally there is a cure which doctors cannot explain. But perhaps the greatest miracle of Lourdes is that so many people from all over the world gather there to pray, for people are often helped when they pray together. We remember the example given by the early Church and how they could then perform miracles in the strength of God.

Bible Reading: Acts 1: 12–14

O Lord, who taught your people how to pray, and promised that their prayers would be heard, hear us as we pray for those who are distressed in body, mind or spirit, and grant unto them your comfort, peace and guidance. We pray for ourselves, and ask that we may have strength, not to live selfishly but in the service of others; for Jesus Christ's sake. *Amen.**

Closing prayer No. 16

Hymns we enjoy (1)

PRAISE AND TRUST IN GOD   *Henry Francis Lyte*

Bible Reading: Psalm 117

This short psalm is one of the hymns of praise that were sung by the people of the Old Testament. Today, when a hymn of praise is required for an important occasion or for an official ceremony, the hymn that is often chosen is *Praise, my soul, the King of Heaven.*

This hymn was written by the Reverend Henry Francis Lyte, while he was curate of the little fishing village of Brixham, South Devon.

But if this hymn is well known, another hymn by the same writer is equally well known and loved by English-speaking people all over the world—*Abide with me.*

It was the last hymn he wrote and came near to being unfinished. Lyte was taken ill and had to go abroad in the hope that his health would improve. On 4th September, 1847, he took Holy Communion with his people for the last time, then strolled by the sea until sunset, thinking of the hymn he had begun to write some time before. Though tired when he reached home, he determined to complete the hymn, which he handed to his family when he left. It was as well that he finished it, for he died two months later.

Abide with me—the hymn sung by thousands of people at the F.A. Cup Final for many years, has been a great comfort to many people; Nurse Cavell before she faced the firing squad, Shackleton before he died, the doomed passengers on the sinking *Titanic* and others who have found it a helpful reminder that God remains always with those who trust him.

O Lord, whose way is perfect, help us, we pray thee, always to trust in thy goodness; that, walking with thee and following thee in all simplicity, we may possess quiet and contented minds, and may cast all our cares on thee, for thou carest for us; for the sake of Jesus Christ our Lord. *Amen.*

Christina G. Rossetti

Benediction No. 46

Hymns we enjoy (2)

THANKING GOD   *Martin Rinkart*

In our reading this morning, the psalmist praises God for his goodness and for hearing his prayers.

Bible Reading: Psalm 138: 1–5

On 21st October, 1648, the Peace of Westphalia was signed, which brought to an end a war which had lasted for thirty years and has become known as the Thirty Years' War.

None can have been more pleased than the Reverend Martin Rinkart, the minister of Eilenburg in Saxony, now part of Germany. His town was a small one with a wall round it and, when war came to that part of the country, people flocked into Eilenburg for safety.

The town became overcrowded; food was scarce; and there were outbreaks of plague. During those thirty terrible years, over eight thousand people died in Eilenburg and the Rev. Martin Rinkart had the sad duty of having to bury most of them, sometimes as many as fifty funerals in a day.

When peace came at last, thanksgiving services were held and ministers throughout the country were asked to preach on the text, 'Now bless ye the Lord of all, who everywhere doeth great things'.

For Martin Rinkart, the words had a very special meaning. Not only did he preach on the words but he was inspired by them to write his well-known hymn:

> *Now thank we all our God,*
> *With hearts, and hands, and voices,*
> *Who wondrous things hath done,*
> *In whom his world rejoices . . .*

O God our Father, we thank you that there is no part of our life in which you are not found. In times of difficulty grant us guidance; in times of weakness, give us strength; in times of danger, grant us your protection. Teach us to pray, to praise you and learn of you; so that we may know you as Father and Friend; through Jesus Christ our Lord. *Amen.**

Benediction No. 55

Hymns we enjoy (3)

Isaac Watts

Bible Reading: Psalm 67

Isaac Watts, the writer of some of the finest hymns in our language, was born on 17th July, 1674. As a boy, in Southampton, he learned Latin, Greek and Hebrew. He was also very fond of expressing himself in verse.

This sometimes got him into trouble, because it annoyed his father, who thought that young Isaac was being cheeky. Once, it is said, his father became so angry that he put the boy across his knee and was about to give him a good hiding when the boy cried:

> 'Pray, father, do some pity take,
> And I no more will verses make!'

Later, he put his verse making to good use. He was far from satisfied with the hymns that were sung in his day and he determined to write better ones himself. Many of these are sung regularly today, over two hundred years after his death.

> *Jesus shall reign, where'er the sun*
> *Doth his successive journeys run*

is, in fact, sung throughout the world. Another of his well-loved hymns is *O God, our help in ages past*, while *When I survey the wondrous cross* has been described as the finest hymn in the English language.

Most of his hymns and other works were written in the latter half of his life after an attack of fever had left him an invalid.

Isaac Watts died in 1748 and a memorial to him was erected in Westminster Abbey but his greatest memorial is to be found scattered through the pages of almost every hymn book.

Here is a prayer taken from a hymn written by Isaac Watts:

> O God, our help in ages past,
>   Our hope for years to come,
> Be thou our guard while troubles last,
>   And our eternal home.   *Amen.*

Closing prayer No. 26

Hymns we enjoy (4)

SOLDIERS OF THE CROSS   *George Duffield*

When we sing our hymns we do so because we enjoy them and we probably give very little thought as to how or why they were written. Some were undoubtedly written by people who sat down with the one intention of writing a hymn. Others were written on a sudden inspiration following a pleasure or a tragic event.

One of the most rousing Christian hymns is *Stand up, stand up for Jesus*. George Duffield, its writer, was born on 12th September, 1818 and served as minister of a number of churches in America before he died in 1888.

One day in 1858, George Duffield listened to a young minister preaching to a group of men and he was very impressed with what the young man had to say. A few days later, the young minister was dead. He had gone into a barn where a mule was working a piece of machinery. Reaching out to pat the animal, his sleeve was caught in the machinery and the minister was dragged into the machine and killed.

Duffield thought what a tragic end this was for a soldier of Jesus Christ. He turned in his Bible to the place where St. Paul wrote these words to the people of Ephesus:

Bible Reading: Ephesians 6: 11–17

The following Sunday, when George Duffield was himself preaching, he took this as the subject of his sermon and finished with the words that had come to him only a couple of days earlier and with which we are so familiar:

> *Stand up, stand up for Jesus*
> *Ye soldiers of the cross . . .*

O God our Father, we confess that so often we have taken the easy way out instead of standing firm as good soldiers of Jesus Christ. Teach us to put on the whole armour of God, so that we may be protected from evil and be able to lead full and useful lives in your service, now and evermore. *Amen.**

Closing prayer No. 11

Hymns we enjoy (5)

ONWARD, CHRISTIAN SOLDIERS   *Sabine Baring-Gould*

A little over a hundred years ago, the curate of the little village of Horbury Brig, in Yorkshire, sat down to write a hymn that could be sung by the Sunday School children as they walked in procession through the village.

The result was the popular hymn *Onward, Christian Soldiers* and the curate, the Reverend Sabine Baring-Gould, would have been staggered if he could have known how popular his hymn was to become especially when sung to the rousing tune composed by Sir Arthur Sullivan.

Nowadays, some people criticize this hymn because it speaks of Christian soldiers, but we have to remember that it does not suggest fighting people, but all the evils that are present in the world. Listen to this advice which St. Paul gave to Timothy:

Bible Reading: 2 Timothy 2: 1–4

While at Horbury Brig, the Reverend Sabine Baring-Gould held a night school in his little house for children and their parents who had to work all day. And he was such a popular story teller that his school overflowed from one room, down the stairs and into the kitchen below.

At the end of school, they would sing a hymn before going home. The curate wrote a special hymn for this purpose too, the well-known *Now the day is over*.

Later in life, he inherited land from his father in Devon, where he later became rector. He wrote many books and other works, having about one hundred and fifty published, but few can have become as well known as these two hymns. He died on 2nd January, 1924.

O God our Father, we thank you for all that you have given us and especially today for the gift of singing. We thank you for those who have written hymns and those who have set them to music so that we might worship you in song. Help us to praise you always, not only in our singing but in everything we do; through Jesus Christ our Lord. *Amen.**

Closing prayer No. 23

Thank you for these (1)

St. Luke

If asked what is the most important thing to have in life, most people would reply, 'health and strength'. This is why many people were brought to Jesus.

Bible Reading: St. Luke 4: 38–40

People who are healthy have much for which to be thankful: those who are not are usually thankful for doctors to help them. The day on which many Christian people think of doctors is St. Luke's Day, 18th October.

St. Luke was one who became a Christian in the early days of the church. He was a Greek doctor, who joined Paul on one of his journeys but we know him best as the writer of the third gospel and of the Acts of the Apostles.

St. Luke remained with Paul on his other journeys and then stayed with him while he was a prisoner in Rome. Paul wrote about him in three letters. To Timothy he wrote, 'Only Luke is with me'. It is believed that Luke died in Greece at a good age. One early writer tells that Luke served the Lord constantly and was 'full of the Holy Spirit'.

St. Luke is the patron saint of painters of pictures. Whether he himself painted we cannot tell, but he was certainly able to paint word pictures in his writings, describing very clearly all that happened.

But St. Luke, the medical man, is probably known more frequently as the patron saint of physicians and surgeons, which is why their work is especially in people's thoughts on St. Luke's Day.

A prayer for St. Luke's Day:

O Lord Jesus Christ, healer of the sick and friend to all who sought your aid, we ask your blessing upon all physicians and surgeons, granting unto them all the skill, gentleness and patience that they need. Bless those who suffer, that they may readily submit themselves to the skill of these physicians and surgeons, and so find rest and comfort, healing and peace of mind; for your Name's sake. *Amen.**

Closing prayer No. 32

Thank you for these (2)

Frederic Chopin

Frederic Chopin was born on 22nd February, 1810. His father was French; his mother was Polish; and he was brought up in the city of Warsaw.

When he was young, Frederic learned the piano and could soon play well enough to entertain well-to-do people. When he was only nine years old, he was invited to play before the Grand Duke.

Of course, this was a very important occasion and he was dressed up to look his best in a velvet suit with a fine lace collar. People were amazed as he sat at the piano, for he was such a small boy that he looked no more than six.

At the end of the concert, in which he played some very difficult music, there was a thunderous applause as he bowed. On reaching home, his mother asked about the concert. 'Mummy!' he exclaimed. 'They clapped like anything when they noticed my collar.'

They were not the only people who liked his music. Later, he composed music as well and one who heard his music was the composer Schumann. Schumann wrote about him in a music paper and headed the article, 'Hats off, gentlemen—a genius.'

Chopin, however, did not enjoy very good health and he became steadily weaker. At a shop in London, where he loved to play the piano, someone used to carry him upstairs to save his strength.

Chopin died when he was only 39 but he left behind a large number of pieces of music composed for the piano, which he loved so well. He is one of that large company of composers of fine music for whom we shall always be thankful.

O God, our Heavenly Father, you have filled this world with so many good things: we thank you for all that is lovely in music, in art and in literature, and for everything created for man's enjoyment. Make us aware of all that is beautiful and help us to remember your gifts; for Jesus Christ's sake. *Amen.**

Closing prayer No. 39

Thank you for these (3)

Iron has been used for many tools and weapons for thousands of of years. We can read about it in the first book of the Bible, Genesis and in later books like this:

Bible Reading: 1 Chronicles 22: 2–5

As years passed, iron was used for making such things as cannon, chariots, armour and machinery. The introduction of machinery meant that great skill was needed for, unless each part was accurate, the machine would not work.

But to make the most of iron, we needed not only people who were skilful with their hands but people who could think of better ways of using it. One of these, a great British mechanical engineer was born on 19th January, 1736. James Watt was particularly interested in steam engines and believed he could make much better ones than had been used up to that time. With another engineer, Matthew Boulton, he formed a company which became known for its fine engines.

Then people began to think further. They knew how to make steel from iron and they knew that better and stronger machinery could be made from steel, but the process of making steel from iron was very costly.

The way of making steel cheaply was discovered by Sir Henry Bessemer, who was born nearly eighty years after Watt, in 1813, but who shared the same birthday, 19th January. Since his discovery, steel has been used for a great many purposes.

Watt and Bessemer were just two of the many people who used the brains which God gave them to discover ways of using the natural materials found in the earth.

O God, who in your wisdom filled the earth with an abundance of minerals and sources of power that are beyond our understanding; give wisdom to all who seek to make yet more discoveries; and grant that such discoveries may be used for the benefit of mankind through Jesus Christ our Lord. *Amen.**

Closing prayer No. 18

Thank you for these (4)

If you have ever looked at a great cathedral or abbey, you have probably wondered however anyone could plan such a magnificent building, especially when you remember that many cathedrals were built hundreds of years ago.

During the time of William the Conqueror, plans were drawn and people began building a cathedral just outside the present city of Salisbury at a place called Sarum. It was finished in 1092 but, only five days later it was badly damaged by lightning. Although it was repaired, the position was never really satisfactory and, just over a century later, the building of the present cathedral at Salisbury began.

While the first cathedral was being built the bishop died and a new bishop was appointed to take his place. His name was Osmund —a learned priest who had been Chancellor of England, the King's chief adviser for four years.

Osmund had no hand in the planning of the cathedral but he had much to say about the way in which it should be run and it is for this that he is especially remembered. It was not to be run by monks, as many cathedrals were but by a brotherhood or Chapter of Canons with a Dean in charge. A Precentor was responsible for the music and a Treasurer for everything of value. A Chancellor acted as secretary besides looking after the schools and the library. This worked so well that it was copied for other cathedrals too.

Bishop Osmund died in 1099 and was laid to rest in his cathedral. In later years he was known as St. Osmund and 4th December became his feast day. Today we are thankful for people of the past who planned places of beauty and for those who saw that they were looked after well.

A prayer from the Sarum Breviary (Service Book) of the Middle Ages:

In this hour of this day, fill us, O Lord, with thy mercy, that rejoicing throughout the whole day, we may take delight in thy praise; through Jesus Christ our Lord. *Amen.*

Closing prayer No. 9

Thank you for these (5)

Samuel Johnson

The first thing that strikes the visitor to Lichfield, in Staffordshire, is the magnificent cathedral, with its three spires towering above the city.

The second is probably the fine statue in the centre of the city, bearing the seated figure of Dr. Samuel Johnson, facing the house in which he once lived. Dr. Johnson was born at Lichfield on 18th September, 1709, the son of a bookseller, and he went to school in the city before attending University at Oxford.

Johnson's early life seemed doomed to failure. He had to leave Oxford without a degree because he had not enough money to remain there; he obtained a post in a school, which he disliked so much that he left it; he tried working for a publisher in Birmingham, which brought him in precious little money; and then he opened a school, which was attended by only three boys.

There was nothing for it. He would go to London to seek his fortune. There he spent much of his time in writing books and articles for magazines. By far the most important of his works was his great *Dictionary of the English Language*, published in 1755, which was of very great importance in the history of the English language.

Johnson's fortune changed. He became rich and received many honours. Not the least of these was that when he died in 1784, he was not only buried in Westminster Abbey, but a monument was erected to him in St. Paul's Cathedral.

Today we are thankful for many scholars and writers of the past who have given us books and knowledge and who have taught us the importance of learning. Like Samuel Johnson, we may have our setbacks but success may lie round the corner if we persevere.

A prayer written by Samuel Johnson:

Make us to remember, O God, that every day is thy gift and ought to be used according to thy command: through Jesus Christ our Lord. *Amen.*

Benediction No. 54

5 Citizenship and Service

There are sixteen themes in this section concerned on the whole with international, national and community affairs as well as with social relationships and service to others.

International friendship	*International days*
War and peace	*Peace and brotherhood*
Crimes against humanity	*Battles to be fought*
Those in authority *Freedom*	*Justice and fair play*
Determination *Chivalry*	*Ready to change*
Saving life	*Hospitals and healing*
Conquering pain and disease	*Deeds of bravery*

All are of five topics except international days, these being days of specific commemoration.

The general thought underlying this section is the adoption of right attitudes of mind in individual, local, national and international relationships.

International friendship (1)

THREE PEOPLES—ONE NATION   *Quebec and Canada*

Bible Reading: Romans 12: 18–21

For people of different races, with differing customs and outlooks, to live together in peace a great deal of understanding and patience is needed.

Just over two hundred years ago, the land we now know as Canada was occupied by the British and the French, each of whom wished to gain control of the whole country. Around them were Red Indians, who were friendly towards one or the other or not very friendly toward either.

The strongest French settlement was Quebec, standing on high cliffs known as the Heights of Abraham. To be masters of Canada, the British must take Quebec. On 27th June, 1759, Wolfe landed near Quebec but he was unable to take it; it was too well defended.

Wolfe was not a man to give in easily and at last he worked out a plan of action. Under cover of darkness, he took his men in small boats to the foot of the cliff and led them up a narrow path. In the morning, the French were amazed to find Wolfe's army in a position for battle.

In the battle, Wolfe was mortally wounded but not before he knew Quebec was taken. That day, 13th September, marked the death of Wolfe but the beginning of a new era in Canada. In the years that followed, British, French and Indians learned to live together until today, when Canada Day is celebrated on 1st July, these and people of many other nationalities who have made Canada their home are all recognized as citizens of one country.

We thank you, God our Father, that people are not all the same but are of different races and colours, speak different languages, and have their own special gifts and abilities. Help us to understand and respect one another and to live in friendship and peace; in the Name of Jesus Christ, in whose sight all are equal. *Amen.**

Closing prayer No. 3

International friendship (2)

Earl Mountbatten

On 25th June, 1900, a baby son was born to Admiral of the Fleet Prince Louis of Battenburg. Perhaps the admiral hoped that his son might also serve in the Royal Navy.

He could hardly have imagined that his son would become Admiral of the Fleet The Earl Mountbatten of Burma, with a dozen rows of medal ribbons on his uniform and many honours—Knight of the Garter, Privy Councillor, Knight Grand Cross of the Bath, Knight Commander of the Star of India, Knight Grand Commander of the Indian Empire, Knight Grand Cross of the Royal Victorian Order, Distinguished Service Order and so on.

In a distinguished career in the Royal Navy, he commanded several ships and, in 1943, was given charge of all allied forces fighting in South-east Asia.

Then, in 1947 came a very important task. The war was over but there was something that required his skill. For almost two hundred years, India had been British, with a Viceroy to act on behalf of the King or Queen. Now it was to have its own government. Earl Mountbatten became the last Viceroy of India and as such he played a very important part in transferring power to the new governments of India and Pakistan, enabling it to be done very smoothly.

Many nations are thankful for men of vision who have been able to guide them through difficult times. The writer of the Book of Revelation also had a vision of the way nations would one day live in peace through God.

Bible Reading: Revelation 21: 1–7

O King of kings, and Lord of lords, hear us for the nation to which we belong. Guide the Queen and her counsellors, show them the path of wisdom, that we may still be worthy to play our part among the peoples of the earth. Especially do we pray that, through the endeavours of the men of goodwill in all nations, the world may be led into paths of peace; through Jesus Christ our Lord. *Amen.*

Rydal School Hymnal

Closing prayer No. 21

International friendship (3)

Sir Robert Menzies

St. Paul made many friends by writing letters and by visiting people. Here is part of one of his letters.

Bible Reading: Romans 15: 23–29

Today people can travel more easily than St. Paul and it is possible for people all over the world to keep in touch with each other and for nations to show their friendship for other nations.

One man who has always been pleased to show his friendship toward Britain is Sir Robert Menzies. Born on 20th December, 1894 in the village of Jeparit, in the State of Victoria, he studied law before becoming a member of the state parliament, then a member of the federal parliament and, in 1939, Prime Minister of Australia. Though defeated in 1941, he became Prime Minister again from 1949 until he resigned in 1966.

One especial honour was conferred on him in Britain. Around the south-east coast of Britain there were five ports, known as the Cinque Ports. These five, Dover, Hastings, Hythe, Romney and Sandwich, with two ancient towns, Rye and Winchelsea enjoyed special privileges in return for providing ships needed by the King. The office of Lord Warden of the Cinque Ports survives to this day and is usually held by someone important. A recent holder was Sir Winston Churchill and he was followed in 1965 by Sir Robert Menzies as a token of appreciation.

Menzies has not only been a strong supporter of Britain but also of the Commonwealth, the family of nations to be found in all parts of the world.

Almighty God, we thank you for the Commonwealth [*or the community of nations*] of which our country is a member. Give us a spirit of understanding, love and peace toward one another. Grant unto the leaders of the nations the inspiration of your Holy Spirit, so that they may realize their responsibilities to work together for the common good and the glory of your holy Name. *Amen.**

Benediction No. 41

International friendship (4)

Universal Postal Union

One of the best ways of ensuring friendship between two peoples is for them to work together. There is a story in the Old Testament which tells how Solomon asked help from another king.

Bible Reading: 1 Kings 5: 2–6

Solomon began by sending a message. St. Paul kept in touch with his many friends by letter. Letters still play an important part in our friendships. Many people have made friends in other countries by finding 'pen friends' to whom they can write. In this way we can learn quite a lot about people of other countries and see how their ways of life are similar to or different from ours.

Have you ever wondered how a letter can pass through many countries without extra charge? It is because of an international organization known as the Universal Postal Union, which was agreed upon in October 1874 and came into use on 1st July, 1875.

The Postal Union, often called simply the U.P.U., has two main principles. One is that every country should be able, for a payment, to use the postal services of another. The other is that there should be no charge for delivery. Once every three years a check is kept on the amount of mail so that people in the office of the U.P.U. in Switzerland can work out how much each country should pay to other countries for handling the letters.

The Universal Postal Union is just one of several international organizations through which the countries of the world have agreed to co-operate for the benefit of people everywhere.

O God, Father of all men, help us to understand more about other people so that through this understanding and through the knowledge that we are all your children, we may grow in love one toward another and learn to live in peace and friendship; for the sake of Jesus Christ our Lord. *Amen.**

Benediction No. 47

International friendship (5)

Bible Reading: 1 Kings 5: 7–12

So the result of Solomon's working together with Hiram was that the two countries enjoyed peace. This is usually the result of international co-operation.

An example of international goodwill is one of the most famous statues in the world, the Statue of Liberty, which stands on an island in New York harbour and towers about 305 feet above water level.

It is the statue of a woman who has just been given her freedom, suggested by the broken shackles which lie at her feet. In her right hand, held high above her head, is a torch with which she can lighten the world as she steps forward. In her left hand is a book of law, on which is printed the date, July 4, 1776, the date on which the United States of America became an independent country.

To gain their independence, the Americans were helped by France and the idea of a statue to commemorate this was thought up in France one hundred years after the event. In fact the money for making the statue, covered with over 300 copper sheets was raised in France and it was a French sculptor, Frederic Auguste Bartholdi, who made the statue in France to be sent out to America. The American people raised the money required for the granite pedestal on which it stands and the statue was finally dedicated on 28th October, 1886.

The Statue of Liberty serves not only to remind all who enter the harbour of the value of liberty but also of the friendship and co-operation of the people of two lands.

Almighty God, we thank you that though we are all so different we are all your children. Forgive us if sometimes we judge other people because of their background or the colour of their skins and help us to remember that it is not what we look like that is important but what we are. Unite all peoples in a love of peace and freedom and with due regard for one another; and to you be the glory for ever. *Amen.**

Benediction No. 45

International days (1)

May 5th is celebrated as Europe Day, the anniversary of the day in 1949 when the Council of Europe was formed by many of the countries of Europe to help them to work together for the good of each other.

It was none too soon. For hundreds of years the people of Europe have been fighting each other, with the worst wars coming in the present century. It was during the Second World War that Sir Winston Churchill, who was then Prime Minister of Britain, suggested such a council. So, after the war had ended, leaders of the nations met. Sir Winston Churchill addressed them:

'We must aim at nothing less than the union of Europe as a whole, and we look forward with confidence to the day when that union will be achieved.'

Twelve months later the Council of Europe was set up with its headquarters in the House of Europe at Strasbourg, near the border between France and Germany. The Ministers of the Council are the Foreign Ministers of each member state and its assembly or parliament has representatives from each.

Since the Council of Europe was formed, the member nations have worked together in many ways for the good of the people in all their countries.

Some of the countries agreed to work even more closely together in trade and industry in a body known as the European Economic Community, often called 'the Common Market'. In time, Britain and other states applied to join.

The states of Europe are moving closer together. They have already learned some of the advantages of international co-operation and as long as this continues, the Council of Europe will have an important role to play.

Almighty God, as we remember the peoples of Europe with their many different ways and customs, we thank you for the ways in which we have learned to work together and we ask your continued guidance and blessing; through Jesus Christ our Lord. *Amen.**

Benediction No. 47

International days (2)

Commonwealth Day is the day when we remember many people of the Commonwealth throughout the world.

These are nations which, until a few years ago, were part of the British Empire—lands in all parts of the world which, at one time, belonged to Britain.

Some years ago, the British Government decided that any of these countries which could govern themselves should have their own government and become independent nations. The first to do so were Canada, Australia, New Zealand, and South Africa. Later, came India, Pakistan, Ceylon, Nigeria, Ghana, and many other lands in Africa, Asia and America.

Although these countries no longer belonged to Britain, they were given the choice to remain in the group of nations known as the Commonwealth, and most of them decided to do so. Some decided that the Queen of Britain should be their Queen too; others decided to have a president instead, but still regard the Queen as head of the Commonwealth.

Commonwealth Day gives us the opportunity to remember the many lands, great and small, which form this great family of nations. The members of the Commonwealth speak different languages, they are of many different races, colours and beliefs.

Yet, for all their differences, these countries meet together for discussion and offer help in a way that is without parallel in the history of the world.

Here could be read the Queen's Message to the Commonwealth.

Almighty God, we remember before you the peoples and nations in many parts of the world who form the Commonwealth. In this changing world, grant that each of these nations may have a spirit of understanding and peace toward the others. Grant unto all the inspiration and guidance of your Holy Spirit so that ties of friendship formed in the past and responsibilities toward the present age may enable member countries to work together for the common good and the glory of your holy Name. *Amen.**

Benediction No. 45

International days (3)

International days

UNITED NATIONS DAY   *24th October*

Several hundreds of years before the time of Jesus, the prophet Isaiah foretold a day when people would live together in peace.

Bible Reading: Isaiah 2: 2–4

Today, nearly two thousand years after the time of Jesus, people have still not found peace and we hear of wars in one part of the world after another.

We have to remember that people the world over are very different and there are many people who are not prepared to see things from the point of view of others. Some fight because they want something that belongs to another nation. Some fight in order to protect what they already have.

Sometimes disputes are taken before the United Nations Organization, which was set up in 1945 to try to keep peace in the world and sometimes a solution is found.

The United Nations, however, has much more to do than settle disputes. Its task is to try to obtain the highest possible standard of living through its departments, such as the United Nations Educational, Scientific and Cultural Organization. The Food and Agricultural Organization seeks to fight world hunger.

The U.N. declares that everyone has the right to freedom from want, freedom from fear, freedom of speech and freedom of worship, but there are many lands in which people are not free in these ways.

Each year, 24th October is kept as United Nations Day, when people remember the work of the U.N. and pray that the world might find peace.

O God our Father, hear our prayer for all peoples of the world. We remember especially people not as fortunate as ourselves, who suffer hunger, poverty or warfare. Bless the United Nations Organization and all who work to bring peace and prosperity to the world; and grant that we, who have so much, may show our gratitude by doing what we can to help others; through Jesus Christ our Lord. *Amen.**

Closing prayer No. 15

War and peace (1)

King Edward I

How many people can say that they have never been involved in a fight? We may excuse ourselves on the grounds that someone else started it or that we had good reason for it because of something that another person did to us. But does fighting really settle problems? Moses found that his fighting had far reaching results.

Bible Reading: Exodus 2: 11–14

In a fight, someone is sure to get hurt or even killed. Fighting may take the form of a battle in which many people are killed—people who are only fighting because their leader has ordered them to. The pages of history are filled with battles such as these ... and they continue to this day.

Some people make a name for themselves as fighters. One of these was King Edward I of England, who was crowned on 19th August, 1274. His coronation had been delayed because he was away fighting in one of the crusades and in the years that followed he had many battles against the Welsh, the French and the Scots. In fact he earned himself the title of 'Hammer of the Scots'. Edward liked fighting, but it was his followers who were killed in the battles.

King Edward I was a great warrior king, and one who did many good things for his country.

But times change. Nowadays we tend rather to respect those who are able to live and work for peace. As Jesus once said: 'Blessed are the peacemakers: for they shall be called the children of God'.

Help us, O God, to live at peace with others;
To keep from saying unkind words which hurt;
To refrain from actions which cause bad feelings;
To control our tempers when we become angry;
To look always for the best in others;
To forgive those who hurt us in word or deed.

Make us to become peacemakers so that we may be called your children; through Christ our Lord. *Amen.**

Benediction No. 51

War and peace (2)

First World War

For some people even fighting is not enough: they must kill those who offend them. Murder is the subject of one of the earliest Bible stories.

Bible Reading: Genesis 4: 2b–8

On 28th June, 1914, a student stood by the roadside in Sarajevo, Bosnia. He was filled with hate for the great Austrian Empire. As the Archduke Ferdinand, heir to the Austrian throne stopped his car, the student pulled out a gun and killed the Archduke and his wife.

Soon almost the whole of Europe was at war. Those shots, fired in Sarajevo, started the war which lasted over four years and cost ten million lives.

Of course there was more behind the war than those shots. They just provided the excuse for nations that had been straining at each other's throats for years.

Soldiers fought from trenches in the battlefields; tanks and aeroplanes were used in war for the first time; poison gas caused great suffering; and submarines sank many a fine ship. At last, on 11th November, 1918, the fighting stopped.

June 28th is also remembered as a day of peace, for it was on 28th June, 1919, that peace was made, five years to the day from the firing of the shots which had started the war.

People believed that this would be a war to end wars but we know otherwise. People have still not learned to settle their differences by peaceful means and, because of this, untold suffering has been brought to thousands of people.

Almighty God, from whom all thoughts of truth and peace proceed, kindle, we pray thee, in the hearts of all men, the true love of peace, and guide with thy pure and peaceable wisdom those who take counsel for the nations of the earth; that in tranquillity thy kingdom may go forward, till the earth be filled with the knowledge of thy love; through Jesus Christ our Lord. *Amen.*

Francis Paget

Benediction No. 47

War and peace (3)

September 15th is Battle of Britain Day, when people recall the air attacks on Britain in the summer of 1940. Those were difficult times. Britain, together with other countries had gone to war with Germany in September 1939 to prevent more lands from being taken by the German dictator, Hitler.

British and French armies faced the German ones, but the defences were not strong enough. Within a short time, France was overrun, British soldiers were being rescued from the beaches at Dunkirk. Holland and Belgium fell; Norway and Denmark were invaded; and Britain stood alone.

Every day the invasion of German troops was expected but did not come. The German leaders decided first to destroy Britain's aircraft from the air so that an invasion by sea would be possible. The attacks began on 8th August. Day after day large numbers of aircraft attacked. The Royal Air Force was small. The Germans expected to have wiped it out within a week. But they had reckoned without the handful of pilots who were determined not to be beaten. At last, the Germans changed their plans. They had lost 1,733 of their aircraft; the R.A.F. about half that number.

Winston Churchill, the Prime Minister, in tribute to the pilots of the Royal Air Force, said, 'Never in the field of human conflict was so much owed by so many to so few'. Today many thankfully remember how 'the few' probably saved Britain from defeat.

We thank you, O Lord, for our country and for all the blessings which are ours today. We thank you too for people of past years who have fought to give us the freedom which we now enjoy. We pray for those who still suffer because of war and for those with bitter memories. Grant that the day may soon come when men shall learn to live together in peace and share such good things as they have so that the world may become a better and a happier place; through Jesus Christ our Lord. *Amen.**

Closing prayer No. 4

War and peace (4)

The Second World War was fast coming to a close. Fighting had ended in Europe, but the Japanese would not surrender.

On 9th August, 1945, an American Superfortress bomber headed for Japan. It carried a single bomb which was intended for the city of Nagasaki. The crew of the plane knew what to expect, for a similar bomb had been dropped on Hiroshima three days before. As the bomb was released, they put on dark glasses to protect their eyes. There was a brilliant flash and a great cloud of smoke above the city.

Then the smoke cleared: the city had gone. In that moment of time, tens of thousands of people had been killed, just as there had been in Hiroshima. And for those outside the area of the explosion, there were dreadful effects which would kill many more.

A few days later, Japan surrendered and the whole world was left with a great problem. Now that such a dreadful weapon had been invented, how could it be controlled? It is a problem that has remained with people ever since, especially as other bombs have been invented which are much more powerful than those dropped in 1945.

Since then, of course, other countries have also learned to make nuclear weapons and aeroplanes are no longer necessary to drop them. Meetings of nations have been held to find ways of controlling such weapons. One thing is certain. Either people learn to live together or the world could be destroyed. The prayer of most people today is that the nations of the world can live in peace.

Almighty God, who taught us by your Son to do what is good and noble and just, and to live at peace with our neighbours; fill our hearts and the hearts of all people with your spirit of peace, so that we may live together in brotherhood. Take from us all hatred, envy and whatever could cause offence, and make us more truly your children; for Jesus Christ's sake. *Amen.**

Closing prayer No. 6

War and peace (5)

Remembrance Day

Each year, on the second Sunday in November, services are held at the Cenotaph in London and at war memorials throughout the length and breadth of Britain. People gather to remember those who lost their lives in the two world wars and to pledge themselves to work for peace so that such things do not happen again.

The fighting in the First World War ended on 11th November. It was felt that it would be fitting each year to remember, during two minutes' silence, to be held at eleven o'clock on the eleventh day of the eleventh month, those who lost their lives.

To help those who had been badly disabled, a fund was started. Money was raised for this by selling poppies—a reminder of the poppies which grew near the battlefields.

Then it happened again. War raged from 1939 to 1945 and many more were killed. Now instead of keeping 11th November as 'Armistice Day', we keep the nearest Sunday to it as 'Remembrance Sunday', when we remember those killed in both world wars.

As it happens, 11th November is the day on which the Christian Church remembers another soldier. But St. Martin, who lived sixteen hundred years ago gave up the soldiering that meant killing others so that he could fight a different kind of battle as a 'soldier of Jesus Christ'.

No doubt the world would be a happier place if people followed the example of St. Martin or heeded this advice which St. Paul gave:

Bible Reading: 2 Corinthians 13: 11–14

Grant, O God, unto all your people
Freedom from hatred and suspicion;
A desire to live together in peace;
A respect for the views of one another;
A true regard for your holy Word;
　　And may your peace be with us all. *Amen.**

Closing prayer No. 16

Peace and brotherhood (1)

A PRIZE FOR PEACE   *Alfred Nobel*

Many schools and organizations have a prize day, when awards are offered to those who have done particularly well during the previous year. December 10th is the prize-giving day for the whole world and the prizes are worth thousands of pounds each. They are the Nobel Prizes, awarded to those who, during the previous year, have done the most to benefit mankind in science, literature and peace.

They are the gift of Alfred Nobel, who was born in Sweden on 21st October, 1833 and died on 10th December, 1896.

Nobel's father was an inventor who, at the time of Alfred's birth was almost penniless. Like his father, Alfred became interested in explosives and he made some interesting experiments with a substance known as nitro-glycerine, which he was able to explode under water.

But nitro-glycerine was difficult to handle and sometimes exploded accidentally. Quite by chance, Nobel found a means of changing nitro-glycerine into a solid form, which was far easier to handle. Nobel had invented Dynamite.

Nobel made his fortune. He was a man of peace, who longed for the day when war would be no more. He arranged for prizes to be given to those who helped mankind but the prize that is most highly regarded is the prize for peace, awarded to the one who has done most to encourage brotherhood between the nations of the world.

In his letter St. James has this to say about the wisdom of being peacemakers and loving peace:

Bible Reading: James 3: 16–18

Almighty God, who lovest all mankind, help us to make the world a better and cleaner place, and a fitter dwelling for thy children upon earth; through Jesus Christ our Lord. *Amen.*

Source not known

Closing prayer No. 27

Peace and brotherhood (2)

THE HAND OF FRIENDSHIP *William Penn*

Bible Reading: Micah 4: 1–5

It is difficult for us to imagine the kind of times of which the prophet spoke, in which war would be no more. Yet we can find instances in history when the most unlikely people learned to live together in peace.

About three hundred years ago, the Red Indians of North America were angry because white people from Europe had settled in their land and were taking it from them. There were frequent quarrels, especially when the white people treated the Red Indians as savages and cheated them out of their possessions.

The Indians came to regard all white men as their enemies. They attacked and set fire to their settlements, killing men, women and children.

Imagine the surprise of some of these Indians to receive a letter addressing them as friends. It told them that the writer had been given land by the king but he wished to pay them for it. The writer was William Penn and the land was the part of America now known as Pennsylvania.

On 23rd June, 1683, William Penn signed a treaty of friendship with the Indians. The land should belong to the red man and the white and they would live in peace. Indians and Christians would treat each other as brothers.

Penn soon found that Indians, who could be cruel enemies could also be loyal friends. This treaty brought peace and brotherly love to Pennsylvania.

O God, send thy Spirit into men's hearts that they may hate war and love peace. Teach the people of every land that it is better to love one another than to fight, so that war may cease and thy Kingdom of love and brotherhood may be set up through all the world, for the sake of Jesus Christ, our Lord. *Amen.*

Junior Worship

Closing prayer No. 24

Peace and brotherhood (3)

Sir Rabindranath Tagore

Bible Reading: Psalm 96: 1–8

Throughout the centuries there have been people, such as the writer of this psalm, who have looked around them at the world in which they live to find it a place of beauty, filled with the wonders of creation.

Such a person was Sir Rabindranath Tagore, a great Indian poet, author and thinker, who was born in Calcutta in 1861. He was sent to England to study law and then returned to India, where he began his writing. In 1913, he became the first Indian to be awarded a Nobel Prize for Literature.

Those were troubled days in India and many people were anxious to make their country a better place. Tagore was one of these. Some thought it could be done by fighting; others by making themselves awkward to those in authority. Tagore believed that most of the problems could be overcome by love and understanding.

He was very interested in education and spent much of his money on a school. Later he founded a university for he believed that men of different races and civilizations could study together in an atmosphere of peace and so learn to understand each other.

When he was not writing, Tagore spent much of his time in travelling and lecturing. He also took up painting.

Sir Rabindranath Tagore died on 7th August, 1941, leaving behind him much of beauty in art, in writing and in his thoughts.

A prayer written by Tagore:

Give us the strength lightly to bear our joys and sorrows. Give us the strength to make our love fruitful in service. Give us the strength never to disown the poor, or bend our knees before insolent might. Give us the strength to raise our minds high above daily trifles. And give us the strength to surrender our strength to thy will and love. *Amen.*

Closing prayer No. 57

Peace and brotherhood (4)

Treaty of Waitangi

Each year, on 6th February, the people of New Zealand celebrate their National Day, marking the anniversary of an important event which took place in 1840.

For nearly a thousand years, New Zealand had been the home of the Maori people, who lived in small villages, each with its own chief.

Then, white traders visited the country and, in 1814, Samuel Marsden became the first missionary to teach the Maoris about Christ. In 1840, the British Government sent Captain Hobson to persuade the Maoris to accept Queen Victoria as their queen.

A meeting took place in a large marquee at Waitangi on 5th February, between the British and a large number of Maoris who lived in the northern part of New Zealand. On the following day they returned and forty-five chiefs signed the Treaty of Waitangi. This meant that New Zealand became a British colony and the British Government promised to safeguard the rights of the Maoris.

Not surprisingly, there were difficulties to be overcome. A few years later, there were several outbreaks of fighting between the Maoris and the Pakeha ('the white man'). We must remember that here were two groups of people, each having an entirely different way of life.

Today, both white men and Maoris work together and share the government of the land in which both races are proud to be called New Zealanders.

The people of New Zealand have shown the world that it is possible for people of different races and backgrounds to live side by side in peace and learn from one another.

Almighty God, we thank you for those places where people of different races have learned to live together in peace. We pray for those in lands where today there is fighting or mistrust, until all men learn to live in brotherhood; through Jesus Christ, who is the Prince of Peace. *Amen.**

Closing prayer No. 33

Peace and brotherhood (5)

BLACK AND WHITE   *James Kwegyir Aggrey*

Bible Reading: St. Luke 9: 51–56

In the time of Jesus there was bad feeling between the Jews and the Samaritans. Bad feeling still exists today between nations or people of different races, sometimes of different colours.

James Kwegyir Aggrey, in the Gold Coast, now Ghana, discovered this. He was the son of an important man at court. As a Christian, there was one thing which worried young Aggrey. He was getting on very well with his studies but there were some white people who thought that, just because his skin was black, he should not be able to do anything worth while.

'The white people do not understand the ways of the black people,' he thought, 'and the black people cannot understand the white.' He determined to spend his life in trying to get a better understanding.

He knew very well that black people and white people could get on very well together. He had done so himself and had become vice-principal of a college in his own country.

Aggrey used to explain it like this. 'God knew what he was doing when he made me black. He did not want me to be grey or white; He wanted me to be black. On a piano you cannot play a good tune using only the white notes: you must use the black and white notes together. God wants to play tunes with both his white notes and his black notes.'

Dr. Aggrey died on 30th July, 1927. Today we could learn much from the lesson he taught. If all people did so, the world would be a much happier place.

O God our Father, who in your wisdom made all people different, help us to see the points of view of one another. May we remember that this is your world and that we can all work to make it a better place until discord and misunderstanding have given way to unity and love, so that all peoples may live in peace and brotherhood; through Christ our Lord. *Amen.**

Closing prayer No. 39

Crimes against humanity (1)

Judge Jeffreys

There are certain things that we always expect of people and the most important is that they should be just in their dealings with others. Here are the words of one of the Old Testament prophets:

Bible Reading: Micah 6: 6–8

Sometimes people are unjust and it is unpardonable when those people are ones responsible for justice. On 18th April, 1689, there died in the Tower of London, one of the unpleasantest characters in the history of England. He was Judge Jeffreys, whose brutal judgements caused his court to become known as the 'Bloody Assize'.

Out of court he was a drunkard who revelled with brutal companions: in court he ranted at witnesses who were terrified by his blazing eyes and bellowing voice so that they sometimes answered wrongly and were given barbarous sentences.

After a rising against the King, Judge Jeffreys went to the West of England to try those concerned. At Winchester he sentenced an old lady to be burned; at Dorchester 292 people were sentenced to death or slavery; at Exeter 243 prisoners were sentenced in one batch; and at Taunton 233 were hanged. Eight hundred and forty three were sent as slaves to the West Indies, including a party of schoolgirls.

When King James II fled from England, the judge thought it wise to follow his example, but he was recognized and nearly lynched before being imprisoned in the Tower. Judge Jeffreys, like some others in history, had great power but he used his power for evil rather than good.

We remember before you, O God, all who are called to rule our nation and those who are appointed to positions of power and authority. Grant unto them wisdom and self-control, discipline and patience, wise judgement and a sense of responsibility; so that we may be free from fear, injustice and hatred and so live full and happy lives to the glory of your holy Name. *Amen.**

Closing prayer No. 22

Crimes against humanity (1) 197

Crimes against humanity (2)

CRIME AGAINST HOSPITALITY   *Massacre of Glencoe*

Some of the grandest scenery in the British Isles is to be found in the west of Scotland, where lofty mountains, purple with heather in autumn and snow-covered in winter, sweep down toward the still waters of the lochs. Between the mountains lie the lonely glens where few people live, and of these, one of the finest is Glencoe which, on 13th February, 1692, became the scene of a cold-blooded massacre.

William III had become King and all the Highlanders were ordered to take an oath of allegiance before 1st January of that year. The old leader of the Macdonalds, who lived in Glencoe left it until the last minute and then was delayed by snow. Others, who had suffered at the hands of the Macdonalds saw their opportunity to get their own back.

At the beginning of February, one hundred and twenty soldiers of Clan Campbell rode into Glencoe, where for twelve days they received true Highland hospitality. Then, at five in the morning on February 13th, they rose from their beds, shot the chief, slew about forty more and drove some 300 others into the mountains, where many more perished in the snow.

The massacre served as a lesson to other Highlanders but it goes down in history as one of the worst crimes against hospitality and friendship. In most countries it is the custom to respect and protect those who stay in a house as guests.

We can read in the Bible how Saul sought to kill David, who was staying in his house, but how David was helped to escape.

Bible Reading: 1 Samuel 19: 8–12

Help us, O God, in all our dealings with others to be fair and just. May we never repay friendship with unkindness but in all our doings seek only that which is pleasing in your sight; through Jesus Christ our Lord. *Amen.**

Closing prayer No. 24

Crimes against humanity (3)

Julius Caesar

One of the best-known characters in history is Julius Caesar—the man who did so much to build the mighty Roman Empire.

As a young man, he showed great interest in anything to do with the people of Rome and proved himself to be a great speaker and leader. But it was as a general in the Roman army that he won fame for himself and earned great popularity.

It was in Gaul—the land now known as France—that he served. Not only did he conquer the country but he invaded Britain and neighbouring lands, thus adding to the already large Roman Empire. Soldiers were happy to fight under the man who never demanded of them hardships he himself would not face.

When he returned to Rome it was in great triumph. The only other general with similar powers fled, leaving Julius Caesar to be ruler over the whole Empire.

Caesar the general, the great speaker and leader, was showered with honours and given powers greater than any Roman had ever held before.

His triumph, however, was short-lived. Some of the nobles became jealous of his powers, fearing that he was becoming a dictator. They believed he must be put out of the way, so they plotted to kill him in the Senate on the day in their calendar called the Ides of March (15th March).

He did not heed the warnings to beware this day but went to the Senate, where he was stabbed to death—destroyed not only by enemies but by some whom he had called friends.

We recall how Jesus was let down by his friends and betrayed by one of them.

Bible Reading: St. Mark 14: 32–35 and 37–46

Forgive us, O Lord, for every unkind thought, every selfish act, and every hurtful word. Fill us with your Spirit, so that our thoughts may become as your thoughts and our ways as your ways, until Christ may be seen in all that we do. We ask it in his Name. *Amen.**

Closing prayer No. 1

Crimes against humanity (4)

Pearl Harbor

At the end of 1941, when the world was involved in war, representatives of the Japanese government were talking peace with those of the United States. Without warning, on Sunday, 7th December, disaster struck the United States military and naval base at Pearl Harbor in the Hawaiian Islands.

At 7.55, a single Japanese aircraft flew over the base. It was followed by nearly two hundred bombers, fighters and torpedo aircraft, all from aircraft carriers.

Suddenly all hell was let loose, with the whine of bombs, the roar of aircraft and violent explosions on land and on the ships. Soon smoking and sunken ships filled the harbour and shore buildings were ablaze.

On the airfield, 126 aircraft were lined up: only 43 remained. Over three thousand army and navy men were killed or wounded.

The world was shocked because the two countries had not been at war. In this way the Japanese declared war and put part of the American fleet out of action at one and the same time.

The war brought sorrow and disaster in many parts of the world but this unexpected attack on Pearl Harbor is considered by most people to be one of the most treacherous acts of the war. There are, of course, always two ways of looking at things and no doubt the Japanese leaders felt this was necessary.

In life we do well to be on our guard for evil always strikes in unexpected ways when we are unprepared. We do well to ask, as the psalmist did in the Old Testament, that God will protect us from evil and that he will keep us from doing evil ourselves.

Bible Reading: Psalm 34: 11–15

Make us strong, O Lord, and help us to stand firm against temptation and wrong. Make us watchful so that we may never be taken unawares. Make us ready to place ourselves in your hands, so that we may know your power. May we take to ourselves the whole armour of God, after the example of Jesus Christ, to whom be the glory for ever. *Amen.**

Closing prayer No. 10

Crimes against humanity (5)

One of the worst things we can do is to think that we are always right and therefore others must be wrong. Here is some good advice given by St. Paul.

Bible Reading: Philippians 2: 3–4

If you have watched films about white men and Red Indians in North America, you may have come to the conclusion that the white people were always right and the red people were always bad. This is quite wrong.

The Indians were a proud people and resentful of losing the land which the tribes had held for hundreds of years. None was prouder than Sitting Bull, chief of the Prairie Sioux, who became principal chief of all the northern Sioux tribes in 1866, when he was about thirty-five.

Sitting Bull had always been a great leader, fearless in battle and ready to uphold the rights of his own people. In 1868 he made friends with the white men, only to be forced from his own land into a reservation. This he would not have. The U.S. army was sent to compel him but the army, led by General Custer, was cut to pieces in a battle which has become known as 'Custer's last stand'. Sitting Bull, fearing reprisals, fled to Canada until famine forced him to return and surrender.

On the reservation, things were little better. Hunger, disease and rumours of an Indian Messiah who would drive out the white men caused unrest amongst the Sioux. The government, fearing an up-rising, sent Indian police and soldiers to arrest Sitting Bull.

On 15th December, 1890, they seized the chief and took him prisoner but he was shot and killed as his warriors tried to rescue him.

Take from us, O God, the pride which makes us think that we are right and therefore those who disagree with us must be wrong. Help us to be ready to see the points of view of others and to respect their way of life. Keep us from covetousness, hatred, envy and any attitude that leads to strife and so make us more truly your children; for the sake of Jesus Christ our Lord. *Amen.**

Benediction No. 41

Battles to be fought (1)

Bastille Day

In France, 14th July is kept each year as a public holiday. It is known as Bastille Day—the anniversary of the day in 1789 when the people of Paris stormed the Bastille—a great fortress which stood on the east side of Paris. It had eight great towers, each a hundred feet high, and thick walls of the same height linking the towers. Around the fortress was a moat eighty feet wide.

It had originally formed part of the defences of the city but, as time passed, it came to be used as a prison—a kind of top-security prison for enemies of the state from which it was almost impossible to escape. These prisoners were not ill-treated. In fact they were able to feast and entertain their friends, but they could do no harm to the state from there.

In May 1789, the French Revolution broke out and the people were anxious to obtain arms and ammunition, which they believed were stored in the Bastille. On 14th July, they asked the governor to let them have what they wanted. He refused. The revolutionaries then took matters into their own hands and the governor with his few soldiers were soon overcome. The Bastille was broken open and later destroyed.

For many years the great stone fortress had seemed to stand for all that was evil. Its destruction was a blow for freedom and a cause for rejoicing—a good enough reason for keeping Bastille Day as a public holiday.

Today there is much that is evil in the world but in the strength of God we can overcome it and rejoice, as King David did in Old Testament times after he had been delivered from evil enemies.

Bible Reading: Psalm 18: 1–6

Almighty God, you know us to be set in the midst of so many diffi-culties and dangers, and ever at the mercy of the forces of evil; equip us we pray with your whole armour, so that we may do battle with evil and stand fast for righteousness and truth; in the Name of Jesus Christ our Lord. *Amen.**

Benediction No. 50

Battles to be fought (2)

American Independence Day

July 4th is known in America as Independence Day, and it is kept as a holiday because it is the day on which the United States was 'born' in 1776.

Of course there had been people living in America long before that. It was the home of Red Indians before English, French, Dutch and Spanish settlers made their homes there.

The English settlers lived on the Atlantic coast, in colonies such as Virginia, New England, Pennsylvania, Maryland, Carolina and Georgia. The British government demanded that the people who lived there should pay taxes to cover the cost of the soldiers who had gone to America to protect the colonists. The Americans said 'Why should we?' and refused to pay.

The British government may have been right in expecting the Americans to pay for their protection: the Americans may have been right in refusing to do so when they had no say in the government. Neither was prepared to see the point of view of the other.

War was the result. Before long, representatives of the thirteen colonies met and, on 4th July, 1776, issued a Declaration of Independence, stating that they were no longer under British rule but were the United States of America—just a small part of the present United States. Britain lost her colonies because she failed to see their point of view.

Are we ready to see the points of view of those with whom we disagree? Intolerance of others causes many of the world's problems. If Jesus had been as intolerant as his fellow countrymen, we would never have heard of Zacchaeus.

Bible Reading: Luke 19: 1–10

Help us to remember, O Lord, that so many of this world's problems arise because people refuse to see the points of view of others. Teach us that we are not always right; make us tolerant of others; and grant us wisdom in all we do or say. Help us to be kind, courteous and at peace with our neighbours through the guidance of your Holy Spirit; through Jesus Christ our Lord. *Amen.**

Benediction No. 56

Battles to be fought (3)

The Dutch in the Medway

Look out across the Thames estuary and you may be amazed at the number of ships sailing to and from their berths in the Thames and the Medway. There are ships of many kinds and of many nationalities and all are welcome.

It was not always so. At times there have been some very unwelcome visitors and none have been more unwelcome than those which sailed up the Thames estuary in June 1667.

These Dutch ships had come to strike a blow at the English navy. On 12th June, they broke through the chain across the Medway which gave protection to the English ships. Several were set on fire; others were blown up; whilst the great ship *Royal Charles* was towed away to become the Dutch Admiral's flagship. Later another Dutch fleet sailed up to Tilbury.

Samuel Pepys wrote in his famous diary, 'It is a sad sight to see so many good ships sunk in the river, while we would be thought to be masters of the sea'.

Why did it happen? Simply because people had become careless and had taken too much for granted. They learned their lesson. When war broke out five years later, England was prepared. The Dutch dared not repeat their attack.

When we look back into history, we find that many disasters happened just because people thought 'That could not happen to us.'

We can read how Jesus gave a warning to people not to become careless about good living: that, too, could be a dangerous thing.

Bible Reading: St. Matthew 24: 37–39 and 42–44

O God our Father, we do not know what today will bring, nor what dangers and temptations lie before us. Guide us therefore, we pray, so that we may seek your will and be prepared to do it, knowing that you will be our shield and defence against the forces of evil; through Jesus Christ our Lord. *Amen.**

Closing prayer No. 31

Battles to be fought (4)

AGAINST ENMITY   *Jan Christiaan Smuts*

One of the hardest things to do in life is to forgive and forget. It is one thing to say we will forgive; it is another to let bygones be bygones and to love our enemies. Yet this is what Jesus taught.

Bible Reading: St. Matthew 5: 43–45 (or 48)

History tells of some people who remained enemies all their lives. It also tells of some who made friends with those who were once enemies. One of the latter was Jan Christiaan Smuts.

Smuts had been a fighter in more ways than one. As a lawyer he fought for what was right in courts of law for, after studying law in England, he became a lawyer in his own country—South Africa.

Soon he was involved in another kind of fighting, for war broke out between Britain and the Boers who lived in South Africa. Smuts was a Boer and he took up arms with others of his race.

When the war was over, he fought for peace and for a better understanding between the two nations. Before many years had passed, he was fighting again, this time on the side of Britain against the German armies. In the Second World War, he again supported Britain, this time as Prime Minister of South Africa.

When he died on 11th September, 1950, it was not only the people of South Africa who mourned his death but people throughout the world. During his lifetime he had held many honoured positions and received a number of awards but one of the greatest was to be honoured as a friend by those who had once regarded him as an enemy.

Teach us, good Lord,
To live in harmony and at peace with our neighbours;
To avoid all things which may cause offence;
To love those whom we find it difficult to love;
To forgive those who hurt us by word or deed;
To put friendship in place of enmity;
To follow the example of Jesus Christ
In whose name we offer this prayer. *Amen.**

Benediction No. 44

Battles to be fought (5)

FOR JESUS CHRIST   *St. Ignatius Loyola*

In one of his letters, St. Paul urged Timothy to forget things which were not important and serve Christ.

Bible Reading: 1 Timothy 6: 9–12

Many years later, in 1521, a young Spanish officer was urging his soliders to fight the French, when he was seriously wounded in the leg. For a long time he lay in bed unable to do all the things he wanted to and longing to be back at court or enjoying himself with his friends.

As he became bored, he asked for books to read. He did not mind what they were—romances, stories—anything would do. Among the books was one about the life of Christ and young Ignatius found that he did not want to put it down. He had been a soldier of his country; now he wanted to be a soldier of Jesus Christ.

He read about some of the great Christian people. If they could serve God so could he. As soon as he was well enough he went on a pilgrimage to Jerusalem. Then he set himself to study.

In Paris where he was studying he formed a group of students who were determined to go to the Holy Land to preach about Christ but war prevented their journey. Instead they formed themselves into a group known as the Society (or Company) of Jesus. There were ten men then but in the next fifteen years they became a thousand, travelling to many lands to preach and teach, founding schools and colleges.

On 31st July, we remember St. Ignatius Loyola, whose prayer reminds us that he never forgot he was a soldier of Jesus Christ.

A prayer of St. Ignatius Loyola:

Teach us, good Lord, to serve thee as thou deservest; to give and not to count the cost; to fight and not to heed the wounds; to toil and not to seek for rest; to labour and not to ask for any reward, save that of knowing that we do thy will: through Jesus Christ our Lord. *Amen.*

Closing prayer No. 9

Those in authority (1)

Charlemagne

Some rulers make a name for themselves for their wisdom, some for the magnificence of their court and some for their good sense or lack of it.

In the Bible we read of the greatness and wisdom of King Solomon, whose fame spread far and wide.

Bible Reading: 1 Kings 10: 1–7

On 28th January, 814, one of the greatest rulers of the Middle Ages died. He was Charles I, King of the Franks, more commonly known as Charlemagne—Charles the Great—the 'Emperor of the Romans'.

How he came to be known as Emperor of the Romans is a long story for the Roman Empire had fallen apart long before. Charlemagne was King of the Franks, who lived in the land we now call France. Soon he was also king of some German tribes, the Lombards who lived in Italy, and others. His armies also marched into Spain which, for some time had been taken over by the Moors, who were not Christian.

It was at this time that the Pope believed there should be another Emperor of Rome. Charlemagne was invited to Rome, where, on Christmas Day, 800, he was crowned as Emperor of the Romans. His empire, known as the Holy Roman Empire, consisted of France, Germany and Italy.

But Charlemagne was more than a soldier. He was a scholar who encouraged learning and ruled wisely for 46 years.

He died in his capital city, Aix-la-Chapelle and was buried, sitting on his throne, under the dome of the cathedral which had been built on his instructions.

A prayer of Charlemagne (Gallician Collect) (written 1200 years ago):

O most merciful God, incline thy loving ears to our prayers, and illumine the hearts of those called by thee, with the grace of the Holy Spirit ... that they may love thee with an everlasting love, and attain everlasting joys; through Jesus Christ our Lord. *Amen.*

Closing prayer No. 2

Those in authority (2)

Frederick the Great

Some rulers in history are referred to as 'the Great'—a title which is usually reserved for those who have done great things for their country or who have had great qualities as rulers.

One who was given this title was Frederick the Great, King of Prussia, who died on 17th August, 1786. His kingdom was a small one but it was not long before it became very much greater and a power to be reckoned with in Europe—a country which joined with others in later years to become Germany. Frederick himself was one of the most important and influential rulers in Europe in his day. For this reason he may be called 'the Great'.

Yet there is another reason too. For all his power, he was a very understanding kind of man who ruled his country well. It may have been because of his very strict upbringing or it may have been because of his regular habit of rising early in the morning and spending long hours about the business of his kingdom. He also made a point of choosing loyal and energetic people to work for him.

Moreover, he had a sense of humour. A story tells how one day he asked a woman to bake him a Dutch pasty. 'What!' she exclaimed. 'How do I know you can pay for it?'

Frederick's companion said that he could easily make the money by playing on his flute; so the woman demanded to hear him. When Frederick played, the woman agreed and went off to bake the pasty, little knowing that she had been talking to a king.

Frederick the Great was a man who kept complete control of his kingdom but he ensured that justice was done and whatever power he had was used for the good of his people.

Help us, O God, never to think too highly of ourselves, nor look down on those who are less able than we are. Help us to use our talents wisely in the service of others and for your glory, remembering that all we have is a gift from you and should be offered to you; through Jesus Christ our Lord. *Amen.**

Closing prayer No. 22

Those in authority (3)

King James II

At three o'clock in the morning on 11th December 1688, a darkly dressed figure crept stealthily from the royal palace, clutching a bag which contained the Great Seal, used to give royal consent to all new laws.

A waiting coach carried him swiftly to the bank of the River Thames, where a ferry boat waited to carry him across. As he passed Lambeth, he dropped the bag into the river, believing that Parliament would not be able to pass any more laws. Then he took a coach to Sheerness to join his wife and son.

This was the last desperate act of King James II, who had seen his kingdom gradually slipping away from him as a result of his own foolishness. James was a clever man and could have ruled well if he had learned a few lessons from the past but, like so many people, he thought he knew best.

Like other Stuart kings, he believed that he could have his own way, even though his father, Charles I had been beheaded for acting in that way.

He knew that people felt very strongly about their religion, yet he did certain things which angered many in the church.

At last some Members of Parliament made it clear that they wanted James's daughter Mary and her husband William to reign as King and Queen in his place. James was deserted by his friends and even by his courage. He fled.

King James discovered too late that no one, not even a king, can do just as he pleases.

Help us, O God, to remember
That we cannot do just as we please;
That we have responsibilities toward others;
That we should always act and speak wisely;
That pride often goes before a fall.

Take from us all pride, all selfishness, and all that would offend others, so that we may serve our neighbours and seek your perfect way; after the example of Jesus Christ our Lord. *Amen.**

Closing prayer No. 29 (a prayer of King James's father)

Those in authority (4)

Duke of Wellington

When the Duke of Wellington died in 1852, the British people felt that they had lost a great national hero. It was only fitting that he should have a state funeral and be buried in St. Paul's Cathedral.

Yet it is quite possible that, had it not been for his brother, there might never have been a Duke of Wellington.

As a young man out of school, the Duke, then just plain Arthur Wellesley, joined the army. His older brother, who was appointed Governor-General of India, realized that young Arthur was an able leader, so he gave him responsibility as governor of a town and in charge of an army unit. By the time he returned to England, he was Major-General Sir Arthur Wellesley.

He became Member of Parliament for Rye but he was called upon to fight against Napoleon, who was then trying to make himself ruler of Europe. Wellesley fought in Spain and Portugal, where he was very successful. He was made Viscount Wellington in 1809, Marquis of Wellington in 1812, a Field-Marshal in 1813 and Duke of Wellington in 1814.

His greatest victory, and final defeat of Napoleon was at the Battle of Waterloo on 18th June, 1815.

On his return, the Duke of Wellington became the Commander-in-Chief of the British army and later Prime Minister for almost three years. He died at the age of eighty-three, having led his country in war and in peace.

A prayer for those who lead the nations today:

Almighty God, who alone givest wisdom and understanding: inspire, we pray thee, the minds of all to whom thou hast committed the responsibility and leadership of the nations of the world. Give to them the vision of truth and justice, that by their counsels all nations and classes may work together in true brotherhood, and thy Church may serve thee in unity and peace; through Jesus Christ our Lord. *Amen.*

The Kingdom, the Power, and the Glory

Benediction No. 52

Those in authority (5)

　　　　　　　　　　Queen Victoria

Victoria was only eighteen years old and it was quite impossible for her to write in her diary all that she felt, for this was the most important day in her life. She described simply what happened.

'20 June 1837.　I was awoke at 6 o'clock by Mamma, who told me that the Archbishop of Canterbury and Lord Conyngham were here, and wished to see me. I got out of bed and went into my sitting room (only in my dressing gown) and <u>alone</u> and saw them. Lord Conyngham then acquainted me that my poor Uncle, the King, was no more, and had expired at 12 minutes past 2 this morning, and consequently that I am <u>Queen</u>.'

Thus Queen Victoria began her reign, which was to be the longest reign in the history of Britain and in which many important things were to happen.

People wondered just how well Victoria could reign, especially as they had not thought much of the previous sovereigns. They were pleasantly surprised. Even the Duke of Wellington, who had thought as little of them as anyone had, felt compelled to say after Victoria's first public appearance, 'If she had been my own daughter, I could not have wished that she should do better. Why, she not only filled the chair, she filled the room!'

Queen Victoria was indeed every inch a queen. She reigned for sixty-four years, during which she was loved and respected by her people in Britain and in other parts of the world.

When she died in 1901, it was not just her reign that ended but a whole era of British history.

A prayer for the Queen:

O Lord, grant the Queen a long life, that her years may be rich with thy blessing; furnish her with wise and safe counsels, and give her a heart of courage and constancy to pursue them. O prepare thy loving mercy and faithfulness for her, that they may preserve her; so will we always sing praises unto thy Name; through Jesus Christ our Lord. *Amen.*

Archbishop Laud

Benediction No. 54

Freedom (1)

Oliver Cromwell

The one thing that most people want above anything else is to feel free to do as they please. In some things, of course, we cannot please ourselves entirely because we have to think of other people, of our school, our community or our country. But, provided we keep within the law, we are free to go where we wish, to say what we wish and to do the kind of things that we like doing.

It has not always been so. Jesus found so many little rules that people found them difficult to keep. Even the sabbath day, which was a day for rest, became a burden as this story shows.

Bible Reading: St. Mark 2: 23–28

In this country, only a few hundred years ago, people could be fined for not going to church or imprisoned for going to the wrong one. In the time of Oliver Cromwell, many sports and customs, like dancing round the maypole were banned because the people who ruled the country said they were wrong. People were expected to be very serious and have no fun. In fact, when Oliver Cromwell died on 3rd September, 1658, people looked forward to their freedom to have fun and laughter again.

Today we are free to do most things, but people of many lands are not. Many people are working throughout the world to give people this freedom—freedom from want, freedom from fear, freedom of speech, and freedom to worship as they wish.

O God our Father, we thank you for the freedom which is ours to enjoy. Help us to remember that we still have responsibilities to others and to you.

We remember the people of other lands who are not free as we are and we pray that the day may soon come when every man shall have the freedom that is his right; for the sake of Jesus Christ our Lord. *Amen.**

Closing prayer No. 4

Freedom (2)

FIGHTING FOR FREEDOM   *Sir Winston Churchill*

Bible Reading: 2 Kings 24: 10–14

Ten thousand people taken into captivity—a story that was all too common in the distant past, when captivity often meant slavery and maybe death.

Although times have changed, there are still occasions today when people are willing to rise up and fight in order to protect their freedom. The last time the people of Britain did so was in 1939, when Hitler's Nazi German army was continuing its conquest of Europe. Within months it was clear that things were going badly. European countries fell before the Germans; the British were driven out of France; and the British Prime Minister, Neville Chamberlain resigned.

On 10th May, 1940, Winston Churchill was invited to form a government and he accepted. He knew it would be difficult but he loved a challenge and was able to stir up the people and encourage them in a manner which few could have done. In the House of Commons he announced three days later:

'I have nothing to offer but blood, toil, tears and sweat.'

Then, nearly a month later:

'We shall defend our island, whatever the cost may be, we shall fight on the beaches, we shall fight on the landing grounds, we shall fight in the fields and in the streets, we shall fight in the hills; we shall never surrender.'

So people were encouraged by the familiar figure with his cigar and his appearance in bombed streets, on ships or near the battle front, always ready to encourage. Many would feel that 10th May, 1940, was the turning point of the war.

O Lord our God, we know how easy it is to be discouraged when things seem to be going wrong, and how easy it is to give in instead of to fight life's problems. May there always be those who will encourage us to press on in spite of difficulties and to overcome temptations, so that we may become more than conquerors; through Christ our Lord. *Amen.**

Closing prayer No. 10

Freedom (3)

Magna Carta

Few people would disagree that King John was the worst king ever to sit on the throne of England.

Before he became King, he was traitor first to his father, Henry II and then to his brother, Richard I, while they were abroad. Then he seized the throne by having his nephew, Arthur, murdered. The Norman barons were so shocked at this that they refused to have him as King and all the Norman lands in France were lost to the English crown.

Then he quarrelled bitterly with the Pope, who ordered that no church services should be held in England. John himself was excommunicated—turned out of the Church—until he begged pardon from the Pope.

The King also used every trick he could find in order to take money or land from the barons, who became angrier and angrier. At last they marched on London and forced the King to meet them on the island of Runnymede, near Windsor.

On 15th June, 1215, the barons laid before the King the Magna Carta, or Great Charter, which decreed that the barons should receive fair treatment according to the law. After reading through it, the King, who could not write, placed his seal upon it, knowing that there was no choice open to him.

The Magna Carta did not affect many of the people of England, who were then serfs or slaves, but it was an important step toward freedom and is generally considered to be one of the great landmarks in our history.

We thank you, God our Father
For all the good things that we have day by day;
For so many blessings that we cannot count them;
For the freedom we have to enjoy these things.

As we thank you for those who won this freedom for us, we pray for those today who work so that others may have the good things of life and to be free to enjoy them; through Jesus Christ our Lord. *Amen.**

Closing prayer No. 14

Freedom (4)

Tolpuddle Martyrs

Bible Reading: St. Matthew 20: 1–14

Although men in this story were given what they had been promised, those who had done the most work felt unjustly treated and said so. Nowadays they would probably complain to their Trade Union or come out on strike.

A century and a half ago, this was not allowed for people were afraid that if workers banded together they would demand too much from their employers. When six farm workers decided to band together to help each other, the law stepped in.

The men lived in the village of Tolpuddle, Dorsetshire, and they decided, in 1833, to form a Friendly Society of Agricultural Labourers but they were arrested in February 1834 on a charge of making illegal oaths.

On 19th March, they were found guilty and sentenced to be sent as convicts to Australia for seven years. They were taken to the convict hulks at Portsmouth and to Australia six weeks later.

But there was an immediate outcry. The six men were regarded as heroes and became known as the Tolpuddle Martyrs. There were demonstrations in London, and elsewhere. Two years later, the sentences were cut and the six returned home, though five later emigrated to Canada.

For many years now, people have been free to belong to a Trade Union and a memorial at Tolpuddle stands as a reminder of those who suffered and so helped millions of others to enjoy the freedom of action which is ours today.

O Lord our God, put into the hearts of all men a desire to give a good day's work for their day's wages and grant that they may be rewarded justly for their labours. Help us as we grow to realize that we cannot expect to receive more than we are prepared to give and that we must work hard and willingly if we are to receive your blessing; through Christ our Lord. *Amen.**

Closing prayer No. 26

Freedom (5)

Houses of Parliament

The visitor to London, standing on Westminster Bridge and observing the majestic building of the Houses of Parliament, might think of this as the building in which the British Parliament has met for centuries.

In fact he would be wrong. Parliament has met on that site but not in that building, which was erected a little over a hundred years ago to replace the former Houses of Parliament which were destroyed by fire in 1834.

Plans were immediately made for a new building and the first stone was laid on 27th April, 1837. Within a few years it was completed with the exception of the great Victoria Tower, which was finished in 1857.

Although the building may be comparatively new, its traditions reach far into the past to the days, seven hundred years ago, when the first commoners were allowed and even before that.

What tales could be told if the remaining parts of the old building—St. Stephen's Chapel and Westminster Hall—could speak! And what secrets of the past might be revealed!

As the years have passed, times have changed, our ideas have moved forward, and our Parliament has become the model on which parliaments in many lands have been based.

On the corner opposite is a statue of Queen Boadicea, who fought for freedom in her day. The Houses of Parliament, with the great clock tower and the sound of 'Big Ben' are often used today as a symbol of freedom and a freedom-loving people.

Today, O God, we remember before you those with the responsibility for governing our land—the Queen and her ministers, the Members of Parliament and the Lords. May your Spirit of wisdom guide them in their various duties and responsibilities toward our nation and the world. May they make wise decisions and good laws so that we may be sensibly governed. May we ever enjoy our freedom and live at peace with our neighbours; through Jesus Christ our Lord. *Amen.**

Closing prayer No. 32

Justice and fair play (1)

The 'Lost' Days

If someone were to ask what happened to England on 6th September, 1752, the answer would be 'Nothing'. In fact there were no dates 4th–14th September in that year. The day after the 3rd September was the 15th.

The reason was that our calendar had been made in Roman times and there was a very slight miscalculation. By 1752, the calendar was eleven days out and the government realized that something must be done about it. It was decided that eleven days should be 'lost'. This, and a slight adjustment in leap years would put matters right.

But many people were very angry and there were riots all over the country by people who believed that their lives had been cut short by eleven days. They demanded that they should be given them back. We can almost hear them shouting, as we hear many people shout, 'It isn't fair! Why should I lose it?'

In the Bible we read of two brothers, Jacob and Esau. Jacob schemed to take away from his brother the birthright and blessing that should have been his. Here is the end of the story:

Bible Reading: Genesis 27: 30–36

Esau, too, could say, 'It isn't fair! Why should I be the loser?'

One of the lessons that we all have to learn is that life is not always fair. Some people always have more than their fair share and others always seem to lose out as a result. But nothing is gained by feeling sorry for ourselves. We have to overcome our difficulties and our disadvantages.

O God our Father, forgive us if sometimes we are envious of others or if we feel hard done by because others have more abilities than we have. Help us to be content and never to despise our one talent but recognize it as a gift we have received from you to be used in the service of others and for the glory of your holy Name. *Amen.**

Closing prayer No. 39

Justice and fair play (1)   217

Justice and fair play (2)

Charles Kingsley

Some of the most popular books written last century were those by Charles Kingsley. They include *Westward Ho!*—a stirring adventure of sailors in the time of the first Queen Elizabeth, *Hereward the Wake*—the English hero in Norman England, and *The Heroes*—a collection of Greek legends.

Like his father, Charles Kingsley was a clergyman and he spent much of his life as rector of the parish of Eversley, in Hampshire. He was a hard worker for the church and very much aware of the social evils of his day. Like other nineteenth-century writers, he mentioned some of these in his books.

One of these was the practice of sending small boys up the huge chimneys to sweep them. Often they hurt themselves; most of them were cruelly treated; and many of them died when they were very young.

It was no doubt the thought of these 'Climbing Boys' that led Kingsley to write his most famous book, *The Water Babies*, in which Tom, a little climbing boy, ran away from his bullying master. This proved to be one of the most successful children's books ever written.

Kingsley was never very strong, even as a child, and he suffered from bad health all his life, but this did not stop him from fighting anything which he thought to be unjust and unfair. He firmly believed, as did the prophet Jeremiah in the Old Testament, that God's blessing would be given to those who sought a square deal for the needy:

Bible Reading: Jeremiah 7: 5–7

When Kingsley died on 23rd January, 1875, the poor and the underdogs lost one of their champions.

A prayer of Charles Kingsley:

Guide us, teach us, and strengthen us, O Lord, we beseech thee, until we become such as thou wouldst have us to be; pure, gentle, truthful, high-minded, courteous, generous, able, dutiful and useful; for thy honour and thy glory. *Amen.*

Benediction No. 49

Justice and fair play (3)

William Wilberforce

Most of the great changes in history have come because someone saw further ahead than other people of his day.

Nowadays, for example, we are horrified at the thought of people being kept as slaves or harshly treated by other people, yet it is not a couple of hundred years since slavery was the accepted thing, as it had been from the beginning of time. We can read of slaves in the earliest chapters of the Bible and we know that most of the great empires of the past were filled with slaves who had been conquered in battle. We even read how Joseph's brothers sold him into slavery:

Bible Reading: Genesis 37: 23–28

More recently, slaves were those taken from their homes in Africa and sold to work in the American plantations. Most people accepted this, but William Wilberforce was one who was horrified by the brutality of it and believed it to be a blot on civilization.

As a Member of Parliament, he found some support but a great deal of opposition. It was some years before Wilberforce was able to persuade Parliament to prevent, in 1807, the carriage of slaves in British ships.

It was a beginning. Wilberforce fought on. In 1833, as he lay dying, he learned that all slaves on British soil were to be freed. Wilberforce, crusader against slavery, died on 29th July, knowing that he had won a great victory.

Soon, thousands of slaves were rejoicing in their new freedom and people in many places were beginning to realize that everyone had a right to enjoy a full, free life.

O God, our Father, we thank thee that thou dost show thyself in Jesus Christ. We thank thee, too, for people we can see today who show us something of thyself in their kindness and goodness, their strength and their love. We pray that our lives may show that we are thy children. *Amen.*

Devotions for Company and Camp

Closing prayer No. 37

Justice and fair play (4)

Abraham Lincoln

One of the greatest names in American history is that of Abraham Lincoln, the poor country boy who became President of the United States.

Lincoln was born in Kentucky, where his father had a farm. His mother died when he was nine, so 'Abe' had to rough it, frequently going bare-footed, dressed in skins and doing the rough work on the farm.

He had little time to go to school but used his spare moments to teach himself to read and write. He had a strong character and people came to know him as 'Honest Abe'. Later he worked as a storekeeper but studied law so that he could better himself and eventually became a lawyer in Illinois, where he was elected to the state government.

One thing, however, troubled him greatly. In his early years he had made trips to New Orleans, where he saw negro slaves working for white bosses and he did not like what he saw. He worked hard to prevent slavery from spreading to other states.

Soon he came to the notice of the Republican Party, which opposed slavery and he was elected President of the U.S.A. in 1860. Almost at once civil war broke out between the slave states and those which opposed slavery.

This lasted until 1865, when those who opposed slavery were victorious. A few days later, on 14th April, Lincoln went to a theatre, where he was shot by an actor. The champion of justice died the following morning.

Jesus once told a parable about people who were quite ready to kill to get what they wanted—a parable about himself and the way in which he would be killed.

Bible Reading: St. Matthew 21: 33–40

Almighty God, by whom we are taught that all men are equal in your sight; help us to fight injustice wherever we may find it, to respect the opinions of others that may differ from our own, and live at peace with our neighbours, for Jesus Christ's sake. *Amen.**

Closing prayer No. 33

Justice and fair play (5)

John F. Kennedy

John Fitzgerald Kennedy was elected President of the United States of America in 1961. At forty-four, he was the youngest president to be elected, and people wondered what to expect of him.

They discovered that he was a very determined man who could stand up to great opposition.

In foreign affairs he had to be strong, because the two great powers, the U.S.A. and the U.S.S.R. were very suspicious of each other and even a small matter could have sparked off a war between them.

At home, he had to be equally strong to make changes that he felt were needed. He believed that every United States citizen should have the same rights, whatever the colour of his skin. There were some places, especially those where negroes had once been slaves, in which equal rights were unknown. Some people thought that Kennedy was right and went all the way with him: others thought he was wrong and became very bitter.

Then, on 22nd November, 1964, as he was riding with his wife in a great motorcade through Dallas, in Texas, he was struck by a sniper's bullet and killed—the fourth president of the United States to be assassinated. The action of one man with a chip on his shoulder, robbed the country of a good leader.

Within a few years, Kennedy's brother was also shot dead and so were others who were prepared to fight against injustice. There are too many people in the world today who think that a murder weapon is the answer to everything.

But this is nothing new. We can read of this happening in the first book of the Bible.

Bible Reading: Genesis 4: 1–8

O Lord Jesus Christ, we thank you for your example of unselfishness and love even to those who opposed you. Teach us to bear with one another; to forgive those who have offended us, and to repay unkindness with love; even as you have loved us. *Amen.**

Benediction No. 53

Determination (1)

Robert Bruce

Do you sometimes feel like giving in? You feel quite sure that you can never do something no matter how hard you try? There is an old saying, 'If at first you don't succeed, try, try, try again'.

Moses must have felt that his task was impossible when God sent him to ask Pharaoh to free his slaves.

Bible Reading: Exodus 6: 28–7: 7

Moses must have been very down-hearted when Pharaoh kept saying 'No'.

The only thing that many people can tell about Robert Bruce is that he watched a spider whilst hiding from his enemies. Time and time again the spider tried to make its web and each time it failed. At last, after many attempts it succeeded. Bruce thought to himself that if the spider could go on trying so could he.

Bruce, the Scottish hero was born on 11th July, 1274, into a noble family. His grandfather had once claimed the crown of Scotland. When the English attacked Scotland, Bruce had defended his country and had been lucky to escape when other leaders were taken prisoner and treated shamefully. The Scottish people looked to Bruce to lead them but he could not drive the English away. It was then that he was forced to hide away.

Now, with a new determination, he captured castle after castle before meeting up with the English king at Bannockburn, near Stirling. There he inflicted a shattering defeat upon the English armies and rightfully earned the crown of Scotland. The Scots were free—thanks perhaps to a lesson learned from a spider which refused to give in.

Heavenly Father, thou knowest that life is often very hard and difficult. Help us not to lose heart, but to realize that our difficulties are opportunities to prove our courage, trust and faithfulness. Make us strong to bear, and steadfast to endure, and by thy grace, grant that we may be more than conquerors. *Amen.*

Devotions for Company and Camp

Benediction No. 40

Determination (2)

Joan of Arc

Joan was the daughter of the Mayor of Domremy in France and lived at a time when the King of England was trying to conquer France. Had she been a boy, she might have been fighting in the French army but, as she was a girl, she looked after her father's animals.

One day it seemed to her that she could hear voices telling her to go to help the young prince, or Dauphin, whose father, the old King of France, had recently died. 'How can I?' she thought. 'I am only a girl.' But her voice told her it was God's will and he would enable her to do it. It seemed even more difficult than David facing Goliath.

Bible Reading: 1 Samuel 17: 31–35

Some people laughed at David but he killed the giant. Some people laughed at Joan but not the Dauphin, who put her in charge of his army. So Joan of Arc as she was called, led the army to victory at Orleans; she fought her way into the cathedral city of Rheims, where the Dauphin was crowned King of France; and she determined to drive the English out of France.

But some were jealous of her success. She was captured, imprisoned and put on trial as a witch who claimed that God had spoken to her when he had done no such thing. The trial was rigged; Joan was found guilty; and she was burned to death in the market place at Rouen on 30th May, 1431.

The English thought they had won a great victory but within a few years, their armies had been driven out of France. Joan of Arc had beaten her giant.

Many of the people who have left their mark on the world have been those who were quite sure what God wanted them to do and refused to be put off.

Grant unto us, O God, to walk with thee as our Father, to trust in thee as Saviour, to worship thee as Lord, that all our works may praise thee, and our lives may give thee glory. *Amen.*

Devotions for Company and Camp

Benediction No. 56

Determination (2)   223

Determination (3)

Elizabeth Fry

On 21st May, 1750, a daughter was born to John Gurney, a rich banker who lived near Norwich. He was a Quaker and little Elizabeth was brought up as a Quaker too.

But it was not as Elizabeth Gurney that she became famous. When she was about twenty, Elizabeth married Joseph Fry, also a Quaker, and moved to London, where she lived at Upton House, in the part of London now known as West Ham.

Some years later, she obtained permission to visit Newgate prison, a grim, stone building in the heart of London. What she saw horrified her. Women in rags, with nothing to sleep on but heaps of dirty straw, fought each other at the iron barred gates just to get a glimpse of someone from the outside world. Many were starving: others were ill. There was no fresh air, very little water, and the whole prison smelt vile.

Elizabeth Fry wanted to do something for these people but there were those who tried to discourage her. But Mrs. Fry was not to be put off. She paid for clothing and fresh straw and she began thinking what else could be done. She started a school for the children, then provided work material for the women prisoners and paid a matron to look after them.

More important still, she spoke to many influential people about the state of the prisons and would not rest until something had been done to improve them. It was largely due to the untiring efforts of Mrs. Elizabeth Fry that the attitude of people to prisons and prisoners began to change.

O God our Father, we thank you for those men and women who have seen the distress of others and have had the courage to do something about it; for men and women of patience, understanding and compassion, who by their work have brought some cheer into the dark places of this world. Inspire all people by your Holy Spirit so that your light is spread abroad and the world becomes a better place; for Jesus Christ's sake. *Amen.**

Closing prayer No. 2

Determination (4)

IN THE CAUSE OF MEDICINE   *Dr. Ronald Ross*

Dr. Ronald Ross, a member of the Indian Medical Service, had few official duties, which suited him very well, for he would sooner write poetry than work as a doctor. Then one day a missionary spoke to him about the thousands of people who died from malaria because nobody knew the cause of the disease.

Ross set aside his poetry. How could he write when so many people were dying? He would try to find out about malaria. His next holiday in England was spent not on his own pleasures but in learning about bacteria, so that when he returned to India he could do something about it.

Somehow, he believed, there must be a connection between malaria and mosquitoes which swarmed everywhere. Some people thought that malaria was caught by drinking water into which dead mosquitoes had fallen. Ross was not so sure. He was more inclined to believe that the germ was carried inside the mosquito and passed on to people who were bitten.

So he took samples of blood from people who caught malaria and he cut open thousands of mosquitoes but he found nothing. Then, on a sweltering night, the night of 29th August, 1897, he was about to give up his work because he was so hot and tired. He would just examine one last mosquito under his microscope. To his amazement, he saw the germs he had been looking for. His patience and perseverance had been rewarded. He had proved that mosquitoes caused malaria when they bit their victims—a discovery that has resulted in the saving of many, many lives.

We thank you, God our Father, for healthy bodies and active minds. Help us always
    To care for our bodies so that we are fit for life's duties;
    To feed our minds so that we can know what your will for us is;
    To use both body and mind in your service in the Name of Jesus Christ our Lord. *Amen.**

Closing prayer No. 35

Determination (5)

Michelangelo

On 6th March, 1475, Michelangelo Buonarroti was born in Florence in Italy. He was to become one of the world's finest artists and sculptors, besides being a fine architect and poet.

As a boy, he had first shown his genius as an artist by making a drawing of some scaffolding. His master on seeing it, remarked, 'This boy knows more than I do'.

After living for some time in Rome, Michelangelo returned to his home town, where a huge block of marble stood in the cathedral. For forty years it had stood there awaiting a sculptor who could make a statue from it, but most said it was impossible.

Michelangelo's eyes lit up. Yes, he could use it. So screens were set around it and Michelangelo began to work on it. At last it was finished and there were gasps from the crowd as they beheld a huge statue of David the shepherd boy awaiting to fight Goliath. For four hundred years this great statue stood in the city.

Shortly afterwards the Pope sent for him to carve a monument but insisted that Michelangelo should first paint the ceiling of the Sistine Chapel in the Pope's palace, the Vatican. This was over 10,000 square feet and nearly 100 feet above the chapel floor. Michelangelo painted it alone, mainly while lying on his back on the scaffolding, a work which took him four years to complete.

At 72, he became the chief architect of St. Peter's in Rome and he died when almost ninety, leaving behind him many treasures of art and sculpture.

O God, who gave us eyes to see the beauty around us and talents to create works which are pleasing to the eye; we praise you for all who have laboured to give us our heritage of art and craftsmanship, and especially those who have dedicated their talents to your glory. Help us to use our talents in such a way that they may give glory to you and pleasure to those around us; through Jesus Christ our Lord. *Amen.**

Closing prayer No. 5

Chivalry (1)

The story is told that one evening in the year 1348, King Edward III and many of his nobles with their ladies were enjoying themselves at a court ball. During the ball, one of the ladies, thought to be the Countess of Salisbury, lost one of her garters, whereupon the King stooped, picked it up and without more ado tied it round his own leg.

The lady blushed and the rest of the company laughed but the King remarked, 'Honi soit qui mal y pense,' which means in English, 'Dishonoured be he who thinks evil of it'. Then he added, 'I will make of it ere long the most honourable garter that ever was worn'.

Whether this story is correct we cannot be sure, but it was not long before the Most Noble Order of the Garter came into being. It consisted of the King and twenty-five knights—the most noble men in England.

The date on which the Order was started cannot be fixed for certain, but it is generally believed to have been 22nd April, 1348, the day before St. George's Day. Sometimes they were known as the Knights of St. George, and sometimes as the Knights of the Blue Garter. As one died, someone was elected to take his place.

Today, there are various Orders of Chivalry but one of the greatest honours that can be bestowed upon anybody is to make him a Knight Companion of the Order of the Garter—an award often given for outstanding services to the country.

A prayer from the Service of the Knights of the Garter (Fourteenth Century):

O God, Almighty Father, King of Kings and Lord of all our rulers, grant that the minds of all who go out as leaders before us, the statesmen, the judges, the men of learning, and the men of wealth, may be so filled with the love of thy laws, and of that which is righteous and life-giving, that they may serve as a wholesome salt unto the earth, and be worthy servants of thy good and perfect gifts; through Jesus Christ our Lord. *Amen.*

Closing prayer No. 29

Chivalry (2)

Since earliest times, men have been foolish enough to fight to settle an argument or to take from someone else something which is rightfully his. Sometimes the lives of thousands of people are lost to satisfy the desires of one person.

One of the lengthiest wars in history is the Hundred Years' War, fought because the English kings thought they should also rule over France. One of the bloodiest battles in this war was the Battle of Crécy, fought on 26th August, 1346.

The English king had formed up his army of over 25,000 men near the village of Crécy: the French came to meet him with 70,000. Many were slain by the English bowmen before part of the French army broke through to attack the section led by the Black Prince. A knight hastened to the King to suggest that help be sent to his son, the Black Prince.

'Return to those who sent you,' the King ordered, 'and tell them not to send again for me this day ... and say that I command them to let the boy win his spurs, for I am determined, if it please God, that all the honour of this day shall be given to him, and to those into whose care I have entrusted him.'

That day, the Black Prince, a lad of sixteen, proved himself to be a courageous and skilful knight.

Today there are many battles to be fought, not against men but against all that is evil in the world. These, too, require courage and determination if they are to be won. Listen to the words of St. Paul:

Bible Reading: Ephesians 6: 11–13

O Lord God, when thou givest to thy servants to endeavour any great matter, grant us also to know that it is not the beginning, but the continuing of the same unto the end, until it be thoroughly fininshed, which yieldeth the true glory: through him who for the finishing of thy work laid down his life, our Redeemer, Jesus Christ. *Amen.*

Sir Francis Drake

Benediction No. 50

Chivalry (3)

St. Hallvard

One day in the year 1043, Hallvard Vebjörnsson, the son of a rich Norwegian landowner, was about to step into his boat to cross a fjord, when he noticed a woman running toward him. 'Please help me,' she cried. 'Take me across the fjord as quickly as you can.'

'Step in the boat,' Hallvard replied. Then he took the oars as the woman sat in the fore part of the boat.

Soon some men appeared upon the shore, who looked very angry. The woman told Hallvard that they were accusing her of stealing but that she was innocent. 'Do hurry,' she urged.

But the others, who had entered another boat, were quickly overtaking Hallvard. They called out.

'How is it, Hallvard, that a well-bred boy like you can help a miserable wretch like her. Let us have her so that we can kill her as she deserves.'

By now the boats were close together. Hallvard pleaded the woman's cause but the other men, fully believing themselves to be right, gradually lost patience. One of them raised his bow and shot Hallvard. Then they killed the woman and cast Hallvard's body into the water. The body when found was laid in the church in the little village of Oslo, which was one day to become the capital of Norway.

St. Hallvard became the patron saint of the diocese of Oslo, where, on 15th May, the people remember the youth who died defending someone who was unable to defend herself. In the Bible we have a story of the way in which Jesus defended a woman who was being accused by the leaders who thought she should be put to death.

Bible Reading: St. John 8: 3–11

Jesus, friend of the friendless, helper of the poor, healer of the sick, whose life was spent in doing good, let me follow in thy footsteps. Make me strong to do right, gentle with the weak, and kind to all who are in sorrow: that I may be like thee, my dear Lord and Master. *Amen.*

                                                    The Daily Service

Closing prayer No. 16

Chivalry (4)

St. John of Nepomuk

How well can you keep a secret? Or would you be like the man in this story of Jesus?

Bible Reading: St. Luke 5: 12–15

Most people have some secrets that they wish to keep from others. But sometimes it helps to tell someone of our problems if we can be sure the person we tell will honour our confidence and not disclose our secrets.

A doctor, for example, takes an oath that he will not disclose anything a patient tells him unless the patient is willing that he should do so. A priest, or minister of religion is also one to whom we can speak and know that what we tell him remains secret. In some churches there are special times when people go to a priest to confess their sins, and no priest would disclose what had been said during confession.

About six hundred years ago, a boy was born in a village of Bohemia called Nepomuk, and was named John. After studying, he became a priest who held some important offices, one of them being the priest to whom the Queen confessed.

One day, when the King was in a drunken rage, he ordered John of Nepomuk to tell what sins the Queen had confessed. Of course he refused to do so, though he was tortured and imprisoned. The Queen begged successfully for his release, but he was taken again a few days later, tied hand and foot and thrown in the river, where he drowned.

Today, St. John of Nepomuk, the one who died because he refused to betray a confidence, is remembered on 16th May.

Help us, O Lord, always to stand firm for what we know to be right. Teach us what things are good and honourable; then help us to perform them faithfully in face of all opposition to ourselves, to our friends, to all who trust us, and to you; for Jesus Christ's sake. *Amen.*

Closing prayer No. 36

Chivalry (5)

Sir Philip Sidney

Sir Philip Sidney, who lived during the reign of the first Queen Elizabeth, was a young man who seemed almost too good to be true. He was handsome, clever, brave, kind and very popular.

He numbered foreign royalty among his friends and, through his uncle, the Earl of Leicester, he was introduced to the Queen. In one sense this was a disadvantage, for young Sir Philip was a man who liked adventure and there was precious little of that at court. His opportunity came when he was sent as part of an army to the Low Countries to fight against the Spaniards.

It was there that something happened for which Sir Philip will always be remembered. The army was besieging the town of Zutphen, when it was learned that help was being sent to the town. Sir Philip was sent with some men to stop these reinforcements but became lost in the fog. When it lifted, he found himself close to the walls of the town.

Almost at once he felt a sickening pain as he was shot in the leg. He struggled dizzily to the back of the English lines, gasping for water, which was brought to him. He was about to drink, when he heard a groan and saw a wounded soldier looking longingly at the bottle. Without tasting a drop, Sir Philip handed over the bottle, saying, 'Your need is greater than mine'.

Sir Philip died soon afterwards but those words, spoken on 23rd September, 1586, have been remembered ever since.

Here are some words of Jesus about our attitude to others.

Bible Reading: St. Luke 6: 35–37

Help us, O God our Father, always to count our blessings and, if at times we feel sorry for ourselves, to remember the many who are less fortunate than we are. Show us how to help them and in so doing find true happiness for ourselves; in the Name of Jesus Christ our Lord. *Amen.**

Closing prayer No. 7

Ready to change (1)

During the summer months lots of people like to cruise in small boats on the canals and inland waterways of Britain at a leisurely pace which allows them to take notice of and enjoy the countryside.

But these canals were not built for pleasure; they were built for business. In days when roads were bad and travelling difficult, canals proved to be a cheap form of transport. A little over two hundred years ago many were built through the heart of Britain, linking the midlands with rivers and seaports. One of the most important was the Grand Trunk Canal, for which the first spade-cut was made on 26th July, 1766.

Nearly one hundred years later, a Frenchman named Ferdinand de Lesseps, dreamed up an even greater canal, to be dug through the desert of Egypt and link the Mediterranean Sea with the Gulf of Suez. This meant that ships travelling between Europe and the East would no longer have to travel right round Africa and many days' travelling time could be saved. For many years Britain maintained this canal but it was nationalized by President Nasser of Egypt on 26th July, 1956. A few years later, during fighting between Egypt and Israel, the canal was blocked and closed.

Today many of the canals in Britain are used no longer. Railways and better roads provide quicker transport. Today too, with bigger and faster ships, the Suez Canal is no longer of great importance.

Times change but while earthly things are continually changing, God remains the same and his ways are always of great importance.

Bible Readings: Psalm 119: 137–144 *and* Psalm 90: 1 and 2

Almighty God, we praise you because you are always the same and when we are not sure of ourselves we can always turn to you for guidance. Help us to place our trust always in you, so that we can say as the psalmist of old, 'the Lord is good; his mercy is everlasting; and his truth endures to all generations'; through Jesus Christ our Lord. *Amen.**

Benediction No. 40

Ready to change (2)

Richard Arkwright

Richard Arkwright, who was born on 23rd December, 1732, had a poor start in life as the thirteenth child of a poor working man. While still very young, he began working in a barber's shop for very little money.

As he grew older, he opened his own shop in Bolton, where he did well. He was an expert wig-maker and all gentlemen in those days wore wigs. They were pleased with his work and paid him well. But gradually wigs went out of fashion and Richard knew he must find other work.

He remembered the weavers who lived near his home. Always grumbling they were. How could they make things with cotton thread that kept breaking? Arkwright decided to try to make a machine which would give the strong thread that they needed.

Night after night he experimented until he had built a machine which worked. But it was large and needed two horses to provide the power to drive it. At last he hit upon the idea of using water power instead. So he built a mill by a stream near Derby. It was so successful that others wanted machines like it and Richard Arkwright became a rich man—one of the richest in the country.

Arkwright, and others like him who invented new machines for the factories, are remembered as men who left their mark on Britain and brought great changes in the lives of a great many people.

Jesus Christ was also a man who made great changes in his day, not by building machines but by all he did.

Bible Reading: St. Matthew 11: 2–6

And that was only a small part of His work. He showed the way to a better world and invited others to do likewise.

Help us, O Lord, to make some mark upon the world in which we live. We may not become great or famous but we shall certainly affect the lives of others. May all we do be for good and not evil, bringing happiness to all with whom we come into contact; and to you be the glory for ever and ever. *Amen.**

Benediction No. 49

Ready to change (3)

The 'Great Eastern'

Isambard Kingdom Brunel was a great engineer with big ideas, one of them being to build a ship larger and faster than any ship in the world.

The keel was laid at Blackwall on the Thames and gradually the great ship took shape. She was 693 feet long and built so that she could be launched sideways into the river.

After three years, in the summer of 1857, she was ready for launching. On 3rd November a great crowd gathered for the ceremony but the *Great Eastern* refused to move. After many attempts, she finally floated free seventy-nine days later.

Then there was not enough money to finish the ship and more had to be raised. Brunel became ill with worry and overwork. A few months later he died.

At last, on 17th June, the *Great Eastern* sailed on her maiden voyage to America. The great ship was a magnificent sight, with five funnels belching smoke and with sails on her six masts. But she was never clear of trouble. Some of her crew were killed by an explosion; her captain was drowned; she was battered in a great storm; and she struck some rocks.

The *Great Eastern* was a brilliant idea but a failure as a passenger liner. She did, however, serve a very useful purpose in laying telegraph cables across the Atlantic and in other parts of the world before being broken up.

Perhaps we have big ideas for our lives but sometimes we find that there is something different in store. This was the experience of St. Paul, who had his plans changed for him by God.

Bible Reading: Acts 22: 3–10

We thank you, God our Father, that we can plan great things for our lives. Let us never be contented with little things but grant us the strength, courage, wisdom and patience to succeed. And if we are not successful, grant us to know that there is more than one way of living a useful life in your service; through Christ our Lord. *Amen.**

Closing prayer No. 5

Ready to change (4)

Girolamo Savonarola

When the people of Florence went to hear the new preacher they were sadly disappointed. In fact his preaching was so dull that the congregation gradually dwindled until few were left. The monk, Savonarola, had to admit that as a preacher he was a dismal failure.

But he did not give up. He believed that God had something for him to say and he made up his mind that he would improve his preaching until people would listen. A few years later he returned and people could hardly believe that this was the same man.

Savonarola now preached against all the wickedness that he saw in the city and demanded that people should change their ways. Many listened to his words of wisdom. Even the ruler of Florence, Lorenzo, could not ignore Savonarola and tried unsuccessfully to bribe him to keep quiet.

But Lorenzo died and his son had little idea how to rule. The people turned to Savonarola and demanded that he become their ruler. One of his greatest victories was when he persuaded the people to pile their books of magic, indecent books and pictures, together with anything that reminded them of the evils of the past, on a huge bonfire in the centre of the city.

But some people did not like the way in which Savonarola spoke out against them, among them the Pope. Savonarola was taken captive and, on 23rd May, 1498, put to death—killed for doing what he believed to be right.

In the Bible we read how John the Baptist spoke out in his day, offended the king, and was put to death for doing so.

Bible Reading: St. Mark 6: 17–27

O thou, who art the Way, the Truth and the Life, make thy way plain before our face. Teach us to live boldly, that we may be free from fear and favour, strong in thy love and power. *Amen.*

The Splendour of God

Closing prayer No. 20

Ready to change (5)

William Gurney, a twenty-five-year-old Sunday School teacher, was discussing Sunday Schools with some of his friends.

'We ought to improve our Sunday Schools. Your Sunday School is better than ours, and you tell me there are schools better than yours. Why should we not get Sunday School teachers together and try to improve, if possible, our plan of instruction, and stimulate others to open new schools in London.'

His friends thought this a good idea and so a meeting was called on 13th July, 1803, when it was decided to form a Sunday School Union, with Mr. Gurney as the first secretary.

In those days, of course, Sunday schools were not as we know them today. Most children had no schooling except in Sunday schools where they could learn to read and write.

The Sunday School Union served any Sunday schools, regardless of the kind of church to which they were attached. It published hymn books, lesson books, spelling books and a scheme of reading. It tried to open new Sunday schools and to improve old ones. In time it became the National Sunday School Union.

But times change, and the National Sunday School Union has changed with them. Today it is known as the National Christian Education Council and it continues to provide all sorts of books, notes, pictures and other materials which are needed by Sunday School teachers and other Christian workers if they are to do their work as efficiently as possible.

O God our Father, we praise and thank you for all who have founded schools and Sunday schools where children and young people could learn to equip themselves for life and to hear your Word. Help all who continue this work today and grant them the joy of seeing the fruits of their labours. May your Name be glorified through their work; for the sake of Jesus Christ our Lord. *Amen.**

Closing prayer No. 32

Saving life (1)

First Parachute Jump

From what height would you be prepared to jump to the ground? Most people would hesitate before jumping more than a few feet in case they should hurt themselves. To jump from higher is to court trouble and many people have been killed in doing so.

Yet there have been strange cases of people who have lived after jumping from very great heights.

The most remarkable of these was in 1944. A British bomber was blazing over Germany, while flying at 18,000 feet (over 3 miles) above the earth. The flight-sergeant had no parachute but did not wish to be burned to death, so he jumped out. After falling to the earth at a speed of about 120 m.p.h., he hit a fir tree and rolled off into a small bank of snow. Three hours later, he was able to examine himself and was amazed to find that not a single bone was broken.

Needless to say, most people would prefer to use a parachute if they had the opportunity to do so. Parachutes are as old as men's first flights in balloons. One was demonstrated in 1783 and an attempt to drop from a balloon by parachute was made in 1793 but the parachutist broke his leg. The first successful parachute jump was on 22nd October, 1797, since when hundreds of lives have been saved by means of parachutes.

For the airman, the parachute is a sensible safety precaution reducing the risk to his life if anything goes wrong in the air.

We may never need to rely upon a parachute but we do need to remember other safety rules, for to risk life anywhere is a foolish thing to do.

Almighty God, the giver of all life, teach us to live our lives wisely, avoiding those risks which may harm us, and remembering all common sense rules which are designed for our safety. Help us to live according to the teachings of our Lord Jesus Christ, who alone is the Way, the Truth and the Life, and so learn the secrets of true living; through Jesus Christ our Lord. *Amen.**

Closing prayer No. 28

Saving life (2)

John Smeaton

Standing on Plymouth Hoe, high above the water, is a lighthouse which gives no warning light, for its place was taken many years ago by a more modern Eddystone lighthouse.

For over a hundred and twenty years, the tower had stood out at sea, its friendly light guiding ships safely into Plymouth. Then, when the new one was built, it seemed fitting that the old one should be rebuilt in sight of the waters in which it had stood. Even now, the stump of this old tower can be seen beside the newer one.

The old tower also stands in memory of John Smeaton, its builder. Born in Leeds on 8th June, 1724, it was expected that he would become a lawyer like his father. John, however, was far more interested in engineering and spent his life at it.

Besides building the Eddystone lighthouse, Smeaton built bridges and planned hundred of miles of canals which were used in England for the transport of goods in days when roads were bad and railways had not yet been invented.

We owe much to engineers like John Smeaton for things which are important today—things like good roads and bridges, railways, ships and motor cars, which are so familiar that we take them for granted.

In these days of reliable lighthouses around our coasts, most sailors probably take them for granted too, but they owe a debt of gratitude to people of past days who began building warning lights to guide ships clear of danger.

Almighty God, our heavenly Father, we thank you for all who make our shores safe for sailors: for those responsible for the upkeep of lighthouses, lightships and buoys; and for lighthouse and lightship keepers who are often at the mercy of the sea and separated from families and friends. Bless them in their work as they safeguard others; and to you be the glory for ever and ever. *Amen.**

Closing prayer No. 26

Saving life (3)

Sir William Hillary and R.N.L.I.

Bible Reading: Psalm 107: 23–31

Sir William Hillary, soldier, traveller and writer, used to sit in his home at Douglas in the Isle of Man and watch huge waves being driven by stormy winds into the bay. If the lifeboat were called out, Sir William could be counted upon as a regular member of the crew. Once he was washed out of the boat, broke six ribs and still continued to rescue shipwrecked people.

The Douglas boat was one of a number of boats which could be found around the coasts of Britain, each of which was run by local people. Hillary believed that there should be one organization responsible for all lifeboats and he described his ideas in an appeal which he published in 1823.

In the following year, he met a Member of Parliament who became interested and called a meeting in London on 4th March, 1824. It was agreed that one body should be formed, known as the National Institution for the Preservation of Life from Shipwreck. Thirty years later, it became the Royal National Lifeboat Institution, the name which it bears today.

This Institution is a voluntary organization, receiving no money from the government and depending entirely on gifts, subscriptions and flag-days. Lifeboat men freely give their service when needed.

Thousands upon thousands of people have been rescued by lifeboats since the service as we know it was formed, and many have cause to be thankful today.

Almighty God, we thank you
For those by whose wisdom the lifeboat service was formed;
For those who are responsible for it today;
For those whose gifts have provided the boats;
For those who volunteer to form the crews;
For all who are concerned with saving life at sea, including helicopter and rescue services;
Grant unto each your blessing and divine help; for Jesus Christ's sake. *Amen.**

Closing prayer No. 7

Saving life (4)

Great Fire of London

Very early in the morning on Sunday, 2nd September, 1666, people living near London Bridge were awakened by the smell of burning wood or the shouts of those who were trying to put out the fire which had started in a baker's shop in Pudding Lane.

By morning, about three hundred houses had burned down and the streets were filled with clamouring people, trying desperately to save their belongings from the path of the fire. Others bundled their belongings into boats and made their way across the Thames.

Attempts to stop the fire were useless. Buckets of water and squirts could do nothing to stop the flames spreading along narrow streets and through timbered houses. Houses were hastily pulled down but the flames, fanned by the wind, spread too quickly. At last, after three days, the King ordered the army to blow up houses with gunpowder and so make a space across which the flames could not pass.

By the time the Great Fire of London ended, 13,200 houses had been destroyed, besides many churches and other buildings, including the old St. Paul's Cathedral.

People were anxious that such a thing should not happen again. New houses were built of stone and brick instead of wood; and steps were taken toward improving methods of fire fighting. Eventually fire brigades were formed with much better equipment. Today, with fast machines and good organization, firemen can be in action within minutes of receiving the call, so that big fires can be prevented from spreading and many lives can be saved.

We thank you, God our Father, for all whose lives are spent in the protection of life and property. We remember all members of the fire services and pray that they may be kept safe while working in dangerous situations. May we help them by taking care not to start fires which may get out of control and by remembering simple rules of safety in the home; through Jesus Christ our Lord. *Amen.**

Closing prayer No. 14

Saving life (5)

One of the best-known emblems in the world is a white flag bearing a red cross. It is flown on hospitals in battle areas; it is painted on ambulances or hospital ships; it is seen on fairgrounds, at sports meetings or on the beach. It is the emblem of the International Red Cross Organization, of which the British Red Cross is one member.

It came into being over a hundred years ago, on 22nd August, 1864, after a conference at Geneva, Switzerland. The Red Cross flag was adopted because it could easily be recognized and this was especially important in time of war, when the flag would indicate a place in which the injured were being cared for.

Most countries agreed that Red Cross people would be allowed to do their work and would not be fired upon by enemy guns.

But the Red Cross is far more than an organization for looking after war injured. It has many jobs to do in peacetime as well. If there is an earthquake or some other disaster, the Red Cross is quickly on the scene with whatever comforts are needed and it can provide urgent medical supplies.

The Red Cross always ensures that there are men and women trained in first aid, who can be called upon when needed. Often their members assist at public meetings. They also do a great amount of work in their district, helping the old, the poor and the sick. For all of this they need money and are grateful for gifts and money collected on flag-days, which enable them to continue their work. [*Details could be given of any collection being made in school.*]

O God, our Father, we thank you for those who freely give of their service for the benefit of others. Today we remember especially the work of the Red Cross and ask your blessing upon it. Guide its members as they help those in need and grant them the knowledge that what they do for others is done for you; through Jesus Christ our Lord. *Amen.**

Closing prayer No. 38

Hospitals and healing (1)

A NEW HEART   *Professor Christiaan Barnard*

Bible Reading: St. Mark 1: 23–28

In Bible times, people knew very little about diseases and their cure. Many illnesses, they believed, were caused by evil spirits and the sick persons could only be cured by casting out these evil spirits.

Today we know that we can visit a doctor or attend a hospital and find a cure for most illnesses. It is even possible now to be given an organ from the body of another person if our own ceases to work.

For some years, people have been given back their sight by transplanting the cornea from the eye of a dead person. Other people have been given a kidney to replace a diseased one.

But history was made on 3rd December, 1967, when, for the first time, a man was given a new heart. The operation was performed by Professor Christiaan Barnard at the Groote Schuur Hospital in Cape Town, South Africa. The patient died after a couple of weeks but later operations were more successful.

Nowadays it is common to hear of transplants of many different organs, though not all are successful.

On 20th February, 1969, for example, doctors in New York transplanted the heart, two kidneys and liver of a man who had died into four other people, while the corneas of his eyes were frozen for future use. On the same day, a similar operation was being performed in Los Angeles.

This kind of surgery has only become possible through the research of very many people and because there are fine hospitals with modern equipment and doctors with skill to be able to save life.

O God our Father, accept our thanksgiving
For healthy bodies and active minds;
For doctors who help us when we are ill;
For hospitals where we can be well cared for;
For all the medical knowledge given to mankind;
For the skill that enables lives to be saved;
    For all such blessings, we praise your name, O God. *Amen.**

Benediction No. 45

Hospitals and healing (2)

St. Camillus

Camillus was a big man with a very hasty temper. He never minded a fight and he was not particularly concerned about who he fought. So, for eight years, he became a soldier of fortune, fighting for whoever was prepared to pay him.

He was also a born gambler and eventually lost everything that he had. To earn some money, he found work as a labourer, helping to build a monastery.

It was then that his life began to change. As he watched the monks, he decided that he too would like to do something that was useful for a change. He tried to join the Franciscan friars but he was unable to do so because of a disease in his leg resulting from an old battle injury.

He decided that he might be able to help those who suffered as he did and so he attached himself to a hospital. He soon discovered what shocking places hospitals were, filthy, ridden with disease and having brutal men to nurse the sick.

In 1584, Camillus became a priest and leader of a band of men, known as Ministers of the Sick, who pledged themselves to help the sick and injured. Camillus sent out the first unit ever to tend the injured on the battlefield. His followers wore a red cross, the emblem of the Crusaders.

When he died, in July, 1614, he had about three hundred others, all pledged to do this great work. Today, he is known as St. Camillus, the patron saint of nurses and the sick and his feast day falls on 18th July each year.

O Lord Jesus Christ, who ministered to all who were in need, bless all who minister to the sick or injured today. We pray for doctors and nurses, asking that they may have skill and patience; for the Red Cross and other organizations which help where there is distress; for ambulance workers and all who assist in emergencies: and to all who are sick or injured, grant your peace. *Amen.**

Benediction No. 55

Hospitals and healing (3)

One of the most popular people at the court of King Henry the First of England was Rahere, whose fun and humour raised many a laugh from all at court.

Then after King Henry's son was drowned in the *White Ship*, things were never the same. Rahere decided to go on a pilgrimage to Rome. There he caught a fever and was nursed back to health by the monks of the Hospital of the Three Fountains.

Rahere was so impressed by the work of these monks, that he decided to build a similar hospital in London. Then he had a dream, in which St. Bartholomew, one of the original disciples of Jesus, blessed his plan, telling him where it should be built, on a piece of land belonging to the King.

His former friends were amazed when he returned to England dressed not in his finery but in the coarse clothing of a monk. He told his story to the King, who readily gave him the land he required, known as the Smooth-field, or Smithfield, just outside the city of London.

Rahere began clearing it with his own hands, but as the news spread, others offered to help him. Some gave their labour; others gave money to pay craftsmen.

Gradually the buildings rose—a simple hospital, a church and a priory, named after St. Bartholomew. When Rahere died, on 20th September, 1144, he was buried in his church. Today the visitor to Smithfield can see the great St. Bartholomew's hospital, which is one of the important London hospitals and, next door, the church dedicated to St. Bartholomew.

O Lord Jesus Christ, to whom the sick were brought for healing and who showed compassion toward all who suffered; look down upon all who suffer today in body, mind or spirit; and let your healing hand rest upon them so that they may receive your blessing. Work through your servants who have the gift of healing so that miracles may be seen in our day; and to you be the glory for ever. *Amen.**

Benediction No. 55

Hospitals and healing (4)

BETTER HOSPITALS   *Florence Nightingale*

On 5th November, 1605, Guy Fawkes was caught as he tried to blow up King and Parliament. The day is still celebrated today with bonfires and fireworks.

November 5th, 1855, marked another event which was to cause the sparks to fly in a different sense. Florence Nightingale and her band of nurses stepped off the ship at Scutari, to nurse the soldiers who were wounded in the Crimean War.

Her hospital was an old Turkish barracks with no beds but mattresses on the cold floor, no basins, no soap, no clean linen, poor cooking and laundry facilities and rats scurrying across the floor.

The army made no secret of the fact that the nurses were not welcome: Florence Nightingale made it equally clear that they were there to stay and to do the job they had been sent to do. When they said, 'It can't be done', she retorted, 'It must be done'—and something usually happened.

Soon she had turned the hospital upside down and the authorities had to admit that there was a great improvement. As for the soldiers, they loved the Lady with the Lamp, who found time amid the business of the hospital to visit them whenever she could.

And it was not just the hospital at Scutari that was changed. When the war was over, she began schools for nurses in Britain. Florence Nightingale found a nursing service that was despised: she left one that was highly respected, in which thousands upon thousands of women have been pleased to serve.

O God our Father, we remember before you all who have dedicated themselves to the service of nursing the sick and suffering. Keep them faithful to their calling, and grant unto them patience, tenderness, compassion and wisdom, so that they may bring comfort and peace of mind to those entrusted to their care. Give them the joy of knowing that service given to others is service given to you, as taught by our Lord and Master, Jesus Christ. *Amen.**

Closing prayer No. 2

Hospitals and healing (5)

William Harvey

If you cut your finger or graze your knee, it is not long before the blood comes trickling out. The first thing you do is to wash and dress the wound to stop the bleeding.

If the bleeding does not stop, you become worried and try to do something about it, like the woman in this Bible story.

Bible Reading: St. Matthew 9: 20–22

In olden times, people had some strange ideas about the blood. Some thought that it gave life to the body. Others thought that by cutting a person and letting out some blood, one could also let out diseases.

One man who made an exciting discovery about blood was William Harvey. He knew that blood travelled from the heart, through the arteries and back through the veins. He decided that the heart must be a pump, which pumped blood to many parts of the body, that the blood returned to the heart and was pumped out yet again. He was the first man to discover what we call circulation of the blood. Harvey, who died on 3rd June, 1657, had made an important discovery.

That was over three hundred years ago. Since then, medical scientists have learned many other facts about the blood. They know, for example, that there are several different blood groups and that it is possible to give a transfusion of blood from another person with the same kind of blood. Knowledge like this has been the means of saving many lives.

Nowadays, many people give pints of their blood, which can be stored in a blood bank until it is needed to help save someone's life.

We thank you, God our Father, that today we know so much about our bodies and the way they work. Help us to look after our bodies and to take whatever precautions we can against illness and infection, so that we can be fit for life's work and for your service; through Jesus Christ our Lord. *Amen.**

Closing prayer No. 17

Conquering pain and disease (1)

ANAESTHETICS   *James Simpson*

One day, Professor James Simpson of Glasgow invited two of his friends to an unusual party. In front of each of them, as they sat in Simpson's dining-room, was a bottle containing a liquid. As they sat and talked, they each breathed the fumes that were coming from the bottles. Gradually their conversation became much livelier; then they all started talking at once; then suddenly all three fell unconscious to the floor. When they woke up, they were delighted and tried again, just to make sure they were right.

They were not trying to drug themselves, but were testing an idea which could be of the greatest benefit in hospitals for killing pain. The bottles on the table contained chloroform, which Simpson believed could be used to put people to sleep while operations were being performed.

Until a year before, there had been no effective means of deadening pain. Limbs were taken off accompanied by the most dreadful screams from the patients. A year before, ether had been used in America for putting people to sleep, but Simpson was sure that chloroform would be better. As a result, on 12th November, 1847, chloroform was first used as an anaesthetic in an operation in Britain.

Nowadays many new anaesthetics are known and used. Operations are done painlessly and without need of fear. The world owes much to Simpson and others like him who experimented, often on themselves, to make these things possible.

Today, O God, as we thank you for all the discoveries in the field of medicine, we pray for those who use them today:
      For all doctors, who seek to relieve pain;
      For nurses and all who care for the sick or injured;
      For medical scientists, who seek new and better cures;
      For all patients in hospital, especially any that are known to us, and ask that they may be restored to health, thankful to all who have helped them and glorifying your holy Name; through Jesus Christ our Lord. *Amen.**

Closing prayer No. 26

Conquering pain and disease (2)

VACCINATION   *Edward Jenner*

In these days, there are few children in this country who have never had vaccination, inoculation or some similar means of preventing disease. For this, we have to thank Edward Jenner, who was born in the village of Berkeley, Gloucestershire, on 17th May, 1749. He studied under a local surgeon, then under a great London doctor, but it was in his native Gloucestershire that he did most of his work.

One thing that did concern him was the large number of people who died of smallpox. Nowadays we seldom hear of anyone in Britain dying of smallpox unless it has been brought from abroad but in Jenner's day about 2,000 died of it every year in London alone.

As he visited the farms, he discovered that many people caught a mild disease known as cowpox as they milked the cows. They laughed when he spoke of smallpox. 'We'll never catch that,' they said, 'not if we have had cowpox.'

They seemed to be right but that was not good enough for the doctor. He had to be sure. So he took some cowpox germs from a milkmaid and injected them into a boy. A few weeks later, he injected smallpox germs into the same boy—but he did not take the disease.

Soon Jenner became famous in many lands. Today, by being vaccinated against smallpox, there is no danger of catching the dreaded disease or of carrying it to others, thanks to Edward Jenner.

Since the time of Jenner, other scientists have experimented and found ways of preventing other serious illnesses which have killed many people in the past. We may not like being vaccinated or inoculated but it is far preferable to catching killer diseases.

Give us wisdom, O Lord, to look after our bodies, to remember the value of cleanliness and wise habits, and to take advantage of all medical knowledge, so that we may reduce the dangers of disease and thus live healthy and contented lives to the glory of your Name. *Amen.**

Benediction No. 43

Conquering pain and disease (3)

TO WAR AGAINST GERMS   *Louis Pasteur*

Bible Reading: St. Luke 7: 18–23

Jesus often healed people who came to him, giving them health and strength, healing diseases or casting out evil spirits. Nowadays we do not often hear people speaking of evil spirits: we are more likely to hear of people having a virus, or a germ, or a 'bug'.

On 28th September, 1885, the world lost one of its greatest scientists, Louis Pasteur, who was especially concerned with germs.

He noticed, for example, that when a substance went sour or bad it was because of germs. He discovered that, if the contents of bottles were sealed and heated, the germs would be killed and others could not get in. This process is used with milk today, and the milk is said to be 'Pasteurized'.

Pasteur put his studies to good use in hospitals, where many patients died after operations. Lord Lister, in England, learned much about germs from Pasteur, then showed how they might be killed. Pasteur noted what Lister proved and carried his work still further.

For a hundred years, people had been vaccinated against small-pox. Pasteur tried inoculation against other diseases and was successful. His last words were, 'I am sorry to die. I wanted to do so much more for my country.' Pasteur believed that science was a means of serving God. He spoke of 'science which brings man nearer to God,' and he freely gave his service wherever it was needed.

O God, our Father, we thank you for those who under your guidance have used their talents to teach us more about the world, and have given us the means of overcoming disease and pain. We thank you especially for those who have freely given their service to others. Help us to know the blessedness of sharing our gifts and the joy of service; through Jesus Christ our Lord. *Amen.**

Benediction No. 48

Conquering pain and disease (4)

Joseph Lister

When Joseph Lister was a young man studying to be a doctor, he saw the first operation being performed in Britain in which the patient was first put to sleep using ether as an anaesthetic. Here was a great step forward but Lister was horrified to learn how many people died after having operations—about three people in every four. He asked himself why.

Then he read of the work of Louis Pasteur in France and he realized that wounds made during operations could be infected by bacteria, or germs.

Lister declared war on germs! Every instrument he used was first boiled in carbolic acid and the air was sprayed to kill any germs. Then, perfectly clean dressings were put on the wounds. This was just a beginning. Once people realized that Lister was right, they looked for new ways of killing germs and built operating theatres in which everything could be sterilized to prevent infection.

In 1877, Lister moved from Scotland, where he had been working, to London where, in 1897, Queen Victoria made him a baron. Modern surgery owes a lot to Lord Lister, who died on 10th February, 1912.

Nowadays more people realize the value of cleanliness. Germs not only attack open wounds, but can cause illness if we do not wash our hands before handling food or after using the lavatory. Cleanliness is essential for healthy bodies.

The Bible tells us that we can also be harmed by sin and that we need to ask God to wash away our sins. This was what St. Paul was told he must do.

Bible Reading: Acts 22: 14–16

O God our Father, help us
To keep our bodies clean and fit;
To keep our minds clean and pure;
To keep our words clean and pleasant;
To keep our lives clean and honourable;
   Through him who cleanses all our sin,
Jesus Christ our Lord. *Amen.*

Benediction No. 42

Conquering pain and disease (5)

THE DISCOVERY OF X-RAYS   *Wilhelm Röntgen*

On 8th November, 1895, Professor Wilhelm Röntgen was working excitedly in his little laboratory, anxious to find out about something which had happened by accident. He had been reading a book and laid it down with a key to mark his place. Absent-mindedly, he put an electric tube, known as a Crookes tube on the book which, by chance, was resting on a photographic plate.

When he moved the tube and the book he discovered that he had, on the photographic plate, a picture of the key, which had been inside the book. He tried it again and the result was the same.

Röntgen began thinking. If rays from the tube could pass through a book, could they also pass through other substances? Why not examine metals in this way to see whether there were any faults in them? Then another thought. What would happen if the rays passed through a person's body? The thought was really exciting. Within a short time, Röntgen proved that his mysterious rays could pass through flesh and leave a photograph of the bones and of other objects. As he did not know what to call these rays, he called them X-rays, the name by which they have been known ever since.

Nowadays, X-rays can pass through metals over a foot thick, but their greatest value has been to enable doctors to see inside the human body and so operate with great accuracy. Things which are otherwise hidden are revealed by X-rays.

The Psalmist tells how things which we think are hidden in our minds are all seen by God:

Bible Reading: Psalm 139: 1–12

Help us to remember, O God, that nothing about us is hidden from you, and even the innermost thoughts of our hearts are no secret from you. May we so order our lives that everything we say, everything we do, and everything we think may be pleasing to you. Teach us to place our trust in you, whose knowledge is beyond our understanding. We ask this in the Name of Jesus. *Amen.**

Benediction No. 49

Deeds of bravery (1)

Jack Cornwell, V.C.

Jack Cornwell was born in East Ham in 1899, and there were few things he liked better than to watch the ships sailing down the Thames near his home bound for far-away places. One day he, too, would go to sea.

His opportunity came when war broke out in 1914. Jack joined the Royal Navy to learn to be a sailor and he trained as a gunner.

There was no prouder moment than when he found himself a member of the crew of H.M.S. *Chester*, a brand new cruiser. He joined the ship on Easter Monday 1916 and his particular duty was on the foremost gun, passing on the orders from the gunnery officer. His was a responsible job for a lad of sixteen.

In a matter of weeks, the *Chester*, with many other ships, engaged the enemy in the Battle of Jutland. The *Chester*, being in the front, received the full force of the enemy gunfire. The fore part of the ship was hit time and time again. The crew of the gun fell dead or wounded and the gun was put out of action. Jack himself was also seriously wounded but he stood at his post until the battle ended. Two days later, on 2nd June, 1916, Jack Cornwell died of his wounds.

His bravery had not gone unnoticed. Admiral Jellicoe reported to the Admiralty on what he described 'a splendid instance of devotion to duty'. John Travers Cornwell was awarded the Victoria Cross.

There are few braver people and few more respected by their fellows than those who are prepared to stand firm in the course of their duty, especially when it endangers their lives. And this can happen in peaceful occupations just as easily as it can in war.

Grant us, this day, O God, clear sight to see the way we ought to take, and courage and perseverance to follow it to the end. Give us humility to ask what is your will for us, and give us trust and obedience to say, your will be done: through Jesus Christ our Lord. *Amen.*

Dr. William Barclay

Closing prayer No. 9

Deeds of bravery (2)

St. Crispin

St. Crispin's Day, October 25th, is a day remembered in history for more things than one. It was on this day in 1854 that the famous Charge of the Light Brigade took place. It was also on this day, in 1415 that the Battle of Agincourt was fought between the English and the French armies. Shakespeare, in his play, *Henry V* tells how the King spoke before battle:

> *This story shall the good man teach his son;*
> *And Crispin Crispian shall ne'er go by,*
> *From this day to the ending of the world,*
> *But we in it shall be remembered,—*
> *We few, we happy few, we band of brothers;*
> *For he today that sheds his blood with me*
> *Shall be my brother; be he ne'er so vile,*
> *This day shall gentle his condition:*
> *And gentlemen in England now a-bed*
> *Shall think themselves accurs'd they were not here,*
> *And hold their manhoods cheap while any speaks*
> *Who fought with us upon St. Crispin's Day.*

But St. Crispin's Day also serves as a reminder of two others who fought a battle of a different kind. They were the brothers, Crispin and Crispinian, who were faithful to their call as followers of Jesus Christ in the early years of the Christian Church and were ready to face death for the cause to which they had given their service. No one then could expect an easy time and had to be ready to bear hardship in Christ's name. Listen to the words of St. Paul:

Bible Reading: Acts of the Apostles 20: 22–24

Today, O God, help us to brace ourselves for battle; to seek what is just, honourable and noble and to devote our lives to the battle against the forces of evil. Make us strong to do right and able to resist temptation, so that we may remain faithful to you. So bring us to the end of this day, knowing that you have blessed our every endeavour; through Jesus Christ our Lord. *Amen.**

Closing prayer No. 37

Deeds of bravery (3)

Earl of Suffolk

Charles Henry George Howard, twentieth Earl of Suffolk and thirteenth Earl of Berkshire, succeeded to the title at the age of eleven, when his father was killed in action in 1917. He inherited over 10,000 acres of land, including the family seat at Charlton Park, Wiltshire.

He was a man of the open air, who loved sailing and riding. He sailed on one of the last of the great clipper ships, held a commission in the guards until ill-health forced him to retire, then ran a sheep station in Australia. When war broke out in 1939, he could not rejoin the army, so he took up scientific work.

One day a bomb fell on Deptford Power Station, London, but failed to explode. Suffolk asked if he could watch those who took out the fuse to make it safe.

Here was a useful job he could do, saving lives by taking the fuses out of unexploded bombs. So he set to work to learn all he could about fuses and bombs.

A new experimental unit was formed with a motor van containing all the equipment needed for recovering fuses. Suffolk was placed in charge of it. As the fuses were removed and examined, information could be passed to bomb-disposal units in Britain and overseas.

It was very risky work. No one knew what the fuse would be like, but the lives of many people depended upon Suffolk's work. Every precaution was taken out but, on 12th May, 1941, one exploded. Nothing was left of the Earl, his team or the van. The Earl was awarded the George Cross for the important work in which he had risked and lost his own life for the safety of others.

Today, O Lord, grant us
Courage to face the things which make us afraid;
A spirit of adventure to face the things unknown;
A willingness to take risks without being reckless;
The will to think more of others than we do of ourselves;
And the knowledge that you are always with us in
times of difficulty, distress or danger.
This we ask for Jesus Christ's sake. *Amen.**

Closing prayer No. 5

Deeds of bravery (4)

On 19th October, 1922, a north-easterly gale cut across the east coast of England, whipping the seas into a frenzy as they broke across the sandbanks off the Norfolk coast.

There, after dark, the Newcastle steamer *Hopelyn* was driven onto the sands off Caister and lay at the mercy of great waves, which battered relentlessly.

Coxswain William Fleming of Gorleston manned his lifeboat and set out for the Scroby Sands. There was no sign of life on board and little could be done in the darkness but he stood by until dawn. Then, after fighting the gale for ten hours he returned to harbour.

Barely had he come ashore, when it was reported that a flag was flying from the wreck. Forgetting their weariness, Fleming and his crew set off once more. Six hours later he was still standing by but could not get near. The Lowestoft motor lifeboat was then called out. As his own boat was damaged, Fleming transferred to the Lowestoft boat and sent his own boat home.

All night they stood by, eventually rescuing the crew, only to be swamped by a great sea which threatened to drag men from the lifeboat. Mercifully none was lost.

For thirty-six hours Coxswain Fleming had stood by to make this rescue. Later he received the Lifeboat Institution's Gold Medal and an Empire Gallantry Medal, which was exchanged in 1941 for the new award, the George Cross.

The story of Coxswain Fleming is only one of a large number of stories which could be told of unselfish bravery on the part of lifeboatmen, who risk their own lives to save others.

O Lord Jesus Christ, who stilled the storm and brought peace to the troubled hearts of your disciples; grant your merciful protection to all who do battle with the sea to save the lives of others. Grant unto them courage in time of danger, strength to fight the raging seas, and a safe return at the end. We ask it in your Name. *Amen.**

Benediction No. 46

Deeds of bravery (5)

P.C. John Pitcher

Imagine yourself looking into the barrel of a sawn-off shotgun and ask yourself what you would do. Common sense would suggest that you keep quite still. But imagine that there was a baby likely to get hit by a shot . . . That might be a different story.

That was, in fact, the position in which Police Constable John Pitcher found himself on 15th December, 1970. In the course of his day's work, he was suddenly confronted by a gang of robbers, busily raiding a bank and robbing it of £70,000. They clearly meant business and were not going to let go of that amount of money. There were seven of them, armed with sawn-off shotguns, and wearing stocking masks under their balaclava helmets. P.C. Pitcher was armed with a truncheon and could do nothing.

Then he noticed the baby in a pushchair, right in the gang's path. Keeping very cool, the policeman walked up toward one of the bandits. Without a word he pointed the truncheon toward the baby. The gunman nodded. P.C. Pitcher stooped, picked up the pushchair with the baby in it and walked to safety. His action had possibly saved the baby's life.

This was not the first time that P.C. Pitcher had faced danger in the course of his duty. Nor is he the only policeman to have done so. Many, armed only with a truncheon have tackled desperate armed gunmen and some have lost their lives in doing so. This is the price that must sometimes be paid by those who endeavour to keep law and order in our land.

O Lord our God, bless the members of our police forces and all whose responsibility is to keep the law in our land. Give them patience in dealing with matters of difficulty, impartiality in the doing of their duties, cool judgement when quick decisions must be made, and courage when danger stands in the path of duty. Keep them in your care and grant them your guidance, so that we may know peace and security now and all our days; through Jesus Christ our Lord. *Amen.**

Benediction No. 55

6 Christian and Personal Qualities

This section of fourteen themes is concerned with qualities and attitudes in life. These are qualities which should be expected as characteristic of those who call themselves Christian and are the kind of relationships taught by Jesus Christ.

This does not mean, of course, that they are exclusively Christian. Other faiths demand equally high standards of those who are sincere in their beliefs. These themes are therefore concerned with the personal qualities of all who have a sincere regard for God and their fellows.

Christian qualities
Friendship and loyalty
Courage of one's convictions
Perseverance
Rules for living
Life's challenge
True values

They shall inherit the earth
Faithfulness
Bravery
Foolishness and wisdom
Making the most of life
Aims and ambitions
Humility

Christian qualities (1)

Frances Ridley Havergal

There are certain things that are required of anyone who would call himself a Christian. One of the most important is a willingness to offer to God whatever abilities he has given us.

Take for example Frances Ridley Havergal, the daughter of a Worcestershire clergyman, who was born on 14th December, 1836. It was soon clear that she was a young lady of great talent. At the age of four she could read the Bible for herself and in later years she memorized much of the Bible. She also learned to speak five languages besides English.

Frances was a clever musician, too. She sang well, composed tunes for herself, and was able to play on the piano from memory some very difficult tunes.

When she was fifteen, she dedicated herself to God. She wrote, 'I committed my soul to the Saviour, and earth and heaven seemed brighter from that moment'. A few years later, while sitting in the study of a German minister she noticed a cross on the wall with the words: 'I did this for thee; what hast thou done for me?'

She took a piece of paper, wrote quickly a verse of a hymn, then, not being satisfied, screwed it up and threw it into the fireplace. Later the paper was found and her father not only encouraged her to write the rest of the hymn, which begins 'I gave my life for thee' but himself wrote the tune to which it is still sung to this day.

Frances wrote many hymns and verses during her short life. She died at the age of 42, having spent her life in many ways in the service of God, to whom all her talents had been dedicated.

Almighty God, who hast created us for thy glory and service; give us grace, we pray thee, to hallow every gift and improve each talent thou hast committed to us, that with a cheerful and diligent spirit we may ever serve thee; and whatsoever we do, do all in the Name of Jesus Christ our Lord. *Amen.*

Source not known

Closing prayer No. 19

Christian qualities (2)

St. Ignatius

Anyone who has dedicated his life to God must be ready to face whatever comes his way. It may be very difficult. Jesus himself told his disciples that they would face grave dangers:

Bible Reading: St. Matthew 24: 7–14

On 1st February, the Church remembers one who faced great hardship for Christ. He was Ignatius, Bishop of Antioch in Syria, who was seized by the Roman governor of that country and sentenced to death by being thrown to the lions in Rome, which was hundreds of miles away.

For week after week, the old man—he was over sixty—was compelled to walk in chains, surrounded by soldiers who, he said, were worse than leopards. At any stage of the journey he could have been released if he had been willing to disown Christ but he remained faithful.

On the way he wrote several letters, including one to Christians in Rome, whom he begged not to wangle his release. 'I bid all men know,' he wrote, 'that of my own free will I die for God, unless ye should hinder me ...'

In Rome there was a delighted roar at the games when it was known that the Christian Bishop of Antioch was being led out to face the lions. It is said that he prayed as the lions rushed upon him, 'Lord, lay not this sin to their charge; for they know not what they do'.

Thus St. Ignatius died about the year A.D. 107, as thousands of other martyrs did because they remained true to what they believed, though few had to suffer such a journey before reaching the arena.

O God, we thank you for those who faced danger and death and remained faithful to the end. Grant us strength in time of weakness, courage in time of danger, and the knowledge that you are with us all the days of our lives. We ask this for Jesus Christ's sake. *Amen.**

Closing prayer No. 18

Christian qualities (3)

St. John Baptist Vianney (Curé d'Ars)

Here is some good advice which St. Paul wrote to Timothy:

Bible Reading: 2 Timothy 2: 22–25

A Christian must always be patient and ready to listen to the problems of any who come to him. Such was the fame of a farmer's son, John Baptist Vianney, who chose to be a priest rather than work on the family farm not far from Lyons in France.

He was no great scholar. In fact his studies lasted from 1806 to 1815 and when he was made a priest it was not for his learning but because of his sincere attitude to the church and his willingness to help others. His post was to a small out-of-the-way village called Ars-en-Dombes. And if people had never heard of it they soon did because John Baptist Vianney, the Curé, or Vicar of Ars, proved to be a most unusual person.

He worked hard for the people of his parish. When they were in trouble they asked his advice; when they wanted someone to talk to he listened; when they wanted to confess any wrong doings he listened patiently, then gave them good advice.

In time, people from beyond the village came to him and not only from the district around his village but from the whole of France—about twenty thousand visitors a year.

For sixteen to eighteen hours a day, he listened to those who came. Then, on 14th August, 1859, he died, having spent himself in the service of others for forty-one years as Curé d'Ars.

O God we thank you for people of patience and understanding to whom we can take our problems and from whom we can seek sound advice. We recall the words of Jesus, 'Come unto Me ... and I will give you rest'. Teach us to know you, so that we may bring in prayer all our hopes and our fears, our difficulties and our doubts, our joys and our sorrows; and grant us your peace, through Christ our Lord. *Amen.**

Closing prayer No. 23

Christian qualities (4)

St. Thomas Becket

A Christian must always guard himself against doing things that are unworthy of him and must often exercise self control, especially in what he says.

Bible Reading: James 3: 1–6

One man who lived to be sorry for his hasty words was King Henry II, who had as his chief adviser a learned man named Thomas Becket.

Becket decided early in life to use his education in the service of God and he was an obvious choice for the important post of Chancellor to the King.

For seven years Becket served the King and was his constant companion. Because of the gifts that were showered upon him, Becket became very rich, so that people said openly that, if the chancellor were as rich as this, however rich must the King be.

Then Becket was made Archbishop of Canterbury and he had to stand up for the Church against some decisions made by the King. While in France, the King heard that Becket had done something which displeased him. In a rage, he exploded, 'Will no one rid me of this turbulent priest?'

Four knights hurried back to England and found the Archbishop in Canterbury Cathedral, on 29th December, 1170. Drawing their swords they murdered the Archbishop on the altar steps.

The King was grieved. This was not what he had wanted. If only he had not uttered those hasty words ... but it was too late. It would have been better if he had kept his temper and controlled his tongue.

Help me today, O God,
To keep my temper and to control my tongue;
To keep my thoughts from wandering and my mind from straying;
To quarrel with no one and to be friends with everyone.

So bring me to the end of today with nothing to be sorry for, and with nothing left undone, through Jesus Christ my Lord. *Amen.*

Dr. William Barclay

Closing prayer No. 11

Christian qualities (4)

Christian qualities (5)

Toyohiko Kagawa

This is what Jesus had to say of anyone who would be known as a disciple:

Bible Reading: St. Matthew 10: 37–42

One who was prepared to do that was Toyohiko Kagawa, who was born on 10th July, 1888, in the Japanese port of Kobe. At the age of about four he lost both his parents and he was brought up by a rich uncle whose wish was that the boy should inherit his business.

Kagawa, meanwhile, had joined a Christian Bible class, through which he learned about Christ. He determined to try to follow Christ's example. In the slums of Kobe people lived in appalling conditions. 'If Christ were here, he would help them,' he thought, 'and so must I.'

But when he told his uncle, he was so angry that he cast Kagawa out of his house without further ado. Kagawa had lost all he might have had for Jesus Christ.

He went to live in the slums, where his home was a broken-down shack, his neighbours were gamblers, thieves and beggars, and where there were frequent outbreaks of plague, cholera, small-pox, typhus and other diseases. Gradually people came to realize that Christianity was not just a religion for rich people. Kagawa showed them that it was a way of life based on love and service. This was something new!

At first the police were suspicious of Kagawa, but like others they came to realize that this work of improving the lot of others was Kagawa's way of showing God's love toward those who needed him.

Almighty God, we thank you
For your love to us in sending Jesus Christ;
For his example of service to others and to you;
For others who have followed that example.
    Teach us always
To love all whom we know and whom we meet;
And to show our love in service to them and to you;
    Through Jesus Christ our Lord. *Amen.**

Closing prayer No. 12

They shall inherit the earth (1)

St. Swithun

One of the best-known passages in the New Testament is the opening passage of the Sermon on the Mount.

Bible Reading: St. Matthew 5: 1–12

'Blessed are the meek ... for they shall inherit the earth.' Some of the greatest Christians are those who have been meek, or humble and one who will be remembered as such is St. Swithun.

St. Swithun's Day is 15th July, a day on which people give an eye to the weather for tradition says that whatever the weather is like on St. Swithun's Day, it will continue so for the next forty days. There is an old rhyme which reads:

> *St. Swithun's Day, if thou dost rain,*
> *For forty days it will remain;*
> *St. Swithun's Day, if thou be fair,*
> *For forty days 'twill rain na mair.*

But St. Swithun had little to do with the weather and records show that the rhyme is not always correct. He was a Bishop of Winchester in Saxon times, who became the chief adviser of the king on religious matters. Though born of a noble family and a friend of kings and princes, he was a very humble man, who is said always to have walked wherever he went instead of riding. When he was dying, he asked to be buried outside the church instead of in a place of honour and this wish was granted.

About a hundred years later, the cathedral was rebuilt and the remains of St. Swithun were carried into the cathedral. It was 15th July, 971 and it is on this day that he is still remembered—a good man and a kindly bishop, who gave himself in the service of both kings and ordinary folk.

Grant to us, Almighty God, that into whatever service you call us, we may enter with willing hearts; seeking to do good wherever we are able, showing kindness to all whom we meet, being humble regardless of our position, and serving you and our fellows with gladness; after the example of Jesus Christ our Lord. *Amen.**

Closing prayer No. 9

They shall inherit the earth (2)

St. Richard of Chichester

Richard was the second son of well-to-do parents, who lived at Wych, now Droitwich, in Worcestershire. He was born about 1197 and spent the earlier part of his life at home, helping to run the family estate after his father had died.

Then, in spite of the suggestions of his brother that he should marry a certain noble lady, Richard of Wych decided to go to Oxford to study to become a priest. He had the misfortune to have his money stolen and had therefore to live at Oxford in poverty. It is said that he and two other students had only one warm tunic and one gown between them, so they had to take it in turn to attend lectures.

In 1235, he returned to Oxford, but was soon called to become chancellor, or secretary, to the Archbishop of Canterbury. The Archbishop had a disagreement with the King and decided to leave England for a time. Richard went with him.

Some years later, the King wanted a certain man made Bishop of Chichester, but the new Archbishop of Canterbury refused and appointed Richard of Wych. The King was so angry that it was two years before Richard could take up his post. Meanwhile, he travelled Sussex on foot.

Once he had taken office, he was renowned for his courtesy and gentleness, but he would never allow himself to be dictated to by the King.

He died at Dover in 1253 on 3rd April, the day on which he is still remembered as St. Richard of Chichester, the writer of a prayer which is very well known:

St. Richard of Chichester's prayer:

Thanks be to thee, our Lord Jesus Christ: for all the benefits which thou hast given us; for all the pains and insults which thou hast borne for us. O most merciful redeemer, friend and brother: may we know thee more clearly, love thee more dearly, and follow thee more nearly, now and ever. *Amen.*

Closing prayer No. 12

They shall inherit the earth (3)

Jesus once taught his disciples a very clear lesson in humility by his own example.

Bible Reading: St. John 13: 5–9

Bishop Oswald of Worcester liked to remember this story and the way in which Jesus told the disciples to do likewise. So, each day in the season of Lent, Oswald invited twelve poor men to a meal, before which he washed their feet. On 29th February, 992, he had just finished this humble act when he fell dead.

Oswald had been Bishop of Worcester for thirty years. For the last twenty of these, he was also Archbishop of York but it is with Worcester that he is chiefly remembered.

One of his first tasks on going to Worcester was to arrange for the building of a new church for the monks who lived there. This church, on the banks of the River Severn, became his cathedral. The cathedral which stands in Worcester today is on the same site but is of a much later date, Oswald's cathedral being destroyed by Danish raiders.

Oswald himself had been educated in a monastery in France, so it is not surprising that he spent much of his time in encouraging the monks, not only at Worcester but in other parts of the country too. Soon after he died, his life story was written and from this we learn that St. Oswald was especially remembered for his gentleness and his kindness and that the people of Worcester had a very high regard for their bishop. Because 29th Februrary only falls once in four years, St. Oswald's feast day was fixed for 28th February.

O God, our Father, we thank thee that thou dost show thyself in Jesus Christ. We thank thee, too, for people we can see today who show us something of thyself in their kindness and goodness, their strength and their love. We pray that our lives may show that we are thy children. *Amen.*

Devotions for Company and Camp

Closing prayer No. 21

They shall inherit the earth (4)

St. Bartholomew

One of the most famous of the London hospitals is St. Bartholemew's Hospital, founded as long ago as 1123. Nearby a famous fair used to be held, where people gathered to buy, sell and amuse themselves, until it had to be closed because of the rowdiness of those who attended. It was called St. Bartholomew's Fair and it was held each year around St. Bartholomew's Day, 24th August.

But who was St. Bartholomew? Very little is known of him except that his name is given in some of the lists which appear in the Bible of the names of the twelve apostles. Those are the only occasions when his name is mentioned.

However, in the lists where his name is not shown, there is included the name of an apostle, Nathanael, and it is quite likely that this was the same man as Bartholomew because the name Bartholomew simply means 'Son of Tholomew'.

If so, we have a very good account in St. John's Gospel of the way in which Nathanael or Bartholomew met Jesus.

Bible Reading: St. John 1: 45–49

As a result of this meeting, Nathanael decided that he would be a disciple of Jesus. Legend tells us that Bartholomew travelled as far afield as India in order to spread the Gospel but that he was put to death for his faith.

There are many ways in which people can be remembered but there can be few greater than to be recognized by Jesus as one who is pure in heart. Jesus once said, 'Blessed are the pure in heart: for they shall see God'.

O God, who can see into the hearts of all people, grant that what is seen in us may be pleasing to you. Cleanse us of all that is impure and help us to grow like our Lord and Master, Jesus Christ, in whose name we ask this prayer. *Amen.**

Closing prayer No. 36

They shall inherit the earth (5)

It is the ambition of many authors to write a 'best seller', but one man who succeeded in doing so was quite unaware of the fact.

Thomas Hämerken was born about 1379 at Kempen, near Düsseldorf, in the country we know as Germany. He became known as Thomas of Kempen, or Thomas à Kempis.

At the age of twelve, he went to Deventer, in the Netherlands, to complete his education at a school run by a religious order and, in the seven years that he was there, he was greatly influenced by the religious atmosphere in which he learned. When he was twenty, he decided to make his home in the monastery of Mount Saint Agnes, where his brother was the prior. There he spent the rest of his life, until he died on 8th August, 1471, aged over ninety.

He was a small man, very capable in his work, kind and gracious to all who met him, but extremely reserved. In fact, he much preferred to be left alone with his books and his studies.

Thomas à Kempis wrote many sermons, hymns and a history of his monastery, but his greatest work was a book, written, as was all his writing, in Latin and entitled *Imitatio Christi* or, in English, *Of the Imitation of Christ*.

In the thirty years following his death, at least eighty editions were published and there have since been thousands of editions in many languages. This book, which has been of great help to millions of people, is the next best seller in the world to the Bible.

A prayer of Thomas à Kempis:

Grant to us, O Lord, to know that which is worth knowing, to love that which is worth loving, to praise that which can bear with praise, to hate what in thy sight is unworthy, to prize what to thee is precious, and, above all, to search out and do what is well-pleasing unto thee; through Jesus Christ our Lord. *Amen.*

Closing prayer No. 35

Friendship and loyalty (1)

Sir Francis Bacon

A person who has many friends can count himself fortunate for true friends can often be a help and comfort and a person with friends will seldom feel lonely. A true friend is one who remains loyal and is ready to put up with our strange ways. He is also one who stands by in time of trouble.

Jesus had friends who travelled with him but even they let him down in his most difficult hours.

Bible Reading: St. Matthew 26: 47–50 and 55–56

There are, of course, friends who only want your friendship for what they can get out of it. These are false friends.

Such a man was Francis Bacon, born on 22nd January, 1561, and one of the cleverest men in the time of the first Queen Elizabeth. He found it very convenient to form a friendship with the Earl of Essex, who was a favourite of the Queen. Yet, when Essex fell from favour, Francis Bacon was one of the first to speak against him and put up a far stronger case than would have been expected of one who had been a friend.

But Bacon was like that. He wanted nothing to stand in the way of his path to success. By and by he became a Viscount and the Lord Chancellor of England.

But he was too clever by half. He accepted bribes and gifts from those who wanted his support in parliament or in courts of law. At last the day of reckoning came. He was charged with corruption, banned from sitting in parliament or holding any office and was indeed fortunate to escape further and harsher punishments for his misdeeds.

Lord, grant us the will and the power to do in all things that which is honest and right. Thou who art the truth, help us bravely and sincerely to speak only that which is true and to behave openly, frankly, and loyally to one another. May we never be afraid to admit our faults and to accept the blame. As thou dost keep us in thy care and love, so may we love one another; for thy Name's sake. *Amen.*

Source not known

Closing prayer No. 13

Friendship and loyalty (2)

Flora Macdonald

Bible Reading: St. Matthew 26: 31–35

But they did let Jesus down. It is one thing to profess loyalty to a person or cause: it is another thing to remain loyal when it is dangerous to do so.

In 1745, Bonnie Prince Charlie landed in Scotland, where many believed he should be King of Britain. Some of them took up arms and began to march toward London but, although they met with success at first, they were forced to retreat. At the Battle of Culloden, the prince's army was defeated and he went into hiding.

The government was determined that he should not escape. Warships patrolled the coast of Scotland; soldiers searched the country; and a price of £30,000 was put on his head, to be paid to anyone who would betray him. It was a fortune, but there was not a single Scot who was prepared to give away the secret.

One in particular was prepared to risk everything in order to get the prince to safety. She was Flora Macdonald, who lived on the island of South Uist in the Hebrides, where the prince was in hiding. If the prince were to escape, he must be taken to the isle of Skye and thence to his friends.

So Flora Macdonald, accompanied by her maid, Betty Burke, went to the coast, where they entered a small boat and were allowed to leave. But Betty Burke was none other than the prince in disguise. The prince escaped but Flora Macdonald was arrested and imprisoned in the Tower of London. Later she was released and returned to Skye, where she died on 5th March, 1790.

Almighty God, grant us, we pray, the gift of loyalty. Help us to be loyal to our friends so that we never let them down. Help us to be loyal to our principles, so that people know what to expect of us. Help us to be loyal to our school so that we may always bring credit to it. Help us to be loyal to you, so that those we meet may know that we belong to you and try to serve you; through Jesus Christ our Lord. *Amen.**

Closing prayer No. 28

Friendship and loyalty (3)

Rudyard Kipling

If you want to know how the leopard got his spots or other interesting facts about animals, try reading the Just-So Stories. If it is jungle adventure you are after, turn to the Jungle Books and read the adventures of Mowgli.

Rudyard Kipling, who wrote these books was a wonderful story-teller, who wrote for children and for adults. His books and poems are full of excitement and adventure.

Kipling was born in India, where his father worked. He returned to England for his education and then, at the age of seventeen, he returned to India, where he worked for a newspaper. It is not surprising that many of his stories are about India.

Later, Kipling returned to England, where he found a house in a quiet village in Sussex and there wrote some of his finest work. In 1907, he was given the Nobel Prize for Literature, which only the greatest writers ever obtain.

Kipling had a passionate love for Britain and her great empire throughout the world and this comes out time and time again in his writing. He firmly believed in kindness and the only words in any of his works that hurt are those which speak against unkindness, bullying, cruelty or injustice. His hymns are those which ask God's help to make ourselves and our country the best they can be.

Kipling died on 18th January, 1936, leaving many books, stories, poems and hymns which echo his high ideals of loyalty, devotion to duty and freedom.

Almighty God, we thank you
For the knowledge of what is right and what is wrong;
For the freedom to choose the way we live;
For your guidance in making up our minds.
   Help us
To choose the right, however difficult it may be;
And to be loyal to our ideals, to ourselves and to you;
For the sake of Jesus Christ, who is the Way, the
   Truth and the Life. *Amen.**

Closing prayer No. 4

Friendship and loyalty (4)

Edith Cavell

On 11th October, 1915, an English nurse stood calmly in front of the table at which a group of German officers sat. She knew well what the outcome would be and was not surprised to hear the verdict. She was found guilty of harbouring in her house French and British soldiers and of helping them to escape from the Germans. The sentence was death and, at 2 a.m. the following morning she faced the firing squad.

There was a great outcry in many lands when the news was announced and several attempts were made to prevent her execution, but to no avail. Edith Cavell had been well aware of the risks she took and she knew that she could expect little mercy if she were caught.

For many years, Edith Cavell had been recognized as a fine nurse and, wherever she served, people spoke very highly of her. Often she went out of her way to help those in need.

After working in several hospitals in England, she had been invited to work in a hospital in Brussels and she was appointed Matron in 1907. It was her loyalty to the hospital that caused her to remain there when the war broke out in 1914. She also felt some loyalty to her own country, which was why she helped her countrymen to escape from their enemies.

Moreover, Edith Cavell was loyal to her profession, for, as a nurse, she knew that she must help friend and foe alike, showing the same thoughtfulness to all who suffered.

In one of his letters, St. Peter reminded the people of his time of their responsibility to be loyal and obedient to their rulers and to God:

Bible Reading: 1 Peter 2: 13–17

O God, who put the spirit of loyalty into our hearts; make us loyal to our families and our friends and to all those who trust in us. Teach us to be loyal to those things which we know to be right and do only those things. Above all, keep us loyal to you; through Jesus Christ our Lord. *Amen.**

Closing prayer No. 3

Friendship and loyalty (5)

Mahatma Gandhi

On January 30th, 1948, India lost one of the greatest men in her history. Mohandras Karamchand Gandhi was born in India, studied in London and then worked as a lawyer in Bombay and South Africa.

He was very strict with himself and refused all luxuries. Throughout his life he kept a promise made to his mother that he would not eat meat, drink alcohol or smoke tobacco. He dressed in simple clothes which he wove himself.

In Africa he helped the Indians who were being badly treated and, when he returned to India, he spent his life in trying to help the lowest classes of people. Others called them 'untouchables'; Gandhi called them 'Sons of God'.

He was given the title 'Mahatma', meaning 'Great Soul' and people all over the world took notice of him. At times he fasted for many days and refused to eat until the government or others changed their plans because they did not want him to die.

When the British left India in 1947, there was bitter fighting and many lives were lost. Gandhi fasted. Then, on 30th January, 1948, as he climbed some steps to begin an open-air prayer meeting, he was shot dead by a Hindu who hated the way in which he mixed with 'untouchables'.

His advice had been to say every morning, 'I shall not fear anyone on earth. I shall fear only God. I shall not bear ill-will toward anyone...' Millions of Hindus thought of Gandhi not only as a national hero but as a saint.

We remember how Jesus, too, was criticized because he mixed with the 'untouchables' of his day:

Bible Reading: St. Mark 2: 15–17

O God, we remember how Jesus earned himself the name of 'friend of publicans and sinners' and was never afraid to do what he believed to be right. Grant that we, too, may hold fast to what we believe to be right, in spite of all that others may say, so that we may show ourselves to be true sons of yours. *Amen.**

Closing prayer No. 7

Faithfulness (1)

Cardinal Wolsey

Thomas Wolsey was the son of a butcher, but his father was able to send him to Oxford, where he did well at his studies.

He entered the church and became a favourite of King Henry VIII. He was still quite a young man when he was appointed Archbishop of York. Then, as Lord Chancellor, he became one of the most important men in England.

After a time, the King became tired of his wife, Catherine of Aragon and he wanted the marriage ended so that he could marry someone else. This put Cardinal Wolsey in an impossible position. Roman Catholics do not agree that marriages can be ended and, in any case, the Pope had no wish to anger Catherine's brother, who was King of Spain.

Wolsey now fell from favour. King Henry VIII had no time for anyone who could not get him what he wanted. Moreover, he was somewhat jealous of Wolsey's possessions.

For years, Wolsey had tried to serve two masters, God and the King, and had been successful. Now he could no longer do so. He returned to York, where he remained until Henry summoned him to London to face a charge of high treason. On the way, he became ill at Leicester and was taken into an abbey, where he died on 29th November, 1530

Toward the end of his life, he wrote, 'Had I but served God as diligently as I have served the King, He would not have given me over in my grey hairs'.

Others have learned the same lesson. God remains faithful to those who trust him.

Bible Reading: Psalm 103: 17–22

Almighty God, our Heavenly Father, you have taught us by your Son that no man can serve two masters. Help us to put you first in our lives, to seek your perfect will, to serve you with gladness, to trust you for all things, and to remain faithful to the end; knowing that we may then dwell in your eternal kingdom with the saints of all ages; through Jesus Christ our Lord. *Amen.**

Closing prayer No. 8

Faithfulness (2)

Martin Luther was born in Germany in 1483. He was a very able scholar but he gave up studying law in order to become first a friar, then a priest and finally Professor of Scripture at the University of Wittenberg.

It was there that he discovered some things about the Roman Catholic Church with which he could not agree. He thought the Church had drifted away from the teachings of the Bible.

Then, one day, a friar visited Wittenberg, promising that people would not have to suffer for their sins if they gave money to the Church. Luther was angry. The Bible said that Jesus had died so that people's sins might be forgiven and there was no price to be paid.

Luther made a long list of ways in which he disagreed with the Church and then nailed his list to the door of the cathedral. The Church demanded that Luther should take back what he had said: Luther refused and was put out of the Church.

Many other people were now sharing Luther's opinions and, on 17th April, 1521, he had to appear before the Emperor and other important people at Worms. He refused to take back his words and the following day was outlawed. For a time he was hidden in a friend's castle, where he translated part of the Bible into German and wrote hymns so that the people could learn for themselves about Christ.

Luther, whose teachings had a great influence on the Christian Church, is honoured for his great stand for what he believed to be true.

In the Bible, we read how some of the disciples were faithful to their beliefs.

Bible Reading: Acts of the Apostles, 4: 1–3 and 13–21

Almighty God, whose ways are beyond our understanding, help us to make up our minds what we believe about you and to remain faithful to our beliefs. And if others hold beliefs that are different from ours or like to worship in different ways, help us to respect their opinions as we wish them to respect ours. *Amen.**

Benediction No. 51

Faithfulness (3)

John Wesley

The alarm was given as the roof of the rectory at Epworth caught fire in the middle of the night. All but one walked out, leaving little John, aged six, trapped. A servant, standing on the shoulders of another, was just able to pull him through the window before the roof fell in.

Little did the Reverend Samuel Wesley realize that the boy who was dragged from the flames would one day set England on fire.

At Oxford, John and some of his companions formed a club for prayer and Bible study, which became known as 'the Holy Club'. Because of their regular habits, they were also nicknamed 'Methodists'.

Still John did not find the joy in his heart that he so anxiously wanted. His religion was very flat. On leaving Oxford, he spent two years as a missionary among the settlers in America but it was back in London, on 24th May, 1738, that John Wesley's life was suddenly changed—converted into something much greater. It was as though he was filled with a new spirit. He knew then what he must do for God.

In no time, he was mounted on horseback and riding hither and thither—his aim to save England. He preached to thousands in the open air; he was frequently attacked; he was refused permission to preach in churches. His followers throughout the land became 'Methodists'.

John Wesley travelled 225,000 miles on foot or on horseback, declaring that he regarded the world as his parish, for the world must come to know the God whom Wesley came to know on 24th May, 1738.

The Bible tells how St. Paul told Timothy to remain faithful to his calling.

Bible Reading: 2 Timothy 4: 1–5

Help us to remember, O Lord, that our religion is not for one day a week but should enter into our whole life. May we find a true joy and peace through Christ our Lord. *Amen.**

Closing prayer No. 2

Faithfulness (4)

FAITHFUL IN DUTY   *Reverend G. A. Studdert-Kennedy*

Some of the bitterest fighting of the First World War was in the trenches, which were dug across France and Belgium. On the one side were British, French and other allied troops: on the other were the Germans.

Between the trenches lay 'no-man's land' in which everything had been blasted away. The soldiers knew that every time they were ordered to charge across no-man's land, many would never return. They knew, too, that at any time shells might land in the wet, muddy trench, where they lived, ate, slept and waited.

Some of the most respected men were the ministers of religion, the Chaplains or Padres, who comforted them in their difficulties. Of these, one of the best known was 'Woodbine Willie', who gained the Military Cross for bravery.

He was the Reverend G. A. Studdert-Kennedy, who was also a chaplain to the King and often preached in Buckingham Palace. This verse of a hymn which he wrote illustrates his own attitude to life.

> *To give and give, and give again,*
>   *What God hath given thee;*
> *To spend thyself nor count the cost,*
>   *To serve right gloriously*
> *The God that gave all worlds that are,*
>   *And all that are to be.*

Studdert-Kennedy did, indeed, wear himself out in the service of God. At the age of 45 he caught influenza and died on 8th March, 1929.

St. Paul had this to write about his own service:

Bible Reading: 2 Timothy 4: 6–8

O God our Father, we give thanks for all who have served you faithfully to their life's end, and especially for the example set by Christ himself. Grant that we may follow in his footsteps without counting the cost, so that our lives may be spent in the service of others and for the glory of your Name. *Amen.**

Closing prayer No. 6

Faithfulness (5)

The Victoria Cross

Who has not heard of the Charge of the Light Brigade, in which six hundred men were ordered to ride into the valley to certain death as cannon roared all around?

This was just one of the examples of bravery which was shown during the Crimean War and soldiers returning from the fight had many such stories to tell.

Among those who listened with great interest to these stories was Queen Victoria, who was so impressed that she called her Ministers together to discuss how deeds of great valour could be rewarded.

Campaign medals already existed, but it was felt that something more was needed—a 'highest award' which would take no account of battles fought, length of service or wounds inflicted, but would only be for conspicuous bravery in the face of the enemy. It should be an award which would be 'highly prized and eagerly sought after by the officers and men of our Naval and Military services'.

Thus, on 29th January, 1856, this new award, known as the Victoria Cross, came into being. It was a bronze Maltese Cross, bearing the Royal Crest and a scroll on which were inscribed the words 'For Valour'.

The first awards were for bravery in the Crimean War: many others have been made since for bravery in action in many parts of the world.

The Victoria Cross is greatly prized, and few people are more highly respected by their fellows than those who hold the V.C.

The Bible tells that those who remain faithful to God to the end have their own special award.

Bible Reading: Revelation 2: 7 and 10

Almighty God, who, through Jesus Christ, promised a crown of life to all who remain faithful to you in times of persecution or distress; help us to fight evil wherever we may find it with courage and determination, remaining faithful to the end; for the sake of Jesus Christ our Lord. *Amen.**

Closing prayer No. 20

Courage of one's convictions (1)

Nelson at Copenhagen

People naturally feel sorry for those who are blind and will go out of their way to help them. There are, however, times when people find it very convenient to be blind in the sense that they do not see things which they know they ought to see. We often talk of 'turning a blind eye' when we deliberately avoid taking some action.

One of the most famous occasions of turning a blind eye happened on 2nd April, 1801, in the days when Denmark and other countries had sided with Napoleon against Britain. With the Danish fleet to help him, Napoleon would have a very strong navy, and so a British fleet was sent to attack ships in the Danish port of Copenhagen.

Admiral Parker commanded the fleet and Nelson was his second-in-command. For several hours the battle raged and the Danes seemed to be holding their own. Admiral Parker decided to stop the battle and hoisted a flag signal ordering the firing to stop.

Nelson was amazed. 'Leave off fighting!' he exclaimed. 'You know I have only one eye—I have a right to be blind sometimes.' Then, putting his telescope to his blind eye, he remarked, 'I really do not see the signal.' Then he went on with the battle and won a great victory.

Turning a blind eye may sometimes be convenient for us; it may even be done to help someone else; but it is wrong to do so if somebody else suffers as a result of our shirking our responsibilities.

It is also wrong to turn a blind eye to God's word and purposely to avoid doing his will. Hear what Jesus had to say about people of his day:

Bible Reading: St. Matthew 13: 15–16

O God, we thank you that we have eyes to see and minds to understand. Teach us to observe with our eyes and to understand what we ought to do. May we never, for selfish motives, turn a blind eye to those things which we see to be wrong, but ever live courageously in the way which we know to be right; for the sake of Jesus Christ our Lord. *Amen.**

Closing prayer No. 1

Courage of one's convictions (1) 279

L

Courage of one's convictions (2)

Anselm was the son of a wealthy merchant but he decided, when he was about sixteen, that he wished to become a monk. His father promptly refused permission but, at the age of twenty-three, Anselm travelled to Normandy, where he became a monk at the Abbey of Bec.

There he remained for thirty years, first as a monk, then as prior, and finally as abbot in charge of all in the abbey. During this time, he showed himself to be very wise in his dealing with both old and young. Kings and princes came for his help and blessing.

Often he travelled to England on business and he was known by most important people in this country. It was on one of these visits that King William Rufus demanded that Anselm should be made Archbishop of Canterbury—and Archbishop of Canterbury he became.

The years that followed were ones of continual struggle between Anselm and the Kings of England—William II and Henry I, both of whom led wicked lives.

Anselm, however, knew what he believed to be right and, once he had made up his mind, no amount of threats, promises or pleas would make him swerve to the right hand or to the left. Though once he had to leave the country for three years, people knew that nothing could make Anselm do what he believed to be wrong. He remained true to his principles and to God, just as Moses was commanded to do long years before:

Bible Reading: Deuteronomy 5: 32–33

Anselm, who died on 21st April, 1109, was buried in Canterbury Cathedral. He is now remembered as St. Anselm each year on 21st April.

A prayer of St. Anselm:

O Lord our God, grant us grace to desire thee with our whole heart, that so desiring, we may seek and find thee; and so finding thee we may love thee; and loving thee we may hate those sins from which thou hast redeemed us; for the sake of Jesus Christ. *Amen.*

Closing prayer No. 18

Courage of one's convictions (3)

Stephen Langton

The mention of Magna Carta conjures up a picture of the English barons meeting King John at Runnymede and forcing him to give away some of his powers. We may forget the man who did much to arrange the signing of the charter, Stephen Langton, Archbishop of Canterbury.

King John had never wanted Langton as Archbishop and he was so angry when the Pope made the appointment that he refused to accept it. The Pope was determined to force the King to do so and some very stern measures were taken. England was cut off from the Church, the King was refused any part in Church matters and the Pope threatened to have him removed from the throne. At last, in 1213 the King gave in.

Langton immediately joined the barons, advising them in the wording of the charter. He was a very important person at Runnymede.

Shortly afterwards, Langton left the country, returning a few years later after Henry III had become King. This time he strongly supported the King, though insisting that all the clauses of Magna Carta should be observed.

At times, too, Langton had his differences of opinion with the Pope but this did not worry him overmuch. He was a man with very strong opinions and he would stick to them in spite of all opposition, even though that opposition came from the King or the Pope. Stephen Langton died on 9th July, 1228.

In the Bible we often read how people were bidden to stand fast against all opposition in the name of God who would help them. Here is one instance:

Bible Reading: Deuteronomy 31: 7–8

We too will be wise if we learn always to place our trust in God.

Help us, O God, to know your will and to have courage and strength to do it. Grant us true thoughts, a clear understanding, and a determination to do only that which is right; through Jesus Christ our Lord. *Amen.**

Closing prayer No. 29

Courage of one's convictions (4)

One of the things which impresses us about the life of St. Paul is the willingness with which he suffered hardship and imprisonment for the sake of the truth of the Gospel of Jesus Christ. Here is a part of one of those incidents:

Bible Reading: Acts of the Apostles 16: 22–24

Today in many lands there are prisoners who have committed no crime other than disagreeing with those who are in authority. Some are imprisoned for political reasons and some because of their religious beliefs. Many are people who would hold important offices if they were allowed to do so.

About three hundred years ago, in the reign of King James II, seven bishops were imprisoned because they dared to say that a document issued by the King was illegal. The King was so angry that he had the seven committed to the Tower of London. Then he took every step he could to ensure that a verdict of 'guilty' was given against them.

But in that instance justice was done. On 30th June, 1688, the bishops heard the charges made against them and then awaited the verdict. It was 'Not guilty'. Before long, King James, who had brought the charge against them was fleeing the country.

We believe today that everyone has a right to his own beliefs and that he should be free to act upon them or speak about them. We remember the many who have lost their freedom because they have done just that.

O God our Father,
We thank you for wisdom to know what is right and for strength and courage to do it:
We thank you that we are free to speak and to worship without fearing the consequences:
We pray for those less fortunate than we are and ask that they may again know the joy of freedom:
We ask this in the name of Jesus Christ our Lord. *Amen.**

Closing prayer No. 4

Courage of one's convictions (5)

Latimer and Ridley

Sometimes we do well to count our blessings and to realize just how fortunate we are today, especially in the freedom we enjoy. It is good to know, for example, that we are free to worship God if we want to in whatever way we wish and in whichever church we choose.

It is not so in every country, and it was not so in England in years gone by. In fact there was a time, about four hundred years ago, when it was dangerous to say the wrong things about religion.

What made it even more difficult for the people was that sometimes they were allowed to believe one thing and sometimes another. If the King or Queen were a Protestant, it could be dangerous to let it be known that you were a Roman Catholic. If the sovereign were Roman Catholic it could be dangerous to speak out as a Protestant. Two men who discovered this were Bishop Latimer and Bishop Ridley, who were condemned to be burned at the stake in 1555.

On 16th October, they were burned at Oxford. As the flames sprang up, Latimer turned to Ridley and said, 'Be of good comfort, Master Ridley; play the man; we shall this day light such a candle, by God's grace, in England, as I trust shall never be put out'.

Perhaps he was right. Certainly today we are far more ready to respect another person's point of view even though they may be very different from our own.

Jesus spoke these words of warning against judging other people when we should be looking to ourselves:

Bible Reading: St. Matthew 7: 1–5

O God, our Father, you have told us that we must not judge others, if we ourselves do not want to be judged. Help us never to be too critical of each other. Keep us from contemptuously or arrogantly criticizing the beliefs of others. Help us to remember that there are as many ways to the stars as there are men to climb them; and help us never to laugh at anyone's belief, if that is the way he gets to God. *Amen.*

Dr. William Barclay

Closing prayer No. 8

Bravery (1)

Grace Darling

The night of 6th–7th September, 1838, was a wild one. A howling northerly gale swept furiously down the coast of Northumberland, driving huge waves crashing against the rocks and cliffs of the Farne Islands.

The steamer *Forfarshire* was heading north from Hull to Dundee, and fighting every inch of the way. Suddenly disaster struck. With a sickening crash the ship struck the Big Harcar rock, heeled over to one side and broke in two. Clinging for dear life, those on the fore part of the ship were horrified to see the remainder of the ship disappear beneath the waves, taking with it 43 of the passengers and crew. Nine others climbed into a ship's boat, leaving nine clinging to the wreck.

Early in the morning, Grace Darling, the lighthouse-keeper's daughter, saw the wreck and called her father. She was far from strong and her father was getting old, yet between them they rowed their open boat across a mile of raging sea to the rescue. Five were taken to the lighthouse and then the lighthouse-keeper and two of the rescued men returned in the boat to rescue the others.

Grace Darling became famous as people heard the story of her gallant rescue. She had been quite ready to risk her own life if there was the slightest possibility of saving the lives of others.

Only four years later, on 20th October, 1842, she died but her name lives on amongst the stories of bravery and unselfishness.

O Lord, give us more charity, more self-denial, more likeness to thee. Teach us to sacrifice our comforts to others, and our likings for the sake of doing good. Make us kindly in thought, gentle in word, generous in deed. Teach us that it is better to give than to receive, better to forget ourselves than to put ourselves forward; better to minister than to be ministered unto. And unto thee, the God of love, be all glory and praise, both now and for evermore. *Amen.*

Dean Henry Alford

Closing prayer No. 13

Bravery (2)

St. Edmund

Edmund was chosen to be King of East Anglia when he was still a youth but the nobles seem to have been slow to decide whether to crown him king.

In those troubled times, Danish ships visited the shores of Britain to plunder and carry off such treasures as they could find. As more and more such visits took place, the nobles decided that a king was necessary and so Edmund was crowned.

In A.D. 869, a large number of Danes moved inland and settled around Thetford, which was in the heart of the Kingdom of East Anglia. Edmund knew it was his duty to try to drive them out and so he raised an army and led his troops into battle.

It was a valiant effort but quite unsuccessful. Edmund was captured and taken before the Danish leader. The Danes were quite prepared to offer peace, he was told, provided that Edmund gave him half his treasures and that he recognized the Danish leader as overlord.

The treasure Edmund was quite prepared to give up: the kingdom he was not. He believed that God had chosen him to be king so that he might help his people to live according to the Christian faith. To serve under a heathen Danish leader would be impossible. The Danish leader was furious and ordered him to be tied to a tree, a target for the Danish archers, who filled his body with arrows. He was then beheaded.

The body was later taken to the new monastery at St. Edmund's Bury (St. Edmund's Borough), which is now called Bury St. Edmunds. His feast day is kept each year on 20th November.

Almighty God, we thank you for the example of your servants of old who stood firm for their beliefs. Make us also faithful. We may not be called upon to face death for you, but we may meet criticism, scorn, ridicule or opposition. Give us the courage that they had so that we may remain firm on the side of righteousness to the end of our days. We ask it in the Name of our Lord Jesus Christ. *Amen.**

Closing prayer No. 17

Bravery (3)

The George Cross

On 24th September, 1940, it was announced that King George VI had decided to make a new award, to be known as the George Cross, for outstanding gallantry, when all thoughts of personal safety were forgotten or set aside in the line of duty.

In some respects it was similar to the Victoria Cross, which had been instituted by Queen Victoria in 1856, except that the Victoria Cross was for valour in the face of the enemy, whilst the George Cross was for civilians or for members of the armed forces who acted with bravery but not whilst fighting.

The George Cross is a silver cross with a circular disc in the centre depicting St. George and the dragon and having the words inscribed 'For Gallantry'.

There had previously been an award for gallantry, known as the Empire Gallantry Medal and it was decided that holders of this medal should be able to exchange it for the George Cross.

Holders of the George Cross come from many walks of life and have earned their award in many ways. They include coxswains of lifeboats, firemen, policemen, bomb disposal officers, men who suffered bravely as prisoners of war and women who were dropped by parachute behind enemy lines.

Many, of course, have lost their lives while doing the things for which they were awarded the G.C. Bob Taylor of Bristol, for example, was shot dead whilst chasing some bank robbers and was awarded the G.C. posthumously—that is after his death. But this is to be expected. The George Cross is only awarded to those who endanger their own lives.

O Lord Jesus Christ, who faced hardship, danger and death for the sake of righteousness and the extension of God's Kingdom on earth; grant that we may have courage to face and conquer evil and so obtain the crown of life that is promised to all who remain faithful to the end. We ask this in your Name and for your sake. *Amen.**

Closing prayer No. 28

Bravery (4)

In the days when the Romans ruled Britain, a rich nobleman lived in the town of Verulamium. He was kind, generous and never turned a stranger from his doors.

One night an old man hammered on the gate and was let in by a servant, who knew that this would be his master's wish. Alban soon discovered that the old man was a Christian priest, trying desperately to escape from those who would take his life. Alban ordered that he should be fed, clothed and kept there in secret.

As Alban spoke with the priest, he learned much about the Christian faith and, in the days which followed, as the priest lay safely hidden, Alban came to realize that this was a far greater religion than his own.

One day, however, the word got out and a band of soldiers was sent to Alban's house to fetch the priest. Quickly Alban took the old man's cloak and wrapped it round himself. He knew the priest could do much more to spread the Christian faith than he could.

Thinking they had the priest, the soldiers took Alban before the governor, who was furious. He demanded that Alban should sacrifice with him to the Roman gods but Alban refused. As a Christian he could not do so.

When persuasion and scourging failed, Alban was beheaded on the hill on which stands the cathedral in the city which bears his name—St. Alban's.

Alban, the first British martyr, is remembered each year on 22nd June.

In the Bible we can read how the first Christian martyr died for his faith:

Bible Reading: Acts 7: 55–60

O Lord Jesus, help us to be true to our faith and true to you when things are difficult.

When we stand alone;

When loyalty to you makes us unpopular with our fellow men;

When doing the right thing involves us in the dislike or in the laughter of others:

Help us still to be true. *Amen.*

Dr. William Barclay

Closing prayer No. 37

Bravery (5)

Manche Masemula

Manche Masemula lived in a little village in South Africa, where most of her people followed the old tribal beliefs and were not ready to listen to the words of Christian missionaries.

In fact anyone who became a Christian was in for a very hard time and Manche, who was only fifteen years old, knew this only too well. Yet she became a Christian, though her parents were very angry.

On the day that she was to be baptized, Manche became ill with fever so that she could not attend the service. She was given some medicine by the Mission doctor which made her feel better, though still weak.

'Get up and work,' her mother told her. 'If your Christian God is of any use, the medicine will have made you well.' Both father and mother dragged her to her feet but, although she tried, it was too much and she sank to the ground again.

Soon the news spread around the village and people gathered. They were determined to beat the girl until she gave up all ideas of being a Christian. She had until morning to make up her mind. 'I shall never stop being a Christian,' she said. 'The more they beat me the more I shall laugh.'

The next day she was savagely beaten by her father and then by her mother until she lay dying, still smiling bravely.

The date was 4th February, 1928. Few people will know the name of Manche Masemula: she is one of many who, even in the twentieth century, are ready to face death rather than give up their faith.

We praise you, O God, for inspiring your servants to go into all the world to preach the Gospel. Fill those who serve today with your Holy Spirit and prosper their work. Bless all who hear your word and obey it, especially those who are persecuted for doing so. Make all your people brave and faithful, in the Name of our Lord Jesus Christ. *Amen.**

Benediction No. 46

Perseverance (1)

IN INVENTION   *Rudolph Diesel*

Bible Reading: Ecclesiastes 9: 10

There are many things to which we may give our attention but there is little point in doing them half-heartedly. Anything that is worth doing is worth doing with all our might.

A man who did just that was Rudolf Diesel, born in Paris on 18th March, 1858. He did not have an easy start in life. Because of war, his German parents had to leave Paris and settle in London with no friends and very little money.

When he was fourteen, Rudolf went to Germany to study engineering. He worked so hard that he made himself ill—but he passed all his examinations. In fact, he never seemed to mind how hard he worked if it would help him achieve his ambition, which was to make an engine which would be more efficient than the steam engine. He thought about electric engines and about engines that could use the power of the sun. He worked until his head throbbed with pain and tears streamed down his face. Nothing could stop him.

At last he designed an engine which did what he wanted it to. Like so many new ideas it did not work perfectly at first. At times he was hailed as a genius; at others he had to refund money to people who found that engines bought from him did not work properly. Diesel was famous—and fame went to his head until he began to do strange things and eventually committed suicide.

Today Diesel's memorial is in the giant engines which bear his name.

Grant us, O Lord, a good ambition in life.
In failure, grant us patience;
In difficulty, help us persevere;
In success, keep us free from pride;
In all things grant us a quiet mind
So that in peace we many enjoy our successes;
    Through Jesus Christ our Lord. *Amen.**

Closing prayer No. 26

Perseverance (2)

IN MEDICAL SCIENCE   *Sir Alexander Fleming*

At almost any time of the year, people can find themselves with coughs, colds, runny noses, influenza and other similar uncomfortable complaints. Most of these are caused by bacteria, or germs, tiny living things so small that they can only be seen under a microscope.

For many years people have studied bacteria to find out as much as possible about them. The more that can be discovered about the behaviour of bacteria, the easier it is to find ways of stopping infection by them.

One famous bacteriologist was Alexander Fleming, a Scotsman who became a professor and lecturer at the Royal College of Surgeons and had a laboratory at St. Mary's College, London. In this laboratory, he bred bacteria so that he could study them.

One day, quite by accident, a tiny speck of mould dropped onto one of his plates of bacteria and began to grow. Around the mould was a circle in which no bacteria was growing. This was something that needed to be investigated. Fleming persevered with his experiments and discovered that liquid forms of mould would prevent the growth of certain kinds of bacteria. He called his discovery penicillin.

That was as long ago as 1928 and it was just a beginning. Later, other scientists discovered more about penicillin.

Next time you take penicillin as a medicine, remember the man who made it possible, Sir Alexander Fleming, who died on 11th March, 1955, having spent much of his life and a great deal of perseverance in the study of bacteria, the result of which has been the saving of many lives and making the world a much healthier place.

Father, we thank you for all who have patiently studied the causes of disease and have been able to find means of curing them. Grant your help to all who continue this work today. May they have wisdom, understanding, patience and, in the end, success, so that the world may become a healthier place; through the great Healer of men, Jesus Christ our Lord. *Amen.**

Closing prayer No. 5

Perseverance (3)

Marie and Pierre Curie

Marya Sklodovska was born in Warsaw, the capital of Poland, on 7th November, 1867. As she grew she was keen to learn. She took a great interest in her father's library and was fascinated by his glass case filled with scientific instruments. One day she would learn how to use them.

But learning was difficult. In those days the Russians ruled over Poland and Polish children were not encouraged to learn. Marya, however, was very determined.

At last, when she was twenty-four, she went to Paris to study and it was there that Marie (for she spelt her name in the French way) met Pierre Curie, a French scientist, whom she later married.

Marie and Pierre became especially interested in a substance which gave off certain rays and they wanted to know how to get out the pure 'radium' as they called it. At last, after several years of perseverance and hard work they were successful. Their radium proved to be of great value in the curing of certain diseases. The Curies were soon famous and honoured in many lands.

Only a few years later, in 1906, Pierre was run over by a wagon and killed. Marie, the true scientist, carried on alone until 1934, when she herself died—killed by the radio-active substance that had helped to cure others.

Had they wished, the Curies could have become extremely rich but they decided to make their discovery free for the sake of science and the benefit of many suffering people, thus finding for themselves the riches of life which are far greater than money can ever be.

O Lord Jesus Christ, who taught your disciples to build up treasures in heaven; help us to find those things which will help us to lead rich and full lives:

The use of all the talents God has given us;

The pleasures to be obtained from work well done;

The great joys we can find in helping others;

The blessings we receive as we serve our God.

Hear us and help us, we humbly pray. *Amen.**

Closing prayer No. 12

Perseverance (4)

Louis Braille

Accidents happen so easily; and once they have happened nothing can undo them, no matter how we may regret that they have befallen.

A small boy, who was born on 4th January, 1809, was the victim of such an accident when he was only three years old. His father a harness-maker in a village near Paris, had been boring holes in leather with an awl but had put down his tool for a moment. It was Louis' chance to try it for himself but, instead of making a hole in the leather, he succeeded in making a hole in his eye.

For days he was in pain. Then infection spread to the other eye and that was the last young Louis ever saw. For the rest of his life he was blind. For many that might have been the end of a useful life.

But as soon as he was old enough, he was sent to a school for the blind in Paris, where he was taught to read by touching large raised letters with his fingers. Louis was so successful that he soon found himself teaching others to read by the same method.

But it was not easy. Some people just could not do it. Louis Braille determined to invent another method by which blind people could read. He worked and persevered for many a long hour to try to perfect an alphabet for the blind. When he was twenty years old he succeeded.

The Braille alphabet consists of groups of raised dots, which can be recognized by touching them with the finger-tips. Braille requires much more space than ordinary print and is expensive but it has proved a blessing to thousands of blind people who are enabled to read without using their eyes.

Blind people do not, however, have to buy all their books. It is possible for them to borrow books in Braille from a special library of these books.

O God, our Father, may these few minutes in your presence make us more thoughtful, more considerate, more ready to count our blessings, and more anxious to help others; so that we might follow in the footsteps of Jesus, in whose Name we ask this. *Amen.**

Benediction No. 48

Perseverance (5)

Gladys Aylward

The clerk in the booking office could hardly believe his ears. 'What was that you said, Miss? I haven't got time for jokes.'

'I am not joking,' replied the young woman. 'I want to know what is the cost of a single ticket to China.'

Then, when she learned that it was nearly £50, she was determined to save it. In those days £50 was a great deal of money.

Gladys Aylward was sure that God wanted her to go to China, but she had been turned down by the committee of the missionary society. They did not feel that they could send the little parlour maid to China.

Gladys, however, was sure that God wanted her to go. If the missionary society would not send her, she must get there under her own steam. Week by week she saved her money until she had enough. Then, on 15th October, 1932, she left Liverpool Street Station in London on the long overland journey to China.

In China, she was met by a Mrs. Lawson, to whom she had written letters. Together they turned an old house into an inn where the Chinese travellers could stay. After the evening meal they would tell Bible stories to the travellers.

The story of Gladys Aylward is almost like a fairy story in which amazing things happened. One of the most remarkable was the journey she made with a large band of orphans, taking them to safety in the war-torn country. After a brief stay in Britain, Gladys Aylward returned to the Far East to work amongst the Chinese people whom she loved and it was there that she died in 1970.

Hers is the story of one who heard the call from God and would not be put off by others but persevered to get herself into the place where she was sure God wanted her to be.

Almighty and everlasting God, grant unto us purity of heart, and strength of purpose, that no selfishness may hinder us from knowing thy will, and no weakness from doing it; that in thy light we may see the light, and in thy service find perfect freedom. *Amen.*

Devotions for Company and Camp

Closing prayer No. 24

Foolishness and wisdom (1)

All Fools' Day

April 1st is All Fools' Day in Britain and from early morning people try to make fools of their friends so that they can have the pleasure of calling them 'April Fool'.

How the custom began is not clear and, although various explanations have been offered none is convincing. In some other countries there are similar days.

Most of the April Fool pranks today are played by children and, though most people are on their guard, there are few who can say that they have never been caught out as an April Fool.

Last century, jokes were played on a grand scale, one of the most famous being in 1860, when hundreds of people received by post an invitation to a special ceremony at the Tower of London of washing the white lions. Invitation was by ticket only, the tickets to be presented at the White Gate. So, on 1st April, 1860, hundreds turned up to discover that there is no White Gate at the Tower of London and they were all April Fools.

However, joking ends at noon and anyone who tries it after that is the fool himself. There are no more fools for another year.

Perhaps it would be more correct to say that one may not be an April Fool for another year. It is certainly possible to be a fool in other ways and many people manage to make utter fools of themselves through the year. One such fool, the Bible suggests, is the man who trusts solely in himself without a thought for God.

Bible Reading: St. Luke 12: 15–21

May God not have cause to say to us, 'You fool!'

Teach us, O Lord, how to use our common sense, and so be wise in our ways. Prevent us from speaking unwisely, from acting foolishly and from any form of foolish thinking. Above all, keep us from the foolishness of thinking that we can manage without the help that comes from you; for the sake of Jesus Christ our Lord. *Amen.**

Closing prayer No. 13

Foolishness and wisdom (2)

King James I

Just before Queen Elizabeth I died, she named King James the Sixth of Scotland as her successor and a messenger hastened to tell the King the news.

James was delighted. In fact he had been awaiting the news for he believed that he would now be rich and powerful—King of Scotland and England. From that day to this, the countries have had the same sovereign, though it was over one hundred years before they were to become a united kingdom. On 5th April, 1603, James set off for London.

James had a great disadvantage. Most people had thought very highly of Queen Elizabeth and did not take easily to the new King. He had nothing of the splendour associated with Elizabeth. His appearance was not very imposing; his tongue frequently hung out of his mouth; his speech was not very clear; his legs were spindly; he shambled along, leaning on the shoulder of a courtier; his clothes were shabby and his table manners were dreadful.

Moreover, the King thought himself very wise and other men fools. In fact, he was once referred to as the most learned fool in Christendom. Had he really been wise, James would have made a much greater effort to win over the people of his new kingdom. As it was, he made enemies, including those who tried to blow up King and Parliament on 5th November, 1605.

St. Paul writes of other people who thought they were wise but who made fools of themselves:

Bible Reading: Romans 1: 18–23

Help us this day, O God, to find the wisdom which will tell us what to do and what not to do; when to act and when to refrain from action; when to speak and when to keep silent.

So grant that, guided by you, we may be saved from all wrong thoughts, from all words which we would wish unsaid and from all deeds we would wish undone: through Jesus Christ our Lord. *Amen.*

Dr. William Barclay

Closing prayer No. 10

Foolishness and wisdom (3)

St. Mark's Eve

How many young ladies would like to know who they are going to marry? According to ancient customs and superstitions, 24th April is one of the occasions in the year when they can find out. Some, of course, may have already tried lying on their backs in bed on St. Agnes' Eve, 20th January, or running three times round the churchyard on the even of St. Valentine.

On St. Mark's Eve, 24th April, three young ladies must get together, make and bake a cake in complete silence. As the clock strikes midnight, each girl breaks off a piece of cake and eats it, then walks backward upstairs to bed, still in dead silence, for any word spoken would break the spell.

If the girl is to be married, she should see a shadow of her future husband or hear him knock on the door. However, no shadow or no knock means no husband.

Of course, if it doesn't work, they can always try again with apples at Michaelmas, cakes on St. Faith's Eve, water on Hallowe'en, or onions on St. Thomas's Eve.

Do you believe these work? Most of the important days of the past had some strange customs or superstitions attached to them. Many of these can be amusing—as long as we remember that they are only superstitions.

It is a tragedy that there are people in many lands and even some in this country, who are so superstitious that they live in real fear and terror of breaking these superstitions.

St. Paul, on his journeys, came across some people who were very superstitious. They had many Gods but built an altar to the 'Unknown God' in case they had missed one out.

Bible Reading: Acts of the Apostles 17: 22–28

O Lord Jesus Christ, who often cast out of people's minds the fears and imaginations which made them ill, help us and all people to know that as we trust in you we have nothing to fear, for you have promised peace to all who trust in you. Hear us and help us we pray. *Amen.**

Benediction No. 46

Foolishness and wisdom (4)

St. Columba

It is easy to be a fool. It is also easy to ask God for wisdom. Here are some words of St. James:

Bible Reading: James 1: 2–5

One man who had to learn wisdom was Columba, a member of an Irish royal family, who entered a monastery at an early age and whose favourite occupation was copying manuscripts. He is said to have copied the Gospels about three hundred times.

The story is told how he quarrelled with an Irish king, then called in his family to settle the dispute. The result was a battle in which many people were slain. Columba realized what a fool he had been. He must learn to control his feelings. He decided to leave his homeland for ever and go somewhere where he could work for God.

So, with a handful of monks, he travelled by coracle from Ireland to the little island of Iona amongst the Western Isles of Scotland. On Iona they made a base from which to teach of Jesus Christ.

They began by preaching to some Irish people who lived on the neighbouring island of Mull and who were already Christian. Then Columba ventured further afield until at last he reached Inverness on the far side of Scotland and where, in spite of opposition from the Druids, he persuaded the King of the Picts and many others to become Christian.

In A.D. 597, Columba died on Iona, and he is remembered on 9th June each year. He had learned his lesson and passed it on through cheerfulness, loving deeds and with the joy of God in his heart.

A prayer of St. Columba:

O Lord, give us, we beseech thee, in the name of Jesus Christ thy Son, our Lord, that love which can never cease, that will kindle our lamps but not extinguish them, that they may burn in us and enlighten others. *Amen.*

Benediction No. 54

Foolishness and wisdom (5)

St. Thomas Aquinas

March 7th is the feast day of St. Thomas Aquinas, who lived about seven hundred years ago. He was the youngest son of Count Landulf of Aquino and was born at his father's castle in Italy in 1226. As he was related to the Emperor himself it was expected that he would one day hold an important position so, at the age of five, he was sent to the monastery at Monte Cassino to be educated.

Later, to the horror of his parents, he decided to become a Dominican friar so that he could teach people about God. To prevent this, he was kidnapped by his brothers, taken home and imprisoned in the castle, where he remained for two years. At last his sisters helped him to escape by lowering him from the castle walls in a basket.

Thomas was a brilliant scholar and was sent to study under a great teacher at Cologne. The other students made fun of this fat young man with the big calm face who seldom said anything. They called him 'the dumb ox'.

One day his teacher said, 'You may call him a dumb ox but one day the whole world will listen to his voice'. He was right. Thomas became one of the greatest teachers of religion that the Church has had.

Where did he get his wisdom? As a small boy he had asked one question—'What is God?' He spent his life answering that question for himself and for others, explaining his beliefs in words that the simplest of people could understand.

The Bible tells how the disciples asked a similar question and of the reply that Jesus gave them:

Bible Reading: St. John 14: 6–10

A prayer of St. Thomas Aquinas:

Grant us, we beseech thee, Almighty and most merciful God, fervently to desire, wisely to search out, and perfectly to fulfil, all that is well-pleasing unto thee this day . . . Bestow upon us also, O Lord our God, understanding to know thee, diligence to seek thee, wisdom to find thee, and a faithfulness that we may finally embrace thee; through Jesus Christ our Lord. *Amen.*

Closing prayer No. 19

Rules for living (1)

A SET OF RULES   *Sir Robert Peel*

A set of rules is necessary in almost everything we do and, if we are wise, we keep to those rules. Even the games which children make up for themselves have certain rules which everyone is expected to keep.

When the rules are broken something must be done about it. Children who cannot play fairly find that others will not allow them to play: a footballer who breaks rules may be sent off the pitch. There are also rules or laws which must be kept if people are to live peacefully together. People who break the laws of a country may be put into prison so that they 'cannot play' for a time.

In the Old Testament there are laws which explained how people should regard God and their fellows. The best known of these are the Ten Commandments, which begin like this:

Bible Reading: Deuteronomy 5: 1–11 (to be continued)

There were stiff penalties for those who did not keep the Commandments and all the people helped to see that they were kept. Nowadays all people are responsible for seeing that our laws are kept but we also have a police force which is especially responsible—one of the finest police organizations in the world.

It was first introduced in 1829 by Sir Robert Peel who was then Home Secretary. Peel, who was born on 5th February, 1788, was one of the great politicians of last century and was twice Prime Minister of Britain. But though his government passed important laws, Peel is remembered most for his police force, still sometimes referred to as 'Bobbies' after their founder, Sir Robert Peel, and today playing an important role in keeping the laws of our land.

We remember before you, O God, our police forces and all others who are engaged in the prevention of crime; all judges, magistrates, and those who administer justice; and all who try to help those who have broken the law. May they all act fairly, wisely and speedily so that the laws of the land may be upheld and we may dwell in security and peace; through Jesus Christ our Lord. *Amen.**

Closing prayer No. 9

Rules for living (2)

George Burns

George Burns was amazed to read in his paper that a ship was to sail down the Clyde, driven by steam engines. Such a thing was unheard of in those days. He counted his pennies, decided not to waste them on such a strange ship, but determined nevertheless to watch the *Comet* sail.

Later, George and his brother went into business as merchants and then as shipping agents too, arranging for ships to carry other people's goods.

It was not long before many businessmen were entrusting the firm with their business. George, who looked after the shipping side of the business, proved most reliable. He was thoroughly honest, never overcharged, and never let others down. He was known to many people as 'Honest George Burns'. Later he ran ships of his own.

George had been brought up in a Christian home and was a stickler for what he believed right. Among the Ten Commandments was one dealing with the sabbath day:

Bible Reading: Deuteronomy 5: 12–15 (cont.)

At first George would not allow his ships to sail on a Sunday but, when he found this impossible, he put a chaplain on board so that a service could be held.

One day, George Burns received a visit from a Quaker named Samuel Cunard, from Halifax, Canada. Suppose they started a shipping line to deliver mail from one side of the Atlantic to the other and promise to deliver on time!

And so, on 4th May, 1839, the Cunard Steam Ship Company was formed. Today, its ships on regular voyages serve to remind us of the reliability of 'Honest George'.

Teach us, O Lord, to live according to your holy laws. Make us trustworthy, honest and reliable in all our affairs. Help us to keep our promises, to do nothing dishonourable, and to stand fast in the faith. Let no thought of riches, fear of difficulty or a fainting heart make us turn aside from you; but help us to live to your glory, after the example of Jesus Christ our Lord. *Amen.**

Closing prayer No. 7

Rules for living (3)

Colonel Blood

Are you ever tempted to steal something? Or do you wish you possessed something that belongs to another person? The Ten Commandments have something to say about both.

Bible Reading: Deuteronomy 5: 16–21

Perhaps you have visited the Jewel House in the Tower of London and seen the Crown Jewels, worth millions of pounds, on display. You may have wondered what it would be like to possess, or borrow, or even steal something—but there is little chance of that for the warders who are on duty are on the alert for anything unusual.

Yet there have been plots to steal the Crown Jewels, one of the most notorious being on 9th May, 1671, when Colonel Thomas Blood succeeded in doing so, only to be caught with the crown in his possession.

It is a strange story and difficult to know what really did happen. Colonel Blood spent most of his life in plotting and in adventure. This, it seemed would be his last but, strange as it may seem, he was not only pardoned by King Charles II but was given a large amount of land in Ireland.

There may seem to be a certain amount of glamour about an attempt to steal the Crown Jewels, and it would seem in this case to have paid off. In fact it is all too easy to be attracted to the highwayman or the pirate of history, without remembering that they were no better than the bank robber or the common thief today who has no thought whatever for the distress of the person who is robbed.

We are wise to heed these laws and refrain from stealing or from coveting our neighbour's possessions.

Almighty God, who commanded people not to covet anything which is their neighbour's; keep us from all forms of dishonesty; restrain us from taking anything which is not ours; teach us that only those things for which we work or which are truly ours can bring lasting happiness; and so give us the peace of a quiet mind; for the sake of Jesus Christ our Lord. *Amen.**

Closing prayer No. 1

Rules for living (4)

Henry Fielding

The people of Old Testament times were told that they would prosper if they kept God's laws:

Bible Reading: Deuteronomy 6: 3–7

But some people broke the laws then, just as people have broken laws ever since. Nowadays we have policemen who enforce the law. A little over two hundred years ago, it was not easy to bring criminals to justice. Henry Fielding, who was the magistrate at Bow Street Magistrates' Court in London, decided that the only way of doing so was to employ a reliable body of men who would track down robbers and arrest those found breaking the law.

These men were easily recognized, for they wore red waistcoats as part of their uniform, which, not unnaturally, earned them the name of 'Robin Redbreasts'. However they proved an efficient body of men and became known as the Bow Street Runners.

Henry Fielding himself was a man of great talent who decided to take up writing and it is as a writer that he is chiefly remembered. It was during his time as a Bow Street Magistrate that he wrote some of his finest work. Unfortunately his health broke down and he went abroad to recover but died while in Portugal, on 8th October, 1754.

Henry Fielding was a man who liked to see that justice was done and was determined to track down any offenders. At the same time, he is remembered as a kindly man, who was ready to see the points of view of others and who could be very sympathetic to those who found themselves in trouble.

Today the law often deals kindly with lawbreakers who can hardly be described as hardened criminals.

Give unto us, O most blessed Lord,
The grace to be patient as thou wast patient;
That we may gently bear with the faults of others,
And strive at all times to root out our own;
 For thy mercy's sake. *Amen.*

Rydal School Hymnal

Closing prayer No. 11

Rules for living (5)

George Washington

One of the most honoured names in the United States of America is that of George Washington, the man who won the high regard of his fellow countrymen and was chosen by them to become the first President of the United States—an office which he took up on 30th April, 1789.

George had shown qualities of leadership when he was very young. At sixteen he had to ride out into the open country, directing the work of men much older than himself. At twenty-three, after fighting against the French and the Indians, he was made a colonel.

The Indians thought that he must have a charmed life, for twice his horse was killed under him and four bullets passed through his coat. Washington believed that his life had been spared for a greater purpose.

Some years later, trouble broke out between the people of Britain and those in America. The Americans said that they would no longer be ruled by Britain. They chose George Washington as their leader and he was so successful that it was hardly surprising that the people chose him to be their first president.

For ten years, Washington led the government of the United States so well that the country made remarkable progress. At the end of his second term of office, he resigned.

George Washington, known as 'The Father of his Country', won the hearts of the people by his leadership but also by the uprightness and honesty of his character. These are the qualities that are the mark of true greatness.

Notice what St. Paul had to say on this:

Bible Reading: Romans 12: 12–17

Lord, grant us the will and the power to do in all things that which is honest and right. Thou who art the truth, help us bravely and sincerely to speak only that which is true, and to behave openly, frankly, and loyally to one another. May we never be afraid to admit our faults and to accept the blame. As thou dost keep us in thy care and love, so may we love one another; for thy Name's sake. *Amen.*

Source not known

Closing prayer No. 36

Making the most of life (1)

Queen Elizabeth I

Have you ever wished you were someone else? Someone, perhaps, who has much more than you have? A prince or princess, maybe, so that you could have all the things you wanted? You might be surprised to learn that many a prince or princess has had a hard time in life.

Young Princess Elizabeth, for example, was only three years old when her mother had her head chopped off by order of her father. Then, for several years she was neglected and forgotten. How she must have longed for something better.

When she was fourteen, her father died and her brother became King. She soon found she must be careful how she spoke and what she did for there were plots to use her to cause trouble.

Six years later, her half-sister, Mary, became Queen. Elizabeth was next in line for the throne and Mary, who was unpopular, feared that the people might wish to have Elizabeth instead. So the princess was locked away, first in the Tower of London, then in Woodstock Palace in Oxfordshire before she was allowed to lead a happier life at Hatfield House near London.

In 1558, Mary died and Elizabeth became Queen. The Queen, who knew what it was to have ups and downs, was determined to succeed and she found many ways of doing so until her reign, one of the most colourful in the history of England, ended with her death on 24th March, 1603.

It is not who we are that is the most important thing in life but what we are ready to make of ourselves.

O God our Father, help us to remember that life always has its ups and downs and we must be ready to take the rough with the smooth. In times of difficulty or distress be our guide and inspiration so that we may have strength to face up to every situation. Help us to know your presence and fill us with happiness so that, when the clouds roll away and the sun shines on our life, we may continually praise and bless you, the author and giver of every good thing; through Jesus Christ our Lord. *Amen.**

Closing prayer No. 2

Making the most of life (2)

Charles Dickens

One has only to mention the names of David Copperfield, Oliver Twist, Mr. Pickwick, Little Nell, Pip or Scrooge and one name immediately comes to mind—Charles Dickens, the author who was born at Landport, Portsmouth, on 7th February, 1812, and in whose books they appear.

Some of the characters in Dickens' books may seem strange to us today but people like them did live then. Rogues like Fagin did send boys out to steal; schools in which boys were starved and beaten did exist: and conditions in prison were dreadful, as Dickens learned from his father, who was once imprisoned for debt.

Dickens, himself, had known hardship in a poor home as one of a large family. He was horrified that some people had to live in such dreadful conditions as were known then. He believed that if he wrote about them in his books, people would take notice and do something to improve living conditions.

Many of the characters in Dickens' books needed a square deal, just as Dickens had done as a boy. But Dickens had made the most of his lot by hard work and by seizing every opportunity to better himself. When he died, at the age of fifty-eight, he was given the honour of a burial in Westminster Abbey.

Dickens is remembered, of course, for his many books which are still read today but also as a man who made other people think.

And if sometimes we feel sorry for ourselves, we should count our blessings that we do not live in conditions like those which existed when Dickens was writing his books.

Father of all men, we pray thee for all those who in these days cannot find work by which to live; for all homes where there is want and poverty; for all those who are hungry and ill-clad, and especially for little children. Stir up, we beseech thee, the conscience of this people, till this shame be removed from our land; for Jesus Christ's sake. *Amen.*

Source not known

Closing prayer No. 15

Making the most of life (3)

When Robert Owen was born, on 14th May, 1771, in the little Welsh town of Newtown, Montgomeryshire, his parents scarcely imagined that he would become rich or famous. Theirs was a poor home and Robert went out to work at the age of nine.

From the beginning, life was one long struggle, but Robert decided to seek his fortune in Manchester, where workers were needed in the new cotton mills. There he showed himself to be so capable and willing to work that he was made manager of a mill. His struggle against poverty ended when he married a millionaire's daughter and later owned a mill of his own at New Lanark.

But Robert Owen did not only think of himself. He remembered the struggles that he had experienced. Now he could improve the conditions of those who worked in his mill. He was more concerned with their welfare than with making large profits. Changes came quickly.

When he took over the mill, much of the work was done by poor children, who began at the age of five. Robert Owen would employ no child under the age of ten. Instead he did the unheard of thing of starting a school for these infants. Hours of work for all were reduced and housing conditions were improved. Later, he entered Parliament in order to make laws to improve factory conditions throughout Britain.

Robert Owen worked all his life to bring as much happiness as he could to as many people as possible in a day when most workers were anything but happy. And we can be sure that as he brought happiness to others, he found true happiness for himself.

Bible Reading: Proverbs 14: 21–24

Help us to remember, O Lord, that life is what we make it ourselves; that if we look on the dark side we shall find only discontent, but if we seek happiness we shall find it. Grant us to live happy and contented lives and, having learned the secret for ourselves, to spread some happiness wherever we go; through Jesus Christ our Lord. *Amen.**

Closing prayer No. 17

Making the most of life (4)

On 12th February, 1915, a little old lady of ninety-five died in America and was buried at Bridgeport. Her gravestone bore the words 'Aunt Fanny' and, at the side, the words of Jesus; 'She hath done what she could'.

Nothing very much, yet behind it lies the story of an amazing woman. Fanny Crosby was born in New York in 1820. When six weeks old she caught a cold and the doctor prescribed the wrong treatment, with the result that she was blinded for life. What could a little blind girl do?

She went to a school for blind children in New York and later taught at the same school for eleven years until she married a musician, Alexander van Alstyne, who himself was blind.

When she was only eight years old, Fanny Crosby had one of her poems published and this was the first of many, for she found it easy to write poetry and especially hymns, which were usually written to fit a particular piece of music. Somebody would play a tune and ask her what words it suggested. In no time she had written verses to fit the music.

Soon she was recognized as one of the greatest writers of gospel hymns—and she wrote somewhere in the region of seven thousand of them, including many which are still enjoyed today including *Blessed assurance, Jesus is mine* and *To God be the Glory*.

People used to sympathize with the poor little blind girl in New York but she did what she could and there is no doubt that she found great joy in life or that the hymns which she wrote have helped thousands, maybe millions of people to come to God. Truly Fanny Crosby was a remarkable servant of God.

O God, sometimes we feel a little sorry for ourselves and think that others have much more than we have. Help us rather to think of the blessings that are ours and how best to use them. Teach us that nothing greater could be said of us than that we have done what we could. So help us to use every part of our lives in the service of others and for your glory; for Jesus' sake. *Amen.**

Benediction No. 41

Making the most of life (5)

John Keble

> *New every morning is the love*
> *Our wakening and uprising prove,*
> *Through sleep and darkness safely brought,*
> *Restored to life, and power, and thought.*

John Keble, who wrote these words, was a man who believed that God could make a great difference to the life of any person who believed in him.

Keble was born in the Cotwolds, educated at Oxford, and spent most of his life as vicar of the small parish of Hursley, near Winchester, but he was known to many people outside his village. His letters, books, hymns and other writings were widely known so that he had a great influence on many people of his time.

Keble, who died on 29th March, 1866, has several memorials. The church at Hursley was built and paid for with money he earned by his writing. At Oxford, Keble College was named in his honour. His hymns, *New every morning, Blest are the pure in heart* and others are frequently sung to this day.

We might do well to remember two lines written in the hymn *New every morning* which are omitted in some books:

> *Old friends, old scenes, will lovelier be*
> *As more of heaven in each we see.*

It is always easy to find the bad in people but so much better if we can see the good, especially if we can remember that we are all God's children. Keble had learned, as many others have learned, that the more we can see of God in anyone or anything the better it appears.

A prayer verse written by John Keble:

> Thou, who hast given me eyes to see
> And love this sight so fair,
> Give me a heart to find out thee,
> And read thee everywhere. *Amen.*

Closing prayer No. 30

Life's challenge (1)

Henry the Navigator

Prince Henry was the fourth son of King John the First of Portugal and he proved to be a very capable leader of men. As a young man, he proved his courage by leading an expedition against Ceuta in North Africa. Soon all Europe knew about him.

The King of England, Henry V, invited him to lead his armies; so did the Emperor of Germany. But Prince Henry had other ideas. He was not interested in fighting men; he wanted to do battle with the mighty Atlantic Ocean, which had for long been regarded as the edge of the world.

Prince Henry made his headquarters near Cape St. Vincent, in one of the most desolate parts of Portugal. There, far from the comforts of court life, he studied astronomy and mathematics; he listened to the stories of discovery; he built ships and he trained sailors in navigation.

Prince Henry was no longer the warrior: he was Prince Henry the Navigator. His aim was to send out ships to try to find a way round Africa and so discover a new sea route to India. He also founded the Order of Jesus Christ; its object being to carry Christianity to the people of West Africa.

Year after year, Henry sent out his ships on the unknown seas. 'Go out again,' he urged one captain who had turned back. 'By the Grace of God, you cannot fail to derive from your voyage both honour and profit.'

On 13th November, 1460, Henry the Navigator died, without finding his route to India, but he had paved the way and the route was found twenty-six years later. Henry the Navigator has become known as 'the originator of modern discovery'.

Almighty God, Creator of heaven and earth and all that is within them, we come to you now and speak with you as our Father. Help us to take your hand as we travel through life and step forward with confidence, knowing that what is hidden from us is known to you. *Amen.**

Closing prayer No. 23

Life's challenge (2)

Mungo Park

For some people, life is very dull: for others it is filled with adventure. Most people can find adventure of some kind if only they are prepared to look for it. One who did was a Scotsman named Mungo Park, who was born on 10th September, 1771.

His opportunity came at the age of twenty-three, when an explorer was needed to find out more about Africa. In those days, people knew little about Africa, which was known as 'the dark continent'. They wanted to find out about its forests, about the desert beyond, and about the great rivers that flowed through them.

Little did Mungo Park realize the dangers and the difficulties that lay in his path, but he was a man of great determination, who refused to heed the warnings to turn back.

From the beginning nothing went smoothly. He was held up by catching a fever. The presents he carried were too few to satisfy those whose land he passed and, in any case, he was robbed of most of them. He was attacked, imprisoned, ill-treated, starved and parched with thirst, but still he sought the source of the great river Niger. He was finally defeated by lions, mosquitoes, a worn-out horse and sickness. He returned to the coast and thence to Scotland.

But it was not the end. A few years later, he returned to his exploration—a journey from which he never returned. Mungo Park may not have reached his goal but it was not for want of courage or determination. He had put everything into his quest. No one can do more than that.

These verses from the Bible remind us that Abraham had faith to go where God wanted him to go.

Bible Reading: Hebrews 11: 8–10

Give unto us, O God, we pray thee, the spirit and courage. Help us to face the difficulties, dangers and setbacks of life with good cheer and brave endurance, that we may rise above them, and so encourage others. *Amen.*

Devotions for Company and Camp

Closing prayer No. 26

Life's challenge (2)

Life's challenge (3)

Great Clipper Race

On 5th September, 1866, two ships raced side by side up the English Channel, wearing every stitch of sail that it was possible to carry, for each captain was determined to be the first to dock in London.

In those days, London tea merchants were anxious to obtain the year's crop of tea from China at the earliest possible date and extra money was given to the captain of the first ship to dock.

So, the fast clipper ships had gathered at the Chinese port of Foochow to be loaded with the first crop of tea. On 29th May, *Ariel* was first to get under way, followed closely by *Taiping* and three other ships.

The race was on. Each ship had soon lost sight of the others and there were no radio messages in those days. The captains seldom knew where they were in the race. It was flat out all the way— through the China Seas, across the Indian Ocean, round South Africa and then northwards in the Atlantic, sometimes becalmed, sometimes in stormy seas but always with their goal in view.

All day on 5th September, it was neck and neck up the Channel, with *Ariel* just in the lead, but *Taiping* had a faster tug to tow her to the Thames and so became the winner by twenty minutes after a race which had lasted for $99\frac{1}{2}$ days.

These were magnificent ships and their crews were fine seamen, who had such faith in their ships, their captains and themselves that they were sure they could win.

So in life we can do much if we have faith in ourselves but more especially if we trust God as the captain of our lives.

Bible Reading: Hebrews 12: 1–2

O God our Father, as we take our place in the race of life, we know that we shall have our days of calm and days when we battle against stormy seas. Give us faith in ourselves to know that we can weather the storms but, above all, give us faith in you to know that you will guide us safely to the end of our journey; through Jesus Christ our Lord. *Amen.**

Benediction No. 50

Life's challenge (4)

Sir Francis Chichester

On 28th May, 1967, Francis Chichester sailed his yacht *Gipsy Moth IV* into Plymouth Sound, to end a voyage of some 28,500 miles, which had begun at that very place on 27th August, 1966.

His aim had been to follow the route of the old wool clipper ships. *Gipsy Moth IV*, however, was only a very small ship and Francis Chichester was sailing her single-handed.

The journey to Sydney, Australia, took 108 days and there his friends tried to persuade him not to continue but Chichester was not to be put off. After a month and a half he left for the return journey round the treacherous Cape Horn.

Soon he was battling with mountainous seas and hurricanes. His ship was all but capsized. He rounded Cape Horn in 100 m.p.h. winds, with *Gipsy Moth IV* carrying only a single small sail. He made it successfully.

His return journey took him 119 days. At Plymouth he was greeted by a great armada of small ships, a din of whistles and sirens, fire-floats sending up fountains of water, and a crowd of 250,000 cheering people. They had come to welcome the man who had set himself against the forces of nature and won through. Soon afterwards, he received the nation's tribute by being ceremonially knighted at Greenwich.

It was a lonely voyage but many were ready to keep watch from ships and planes and then report his progress. So, if we find difficulties in life, we can be sure that help is at hand from many people and strength from God himself.

O Lord our God, give us strength to face up to life's adventure. Help us in the storms of life to remember that we do not have to face them alone, for you are with us. Help us, too, in peaceful times to trust in you. Then, at the end of life's voyage, may we receive the reward promised to all who win through; through Jesus Christ our Lord. *Amen.**

Benediction No. 48

Life's challenge (5)

Battle of Hastings

October 14th is the anniversary of the Battle of Hastings in 1066, between the armies of William of Normandy and those of Harold of England.

William had made no secret of the fact that he thought he should be King of England and it was no surprise when his armies set sail from Normandy and headed toward the English coast.

Harold, who had been fighting another battle, hastened southwards and took up his position on a hill at Senlac, ready to withstand the onslaught of the enemy. His seemed to be by far the superior position, for the Normans would have to take the hill, whilst the Saxons on top could fire their arrows down on the Norman army.

William realized that he must lure the English from their stronghold. This he did by pretending to retreat. The English, overjoyed at seeing their enemy in flight, left their positions and gave chase. Only then did they realize their mistake. The Normans turned to fight. The English had lost whatever advantage they had. In a very short time, the battle was over. Harold lay dying on the battlefield and William was indeed the Conqueror. He marched to London, where, on Christmas Day, he was crowned William the First of England.

So, in life, we have the strength of God to keep us but there is many a person who has allowed himself to be tempted away from God, only to find that he has made a great mistake in doing so.

Bible Reading: St. Matthew 4: 1–11

Almighty God, who knowest the many and great dangers by which we are beset, be unto us, both this day and all our days, our strong and sufficient helper. Deliver us from sloth and pride and from all that is false in thought or act, and teach us to watch and pray that we enter not into temptation; through Jesus Christ our Lord. *Amen.*

H. Bisseker

Benediction No. 51

Aims and ambitions (1)

TO BE FIRST   *Robert Falcon Scott*

On 6th June, 1868, Robert Falcon Scott was born at Devonport, one of the main ports and bases of the Royal Navy. Like many a Devonport man, he decided to make the Royal Navy his career and, at the age of fourteen, went to the naval training ship at Dartmouth.

But although he did very well for himself in the Navy, he won fame far away in the icy wastes around the South Pole.

His first voyage to Antarctica was in the *Discovery* in 1901–4, when he began to explore the continent and made a journey with two companions which took him further south than anyone had yet been.

A few years later, in 1910, he set out again in the *Terra Nova*, determined to reach the South Pole. About the same time, a Norwegian explorer, Amundsen, had also sailed and Scott knew that the Norwegian, with a greater knowledge of skiing and with more dogs to pull sledges, had a great advantage.

Nevertheless he pressed on, hoping to be first at the South Pole. His hopes were dashed on reaching it to find that Amundsen had been there a month before him.

The return journey was a nightmare. One member of the party died: another walked out to his death in a blizzard. Scott and his other two companions died in their tent where they had been pinned down by a blizzard.

Their bodies were found some months afterwards and were buried under the snow just where they had been found.

A cross erected to their memory bore the words, 'To strive, to seek, to find, and not to yield'. They were unsuccessful in being first but their endurance will always to remembered.

O Lord God, when thou givest to thy servants to endeavour any great matter, grant us also to know that it is not the beginning, but the continuing of the same unto the end, until it be thoroughly finished, which yieldeth the true glory: through him who for the finishing of thy work laid down his life, our Redeemer, Jesus Christ. *Amen.*

Sir Francis Drake

Closing prayer No. 10

Aims and ambitions (2)

TO BE FASTEST   *Sir Donald Campbell*

Some people have within them a particular ambition and will spare
no effort to achieve it, though they may die in the attempt.

One such man, Donald Campbell, was born on 23rd March, 1921.
His father, Sir Malcolm Campbell, was world famous as the fastest
man both on land and on water when he died in 1948. Donald was
determined to be faster than his father.

His first attempts on water were made in his father's boat, *Bluebird*, but this was wrecked. He knew that if he were to succeed,
he must have a boat of an entirely new design and powered with a
jet engine. So the new *Bluebird* was built with the world record in
mind.

Bluebird proved herself very quickly by taking the world record
at over 200 miles per hour. Campbell was pleased but not satisfied.
He tried again and again until the record of 260·35 m.p.h. was
reached in 1959.

A few years later, in Australia, Sir Donald Campbell achieved
the double. In July he drove his turbine-driven car at 403·1 m.p.h.
and in December he travelled on water at 276·33 m.p.h.

Still he was not satisfied. If it were possible to go even faster,
he would be the man to do it. In January 1967, as *Bluebird* hurtled
across the surface of Lake Coniston, observers were horrified to see
it rise into the air and somersault into the water. Sir Donald
Campbell was killed as he tried to better his own record.

Perhaps you have heard someone say, 'I'm going to do that if
it kills me'. They probably do not mean it in the sense that it
happened to Donald Campbell—rather that they will put every
ounce of effort into their task in the hope of success.

Help us, O God, to know what we want to do and give us the
courage to try it. May we never be satisfied with second-best but
seek always to improve until we have achieved our ambition. Show
us some way of serving others and serving you and keep us true
to our calling to our life's end; through Jesus Christ our Lord.
Amen.*

Closing prayer No. 22

Aims and ambitions (3)

TO PUT THINGS RIGHT   *Josephine Butler and Amelia Bloomer*

If one were to suggest that boys were more important than girls, no doubt all the boys would agree and all the girls would disagree. Yet, if you were to ask the same question in some countries today there would be no doubt about the answer for boys are considered more important.

It was always so in the ancient world. In fact in Bible times women were always kept in their place. Here are some words of St. Paul:

Bible Reading: 1 Timothy 2: 8–12

Today there are people who would say that St. Paul was wrong because we think differently, mainly because certain people fought for women's rights. In America, for example, Amelia Bloomer attended a meeting of women's rights in 1848 and thereafter spent her life in trying to change things that were wrong by her speeches and her writings. She gave her name to a revolutionary kind of dress for women. Her kind of trouser suit, worn instead of a dress became known as 'Bloomers'. By the time she died on 30th December, 1894, she had done much for women.

In Britain, another social reformer died on 30th December but in 1906. She was Josephine Butler, who championed the cause of women and whose speeches and courage brought her thousands of supporters.

And because people like these battled for what they believed, things began to happen. Today there are many people working for other causes—to help those who are down-trodden and to gain equal rights for those who are treated as second-class citizens in many parts of the world.

We remember before you, O God, people of many lands who are oppressed because of their beliefs, their social standing or the colour of their skin. Hasten the day when all shall recognize their brotherhood in Christ and treat all people as equals, and to you be glory for ever and ever. *Amen.**

Closing prayer No. 27

Aims and ambitions (3)

Aims and ambitions (4)

William Blake

William Blake, who grew up to be a great poet and painter, was born in London on 28th November, 1757.

Some of his poems show very deep thinking: others are delightfully simple. 'The Tiger' and 'The Lamb' are two well-known ones. Here is 'The Shepherd'.

> *How sweet is the Shepherd's sweet lot!*
> *From the morn to the evening he strays;*
> *He shall follow his sheep all the day,*
> *And his tongue shall be filled with praise.*
>
> *For he hears the lamb's innocent call,*
> *And he hears the ewe's tender reply;*
> *He is watchful while they are in peace,*
> *For they know when their Shepherd is nigh.*

But Blake was not just a poet, he was a dreamer, and many of the things he wrote expressed his feelings about religion and the evils he saw around him.

> *I will not cease from mental fight,*
> *Nor shall my sword sleep in my hand,*
> *Till we have built Jerusalem*
> *In England's green and pleasant land.*

This was not written as a hymn, nor intended to be one, but it became a popular hymn after it was set to Hubert Parry's music in 1916. It is a challenging hymn, but we need to remember that the new Jerusalem, God's Kingdom, cannot be built by our efforts alone. We need to seek God's help in the task.

Help us, O God, to see what needs to be done and then to do it with all our might. Help us always to be active for the right instead of leaving things to others. Help us to work for the good of all people and the coming of your Kingdom. Help us to remember that we cannot do these things by ourselves but only with your help. So may we offer our lives to your service, and may your Spirit guide us in thought, word and deed; for the glory of your Holy Name. *Amen.**

Closing prayer No. 25

Aims and ambitions (5)

There are few people today who have never heard the name Rolls-Royce. For some it may mean the last word in excellence where cars are concerned: for others it stands for fine aeroplane engines. But how many realize that Rolls-Royce is, in fact, the name of two gentlemen a Mr. Rolls and a Mr. Royce—or, to be more exact, The Honourable Charles Stewart Rolls and Sir Frederick Henry Royce, who joined forces in 1906 to form Rolls-Royce Ltd.

The Honourable C. S. Rolls was a good athlete and he also won prizes in cycle races. Then he became one of those early pioneers of motoring who drove motor cars in the days when a man had to walk in front of any car carrying a red flag as a warning to pedestrians.

Later, he took part in many car races and rallies in England and in Europe. Several times he broke the world speed record and many motoring prizes came his way.

Rolls also liked to get off the ground. In addition to his cars, he owned a balloon and an aeroplane. In 1910, he became the first man to fly the English Channel and back without stopping. He also had another 'first'. He was the first man to be killed in a flying accident. On 12th July, 1910, his plane crashed near Bournemouth.

In his life, he was never satisfied with second-best. No doubt he would have been pleased to know that the double-R badge of Rolls-Royce always stood as a symbol of the highest quality.

In his first letter, Peter tells his readers to aim always for the highest:

Bible Reading: 1 Peter 1: 13–16

Almighty God, who commanded us to be perfect as you, our Father, are perfect; help us to become all that we ought to be. Teach us to be content with nothing less than the best and to seek your way, so that we may be fit to bear the name of Christian, after him, who lived the finest life of all, our Lord and Master Jesus Christ. *Amen.**

Closing prayer No. 14

True values (1)

Mary, Queen of Scots

As evening fell over Loch Leven, in Scotland, on 2nd May, 1568, Lady Douglas sat at supper, unaware that her prisoner, Mary, Queen of Scots, was making her escape. With stolen keys the door was opened to allow the Queen to make her way silently to the water's edge, where a boat waited to carry her from the island to the shore.

Mary, Queen of Scots, is one of the most colourful people in history and this escape was just one of the events in her troubled life.

She inherited the throne of Scotland when she was very young but soon she had to be sent to France for safety from the English. In France she married the French king's eldest son but he died, leaving Mary a widow at the age of nineteen. Back home, she married Lord Darnley and it was their son James who later became King of Scotland and then King James I of England.

The next few years were years of trouble. Firstly her secretary was murdered then her husband. There were many who believed that Mary was in the plot to kill her husband, especially as she married again soon after. She was forced to give the crown to her son at Loch Leven castle and, after her escape, she fled to England.

Mary had made some bad mistakes. She was a beautiful young woman, who used her charm to get what she wanted but she eventually found herself an outcast. Later, when she was beheaded for plotting against Queen Elizabeth of England, there were some who felt that she got what she had been asking for.

There are many reminders in the Bible that the only way to live is uprightly. Here is one:

Bible Reading: Psalm 24: 1–6

O Lord Jesus Christ, who taught men how to live and who suffered through the plots of others; show us that we cannot obtain happiness or true riches by any means other than by living uprightly, honestly and lovingly; and that the greatest blessings come to those who give themselves in the service of others; in your name and for your sake. *Amen.**

Benediction No. 42

True values (2)

King Richard I

September 8th, 1157, was the birthday of King Richard the Lion-heart, King of England from 1189 to 1199.

Of all the kings of England, Richard I must rank as one of the most colourful and romantic, although very little of his reign was actually spent in England.

Richard was a Crusader, leading his armies into battle against those who had invaded the Holy Land. Many stories are told about Richard and the greatest of his enemies, Saladin, each of whom had great respect for the other.

We may recall how Richard was taken prisoner and how his faithful servant travelled through Europe as a minstrel until, passing a castle, he heard the voice of the King in reply from his prison. England had to pay £100,000 for his ransom, which was a huge sum of money then.

Although Richard could be very violent at times, he had many fine qualities, such as great valour and remarkable generosity. Yet, for all his qualities, Richard was a very poor king. He found it far more exciting to go crusading, and left England to the mercies of his evil brother, John, who later became the worst king England ever had.

Perhaps Richard failed to learn the lesson that many another has had to learn. Although there may be many exciting things to do in life, our first responsibility must be to do well any job which we have agreed to do.

Jesus had a parable to tell about those who failed to do their work properly:

Bible Reading: St. Matthew 24: 45–51

Give us, good Lord, a sense of responsibility toward those who should be able to rely upon us:
Our parents and the members of our family;
Those who have chosen us to be their friends;
Those whom we have promised to help.

Make us loyal and responsible to whatever cause we may have committed ourselves and to you, our God and Father; through Jesus Christ our Lord. *Amen.**

Closing prayer No. 5

True values (3)

St. Clare

One of the most important lessons in life is the need for self-control, much as an athlete has to control his habits. Listen to what St. Paul had to say:

Bible Reading: Ephesians 5: 15–21

Many followed his advice, including people like St. Francis, who gave up all luxuries as they tried to serve Jesus Christ. In St. Francis' home town of Assisi, there was a young girl who admired this way of life. Her name was Clare, a girl of noble birth, who could well have become very rich but decided at the age of eighteen to live the strict disciplined life of a nun.

Her family tried to dissuade her but she was determined. She wanted to live as St. Francis lived, with nothing to call her own and it was none other than St. Francis who suggested a way of life for Clare and others who joined her. It was the beginning of the order known as the Poor Ladies, now known as the Poor Clares.

Two or three years later, she obtained permission from the Pope for her ladies to live entirely on the gifts which they were given. No nuns had a harder life than the Poor Clares but they were happy in believing that this helped them to serve God.

Clare herself was sometimes far from well, but we find her always encouraging the other nuns, whom she led for forty years. She died in Assisi in 1253, after which she became known as St. Clare. Today, her feast day is kept each year on 12th August.

Almighty God, teach us this day in all things to remember thee, alike to serve thee and to praise thee in all our work and in all our leisure. Incline our hearts at all times to a firm self-control and a ready sympathy with the needs of others. May we meet the difficulties of life with courage, and by thy strength, resist every assault of evil; through Jesus Christ our Lord. *Amen.*

H. Bisseker

Closing prayer No. 22

True values (4)

Do you sometimes wonder how certain words came into our language? They have done so in many ways. Things which are bright and cheap, for example, we sometimes say are tawdry—a word which came to us through careless speaking.

October 17th was kept as a holy day in the Middle Ages in the city of Ely and a fair was held there in honour of St. Audrey. At this fair, a certain cheap kind of lace was sold, which became known as St. Audrey's lace but, as time passed, St. Audrey's lace became tawdry lace, and the word has been used ever since to mean something cheap or second-rate.

But who was St. Audrey? That was not her real name. Her real name was Etheldreda. Just as today we may call Robert, Bob or Margaret, Peggy, so in those days, girls named Etheldreda were called Audrey by their friends.

Etheldreda was a princess, daughter of a king of East Anglia. Against her will she was made to marry twice. Her first husband died after three years and her second agreed to end the marriage. Etheldreda went to Ely, where she founded a nunnery, remaining its head until she died about A.D. 672.

Sixteen years later, when a new church was built there, the coffin of St. Etheldreda was moved into it on 17th October, the day which became the holy day in Ely.

In Norman times, the great cathedral at Ely was built on the same site. St. Etheldreda, or Audrey, may have given us the word 'tawdry' but there is nothing tawdry about the great cathedral, which was built there for the glory of God.

But then man has always offered his best for the glory of God.

O God, by whom many people have been inspired to give their best in your service; help us to remember that every gift we possess comes from you and that we should dedicate ourselves and our talents to you. May we offer to you nothing that is tawdry or second-rate, remembering that you gave your best to us. We ask this in the Name of our Lord Jesus Christ. *Amen.**

Closing prayer No. 11

True values (5)

William Cowper

William Cowper, who was born on 15th November, 1731, had a very troubled life, which was full of ups and downs. There were times when he walked with his head in the clouds and others when he was in the depths of despair.

Sometimes, when he was in his blackest moods, he felt like committing suicide. Once, it is said, he hailed a cab and asked to be driven to the river, but it became so foggy that the driver lost his way. Instead of finding the river, Cowper found himself back at his own house.

There were other times when he lost his senses and had to spend some time in a mental asylum. At other times, he was able to write fine poetry, full of fun as in *John Gilpin*, or full of drama.

When he was thirty-six, he went to live in the little town of Olney, Buckinghamshire, where he made friends with the rector, Rev. John Newton, who had once been a sailor in a slave ship. Often the rector would kneel in prayer with the poet to bring him through a bad spell.

Between them they composed a number of hymns, known as the Olney hymns. Cowper wrote sixty-seven of them, some being classed with the greatest hymns. One of the best known of these suggests how Cowper longed for the peace and quiet mind which God can give.

> *O for a closer walk with God,*
> *A calm and heavenly frame,*
> *A light to shine upon the road*
> *That leads me to the Lamb.*

St. Paul also writes of the peace of God:

Bible Reading: Philippians 4: 6–9

Grant unto us, O Lord, that our walk through life may be close to you, and give us a perfect trust in you so that our minds may be free from worry or fear and we may know the joy, the sense of calm and the peace of mind, which comes to all who truly know you; through Jesus Christ, to whom be the glory for ever. *Amen.**

Benediction No. 46

Humility (1)

St. Francis de Sales

It is all too easy to consider ourselves to be of greater importance than we really are.

Bible Reading: St. Luke 18: 9–14

The Pharisee in this story fell into the trap of thinking himself to be much better than the publican (tax collector). History has many tales to tell of people who became too big-headed. It is all the more pleasant, therefore, to learn of people who were important but were also humble. One such person, Francis de Sales, was born on 21st August, 1567.

He was born into a wealthy family and attended university before deciding to become a priest. His first work was particularly difficult, for he was sent to his home district to try to change the minds of those people who had turned away from the church.

In four years he met with great success because, as he said, 'whoever preaches with love preaches effectively'. A few years later, he was given the very important position of Bishop of Geneva. But he did not want to let this go to his head. Instead, he said 'I must be Bishop of Geneva in public, but Francis de Sales in private.'

Throughout his life he tried to show that an ordinary life can become holy if everything is done as though for God.

He died at the age of 55, worn out with all the work that he had done. One of the greatest tributes to him came from the minister of a church that had broken away from the Roman Catholic Church.

'If we honoured any man as a saint, I know of no one since the days of the apostles more worthy of it than this man.'

Teach us, good Lord, never to rate ourselves more highly than we ought but to be humble, remembering that all we have is a gift from you. Show us how to use our talents aright so that through them we may give glory to you and help to those that are around us. Guide us by your Holy Spirit, so that we may live according to the example of our Lord and Master, Jesus Christ. *Amen.**

Closing prayer No. 23

Humility (1)

Humility (2)

St. Chad

Jesus told this parable as a warning to those who held a very high opinion of themselves.

Bible Reading: St. Luke 14: 7–11

Long ago in Saxon England, lived four brothers, all of whom were priests. One, named Cedd, became abbot of Lastingham Abbey, in Yorkshire and, when he left to become bishop, his brother Chad took his place.

Chad later became Bishop of York and set himself to study and to preach but unfortunately there had been something wrong with the way in which he was made bishop and the archbishop had to tell him so.

Chad was very humble and replied to the archbishop, 'I willingly resign the office, for I never thought myself worthy of it; but though unworthy I submitted out of obedience to undertake it.'

The archbishop was so impressed by Chad that he later made him Bishop of Mercia, the large kingdom that then covered the centre of England. Chad lived at Lichfield in Staffordshire and faithfully carried out his duties.

He was still very humble, so much so that he always travelled on foot until the archbishop insisted that he ride a horse. Near his church, he built a small place in which he could pray and study with others whenever there was opportunity.

Chad died at Lichfield on 2nd March, 672 and this day is now kept in memory of St. Chad. The remains of this humble bishop now lie in the magnificent cathedral at Lichfield, which was built nearly five hundred years after the saint's death.

O Lord Jesus Christ, who taught us that the humble will be exalted and the proud cast down, and who, by your own example, taught us humility; help us never to think of ourselves more highly than we ought, nor to become proud of ourselves or what we have been able to do, but to remember that we are what we are by the grace of God by whom we have been given all our talents and abilities, and to him be the glory for ever. *Amen.**

Closing prayer No. 6

Humility (3)

Gipsy Smith

Do we sometimes despise humble or simple things and think they do not matter? Paul wrote that God often uses such things for his work.

Bible Reading: 1 Corinthians 1: 26–29

Gipsies are seldom welcomed where other people live for they have earned themselves a reputation for untidiness and sometimes dishonesty. So, in 1860, a gipsy family named Smith camped near Epping Forest and it was there, on 31st March, that Rodney was born.

Like other gipsies he loved the open air. He never went to school but helped the family to make and sell pegs. He was still only a lad when his mother died.

A few years later came an important change in the family. Rodney's father became a Christian and decided to change his ways. No more would he drink, steal or swear. The change was so remarkable that Rodney, too, became a Christian.

He bought a Bible, but could not read, so he had to learn how. He also sang and preached short addresses to which people liked to listen. When he was seventeen, he was invited to preach and work at a mission in London. Gradually he learned to read better, sometimes spending whole mornings reading and praying and the evenings in preaching.

From London, he went to other towns, where hundreds of people gathered to hear him. By this time he was known as Gipsy Smith— a name which was sure to draw big crowds, not only in Britain but in America too.

But although he mixed with important people, he never forgot, nor allowed others to forget his humble childhood, and for all his blessings he never ceased to thank God.

Almighty God, who resisteth the proud, but giveth grace to the humble, grant that we may never be lifted up by pride, nor exalt ourselves above others; but serving thee with a meek and humble heart, may always use thy gifts to thy honour and glory, through Jesus Christ our Lord. *Amen.*

Source not known

Closing prayer No. 5

Humility (4)

There have been sixteen Popes named Gregory, the first and greatest of them, often referred to as Gregory the Great, is remembered by the church on 12th March.

He was born of well-to-do parents in Rome, where, for some years, he was an important magistrate. He showed a great interest in monasteries and gave large sums of money for starting a new monastery in Rome and several others in Sicily.

When he was about thirty-five, Gregory decided to become a monk himself and, some years later, was chosen to be Pope, the first monk ever to hold that high office. For fourteen years as Pope, he worked to make the church stronger and he wrote many books and letters about religious matters.

For one thing he is particularly remembered by the people of Britain. In the days before he became Pope, it is said that he was walking through Rome when he noticed some slave children who were up for sale. Being attracted by their fair hair and skin, he asked where they had come from. 'They are Angles,' was the reply. 'Not Angles, but Angels,' was Gregory's comment.

He vowed to set off himself in order to teach the English people about Christ but he was not permitted to do so. But he never forgot and, once he had become Pope, he sent Augustine and other monks to teach the English.

Though Gregory was a great man, he remembered the words of Jesus that the greatest must be the servant of all and so he called himself 'the servant of the servants of God'—a title used by all Popes since then.

Bible Reading: St. Mark 10: 42–45

This is, perhaps, the most difficult lesson that we have to learn if we would be Christ's disciples.

O God our Father, who taught us through Christ that he who would be greatest in the Kingdom of Heaven must be the servant of all, help us not to think too highly of ourselves but to be ready to serve our fellows; and grant that in service we may find our true reward; through Jesus Christ our Lord. *Amen.**

Closing prayer No. 8

Humility (5)

John Newton was born in London on 24th July, 1725. His father was a very strict sea captain: his mother died when he was seven: he was so badly treated at boarding school that he was glad to run away to sea, which was a hard life in those days.

A few years later, he was caught by a press-gang and forced to serve on a naval ship, which he hated. He was foully treated, deserted, recaptured and placed in irons. Then he obtained permission to transfer to a slave ship.

By this time his behaviour was abominable; he refused to obey orders; his attitude was most unpleasant; he had long since vowed that God did not exist and that he would never go to church or read the Bible. John Newton had sunk about as low as it was possible for a man to sink.

One day he picked up a book which had been left lying about and he glanced through it. It was called *Of the Imitation of Christ*. The words he read struck him very hard and he began to wonder what he should do.

That evening his ship was battered by a violent storm. 'I am too late,' he thought. 'How can God possibly forgive all that I have done?' By morning the gale had died away, the ship was still afloat, and John Newton was a changed man.

It was then that he learned the truth of the words of Jesus. God would forgive anyone who called upon him.

Bible Reading: St. Luke 15: 1–7

Soon afterwards Newton left the sea to become a minister of religion. He became a great preacher, the writer of some well-loved hymns, and one who used his energies to help abolish the slave trade.

Almighty God, our heavenly Father, who of thy great mercy hast promised forgiveness of sins to all them that with hearty repentance and true faith turn unto thee, have mercy upon us; pardon and deliver us from all our sins; confirm and strengthen us in all goodness, and bring us to everlasting life; through Jesus Christ our Lord. *Amen.*

The Book of Common Prayer (adapted)

Closing prayer No. 21

7 Christian Service

The theme of Christian Service develops the previous theme to consider how sincere religious belief should be translated into practical service. Again, there is no desire to suggest that these forms of service are exclusively Christian. They are the attitudes that one should expect of a Christian but also of many others who have a genuine concern for others. There are fourteen themes of five topics:

Concern for others	*When I needed a neighbour*
Called by God	*Make up your mind*
Nothing is impossible	*Giving of one's best*
Good use of talents	*Into God's hands*
Self-denial	*Saints and martyrs*
Saints	*More saints*
Service	*'Go ye into all the world . . .'*

Some of the topics are intended partly to be used in connexion with appeals that may be made from time to time as in Christian Aid Week or for specific Christmas charities. Others are those which teach by the example of those who have offered themselves in the name of God and have devoted their lives to his service.

The last five sections are of topics less closely related than others in the book and they may be readily used as individual stories rather than as themes.

Concern for others (1)

St. Vincent de Paul

Bible Reading: St. Matthew 20: 29–34

This is just one story in which we read that Jesus was deeply moved by people in distress. But Jesus showed that being sorry was not enough if there was something more that could be done.

Many people, following his example, have also been moved to help the less fortunate. One such is St. Vincent de Paul, remembered each year on 19th July. He was a farmer's son who became world famous.

Trained as a priest, he was captured by pirates, sold in a slave market and set to work by his owner, whom he later persuaded to become a Christian. Back in France he eventually became chaplain to the galley-slaves—wretched prisoners who were chained to the oars of the king's galleys and lashed mercilessly if they did not row hard enough.

Having been a slave, Vincent could feel for them more than most. Once he learned of a prisoner who was particularly distressed. Vincent quietly released him and took his place at the oar. What a to-do there was when the Chaplain of the Galleys was found chained to an oar. The convicts came to love and to trust him.

Vincent found many others who also needed help. Paris was full of beggars, unwanted children, old folk and sick. Vincent did what few others could have done. Not only did he persuade rich people to give him money: he actually persuaded them to give their lives to the service of those who were in need.

> Jesus, Friend of the friendless,
> Helper of the poor, healer of the sick,
> Whose life was spent in doing good,
> Let me follow in thy footsteps.
> Make me strong to do right, gentle with the weak,
> And kind to all who are in sorrow;
> That I may be like thee,
> My dear Lord and Master. *Amen.*

The Daily Service

Closing prayer No. 16

Concern for others (2)

When St. Paul wrote to the Romans, he told them how anxious he was to visit Rome because he believed he could help them, as he had helped others, to learn of Jesus Christ.

Bible Reading: Romans 1: 8–12

St. Paul wanted to make his journey to help those who were Christian. A few hundred years later, another man wanted to make a journey because he believed he could help people who were not Christian. His name was Aidan and the people he longed to visit were those living in the north of England called Northumbria.

A missionary to these people from Iona, a Christian settlement on the west of Scotland, had returned to say that the people were so savage that nothing could be done. Aidan was thoughtful, then spoke up.

'Perhaps our brother has been too harsh with them. After all, you feed babies on milk, not meat. He may have taught things which they could not understand.'

So it was agreed that another attempt should be made, this time by Aidan. From headquarters which he set up on Holy Island or Lindisfarne, he travelled far and wide on foot. Never did he force himself upon the people but taught by acts of kindness.

It is said that the king once gave Aidan a horse so that he could travel more easily, but Aidan gave the horse to a beggar. The king was angry, but no one could remain angry with Aidan for long.

Each year on 31st August, the church remembers St. Aidan, who won many for Christ by his sincere and gentle living and by his obvious concern for their well-being.

Teach us, O Lord, that it is not what we say that is important but what we are; that it is not what we believe but what we do about our beliefs; that it is not what we know should be done but whether we are willing to do it. Help us, by the power of your Spirit, to live and act in sincerity, gentleness and love; so that we may show by our lives whose we are and whom we serve; through Christ our Lord. *Amen.**

Benediction No. 43

Concern for others (3)

St. John Bosco

There is an old proverb 'A friend in need is a friend indeed'. From earliest times, poor and needy people have looked to others to help them in their times of need. Here is some advice given early in the Old Testament:

Bible Reading: Deuteronomy 15: 7–8 and 10–11

In 1841, John Bosco, who had just become a priest in Turin, Italy, did not have to look far to find people in need of help. Many were boys and young men who had left their country homes to find work in the city. He could see that they needed education, religious teaching and a place for recreation. Some were already what we would call juvenile delinquents and needed a fresh start.

John Bosco had no building, so he borrowed one to start his work in. Before long he had a large school, a boarding-house for apprentices, workshops and a church—all of it obtained by begging and by sheer hard work. In these he had no less than seven hundred young men, even the worst of them being won over by his cheerful attitude and his readiness to put himself out for them.

Many Christian people came forward to help him and later went to other parts of the world to do similar work. In 1872, with the help of Mary Mazarello, he began a similar work among girls.

He died in Turin on 31st January, 1888, and it is on 31st January each year that the church remembers St. John Bosco—the man who saw that something needed to be done and spared no effort to become a real friend to those in need.

Almighty God, we thank you for giving us various talents which can be used in your service for the benefit of other people. Help us to know what we can do so that we may live useful lives as you intended us to; after the example of the one who always went about doing good, Jesus Christ our Lord. *Amen.**

Benediction No. 42

Concern for others (4)

WHY ME? *Christian Aid*

How much thought do we give to other people who are less fortunate than ourselves?

Jesus once told a story about two men which begins like this:

Bible Reading: St. Luke 16: 19–21

Here was a rich man who had all that he needed and a poor man who begged even for a crust of bread. No doubt the rich man thought, 'Why should I help him. He is nothing to do with me!' The answer to such a question is that if the rich man did not help him there was no one else who could.

We do not have to look far to find people who are poorer than ourselves, yet even these are rich compared with people living in some parts of the world, especially in parts of Asia and Africa, where people exist on a handful of rice a day or on grubs and roots which they dig from the ground. Some live in huts or even in old packing cases. Few of them can expect to reach old age.

Moreover, the countries in which they live can do little about it. They have very little money and not much with which to trade. That is why the governments of countries like Britain which have money give some to help. That is why individual people are also asked to give.

There are various organizations which help to raise and send money. One, particularly associated with the Church is Christian Aid. Each year in Christian Aid Week, money is collected in many ways to help those who are in need and cannot help themselves.

Almighty God, we ask your blessing upon all who seek to help those who are unable to help themselves. [At this time we ask a special blessing upon ...] We pray that those in need will be strengthened and encouraged, and that those who help them will know the joy that comes in serving others; through Jesus Christ our Lord. *Amen.**

Closing prayer No. 14

Concern for others (5)

Christmas is a time of goodwill, when we give and receive presents and send greetings to our friends and people we may not have seen for some time.

It is also the season when we especially remember people in need of help. There are many ways of doing this. Look inside the Christmas cards which come into your house and you may find that some have been sold in aid of a good cause. Examine the Christmas seals which are stuck on envelopes and parcels to see whether these were bought to help anyone. Look on shop counters and you will find collecting boxes or stockings in which money can be placed.

Carol singers, too, often collect for a charitable organization. In all these ways, people are able to help those in trouble or who are ill in this land or overseas.

There are so many people who are in need that it is difficult to decide which to help. There are people who are homeless or hungry; there are people who suffer ill health and there are scientists who need money for research to find new cures; there are children who have no homes and others who are physically handicapped. Each year we are asked for help by many organizations which must rely upon the goodwill of many people if they are to continue their work.

(Details of this year's special appeal)

One thing is sure. Whatever we do for other people we are offering as a gift to Christ himself. He once said, 'Inasmuch as ye have done it unto one of the least of these my brethren, ye have done it unto me'.

We praise you, God our Father, for all that you have given us. Hear our prayer for those who are distressed,—the poor, the sick, the bed-ridden, the hungry, the homeless, the prisoner, the orphan and the friendless. Put into our hearts at this happy time of Christmas a desire to help those in need: [Bless what we do now to help . . .]: and accept what we give as a thank-offering to you; for the sake of Jesus Christ our Lord. *Amen.**

Closing prayer No. 27

Concern for others (5)   335

When I needed a neighbour (1)

HELPING THE PRISONER   *John Howard*

Bible Reading: St. Matthew 25: 31–40

Some of the greatest people in history have been those who have offered friendship and help to those in need.

Take John Howard, for example—a man who was concerned about conditions in which prisoners lived and was anxious to improve them. His interest in prisons had begun when he himself had been imprisoned—for no other reason than that he was a passenger on an English ship that had been captured by the French when the two countries were at war.

Howard learned what it was like to live in damp, dark prisons in dreadful conditions, with little food and with bullying gaolers. It was a lesson that he would remember and one that was to have very far-reaching results.

Nearly twenty years later, he was made High Sheriff of Bedford and had opportunity to visit prisons in that area. He was horrified. There were prisoners declared innocent but not released because they had no money to pay the fees demanded by their gaolers.

Howard determined to see what conditions were like elsewhere and he travelled from town to town, visiting prisons and making notes which he then laid before Parliament. At once laws were passed to improve the prisoners' lot. Later he visited Europe too.

John Howard died on 20th January, 1790, while still seeking to help his fellows. A statue was later erected to him in St. Paul's Cathedral in recognition of his services to prisoners and other sufferers. The work of prison reform goes on to this day.

O God, the loving Father of all men, hear our prayers for all those confined to prisons and for those who suffer in any way today, some because of what they have done and others through no fault of their own. Keep us mindful of the sufferings and needs of others and help us to work for the coming of your kingdom of love; through Jesus Christ our Lord. *Amen.**

Closing prayer No. 15

When I needed a neighbour (2)

Father Damien

On 3rd January, 1840, Joseph de Vuester was born in a poor peasant home near Louvain, Belgium. Nineteen years or so later, he went to visit an older brother who was training as a Roman Catholic priest and he decided there and then that he would do likewise.

His brother was going as a missionary to the Pacific but, at the last moment, was taken ill. Joseph begged to be allowed to take his brother's place. So, at the age of twenty-four, he said farewell to his family and friends whom he would never see again. He was about to do what he believed God wanted him to do under the name of Father Damien.

He found plenty to do on the Hawaiian Islands but one thing grieved him greatly. Some people became lepers and were sent to the island of Molokai, from which there was no return. He had compassion on the lepers, much as Christ had in his day.

Bible Reading: St. Matthew 8: 1–4

Damien could not heal the lepers but he could help them. He asked if he might become priest to the lepers. On Molokai he found a wretched, hopeless group of people. His first task was to improve their living conditions. Houses were built; water pipes were laid; medical aid was given; and a church was built. Twelve years later, Father Damien caught leprosy from which he died.

He had not given his life in vain, for the news spread and people sought a cure for leprosy. Today the disease can be controlled and cured in leper hospitals in those lands where the disease still exists.

Father we thank you for the unselfish example of all who have faced danger or death for the sake of their fellows. We thank you for all who have worked for the relief of disease and pain. We pray for all who today suffer from leprosy or from other dreadful diseases and for all who work among them to cure or comfort; through Jesus Christ our Lord. *Amen.**

Closing prayer No. 7

When I needed a neighbour (3)

HELPING THE BLIND   *Sir Arthur Pearson*

Bible Reading: St. Matthew 9: 27–31

Many blind people owe a debt of gratitude to a man who was himself blind. Poor sight had hindered Arthur Pearson even at school. He loved cricket but could only bowl because he could not see to bat or field.

At eighteen, he went to work in an office of a magazine. Six years later, he branched out to publish his own magazine, *Pearson's Weekly*. Before he was thirty he had other magazines and was a wealthy man.

This gave him an opportunity to do something that he had wanted very much to do. He started a Fresh Air Fund to raise money to take poor children from the East End of London for outings. Thousands were taken to Epping Forest for day visits and thousands of others were given country holidays.

Gradually his sight became worse until he was completely blind. He was now Sir Arthur Pearson and he joined the National Institute for the Blind. Through his magazines he drew attention to the blind and was able to raise large sums of money for them.

Two years later, he met some soldiers, blinded in the war, and felt that he must do something for them. A house was opened in London for four blind men. Before long there were hundreds of blinded soldiers in a home called St. Dunstan's, learning how to live a new full life.

Sir Arthur Pearson died suddenly on 9th September, 1921, but St. Dunstan's is very much alive—a fitting memorial to a great man and a neighbour to many.

O God our Father, we thank you for eyes to see the beauties of your world. Bless those who cannot see and help them to find their enjoyment through hearing and feeling. Guide all who work on their behalf to provide guide dogs, Braille books, and such other aids as the blind may need to lead full, useful and enjoyable lives, to the glory of your holy Name. *Amen.**

Closing prayer No. 38

When I needed a neighbour (4)

HELPING THE NEEDY   *Earl of Shaftesbury*

Bible Reading: St. Matthew 19: 16–22

As Anthony Ashley Cooper walked down the hill from Harrow school, he saw the rough coffin of a poor man being carried up the hill by a group of drunken men. He was horrified as one of them stumbled so that the coffin went crashing to the ground.

There and then he made a promise. 'Henceforth, with God's help, I will give my life to help the poor and friendless.'

His opportunity came in later years when, as Lord Ashley, he became a Member of Parliament. He gave up all chances of holding an important position in the government by his willingness to be a champion of the poor, thus making himself unpopular.

In those days, children worked long hours in factories and mines. Many were ill-treated and forced to work hard. They suffered from bad health and many died at an early age. Lord Ashley took up the challenge.

Firstly he had their hours reduced to twelve per day and then ten. He fought for better conditions for women and children in the mines. He stopped the use of little boys as chimney sweeps. He demanded that poor children should have the right to go to school instead of being forced to work in the fields.

By this time his father had died and Lord Ashley became the Earl of Shaftesbury but he never forgot his promise. When he died on 1st October, 1885, poor people in many places mourned the loss of a real friend.

Today his work is continued by a Shaftesbury Society, which helps those in need—the young and the old who are poor or disabled.

We thank you, O God, for all who have laboured to improve living or working conditions and have been able to recognize the needs of others. Make us aware of the problems of today and ready to do what we can to make our land and the world the better; for Jesus Christ's sake. *Amen.**

Closing prayer No. 39

When I needed a neighbour (5)

HELPING THE HUNGRY   *Oxfam*

Bible Reading: St. Mark 6: 35–44

In that story we read how Jesus had compassion on the hungry people who had been listening to him and in a miraculous way was able to feed them.

Today there are millions of hungry people in the world but no miraculous way of providing them with food or other daily needs. Someone has to pay for anything that is sent to help them.

Yet the story of one group of people and their work may appear little short of a miracle. Many years ago, in 1942, a group of people in Oxford learned that children were starving in Greece and they thought they could raise a little money to help them. They formed a committee known as the Oxford Committee for Famine Relief and they began raising money in a variety of ways.

In time, this particular need came to an end but the work of the committee went on, raising money that could be used to help people in other parts of the world. The work spread from Oxford to many other centres. Thousands of volunteers collected money from their friends; shops were opened for the sale of anything that had been given for this purpose; young and old alike found all sorts of ways to raise money. The Oxford Committee for Famine Relief, which was rather a mouthful, became simply Oxfam, world famous for its relief work.

Perhaps one might say that the miracle is that Oxfam has persuaded so many people to put their hands in their pockets to help those in far off places whose need is really desperate.

Hear our prayer, O God, for the hungry and starving people of the world; for the homeless and the refugee; for the sick and diseased and for all who are in distress. Bless all who make themselves neighbours to such as these—the relief organizations and all doctors, nurses, teachers, scientists and others who have readily offered their services. We ask it in the Name of Jesus Christ our Lord. *Amen.**

Benediction No. 44

Called by God (1)

St. Peter

Simon the fisherman had already been introduced by his brother to Jesus but it was by the side of the Sea of Galilee one day that he became a true disciple.

Bible Reading: St. Luke 5: 1–11

For some time after that, Simon and the other disciples travelled the country with Jesus as he taught, healed and helped people. Then, one day, Jesus asked who the disciples thought he was. Simon answered, 'You are the Christ, the Son of the living God'.

Jesus said to him, 'You are Cephas (a rock) and on this rock I will build my church'. The Greek word for 'rock' becomes Peter in English, and it is by this name that Simon is better known.

Peter, with James and John, shared more time in private with Jesus than any of the other disciples. They were with him on the mountain; they were with him in Gethsemane. Peter was the disciple who drew his sword to defend Jesus but denied him only a short time later.

Jesus's last commission to Peter was to 'Feed his lambs'. This Peter did as well as he was able, becoming one of the leaders of the early Christian Church.

We can read in the Bible how Peter helped other people to know God and we have there two letters which he wrote. Tradition says that Peter eventually went to Rome and there he was crucified in the time of Nero, asking that he be crucified upside down because he was not worthy to die in the same way as his master.

St. Peter is always remembered as the fisherman who left his boats and fished for men. His feast day is 29th June.

We thank you, O Lord, for the example of your servants of old, who readily forsook all they had in answer to your call. Give us open ears to hear you speak and help us to be ready to obey your commands. May we too first learn from you and then teach others, both by our words and by our example; for the sake of Jesus Christ our Lord. *Amen.**

Benediction No. 50

Called by God (2)

St. Cedd

Jesus demanded much from those who would follow Him.

Bible Reading: St. Matthew 16: 24–26

In the many centuries since that happened, there have been many who have given up everything in order to be counted as followers of Jesus.

Some have given up possessions; some have left home and family; some have even lost their lives. These have not been forgotten. Many have become known as saints and have a special day each year on which they are remembered. It is known as their feast day.

January 7th is the feast day of St. Cedd, who is remembered as one of the early missionaries in Britain. He was one of four brothers living in the north of England, all of whom became Christian. With his brother Chad, Cedd went to live in the monastery at Lindisfarne, where they learned from a very great Christian, St. Aidan.

Cedd was one of four priests who were sent to the people living in the part of England which we call the Midlands, then known as Mercia. Later he went to the East Saxons (Essex) and was so successful that he was appointed to be their bishop.

During these years amongst the East Saxons, Cedd was responsible for founding a number of monasteries and churches.

Sometimes he liked to travel north to visit a monastery at Lastingham in Yorkshire, which he had started many years before. It was on one of these visits that he caught plague and died, leaving many people of the East Saxons very sad at heart.

O God, our Father, we thank you that there have been many who answered your call and gave their lives in your service. Bless all who continue their work today so that they may work for your glory and for the coming of your kingdom. Show us what you would have us do and make us willing; for Jesus Christ's sake. *Amen.**

Benediction No. 52

Called by God (3)

David Livingstone

It was 10th November, 1871 and in Africa. The explorer parted the crowd of people and walked slowly toward the man he had been looking for. He noticed that the man was pale, looked worried and was clearly not in the best of health. He noticed the bluish cap with its faded gold band, the red-sleeved waistcoat and the pair of grey tweed trousers. So this was the great explorer who had helped to make Africa known to the world!

The explorer, Henry Morton Stanley, walked deliberately forward, took off his hat, and spoke the words which have become famous, 'Doctor Livingstone, I presume?'

After years of exploring in Africa, David Livingstone had reached the village of Ujiji, wondering how he could possibly go any further. The arrival of Stanley put new life into the tired explorer.

Livingstone had first gone to Africa as a missionary thirty years before. His adventures had begun in South Africa but he did not stay there for long. He journeyed northwards until he reached the Zambezi River. Then he travelled first to the west and then to the east, crossing the whole of Africa. Now, at Ujiji, his work was almost at an end. He died only a year and a half later.

During his time in Africa, Livingstone had explored and mapped lands unknown before to Europeans; he had fought the evils of the slave trade with all the power at his disposal; and he had helped many to know the God whom he served faithfully all his life.

Almighty God, Father of all people, we thank you for those who carried the Gospel to the ends of the earth and for those who continue their work today. We think of the people of lands where they worked, and especially those of Africa and Asia with their many problems. Grant that your blessing may rest upon all who work to bring peace and prosperity to these lands; in the name and for the sake of Jesus Christ our Lord. *Amen.**

Closing prayer No. 24

Called by God (4)

George Fox was born in 1624 in the village of Fenny Drayton, Leicestershire. His father was a weaver and George was himself apprenticed to a shoemaker.

But George was a very troubled young man. He heard talk of religion from men who were ready to fight each other; he saw much that was evil or unpleasant all around him; and he wondered what was the right way to live his life.

Finding no one who could answer his questions, he left his job and wandered the country trying to find someone who could. Then one day it suddenly dawned on him. There was no man who could help him, but Jesus Christ could help anyone, no matter what his condition.

Suddenly George Fox realized that he need look no further. In fact here was something to talk about. He must tell others of the peace which he had found. He spoke in the markets; he spoke at the fairs; he spoke in the churches; in fact he even interrupted preachers in the churches.

Fox and those who followed him recalled the words of Jesus: 'Ye are my friends if ye do whatsoever I command you'. They called themselves Friends of Truth.

Several times Fox was arrested and tried. Once he called upon everyone present to 'quake and tremble at the word of the Lord'. The judge referred to him as a 'Quaker' and the name stuck. To this day, members of the Society of Friends are known as Quakers.

Fox died on 13th January, 1691, leaving behind him a movement which has had a very great influence on the world, for the Quakers have been responsible for some very important reforms.

O God, Father of all, we pray for the guidance of your Holy Spirit so that we may learn to live as you would have us live:
Honest with ourselves;
At peace with our neighbours;
Faithful to you;
For Jesus Christ's sake. *Amen.**

Closing prayer No. 25

Called by God (5)

William Booth

William Booth, who was born in Nottingham on 10th April, 1829, know what it was to be poor. He was apprenticed to a pawnbroker and received precious little money for himself. He also saw the misery of those who came into his shop to pawn their posssessions to borrow money for that day's food.

His apprenticeship over, he moved to London, where he began to preach. He became minister of a church but resigned so that he could work among the very poor and wretched people in the worst parts of the East End of London.

He was shouted down, laughed at, mocked and beaten up but nothing would stop him. For thirteen years he worked tirelessly to win these very people for Jesus Christ.

Then he had an inspiration. He had many things to battle against and to fight you need an army. So he called his mission the Salvation Army and he put all his 'soldiers' in uniform.

Often they were attacked by mobs; their instruments were destroyed; they were ridiculed—but their ranks grew and branches were started in other parts of the country. Little by little, people came to respect the Salvation Army for they discovered how much good it was doing,—sheltering the homeless, feeding the hungry, showing people how to live a new and useful life.

General Booth died in 1912 but his work goes on. People in many towns and villages are familiar with the music and preaching of the Army in the streets on Sundays, whilst throughout the world it continues its great social work of feeding, clothing, housing, helping, and, above all, pointing the way to God.

We ask your blessing O God, upon the work of the Salvation Army and other organizations which bring comfort and help to those in distress. May they find joy in service, knowing that whatever they do for others is done for you; and grant that your love may be seen in all that is done in your Name; through Jesus Christ our Lord. *Amen.**

Closing prayer No. 16

Make up your mind (1)

There are many people who can play the piano but not all of them are able to play in such a way that those who listen are carried away by the music which they play. It takes a real master musician to be able to do that.

One such pianist was the Polish pianist and composer Paderewski, who was born on 18th November, 1860 and who has been described as one of the finest piano players who ever lived. He could play the piano when he was only three; at twelve he went to Warsaw to study; and at eighteen he became professor at the Warsaw Conservatoire (School of Music), having already toured eastern Europe. In later years he played through western Europe. and in America, being greatly admired wherever he went.

In those days his country, Poland, was under the Russians but that changed during the First World War. Paderewski took some hand in the shaping of his county and, when it became a republic in 1919, Paderewski was its first Prime Minister.

This, however, was not to last for long. He resigned from office at the end of the same year and gave up politics shortly afterwards. He was a musician and he knew that to remain a first-class musician he must give more time to it than politics would allow. He had to choose one or the other.

In life we are often faced with choices like this, one of the most important being whether we are to give enough time to our service of God. This is what Jesus had to say:

Bible Reading: St. Matthew 6: 24 (or 24–34)

O God our Father
Help us to know what you want us to do;
Help us to choose the right and reject the wrong;
Help us keep the right always in mind:
Then give us strength to do it
And determination to pursue it
  To our life's end. *Amen.**

Closing prayer No. 6

Make up your mind (2)

John Knox

One of the best-known figures in Scotland a little over four hundred years ago was a bearded preacher who had some very strong ideas and was not afraid to speak them even to the Queen.

His name was John Knox. Although he had been brought up a Roman Catholic, he had done some deep thinking and concluded that he could not agree that the Church was right in its teachings. Nor did he believe that the Pope should be head of the Church in Scotland.

Once he was captured by the French and made to work as a convict on the galleys for about a year until the King of England obtained his release and made him one of his chaplains. The King, Edward VI, had similar beliefs to those held by Knox.

Then Queen Mary, who was a Catholic came to the throne. Knox feared for his life and made his way to Switzerland where he worked with other Protestant leaders. While there, he wrote an attack on women who ruled over countries, especially the Queen of Scotland and her daughter who wished Scotland to remain Roman Catholic.

In 1559, Knox returned to Scotland, where he preached, argued and fought hard for the new Protestant ideas. The Scottish government took notice of him and passed laws to say that the Pope was no longer head of the Scottish Church.

John Knox died in Edinburgh on 24th November, 1572, knowing that he had won his battle.

Whether or not we agree with John Knox, we have to admire a man who made up his mind and then had the courage to speak boldly about his beliefs without fearing the consequences of his words.

O thou, who art the Way, the Truth, and the Life, make thy way plain before our face. Teach us to live boldly, that we may be free from fear or favour, strong in thy love and power. *Amen.*

The Splendour of God

Closing prayer No. 8

Make up your mind (3)

DON'T BE PUT OFF   *St. Thomas More*

It was not necessarily a good thing to become a close friend of King Henry the Eighth, as several people discovered. The King could be very friendly if it suited him to be so but he could not bear to be crossed.

One who discovered this was Thomas More, who rose to hold very high office and held the King's favour. He was a lawyer, Member of Parliament, scholar and author. After several other important posts, he was appointed Lord Chancellor of England.

As a judge he was known for his absolute fairness and he would allow no man to stand in the way of justice. As a man he was gay, friendly and humorous. His friends were among the greatest in the land.

At the time he reached the height of his career, King Henry made it known that he wished to put away his wife, Catherine of Aragon, so that he could marry Anne Boleyn. When the Pope refused him permission to do so, Henry declared that he was now head of the Church in England so that he could have what he wanted.

Like many others, Thomas More disagreed with the King's action. He let it be known and he resigned as Lord Chancellor. Two years later, in 1534, he was arrested, imprisoned in the Tower of London and condemned to death.

On 7th July, before he was beheaded, he declared that he was 'the King's good servant—but God's first'. To the end he allowed no threat to make him agree to what he believed to be wrong.

In the Bible the psalmist gives a reminder that it is better to trust in God than in princes:

Bible Reading: Psalm 146

O Lord, we beseech thee mercifully to receive the prayers of thy people which call upon thee, and grant that they may both perceive and know what things they ought to do, and also may have grace and power faithfully to fulfil the same; through Jesus Christ our Lord. *Amen.*

Gregorian Sacramentary

Closing prayer No. 33 (a prayer of St. Thomas More)

Make up your mind (4)

St. Matthias

About one hundred and twenty of the disciples of Jesus were met together in the upper room of a house in Jerusalem, praying and wondering what would be the next thing for them to do. Before Jesus had left them, He had told them to wait until they were given the power of the Holy Spirit.

Then Peter stood up and reminded the others that there were only eleven apostles left instead of twelve because Judas had killed himself. They needed another, he said, who would take the place of Judas but it must be someone who had been with the apostles from the time when Jesus had been baptized by John until the day he had ascended into heaven.

They found that there were two—Joseph Barsabas and Matthias —but which one to choose? They decided that they must ask God to guide them in their choice. They would cast lots ... today we might say toss up for it ... but ask God to influence their decision so that it would be the right person for doing God's work.

Bible Reading: Acts of the Apostles 1: 23–26

So Matthias was chosen. Like some of the other apostles, he does not appear again in the Bible story and nothing certain is known about him. One legend tells that he worked in Ethiopia and another that he worked in Jerusalem. It is also probable that he was put to death for his Christian faith. He is now remembered as St. Matthias and his feast day is 24th February.

O God our Father, there are lots of things that we have to make up our minds about and the decision is not always easy. Help us to remember the example of your people of old and turn to you for guidance. Help us to place our trust in you, for you know much more about us than we know about ourselves. Let your will be done in our lives for Jesus Christ's sake. *Amen.**

Closing prayer No. 21

Make up your mind (5)

St. Augustine of Hippo

In the days when the mighty Roman Empire was fast coming to an end, a young lad named Augustine was growing up in a small town in North Africa. His mother was a Christian and wanted Augustine to be one as well but young Augustine would have none of it. He would have to give up some pleasures enjoyed by others and this was too great a price to pay.

Remember the words of Jesus when a rich young man had turned away from him?

Bible Reading: St. Mark 10: 21–26

Augustine, however, wanted to be a successful teacher and after studying in Carthage became a professor at Milan, in Italy, where he heard Bishop Ambrose preach. He realized that the bishop not only spoke excellently but what he said was true. Augustine made up his mind that he would be a Christian. No one was more delighted than his mother, who had prayed this would happen for thirty-one years.

Augustine returned to North Africa to the town of Hippo, where he worked in the church before being made Bishop of Hippo. For thirty-four years he worked untiringly, preaching, writing, advising, looking after the church and helping the poor.

He died on 28th August, 430, leaving behind him hundreds of books, letters and sermons, of which two books are still widely read today.

St. Augustine of Hippo, who was one of the greatest Christian teachers of his time, is remembered each year on 28th August, the anniversary of his death.

A prayer of St. Augustine:

O Lord, who though thou wast rich, yet for our sakes didst become poor, and hast promised in thy gospel that whatsoever is done unto the least of thy brethren, thou wilt receive as done unto thee: give us grace, we humbly beseech thee, to be ever willing and ready to minister to the needs of our fellow creatures, to thy praise and glory who art God over all. *Amen.*

Benediction No. 53

Nothing is impossible (1)

The Spanish Armada

King Philip of Spain was angry. Elizabeth of England had refused his hand in marriage; and his ships were frequently attacked by English sea captains. He was determined to teach those English a lesson.

He assembled a great armada of ships—130 all told—including sixty great galleons and a number of galleys, with no less than twenty thousand soldiers on board.

On 19th July, 1588, the Armada was sighted off the Lizard in Cornwall and beacon fires were lit all along the coast to give warning. The English captains were awaiting them at Plymouth. No doubt you know the legend about Sir Francis Drake. This is how Sir Henry Newbolt tells it:

> *He was playing at Plymouth a rubber of bowls*
> *When the great Armada came;*
> *But he said, 'They must wait their turns, good souls,'*
> *And he stopped, and finished the game.*

How true that is we cannot tell, but we do know that on Sunday, 21st July the English fleet of sixty-seven small ships, under the command of the Lord High Admiral, Lord Howard of Effingham, engaged the Armada, which was spread over seven miles of sea.

For a week the smaller English ships battered the Spaniards up the Channel until they had been put to flight. It is worth a thought that courage and determination can often succeed in the face of what might seem to be impossible odds.

Remember David as he faced Goliath?

Bible Reading: 1 Samuel 17: 41–50

Help us this day, O God, to run with patience the race that is set before us. May neither opposition without nor discouragement within divert us from our goal. Inspire in us both strength of mind and steadfastness of purpose, that we may meet all fears and difficulties with unswerving courage, and may fulfil with quiet fidelity the tasks committed to our charge; through Jesus Christ our Lord. *Amen.*

H. Bisseker

Closing prayer No. 32

Nothing is impossible (2)

On 7th May, 1942, Viscount Gort, V.C., arrived in Malta to be the new Governor of the island. In his pocket he carried a small silver cross—the George Cross, awarded to the island of Malta. This was not an award to one person but to the island as a whole—the only case in which an award has been made to a whole country and a special tribute from a king to his loyal subjects.

Accompanying the cross was a letter giving the reason for the award in the following words:

'To the island of Malta to bear witness to a heroism and devotion that will long be famous in history.'

To understand why the award was made, we need to find the position of Malta on a map, to realize that all neighbouring lands were controlled by the Germans and the Italians, and that the nearest British forces were at Gibraltar at one end of the Mediterranean Sea and in Egypt at the other. Maltese airfields were essential for aircraft flying from Britain to Egypt.

To defend the island, the Maltese had four old aircraft, sixteen anti-aircraft guns, four battalions of soldiers . . . and a sheer determination not to be beaten.

From June 1940 until 1943, Malta became a centre for air and submarine attacks on enemy shipping. She was attacked daily by aircraft, ran short of supplies, had nearly 1,500 people killed and more than twice that number injured. Yet she stood firm and the George Cross serves as a reminder of those days of courage and devotion to duty.

There are times when we are surrounded by evil and, like the psalmist, seek God's help to stand fast.

Bible Reading: Psalm 40: 10–13

We thank you, God our Father, that in times of difficulty or danger you have so often inspired people to work together for the common good. Put into our hearts a desire to work together in peace to fight the evils that surround us so that together we may stand firm in the cause of righteousness; for the glory of your holy Name. *Amen.**

Closing prayer No. 38

Nothing is impossible (3)

Christopher Columbus

It is one thing to believe in something yourself: it is another thing persuading others to believe it too. When it was first suggested that the world was round, people laughed. 'Don't be daft,' they said. 'Everyone knows it is flat.'

When Christopher Columbus suggested that he could sail westwards to reach India, people laughed at him. Whoever heard of such a thing? Everyone knows that you must sail east to reach India.

But Columbus was not to be put off. He had made many calculations and he was sure he was right. At last he was able to persuade Queen Isabella of Spain to give him money and ships: but where was he to find crews for them? Nobody in his right senses would sail out of sight of land in the wrong direction. It was a strange crew that eventually set sail.

How many times Columbus wondered whether he was right we shall never know. Certainly some of his crew wept and pleaded to be taken home. Others became mutinous as the days passed and no land appeared.

Then, at last, a dream came true. The dark shape in the distance proved to be land and, on 12th October, 1492, Columbus stepped ashore on Watling Island. The course of history was changed.

The story of Christopher Columbus is the story of a man who had faith to believe that he was right, determination to persuade others, and courage to put his ideas to the test.

We remember how Jesus sometimes faced ridicule or opposition as he taught about the Kingdom of God.

Bible Reading: St. John 6: 38–43 and 47

In everything we do, O Lord,
Give us a desire to seek out the truth;
Give us a willingness to heed the advice of others;
Give us wisdom in reaching any decision;
Give us faith to believe in our conclusions;
Give us courage to put our ideas to the test;
And, if we prove ourselves wrong, give us grace to admit it; for
  Jesus' sake. *Amen.**

Closing prayer No. 31

Nothing is impossible (3)   353

Nothing is impossible (4)

In the days when Jesus was preaching and healing in Galilee and Judea, he chose twelve men to be his close friends and to help him with His work. Of some we learn quite a lot: of others we know almost nothing. One of whom we learn very little is Thomas.

His name suggests that he was a twin, and we know him to be a a man who was very loyal, yet slow to believe anything that was difficult to understand.

His loyalty is shown on the occasion when their friend Lazarus was taken ill in Bethany. Jesus declared his intention of going to Bethany but he was immediately rebuffed by some of the disciples. 'Don't you remember how the Jews sought to stone you? You are surely not going there again!'

But Jesus was determined. Thomas then turned to the others and said, 'Let us also go, that we may die with Him'. It is difficult to find greater loyalty than that.

But although St. Thomas is remembered by the church on 21st December, he is chiefly remembered for his part in the Easter story. When Jesus appeared to the other disciples in the upper room, Thomas was not present. He could not bring himself to believe them. 'Except I shall see in his hands the print of the nails ... and thrust my hand into his side, I will not believe.'

Let the words of the Bible tell what happened when Jesus returned to them, and to Thomas, about a week later.

Bible Reading: St. John 20: 26–31

O God our Father, we come to you as those who must believe without seeing. We cannot see you but we know you are here; we cannot hear you but we know you have ways of speaking to us; we cannot understand all that you have done for us but we know it was because you loved us that Jesus came into the world. Help us to believe what we may not understand; for Jesus Christ's sake. *Amen.**

Benediction No. 49

Nothing is impossible (5)

'Pilgrim's Progress'

Here is some advice which Paul gave to the people of Philippi:

Bible Reading: Philippians 2: 12–16

If they were to be true Christians, it was essential that they remain free of the evils around them and be loyal to Christ. Many have set off in this way but have allowed themselves to be led aside for there are plenty of people who would lead the Christian astray.

One of the most famous books in the world is *The Pilgrim's Progress*, which has now been published in many different languages. It tells the story of Christian, who sets off for the Celestial city, helped by such people as Faithful and Hopeful and having his way barred by many such as Apollyon, a foul fiend, hobgoblins and evil spirits, and Giant Despair who lived in Doubting Castle.

The book was first published on 18th February, 1678. Its author, John Bunyan, was a man who knew what it was like to be thwarted in his work for God. He was a very powerful preacher and spent two spells in prison because he refused to leave off preaching in days when only clergymen were supposed to preach. It was in Bedford gaol that *The Pilgrim's Progress* was written. The book has encouraged many people with God's help to overcome all evils to win eternal life. Here is a verse of Bunyan's hymn:

Hobgoblin nor foul fiend
  Can daunt his spirit:
He knows he at the end
  Shall life inherit.

Then fancies fly away,
He'll fear not what men say;
He'll labour night and day
  To be a pilgrim.

O God our heavenly Father
Teach us ever to walk in your holy ways;
Lead us safely through the paths of life;
Guide and inspire us by the Holy Spirit;
And so bring us to eternal life;
  Through Jesus Christ our Lord. *Amen.**

Closing prayer No. 37

Giving of one's best (1)

Alfred, Lord Tennyson

Alfred, Lord Tennyson, born on 6th August, 1809, became recognized as one of the greatest of our poets, for few men have been able to express such feelings in a few words as he could.

He began writing poetry when he was nineteen, and he never looked back. In the following year he won a medal for a poem and, in 1850, on the death of William Wordsworth, he became the Poet Laureate, the greatest honour a poet can receive.

He wrote poems of many kinds, some of them describing incidents from history, such as 'The Revenge', which tells of the gallant fight of one little ship against fifty-three. Another was 'The Charge of the Light Brigade', in which he captures the smell of battle:

> *Cannon to right of them,*
> *Cannon to left of them,*
> *Cannon in front of them*
> *Volleyed and thundered.*
> *Into the jaws of Death,*
> *Into the mouth of Hell,*
> *Rode the six hundred.*

Tennyson was a deep thinker and many of his poems reflect things which he considered of great importance. He knew something of the importance of prayer, as we can tell from his well-known words:

> *Pray for my soul:*
> *More things are wrought by prayer*
> *Than this world dreams of.*

It was fitting that his funeral should have been held in Westminster Abbey, resting place of many of the greatest poets.

O Lord our God, help us to use the talents you have given us with wisdom and to give such good account of our lives that one day we may hear you say to us. 'Well done, good and faithful servant.' *Amen.**

Benediction No. 43

Giving of one's best (2)

WORKING WITH ENTHUSIASM   *Isambard Kingdom Brunel*

'If a job is worth doing, it is worth doing well.' This sums up the attitude of an engineer with an unusual name, Isambard Kingdom Brunel. Born on 9th April, 1806, he was to become one of the greatest engineers of railways, docks, bridges, tunnels, canals and ships.

He was the son of an engineer, Sir Marc Brunel and followed in father's footsteps, assisting him in building a tunnel under the Thames. But his big opportunity came when designs were invited for a bridge over the river Avon below Bristol.

This bridge would have to span a deep gorge, which was no easy task but Isambard got busy and his plans were accepted. Work began but had to stop because there was not enough money but it was finally completed after Brunel's death as a memorial to him.

Meanwhile, he had become interested in railways and became an engineer for the Great Western Railway, the present Western Region of British Rail. He was responsible for laying about 1,200 miles of railway track, for which he also designed bridges and tunnels.

His railway ran from London to Bristol and beyond. But why stop there? Beyond lay the Atlantic Ocean and America. So Brunel turned his attention to ships and designed several that were capable of crossing the Atlantic. His greatest, the *Great Eastern* was larger than any ship of her day and caused Brunel so much worry that he died in 1859 from bad health.

Isambard Kingdom Brunel was a man of great talent. He was never one to tackle a job half-heartedly, but took pride in his work and entered into every job with great enthusiasm.

O God our Father, we have received so many blessings at your hand and we have so much to thank you for, but we come to ask yet one more thing, that you will help us to use your gifts wisely. Give us enthusiasm for our work, patience when things go wrong, and a desire to do and be the very best we can; for Jesus Christ's sake. *Amen.**

Closing prayer No. 17

Giving of one's best (3)

DETERMINED TO SUCCEED   *Charles Parsons*

Charles Parsons stood by the side of the pond with his fishing rod in his hand—but he was not fishing. On the end of his line was not a baited hook but a two-foot model boat.

Parsons was a great engineer, who had shown how to build huge turbine engines that were used to drive the dynamos used for making electricity. Now he believed that turbine machinery could be used to drive great passenger ships, but first he must try out his ideas and find what shape the ship would need to be.

From each of his experiments he obtained information which would be useful. Then, at last, he had a small ship built, which he named *Turbinia*. He continued his experiments until the *Turbinia* could steam at 34 knots.

But people were not ready to take up his idea. Parsons would not be put off. On 26th June, 1897, a great Naval Review was held at Spithead in honour of Queen Victoria's Jubilee. Great warships of many lands were drawn up in long lines. 'I'll show them', thought Parsons.

Suddenly, against all orders, the *Turbinia* shot between the lines at a speed unheard of before. People were astounded: Navy chiefs were horrified. A Naval ship sent to stop her was just left standing.

Parsons had proved his point. The turbine engine could be used in ships. Within a few years, great battleships and ocean liners were fitted with turbine engines—a tribute to the man who believed in his idea and refused to take 'No' for an answer.

Our Bible reading tells of others who believed in something and refused to be put off:

Bible Reading: Acts 5: 25–32

Help us, O Lord, to use our skill, our imagination, and all the gifts with which we are bestowed. Teach us to experiment without fear of mistakes; teach us not to lose heart when things fail to come out right; teach us patience and perseverance; and teach us to make the most of our talents for our satisfaction, for the benefit of others and for the glory of your holy Name. *Amen.**

Closing prayer No. 58

Giving of one's best (4)

Wolfgang Amadeus Mozart

Most people are prepared to make allowances for children when they sing or perform or play musical instruments and are quite ready to applaud a good effort, even though it may not be very musical. But sometimes they are surprised at the quality of the performance.

On 12th January, 1761, the Emperor Maximilian the Third of Austria was waiting to hear two small children play the piano. He had heard tell of these children but was sure the stories must be exaggerated. He was in for a big surprise. The little girl was only nine and her brother not yet six . . . but how they played!

The boy was Wolfgang Amadeus Mozart, destined to become one of the world's greatest composers. He had begun playing music when he was barely three and his fingers too small to reach the notes on the harpsichord properly. Before he was five he could play simple pieces of music perfectly and he was able to write music before he could write words. His father, who was musician to the Archbishop of Salzburg, encouraged him all he could both by teaching him music and by arranging foreign tours.

Some people thought that a boy of his age could not possibly do all that was claimed of him but, after he had written the music for an oratorio at the age of twelve while shut in a room for a week, they were convinced that he was a genius. Mozart died at the age of thirty-five, having composed an amazing amount of music, including no less than forty-one symphonies to be played by the full orchestra. His musical talents have brought pleasure to millions.

Accept our thanks, O Lord our God,
For the wonderful world in which we live;
For so very many things which give us pleasure;
For those talented people whose work we enjoy.
   Help us to remember
That each one of us has some talent;
That all these talents have been given by you;
That you gave us these talents to use;
   So may we use them for your glory. *Amen.**

Closing prayer No. 39

Giving of one's best (5)

The Venerable Bede

Most people who achieve fame do so by travelling to far away places or by doing something spectacular, but a man who holds an honoured place in the history of England did neither of these.

His name was Bede; he was born in Northumbria; he went as a boy to a new monastery at Wearmouth and later to Jarrow on the Tyne. At Jarrow he became a monk and a priest; at Jarrow he spent the whole of his life; and at Jarrow he died and was buried. It is doubtful whether he ever travelled further north than Lindisfarne nor further south than York.

Bede was a scholar with a gift for writing and for teaching and he made up his mind that he was going to use the talents that had been given in the service of God. As he wrote himself:

'I have devoted my energies to the study of the Scriptures, observing monastic discipline, and singing the daily services in church; study, teaching and writing have always been my delight.'

Of the forty or so books that he wrote, one of the most important was his *History of the English Church and People*, which has given historians a vivid picture of England as it was over twelve hundred years ago. People from many places came to learn from the man who was able to teach Latin, Greek and Hebrew.

Apart from his books, Bede wrote hymns, verses, letters and sermons. He was translating St. John's Gospel when he died.

Bede is remembered by the church each year on 27th May, not as a saint but as The Venerable Bede, that is someone who is worthy of honour.

Almighty God, from whom we have our various abilities and talents: help us to learn to use them wisely. Help us to know that talents kept to ourselves are wasted but those shared bring joy to many. Make us ready to dedicate ourselves and all that we have to your service; for the sake of Jesus Christ our Lord. *Amen.**

Benediction No. 47

Good use of talents (1)

Galileo

Bible Reading: St. Matthew 25: 14–21 (to be continued)

Galileo was a man of many talents and he put them to good use. One day, in the cathedral at Pisa, he watched a lamp swinging to and fro. He noticed that, though the length of the swing became shorter, the length of time taken for each swing was exactly the same. From this discovery, the pendulum was shown to be an accurate method of measuring the time.

He was eighteen at the time and keen to find true scientific facts. He discovered that, whilst some people welcomed his findings, others refused to believe him. As a young man, he angered the professors at the university by telling them that they were wrong.

He borrowed an idea that had been invented by a Dutchman and from it made a strong telescope. He was amazed to find stars that had never been seen before; he found that the moon did not have a flat surface; and he discovered moons moving round the planet Jupiter. He was now sure that the earth moved round the sun and the moon round the earth.

Galileo was thrilled with his discoveries, but other people were not. Some Church leaders were as blind as the professors had been. They said that Galileo had no right to teach things which they said were wrong. They left Galileo with no choice. To save his life, Galileo was forced to tell lies about his discoveries.

He died on 8th January, 1642, having become blind in his old age and unable to see the wonders of the heavens. Yet how much blinder were those who could have seen what he saw but refused to do so.

O God our Father, we thank you for eyes with which to see and for minds with which to think and understand. Forgive us that sometimes we use neither our eyes nor our minds; that we dismiss new ideas without a moment's thought; and that we refuse to admit that we may be wrong. Help us to know the truths about our world and about you; through Jesus Christ our Lord. *Amen.**

Closing prayer No. 31

Good use of talents (1)

Good use of talents (2)

Marconi

Bible Reading: St. Matthew 25: 22–23 (if taken in series)

Marconi was another man who was blessed with talents. He also had the good fortune to have a wealthy father and mother who encouraged him in his ideas. Thus, when he left university, he was able to make his own laboratory in which he could study electricity.

There, and in his garden, he experimented with wireless telegraphy until he felt sure that he could send messages through the air. He then had to persuade people that he had made a useful discovery.

The Italian government showed little interest, so Marconi came to Britain. In 1897, he sent messages through the air across the Bristol Channel, then between the Isle of Wight and Bournemouth and later across the English Channel. But would it work over greater distances? Marconi set out to prove that he could send messages across the Atlantic.

He built a transmitting station at Poldhu in Cornwall and then, with three companions, travelled to St. John's in Newfoundland. There, on a very windy day, a kite was flown, from which an aerial led to the receiving set.

It was Thursday, 12th December, 1901. Marconi and his friends waited patiently. Suddenly there was a click, followed by the letter 'S' in Morse Code, which had travelled thousands of miles through the air from Poldhu.

This first, faint signal introduced a means of sending messages which has been of the utmost benefit to mankind.

Almighty God, our Heavenly Father, we thank you for men of patience, whose persistent experiments have led to discoveries which have brought untold blessings to mankind. Grant, we pray thee, that we too may have patience in the little things that we do, perseverance to keep on trying, and the joy of contributing something worthwhile to the world; for the sake of Jesus Christ our Lord. *Amen.**

Benediction No. 51

Good use of talents (3)

Helen Keller

Bible Reading (Cont.): St. Matthew 25: 24–29

It is all too easy to feel that one cannot do much and to bury one's talents. Most people would not have been surprised if Helen Keller had done just that, for she seemed able to do so little.

She was born on 27th June, 1880 and was obviously intelligent but, within two years tragedy had struck. A serious illness left her totally blind and deaf. What could she possibly do? Most people said that nothing could be done, but her parents refused to believe this. They searched America for someone who would be able to teach little Helen to live a normal life. At last they found a young teacher, Anne Sullivan, who invented her own means of teaching Helen by touch.

Not only did she learn to speak her own language but several others too. She learned Mathematics, Latin and Greek and did so well at school that she went on to university, where she did what she had set her heart on doing. She proved that a blind person could do as well as any other.

Her efforts to help handicapped people like herself have given great encouragement to blind, deaf and dumb people in many parts of the world.

At first it must have appeared that Helen Keller had little to offer the world but by sheer determination she showed that her talents could be used not only for herself but for the benefit of others.

Almighty God, we thank you for the gifts of sight, hearing and speaking enabling us to behold all that is around us and communicate with one another. Grant your blessing upon all who are blind, deaf or dumb. May they be encouraged by those who have conquered their difficulties, and themselves lead happy and profitable lives. Give patience to all who help them and bless their work; for Jesus Christ's sake. *Amen.**

Closing prayer No. 8

Good use of talents (4)

Handel

George Frederick Handel was born in the little town of Halle, in Saxony, on 23rd February, 1685. From a very early age, he showed that he had talent for playing music but his father was not pleased. However, at the age of seven, young George played so well on a chapel organ that the Duke of Saxony persuaded his father to allow George to have lessons.

Handel became a great musician, who played before kings and dukes and set his hand to writing music too. By the time he was thirty, and living in England, his talents were recognized. When a special piece of music was needed, no one could compose it better than Handel. Two well-known examples are his *Water Music* and *Music for the Royal Fireworks*.

But some of his greatest music is that which tells Bible stories. He has been described as a man who 'set the Bible to music'.

None is better known than the *Messiah*, which tells the story of Jesus from start to finish. Working day and night, he took twenty-two days to write it.

When it was first performed in London, King George the Second was listening with great interest. As the wonderful strains of the *Hallelujah Chorus* filled the hall, the King rose to his feet in homage to the King of Kings. As the King rose, the people did also, and still do today as these words and music sound the praise of God.

In the Old Testament we learn how King David also praised God with his whole being:

Bible Reading: 1 Chronicles 29: 10–13

Almighty God, King of kings and Lord of lords, we too stand in homage as we remember the greatness of your love toward us. We praise you for your power and your glory but above all for your Son, who has shown us that we can speak with you as our Father. May we praise you with our whole being; for his dear Name's sake. *Amen.**

Closing prayer No. 34

Good use of talents (5)

IN THE SERVICE OF GOD   *Albert Schweitzer*

There can be few people who are better known for their unselfish use of talents than Dr. Albert Schweitzer, born in Alsace on 14th January, 1875.

Schweitzer was a brilliant scholar with many talents. As a boy he played tunes without using the music. As he grew older he learned to play the organ and became one of the finest players of music by the composer Johann Sebastian Bach.

He proved very able at his studies at university and became a Doctor of Philosophy. He also studied religion and became a Doctor of Theology. For most people that would be plenty, but not Schweitzer. He also studied medicine and qualified as a medical doctor.

Then, just as one would have thought he was at the height of success, he announced that he was going to a remote part of Africa in order to help the people. He must be mad, people thought. Fancy throwing away all his gifts like that. But Albert Schweitzer did not consider he was throwing away his gifts. He believed that God had given him his talents and this was how God would have him use them.

In 1913, he sailed for Equatorial Africa and set up a hospital at Lambarene on the Ogowe River. There he spent the rest of his life except for a few brief absences, some of them to raise money for his hospital and one, in 1952, to receive a very special award, the Nobel Prize for Peace.

Albert Schweitzer, known as the Genius of the Jungle, had no doubts as to how his talents should be used—in Africa, for the Glory of God.

O God, our Father, make us aware of the work that you have for us to do; make us willing to do that work whatever the cost may be; make us courageous to take steps that others may think unwise; make us ready to trust in you for all life's needs; and make us to know the joy that comes to all who serve you faithfully; through Jesus Christ our Lord. *Amen.**

Closing prayer No. 16

Into God's hands (1)

Nicolo Paganini

If you have ever tried to play a violin, you will realize that it is not as easy as it looks. There is more to it than drawing a bow across the strings and placing your fingers in the right place. In fact the violin, which is capable of producing some of the most beautiful music, can do just the opposite in the hands of the wrong person.

October 27th, 1782, was the birthday of one of the world's greatest violinists, Nicolo Paganini. He was born in Genoa, where his father taught him to play both the guitar and the violin, but he could soon play much better than his father and he had lessons from other great musicians. While still only a boy, he appeared on the stage and played his own arrangements of some difficult music.

Not content with arranging the music of other people, he set his hand to composing his own. Meanwhile, he toured Italy, Austria, France, England and Scotland, settling for a time in Paris. He soon became a wealthy man and he gave a considerable sum of money to the composer Berlioz to enable him to work at his music.

In the hands of Paganini, the violin came to life, producing music, either gay or sad, to suit the occasion. In the hands of another, the same violin would have been useless. To get the most from our lives, we need to place ourselves into the hands of God, who can make us to be a joy to others.

We read in the Bible how St. Paul only began to serve God well when he was ready to do things God's way.

Bible Reading: Acts 22: 10–15

O God our Father, we confess our shortcomings: the unkind words we speak; the thoughtless things we do; the displeasure we sometimes give to others. Take us into your hands and teach us your ways; then, as a violin becomes an instrument of joy in the hands of a master musician, make us into instruments of pleasure to all who meet us; through Jesus Christ our Lord. *Amen.**

Closing prayer No. 25

Into God's hands (2)

St. Antony of Padua

Many a person who has given himself into the service of God has found his sphere of service to be different from what he expected it to be. Here is part of a story from the New Testament.

Bible Reading: St. Mark 5: 1–8 and 18–20

Another who was led by God was St. Antony of Padua, remembered by the church on 13th June. He was born near Lisbon, in Portugal in 1195. His real name was Ferdinand de Bouillon, and he was a descendant of one of the great heroes of the first Crusade.

After attending the cathedral school in Lisbon, he worked in a monastery for eight years, then became a priest. One day, five Franciscan friars called at the monastery on their way to Morocco to start a Christian mission. They were followers of St. Francis and had given up their possessions to travel where they could, helping people and preaching the Gospel.

A year or two later, when their bodies were brought back—for they had been martyred—Ferdinand decided to become a Franciscan friar and take their place. When he did so, he changed his name to Antony.

As it happened, he never reached Morocco; God had work for him to do elsewhere. His ship was blown in a storm onto the coast of Sicily and because of this, most of the rest of his life was spent in Italy or neighbouring lands.

Antony had a most unusual gift for preaching, so that vast crowds gathered to hear him, so vast that the market places could not contain them and he had to preach on the hillsides. When he died, aged only thirty-six, worn out by his work, he was buried at Padua, in a great church built in his honour.

Help us, O Lord, to seek what is your perfect will, and having found it to go forth in your name; and may we have the strength of our Lord Jesus Christ and the power of the Holy Spirit to keep us sure and steadfast now and all our days. *Amen.**

Closing prayer No. 19

Into God's hands (3)

GIVING ALL FOR GOD   *St. Bernard of Clairvaux*

Jesus never left any doubt that those who would serve God must be prepared to give all.

Bible Reading: St. Mark 8: 34–37

Nearly nine hundred years ago, a small group of monks agreed to give up all and live very strict lives. They built a place to live in at Citeaux and they became known as Cistercians. But the life they led was so severe that one by one they left until the abbot began to wonder whether he would have to close the monastery.

Then one day, he was amazed to find a large group of men at the door. Had they come in peace or would they make trouble? Their leader stepped forward. 'We come in the peace of God,' he said.

Immediately the abbot opened the door wide and bid them enter. He was astounded to discover that the leader, named Bernard, had brought with him four brothers and twenty-seven friends, all of whom wished to become monks at the monastery.

So Bernard, the son of a rich nobleman, started a new life in which he would have nothing to call his own. Two years later, he was sent with some friends to start a new monastery in a place which was known as the Valley of Bitterness. Bernard changed its name to the Valley of Light or, in French, Clairvaux. That is why he is known to this day as St. Bernard of Clairvaux.

Many came to his monastery, so many, in fact, that there was no room for them all. No less than sixty-eight other monasteries had to be built.

St. Bernard of Clairvaux, beside being a great preacher, scholar, thinker and writer, was a man who was never afraid to speak his mind. He is remembered by the church on 20th August each year.

A prayer verse of St. Bernard of Clairvaux:

> O Jesus, ever with us stay;
>   Make all our moments calm and bright;
> Chase the dark night of sin away;
>   Shed o'er the world thy holy light. *Amen.*

Benediction No. 44

Into God's hands (4)

LED INTO GOD'S SERVICE *George Matheson*

George Matheson was born in Glasgow on 27th March, 1842 and it was soon discovered that there was something wrong with his eyesight. At school he had to sit near the window to read books with large print through very thick spectacles.

Many a person might have given up, but not George. At the Glasgow Academy, he learned by heart the passages which were read to him and he gained prizes for his outstanding work. At University, he was renowned as a speaker and was successful in his studies. He then decided to use his gifts as a minister in the Church.

As minister of the church at Inellan, a holiday resort on the Firth of Clyde, he achieved a fame which led many to go to hear him. 'Matheson of Inellan' was a great preacher and none who heard him went away disappointed.

Every word had to be memorized—hymns, prayers, lessons, sermons—but it was done so well that people soon forgot that the preacher could not see them. Many a person was amazed to be called by name by the man who had neither seen him nor spoken to him for some time.

From Inellan, Matheson was invited to become the minister of a great church in Edinburgh with above two thousand members, most of whom he made it his business to visit in their homes. His cheerfulness was an inspiration to many and reflected his love for God.

Hymn writer, author, sick visitor, powerful preacher, blind for half a century, George Matheson filled every moment with useful and loving service in the name of the God into whose service he had committed his life.

We praise you, O God, because nothing is impossible to you and because you can always do something with any life that is placed in your hands. We thank you for the example set by many who, with your help, have been able to overcome great difficulties and in turn have helped others. We ask you to take whatever talents we have, few though they may be, and use them mightily in your service; in the Name and for the sake of Jesus Christ our Lord. *Amen.**

Benediction No. 45

Into God's hands (5)

A little over a thousand years ago, one of the most dreaded sights was a Viking ship heading for the coast, for people knew that the Vikings would burn, plunder and show mercy to no one.

In a short time, many lands fell into their hands, including the Orkneys and other islands to the north of Scotland.

The Vikings were a warlike people. They believed that if they were to go to Valhalla (Heaven), they must prove themselves in battle. It may therefore seem strange to learn of an Earl, or Jarl, of the Orkneys who was a man of peace. Such a man was Magnus Erlingsson.

In his younger days he had fought as any other Viking, but he was a Christian and realized one day that he should change his ways. Once he sat in front of the king's ship during a battle, refusing to fight because he had no quarrel with those whom the king was fighting.

Magnus ruled one half of Orkney: his cousin Haakon ruled the other half but wanted to rule the whole. It was agreed that they would meet at Easter 1115, each bringing two ships. Haakon broke the agreement and arrived with eight, clearly ready to fight.

Magnus refused to allow his men to be killed, though they were quite ready to fight for him. He met Haakon alone and was killed.

Of all the Orkney Jarls, Magnus stands out as the one who was different. He became known as St. Magnus and the cathedral on Orkney was named after him. He is still remembered there and in the north of Scotland on 16th April.

These words of Jesus tell how disciples of his may be recognized:

Bible Reading: St. John 13: 34–35

O God our Father, we remember that the followers of Christ were first called Christians because people noticed that they were different from others. Help us to realize that we, too, must be easily recognized if we are to bear your name. Strengthen and guide us, we pray, in the name of our Lord Jesus Christ. *Amen.**

Benediction No. 40

Self-denial (1)

Garibaldi

On 11th May, 1860, the great Italian patriot Garibaldi landed at Marsala in Sicily with a thousand men, determined to win Sicily and make it part of the new united country of Italy. An army of some twenty-seven thousand men and several guard ships were unable to stop him and within three months the island was won.

Garibaldi's life had been full of excitement. Years before, he had been forced to flee from Italy in disguise after plotting to capture a ship on which he was sailing. Then he sailed in the French Navy, fought with rebels in Brazil, became a pirate, and defended Rome with a handful of men against a mighty French army.

He was a born leader, quite fearless, and able to encourage others to do what seemed impossible. He never promised comfort but offered a cause that was worth fighting for. On one occasion, as he tried to raise an army, he was asked what his followers would receive.

'My friends,' he said, 'I offer you hardship, hunger, rags, thirst, sleepless nights, foot-sores, long marches, countless privations, disappointments—and the hope of victory in the noblest cause that any Italian ever yet fought for.'

It was the same kind of promise that Churchill offered the people of Britain in the difficult days of 1940; it also reminds us of those early disciples, who were promised nothing but hardship as they sought to win the world for Jesus Christ and make it become the Kingdom of God.

Here is just one of the things that Jesus told them:

Bible Reading: St. Matthew 10: 16–18

Help us to remember, O Lord, that the way of life is never easy; that rewards seldom come to those who sit and wait but rather to those who face up to life's challenge. May we, like your servants of old, be ready to forsake all in your service so that we may be true and faithful servants and receive at last the reward of our labours; in the name of our Lord Jesus Christ. *Amen.**

Closing prayer No. 20

Self-denial (2)

AT THE RISK OF ONE'S LIFE   *Sgt. Michael Reeves, G.M.*

Once, when Jesus was asked the question, 'Who is my neighbour?' he answered by telling the parable of The Good Samaritan.

Bible Reading: St. Luke 10: 25–37

The Samaritan in this story saw a man in trouble and went immediately to his aid regardless of his own safety. If the robbers had returned, he too might have suffered.

There are many real-life examples of people who have been ready to help someone in distress even at the risk of their own lives.

On 17th September, 1967, for example, a training aircraft was flying at 2,500 feet. A young learner-parachutist jumped but, unfortunately, the line attached to the aircraft failed to open the parachute and the man was left hanging on the line sixteen feet below the plane.

The instructor, Sergeant Michael Reeves, thereupon climbed down the line, supported the man and ordered the line to be cut. As they fell, the sergeant opened the other man's parachute before opening his own. For this act of bravery, Sergeant Reeves was awarded the George Medal.

We often read of cases in which people have been willing to risk their lives to rescue others. Some enter burning buildings to do so: others face rough seas, sharks, explosions, or other dangers without considering their own safety.

It is easy to stand by and feel sorry for someone: the priest and the Levite in the story did that. The good neighbour is the person who is ready to do whatever can be done to help.

O God our Father, help us to become good neighbours to those around us, to keep our eyes and ears open for cases of need, and to be ready to help wherever we can. May we never spare ourselves but be ready to offer all that we have in the service of others and for the glory of your Holy Name; through Jesus Christ our Lord. *Amen.**

Closing prayer No. 24

Self-denial (3)

In Bible times, leprosy was such a dreaded disease that anyone afflicted with it was compelled by law to keep away from others so that it would not be passed on. Lepers had to stand their distance.

Bible Reading: St. Luke 17: 11–19

In 1665, tragedy came to the village of Eyam, in Derbyshire, when a box arrived from London, where the great plague was killing many people. Within a couple of days, the man who opened the box was dead. Before long, many others were also dying and there seemed no way of checking the plague.

The Rector of Eyam, Rev. William Mompesson, called the villagers together. There was nothing to stop them leaving the village but, if they did, they risked carrying the plague to other towns and villages. The people agreed on what they should do. They would make an invisible wall round the village. No one would pass in or out of the village. Their needs would be left at this boundary and the money to pay for them placed in water. By not coming into contact with other people, the plague would be unable to spread beyond the village.

The plague struck on 7th September, 1665 and lasted over a year. Of the 350 villagers, over 250 died, including Mompesson's wife. It was a terrible toll, but their end had been achieved. The plague had been contained within the village.

When it ended, those who had been spared, gave thanks to God for their deliverance and for the strength to hold out which they had been given. To this day, a simple service is held in Eyam once a year in thanksgiving for their self-sacrifice.

We thank you, God our Father, for men and women of courage and determination, who have seen the right course and have had courage to take it, after the example of our Lord and Master, Jesus Christ. Help us likewise to follow in his steps and always do the right whatever it may cost; for Jesus' sake. *Amen.**

Closing prayer No. 27

Self-denial (3)   373

Self-denial (4)

Captain Oates

Bible Reading: St. John 15: 12–17

'Greater love hath no man than this, that a man lay down his life for his friends.'

This is just what happened on 16th March, 1912. The man was Captain Oates and his friends were Captain Scott, Lieutenant Bowers and Dr. Wilson.

They were on their way back from the South Pole, having had the disappointment of being beaten to the Pole by Amundsen. Now they were delayed by one thing after another,—the death of their companion Evans, biting winds, blizzards and frostbite.

Oates' feet were so badly frost-bitten that every step was agony and the party as a whole had to travel slowly. Oates knew that he was being a burden to others and begged them to leave him behind so that they could travel faster. Of course they refused.

That night, Oates climbed into his sleeping-bag and hoped that he would not awaken the next morning. He wished that his companions could go on. However, he did awaken to find that it was blowing a blizzard outside the tent.

Turning to the others, he said, 'I am just going outside and may be some time.' He walked out into the snow and was never seen again.

Scott wrote in his diary: 'We knew that poor Oates was walking to his death, but, though we tried to dissuade him, we knew it was the act of a brave man and an English gentleman. We all hope to meet the end with a similar spirit . . .'.

O Lord, give us more charity, more self-denial, more likeness to thee. Teach us to sacrifice our comforts to others, and our likings for the sake of doing good. Make us kindly in thought, gentle in word, generous in deed. Teach us that it is better to give than to receive, better to forget ourselves than to put ourselves forward; better to minister than to be ministered unto. And unto thee, the God of Love, be all glory and praise, both now and for evermore. *Amen.*

Dean Henry Alford

Closing prayer No. 29

Self-denial (5)

Alexander Russell

Few people will know the name of Alexander Russell but what he did has gone down as one of the bravest and most unselfish acts in history.

He was one of hundreds of soldiers, with their wives and children on the troopship *Birkenhead*, when she struck a rock off South Africa on 26th February, 1852 and began to sink. All the soldiers lined up on the decks as boats were lowered and the women and children packed into them, filling every seat. Alexander Russell was ordered to command one of the boats.

As the boats moved away, they watched the troopship slowly sinking until the courageous soldiers, still standing to attention, were sucked into the water as she took the final plunge.

There were terrified cries from the water and in the boats but one was louder than the others and came from within Russell's boat. 'Oh sir! There's my husband—please save him!'

Russell saw the agony in her face and the terrified faces of her children; he saw the appealing eyes of the man in the water; and he looked at his crowded boat. Without a word, he plunged into the water, helped the husband into his own seat and then turned away until he could swim no further.

'God bless you,' murmured many within the boat, as Alexander Russell swam off, never to be seen again.

Alexander Russell knew that he was giving up his own life so that another could be saved. So Jesus knew that in going to Jerusalem, he was going to lose his own life for the sake of others. This is what he told his friends.

Bible Reading: St. Mark 10: 32–34

O Lord Jesus Christ, who taught us always to put others before ourselves, and gave your own life for the sake of sinful men, make us ready to consider the needs of others and to put their needs before our own, so that we may be true children of our Heavenly Father. We ask it for your sake. *Amen.**

Closing prayer No. 39

Saints and martyrs (1)

In the very early days of the Church, those who were known as Christians faced danger and death. Herod was one of the first to persecute them.

Bible Reading: Acts 12: 1–5

In the years that followed, Christians were also regarded as trouble-makers because they said that they must obey God rather than the Roman Emperor. Many excuses were found for putting Christians to death. Some were crucified; some were burned; and some faced wild beasts in the arena.

January 21st is kept as the feast day of one of the most famous of those martyrs in Rome. Her name was Agnes, now known as St. Agnes, who was put to death about the year A.D. 304.

St. Agnes is especially remembered because she was only thirteen years old, yet was ready to die rather than be unfaithful to God. She is said to have spurned an offer of marriage from the son of a Roman official. She was a Christian, she said and her life belonged only to God. The official demanded that she should give up her beliefs but she refused to do so and was sentenced to death.

Agnes was buried in a cemetery in Rome and a church was later built in her memory. If it had not been for the strength and bravery of people like Agnes, the Christian Church might well have been wiped out.

Today, O God, make me
Brave enough to face the things of which I am afraid;
Strong enough to overcome the temptations which try to make me
  do the wrong thing and not to do the right thing;
Persevering enough to finish every task that is given me to do;
Kind enough always to be ready to help others;
Obedient enough to obey your voice whenever you speak to me
  through my conscience;
Help me to live in purity; to speak in truth; to act in love all
  through today. This I ask for Jesus' sake. *Amen.*

Dr. William Barclay

Benediction No. 44

Saints and martyrs (2)

St. Catherine

Have you ever wondered why a certain firework which spins on a pin is called a Catherine wheel?

It took its name from a young woman, who is believed to have lived over sixteen centuries ago at Alexandria in Egypt and whose feast day falls on 25th November.

Many of the tales that are told of St. Catherine are only legends and one cannot be sure which are true. Some we know can only be legends. We are told that Catherine was a very beautiful and intelligent young woman to whom the emperor was very attracted. But Catherine was a Christian and she said that she would have nothing to do with a man who was not, even though he were the emperor. Fifty of the most learned men of the day were called in to make her change her mind but, though she was only eighteen, Catherine broke down all their arguments.

The emperor became so angry that he ordered her to be tortured on a wheel studded with spikes—the Catherine wheel. Afterwards she was beheaded and legend says that she was buried on Mount Carmel which was visited by many pilgrims in later years.

In bygone days, St. Catherine's Day was kept as a day for merry-making and there were various customs associated with it, kept especially by young women who believed that St. Catherine would help them in their choice of a husband.

Those customs belong to the past but today St. Catherine is still remembered as one who went through a great deal rather than give up her faith. She stood firm, just as St. Paul told Timothy he should:

Bible Reading: 2 Timothy 3: 10–15

Lord, grant us the will and the power to do in all things that which is honest and right. Help us bravely and sincerely to speak only that which is true, and to behave openly, frankly and loyally to one another. Make us not afraid to admit our faults and to accept the blame; for the sake of him who is the Way, the Truth, and the Life, even Jesus Christ our Lord. *Amen.*

S. M. E. Trood (Service Book for Youth)

Benediction No. 42

Saints and martyrs (2)   377

Saints and martyrs (3)

St. Blaize

Many people like a good bonfire and find the excuse to have one on 5th November, when they burn the Guy. Hundreds of years ago, long before the time of Guy Fawkes, it was the custom to light bonfires on the hill-tops on 3rd February, and people would try to make their bonfire bigger than those on neighbouring hills.

Their reason for doing so was that 3rd February is St. Blaize's Day and his name suggests a large blazing fire.

St. Blaize, or Blasius as he is also known, was a bishop of the Christian Church at Sebaste in Armenia. We know little about him but legends tell of his ability to heal people and animals. One legend tells how he cured an animal while hiding in a cave. Other animals gathered around the cave and attracted the soldiers who arrested Blaize. He was beaten and sentenced to death after being tortured by having his body raked by iron combs.

Because of this, he became the patron saint of wool combers. There were many of these in England in the Middle Ages and they celebrated St. Blaize's Day not only with bonfires but with processions and feasts in honour of their saint.

The custom of holding these bonfires and processions has long been forgotten but St. Blaize, the Christian martyr is still remembered. He stood firm, faithful to God, much as St. Paul told the people of Philippi to do when he wrote his letter to them. Here are his words:

Bible Reading: Philippians 1: 27–30

Almighty God, we remember before you all who have suffered in the cause of righteousness and have not faltered even in the face of death. Help us to remain firm even when others are unkind to us, or hurt us, or say unkind things about us because of our trust in you. Show us your perfect way and enable us to be your loyal servants to the end of our days; for the sake of Jesus Christ our Lord. *Amen.**

Closing prayer No. 11

Saints and martyrs (4)

St. Apollonia

Paul was able to offer comfort to those who might suffer for the faith. He could do so because he had frequently suffered himself. He once recounted his own sufferings in one of his letters:

Bible Reading: 2 Corinthians 11: 24–27

Many other Christians were also brutally treated. One, who is remembered on 9th February, is St. Apollonia, an old Christian woman who lived in Alexandria. She was taken prisoner, struck in the face and her teeth knocked out. She was then told that she would be burned alive if she did not deny Christ and a large fire was lit. It is said that St. Apollonia offered a short prayer to God, then stepped into the fire where she died.

It is sad to recall that many hundreds of years later it became the custom for people to be burned if they dared to argue against the Christian Church and its teachings. People then believed that if they burned the body of such a person his soul could still go to heaven.

We find that on 9th February, 1555, which was St. Apollonia's Day, Bishop Hooper was burned at the stake in Gloucester and, on the same day, Dr. Rowland Taylor was burned at Hadleigh in Essex. These are just two of many hundreds who met death in this dreadful way.

Today we are much more fortunate. We live in days when people are free to worship God in whatever way they wish without fear of being put to death for doing so. People in some lands, even today, are not free to do this.

We do well sometimes to remember just how fortunate we are and to thank God for our freedom.

Almighty and everlasting God, who dost enkindle the flame of thy love in the hearts of the saints; grant to our minds the same faith and power of love; that as we rejoice in their triumphs, we may profit by their examples; through Jesus Christ our Lord. *Amen.*

Gothic Missal

Benediction No. 54

Saints and martyrs (4)   379

Saints and martyrs (5)

Thomas Cranmer

One of the most important churchmen in the reign of King Henry the Eighth was Thomas Cranmer, Archbishop of Canterbury, whose actions led to great changes in religion in England.

Cranmer, who was born on 2nd July, 1489, was a very learned man. He came to the notice of the King and was appointed Chaplain to the King. He was sent to Rome to put forward the case of the King, who wanted his marriage to Catherine of Aragon dissolved. The Pope refused the request.

Soon afterwards Cranmer was appointed Archbishop of Canterbury. As such, he granted the King's wish and then approved Henry's marriage to Anne Boleyn. At the same time, it was decreed that the Pope was no longer head of the Church in England. Cranmer worked hard to establish the new Church of England. He had the Bible translated into English and he took other measures which were not popular with the Roman Catholics. In later years, he tried unsuccessfully to keep Mary, a Roman Catholic, off the throne of England.

For his trouble, he was imprisoned as soon as Mary became Queen. In order to save his life, he was persuaded to sign a paper in which he admitted his mistakes but, shortly afterwards, while at Oxford, he said that he had been wrong to do so. His mistake was not to remain faithful to what he believed. Cranmer was immediately taken outside and burned. His opponents were able to take away his life, but they could not undo all that he had accomplished in his lifetime.

O God our Father, thou knowest how often we fail because we are afraid. We fear what men will do if we stand for the right; we fear what they will say. We fear that we shall not have strength to go on even if we begin. Forgive us for our weaknesses. Help us to remember our Master Christ and all that he endured for us, so that we, like him, may never be afraid of men but only of sinning against thy love. We ask it for his Name's sake. *Amen.*

A. G. Pite

Benediction No. 50

Saints (1)

St. George, whose feast day is 23rd April, is honoured as the patron saint of England. He is also the patron saint of soldiers and boy scouts.

Ask anyone what St. George did to become famous and the reply is almost certain to be that he fought a dragon and rescued a maiden in distress. It is the kind of thing that any brave knight would have been glad to do but, alas, it did not happen. The story of the dragon was first told several hundred years after St. George had died.

In fact, although St. George is one of the best known of the early Christian martyrs, there is very little that we can learn about him from history. That is why several legends are told about him.

It would seem that St. George was a soldier-saint, who lived in the Holy Land and was probably martyred there about the beginning of the Fourth Century. He also had the reputation of being a very good man.

How he came to be the patron saint of England is not known. His name was known in England long before the Normans came. No doubt, too, the Crusaders heard of St. George when they were fighting in the Holy Land and brought back stories of him. His emblem, of course, is a white flag bearing a red cross—the emblem worn by the Crusaders when they went into battle.

St. George fighting the dragon is often used as a symbol of the fight between good and evil. We still need our Georges to fight the dragons of the present age.

O God my Father, help me in the name of Jesus Christ to do your will.

> Let faith be my shield and let joy be my steed
> 'Gainst the dragons of anger, the ogres of greed;
> And let me set free, with the sword of my youth,
> From the castle of darkness the power of the truth.

Amen.*

(verse by Jan Struther)

Closing prayer No. 10

Saints (2)

St. Andrew

November 30th is St. Andrew's Day, when the people of Scotland remember their patron saint.

St. Andrew was not a Scot, but one of the original apostles of Jesus, probably the first, who introduced his brother, Simon Peter, and probably others to Jesus.

Apart from the stories in the Bible, we have very little information about Andrew. There are various traditions, which tell of places where he preached, and one which tells that he became a bishop, but none of these is reliable.

Andrew is said to have been crucified on an X-shaped cross, but even this is open to question and seems to be a story which was first told hundreds of years later. Certainly St. Andrew's flag has a white diagonal cross on a blue background and a cross of that shape is often referred to as a St. Andrew's cross.

From the Bible, we learn that Andrew was one of the fishermen of Bethsaida in Galilee. One day he heard John the Baptist refer to Jesus as the 'Lamb of God', and he decided to follow Jesus. The first thing he did was to go home and tell his brother, Simon Peter, who also followed Jesus. Here is another story about him.

Bible Reading: St. Matthew 4: 18–22

Often, it seems that St. Andrew was overshadowed by his brother, yet we know that he did a great deal during the life of Jesus and after.

We may think of St. Andrew today as the patron saint of Scotland, or we may remember him as the man who found something really worth having and made sure that his brother found it too.

O God, you have taught us through Jesus Christ to live according to your laws so that we may enjoy full and contented lives. Help us by your Holy Spirit to seek your way for ourselves and, when we have found it, to tell others so that they too may come to know you and receive your blessing. *Amen.**

Benediction No. 52

Saints (3)

St. Patrick

March 17th is St. Patrick's Day, when Irish people all over the world remember their patron saint.

Patrick, as a boy, was playing by a river, possibly the Clyde, when he was carried off by pirates and made to work in Ireland looking after animals. He escaped on a ship which he thought would take him home but which, in fact, took him to Gaul, as France was then called, where he became a priest.

After returning home, he had a dream in which he was told to return to Ireland to make the people Christian. He made his way to Tara, the home of Laoghaire, the chief king. Outside the town, on the evening before Easter, when no fires were permitted to be lit, Patrick lit a great fire. He was ordered to put it out but refused, saying that the light which he had brought to Ireland could never be put out.

Later, he was given a piece of land at Armagh and this became his headquarters from which, as Bishop of Ireland, he spread Christianity far and wide.

One day he was trying to explain to people how God could be three persons—the Father, the Son and the Holy Spirit. Stooping to the ground, he plucked a leaf of shamrock, saying, 'See! This has three leaves but they all come from the same point and make only one leaf. So the Father, Son and Holy Spirit are three persons but one God'.

Thus the shamrock became St. Patrick's emblem and it is always worn by Irish people in many parts of the world on St. Patrick's Day.

A prayer of St. Patrick:

> Christ be with me, Christ be within me,
> Christ behind me, Christ before me,
> Christ beside me, Christ to win me,
> Christ to comfort and restore me,
> Christ beneath me, Christ above me,
> Christ in quiet, Christ in danger,
> Christ in hearts of all that love me,
> Christ in mouth of friend and stranger. *Amen*

Benediction No. 50 (a benediction of St. Patrick)

Saints (4)

St. David

March 1st is St. David's Day, and Welshmen throughout the world celebrate the day of their patron saint.

Many show their loyalty by wearing a leek, which is the Welsh national emblem or a daffodil, the national flower. Others prefer to eat their leeks. How the leek came to be chosen, we cannot be sure as there are several different legends, but one thing is certain, that wherever Welshmen gather together, especially in the Welsh army regiments, there are a good many leeks to be seen.

But who was St. David? David is the English form of his name, which, in Welsh, is Dewi. He was born in the south-west corner of Wales, which today is known as Pembrokeshire.

Very little is known about his early life, except that he gave himself to the service of Jesus Christ and decided to build a monastery near his home. During his lifetime, he founded no less than twelve monasteries in Britain. It is also said that he went on a journey to Jerusalem and was there made a bishop.

At home, he met with some opposition, but he was very well-liked and he became Archbishop of Menevia (now St. David's). From here he was also able to give advice to Irish kings.

St. David is remembered in the cathedral and city which bear his name, but also in the hearts of Welsh people everywhere.

Since the Welsh people love music and singing, this Bible reading seems appropriate:

Bible Reading: Psalm 98

We remember before you, O Lord, the people of Wales, with their love of poetry and singing and their awareness of your presence in their midst. We thank you for the beautiful hymns and music which have spread from the chapels in the valleys to the far corners of the earth. May this land of song continue to sound your praises now and always. *Amen.**

Benediction No. 48

Saints (5)

St. Boniface

One day a small boy overheard the conversation of some monks who were staying at his father's house at Crediton in Devon. As they spoke of their work among the heathen people of Europe, young Winfred decided that he, too, would become a monk and preach the Gospel in Europe.

At first his father opposed the idea, but later he gave his consent. When he entered a monastery, Winfred changed his name to Boniface, the name by which he is always remembered.

At the first opportunity, he sailed for Europe to work among the German tribes living in Friesland, but the king refused to allow him to preach there.

Boniface, therefore, made the first of three visits to the Pope, who gave him the important task of converting the heathen tribes of Germany. Boniface was a powerful preacher and, wherever he went, people were prepared to listen to him.

On his second journey to Rome, Boniface was made the first 'Bishop of all Germany'. For thirty-one years, he worked unceasingly to strengthen the Christian church in Germany and to convert the heathen people. To help him in his task, he sent to England, from where many missionaries, both men and women, were happy to go to his aid.

In time he was made an archbishop, an office which he held for over twenty years.

Then, in the year 754, when he was over seventy, he went, once again, to Friesland, where, soon afterwards, he and his companions were attacked and killed after refusing to fight. Now he is remembered as St. Boniface on 5th June.

Heavenly Father, we praise you for all who have been prepared to leave their homes and serve you in far away places. Bless those who continue their work today and grant them success in their labours so that the whole world may one day acknowledge you as God and Father; and to you be all praise and glory for ever and ever. *Amen.**

Benediction No. 47

More saints (1)

A SAINT FROM CYPRUS   *St. Barnabas*

On 11th June, the Christian Church remembers St. Barnabas, a man who is described as an apostle although was not one of the twelve. Like many of the early Christians, we know little about him except what we can read in the Bible. He was a Jew, born in Cyprus, who sold his land and brought the money to the apostles so that it could be shared among the members of the church.

Barnabas is especially remembered for his work with St. Paul. In the early days after Paul had become a Christian, and when the apostles were worried that this might be a trap set by the Pharisees, it was Barnabas who took Paul to them and explained how Paul had become a Christian.

Later, when the Christians were in danger in Jerusalem, many travelled north to Antioch, where the Church became strong. Among those who went to Antioch was Barnabas and it was he who went to Tarsus to find Paul and bring him to Antioch. We read in the Bible how Barnabas was highly thought of by the church.

Bible Reading: Acts of the Apostles 11: 22–26

Later, when it was decided to take the Gospel to other lands, Barnabas was one who travelled with Paul to Cyprus and on to the cities of Asia Minor, the land we now know as Turkey. Barnabas later visited Jerusalem and then returned to Cyprus.

St. Barnabas is generally considered to be the founder of the church in Cyprus and it is believed that he was put to death there because of his faith—a fate which befell so many of the early Christians.

O God our Father, fill us, we pray, with your Holy Spirit, so that we may be true and faithful, wise and good, strong and courageous: then help us to use these gifts in the service of others for your glory. So may we find peace and joy in our own hearts and know ourselves as your disciples; through Jesus Christ our Lord. *Amen.**

Closing prayer No. 18

More saints (2)

St. Ambrose

During the Fourth Century, a young man who was a lawyer in the Roman courts was appointed governor of that part of Italy, then known as Liguria, with Milan its capital city. His name was Ambrose, a name that was to become greatly respected in the Christian Church.

About four years after he had reached Milan, it was necessary to appoint a new bishop and the Christians met together to choose one. There was no doubt who they would choose. Ambrose had become such a good leader that they wanted him to become bishop. He was not very happy about this because he had not been baptized, but the people would not be dissuaded. As soon as he had been appointed, at the age of 34, Ambrose gave away all his belongings so that he would have nothing to keep his mind off the work that he would have to do.

Every Sunday he preached and people of many kinds came to hear him. Among them was one from North Africa who was so moved by Ambrose that he gave his life to the service of God. In later years, this man became St. Augustine of Hippo, one of the greatest teachers in the church.

Ambrose feared no one, not even the mighty Roman Emperor. He persuaded the emperor not to allow a statue of a goddess to be put up in Rome; he refused to hand over a building when the empress ordered him to; and he spoke against an emperor who had organized a massacre of many people.

St. Ambrose, remembered by the church on 4th April, was more concerned with ordinary people than with emperors and his teachings were such that ordinary people could understand them.

Father of all, we your children come to you in the freshness of the morning to ask your blessing upon all that we do. Help us to show by our words and our deeds that we are your children. Forgive us for our failures and help us to do better. Help us always to love you and to show our love in being helpful to others; through Jesus Christ our Lord. *Amen.**

Closing prayer No. 13

More saints (3)

St. Edward the Confessor

There have been bad kings and good kings, but there are very few who have been regarded as saints. October 13th is the feast day of one who was—St. Edward the Confessor.

He was born almost a thousand years ago, the son of King Ethelred the Unready. His uncle was the Duke of Normandy, and Edward spent most of his life there from the age of ten to thirty-seven.

In the following year he became King of England, but found that there were certain powerful nobles, not the least of which was Godwin, Earl of Wessex, whose daughter Edith the king married.

Later the King and the Earl quarrelled, but Godwin was not an easy man to push on one side. King Edward was always aware that Godwin was around.

As a boy, Edward had been brought up in a monastery at Ely and there is no doubt that he was very fond of life in the monastery. Had he not known that one day he was likely to become King, Edward might well have become a monk. It is no doubt because of his religious outlook and his generosity to the poor that King Edward came to be regarded as a saint.

As king, he built a monastery just outside London on an island in the Thames known as Thorney Island. This island no longer exists and his abbey is no longer there, but in its place stands the present Westminster Abbey, with the shrine of St. Edward the Confessor in a central position.

Like many saints, he had learned the value of living with and for God. St. Paul's words are a reminder:

Bible Reading: Philippians 4: 4–8

O God our Father, help us to learn of you and to fill our thoughts only with those things which are true and noble, just and pure, lovable, gracious and good; so that we may live as you would have us to live under the guidance of your Holy Spirit and with your peace in our hearts; through Jesus Christ our Lord. *Amen.**

Benediction No. 41

More saints (4)

More Saints (4)

A SHEPHERD SAINT   *St. Cuthbert*

Long ago, in Anglo-Saxon England, the northern part of the country was the kingdom of Northumbria and it was there that St. Aidan worked tirelessly to teach people about Christ and make it a Christian kingdom.

One who lived there was a young shepherd named Cuthbert. One night he had a dream in which he saw the soul of St. Aidan being taken to heaven by a band of angels. Cuthbert decided to leave his sheep and become a monk so that he, too, could help people as Aidan had done.

From his first abbey at Melrose, and later from Holy Island, or Lindisfarne, he undertook long journeys either on foot or on horseback to visit those who lived in the lonely parts of the kingdom.

There came a time, at the age of forty, when Cuthbert wanted to be alone with God. He spent eight years on one of the lonely Farne Islands. Then he was called back to work as Bishop of Lindisfarne and he began again actively to help and to heal. One story tells how he healed a child with a kiss; others tell of his friendship with animals and birds.

Cuthbert was bishop for only two years, but those were busy years in the service of others. He became ill, died, and was buried on Lindisfarne.

When Viking raids began, Cuthbert's remains were removed for safety and later laid to rest in Durham Cathedral. Each year, 20th March is kept as St. Cuthbert's Day, when we remember the man who left his sheep to become a shepherd to God's people. Our Bible reading reminds us that this was what Jesus told Peter he should do:

Bible Reading: St. John 21: 15–17

O Lord Jesus Christ, we remember how your life was spent in the service of others, and how you found strength in periods of quietness and prayer. Make us ready to spend our lives in service; teach us to find God in silence and how to pray; then send us out to do your will, to the glory of your Holy Name. *Amen.**

Closing prayer No. 14

More saints (5)

St. Giles

Over twelve hundred years ago, and possibly even fourteen hundred, for we cannot be sure, a Greek man, travelling to Rome, stayed at the home of the Bishop of Arles, a town on the river Rhone, in France.

Aegidius, or Giles as he is better known, decided then that he would become a hermit, living on his own in a cave near the river and feeding on such wild foods as he could find.

The story is told how Giles had a pet deer, which lived with him in the cave. One day the king was out hunting with his hounds, when they picked up the scent of the deer and gave chase through the forest. Seeing the deer, the king drew his bow and sent an arrow speeding through the trees.

When he reached the place where he expected to find the dead deer, the king found instead the deer by the side of Giles, who had himself been wounded by the arrow. On hearing that the deer was Giles' companion, the king ordered the hunting party to leave.

On one of his later visits to Giles, the king was advised by the hermit to build a monastery. This he agreed to do provided that Giles would become its first abbot.

Giles later became known as St. Giles and his special day in the calendar is 1st September. He is known as the patron saint of cripples and beggars. During the Middle Ages, over 150 churches in Britain were dedicated to him, including St. Giles' Cathedral in Edinburgh and St. Giles' Cripplegate, in the city of London.

We thank you, O Lord our God, for all the blessings which are ours and especially for our health and strength. We remember before you those who are unable to do the kind of things that we can do and especially any who, through disablement, are unable to leave their beds or chairs. Grant to them happiness in the many things which they can enjoy, and to those who look after them give patience and strength; through Jesus Christ our Lord. *Amen.**

Closing prayer No. 15

Service (1)

David Lloyd George

On 30th March, 1945, thousands of Welsh people from all corners of Britain gathered on the banks of the river Dwyfor in North Wales for the funeral of Earl Lloyd George of Dwyfor, better known to most of them as David Lloyd George, the man who had spent his life in the service of his country and in the interests of others.

David Lloyd George had a gift for speaking, as a preacher, as a lawyer, and as a politician. When he spoke, he did so in such a way that people could not fail to take notice of him.

He entered Parliament at the age of twenty-seven and he remained there for almost sixty-five years. During that time, he held important offices, including that of Prime Minister during the First World War. On the day that he had been a Member of Parliament for fifty years, when Britain was again at war, he said: 'If there is any service, be it great or small, which I can give to help the nation out of its tribulation and to lead the world again into the paths of peace, justice and freedom, I will do so'.

David Lloyd George is also remembered for the many things he did to help obtain better conditions for the poor and needy. He is remembered for introducing in Parliament the Act which gave out-of-work people unemployment money or sickness benefits.

There were those who thought that Earl Lloyd George should be buried in Westminster Abbey but it was not his wish. He preferred to rest in his own village at the foot of the Welsh mountains among the people who will always hold him in the highest regard.

Almighty God, we do not know what the future holds for us but we do know that it will provide many opportunities for service to others, to our town [*village*] and to our country. Help us so to prepare ourselves that when such opportunities arise we may be found ready and willing to give of our best; in the Name and for the sake of Jesus Christ our Lord. *Amen.**

Closing prayer No. 31

Service (2)

St. Hilda

St. Paul gave the people of Rome a reminder that the greatest possible service was that given to God.

Bible Reading: Romans 12: 1–2

High above the town and harbour of Whitby, in Yorkshire, stand the ruins of what was once an important abbey, famed for its learning, and which played an important part in the growth of the Christian Church.

The first abbess, and founder of the monastery, which was for men and women, was St. Hilda, whose feast day is kept each year on 17th November. She was a royal princess, who decided to give herself into the service of God.

When she was thirty-three, she became a nun in a small monastery beside the river Tweed. A year later she became abbess of one at Hartlepool and it was from there that she went to begin the new abbey at Whitby.

There were others living at the monastery, who were not monks or nuns, but who did other work. One of these was Caedmon, who discovered that he could make songs of Bible stories. When Hilda heard of it, she encouraged him, so that he became the first English religious poet.

Hilda was renowned for her wisdom, kindness, patience and courage. Bede wrote of her that 'she never failed either to return thanks to her Maker, or publicly and privately to instruct the flock committed to her charge'.

So well did she do her work, that five bishops came from her monastery. Hilda had always insisted that those who would serve God must prepare themselves and study the Holy Scriptures regularly—which is still very good advice to those who would serve God today.

O God, help us to prepare ourselves for your service. Help us
To find time to spend in your presence;
To pray and listen for you to instruct us;
To study your Word and so understand your will;
To open our hearts to let you in;
To follow the example of our Lord and Master, Jesus Christ. *Amen.**

Closing prayer No. 32

Service (3)

St. Dominic

St. Dominic, who is remembered by the church on 4th August, was born in 1170 in Castille, one of the kingdoms which later became Spain.

There was nothing particularly outstanding about his early life, except that he was determined to be a priest and as such, helped in running a cathedral.

The important year in his life was 1206, when he went with a bishop on a special mission to France. Their journey took them to Toulouse, where some people known as the Albigenses had strange beliefs and, among these, the bishop and Dominic began to work. They made no fuss about things, but lived simply and took every opportunity to preach the Gospel.

After the death of the bishop. Dominic made his headquarters at Toulouse and there an idea began to take shape. Jesus had sent out disciples to preach.

Bible Reading: St. Luke 9: 1–6

Why not have a group of priests who would be prepared to travel wherever they were needed to preach the gospel?

In 1216 the idea was approved by the Pope and, a year later, the first eleven Dominican friars set out. That was more than half the priests that Dominic had but, within a few years, there were many more. They were known as Black Friars from the colour of their robes.

The district of Blackfriars in London, indicates just one of the many places throughout the world where Dominican friars have preached and helped people, much as St. Dominic did himself during his lifetime.

O Lord, who though thou wast rich, yet for our sakes didst become poor, and hast promised in thy gospel that whatsoever is done unto the least of thy brethren, thou wilt receive as done unto thee; give us grace, we humbly beseech thee, to be ever willing and ready to minister, as thou enablest us, to the necessities of our fellow creatures, and to extend the blessings of thy kingdom over all the world, to thy praise and glory, who art God over all, blessed for ever. *Amen.*

St. Augustine

Closing prayer No. 12

Service (4)

On 20th May, 1867, James Chalmers gazed at the mountains of the island of Rarotonga as they appeared on the horizon. The months and months of waiting were ended. Here was the Pacific island to which he had been sent to work as a missionary.

The ship approached the shore and the passengers were carried ashore. Anxious to announce the name of the new arrival, the man who carried the missionary asked his name.

'Chalmers', he was told. But the man did not get it. 'Tamate', he shouted to his friends on the shore, and it was as 'Tamate' that Chalmers was known for the rest of his life.

For ten years he worked on Rarotonga, but he became restless. Tamate was an adventurer by nature. The more he heard about the cannibals who lived along the Gulf of Papua, New Guinea, the more he wished to go to work amongst them as a missionary. He and his wife knew the dangers but they also knew God, as the psalmist did.

Bible Reading: Psalm 27: 1–4 and 13–14

One of his first eerie experiences was to lie on a bed in the chief's house with human skulls dangling above him. In the years that followed he was to have many tense moments in his dealings with the head-hunting cannibals, many of whom became Christian and changed their ways. Then, after twenty-five years in Papua, the end came suddenly as Tamate ventured into new territory. Sadly, people all over the world learned that Chalmers had been attacked, killed and eaten by cannibals as he tried to teach even more of them the ways of peace and the Gospel of Jesus Christ.

O God our Father, we thank you for all who have heard your call and have gone forth into the far places of the world to teach the ways of love and peace. Bless all who continue the work to this day and hasten the day when people all over the world shall know your peace; for the sake of Jesus Christ our Lord. *Amen.**

Closing prayer No. 37

Service (5)

TO YOUNG PEOPLE   *Sir William A. Smith*

On 4th October, 1883, a number of boys made their way to the Free College Church Mission in Glasgow to see what was going on. Some of them went out of interest; the others went for a bit of a lark, determined to make a nuisance of themselves.

They found three men there, who were anxious to start an organization for boys at the church. One was William A. Smith; the others were two brothers named Hill. Those who had come to play the fool soon discovered that Mr. Smith was a man who understood boys. He was not angered by their tomfoolery but he was quite firm.

On that evening, with three officers and twenty-eight boys, the Boys' Brigade was born.

It was such an outstanding success that other companies were formed, not only in Glasgow but in other parts of Britain. Within a few years it had spread overseas, and today companies of the Boys' Brigade are to be found on every continent.

Moreover, other people became interested in the kind of organization which William Smith had started and similar groups were started for boys—the Church Lads' Brigade, the Jewish Lads' Brigade, the Boy Scouts and many others—besides sister organizations for girls, still enjoyed by children and young people today.

In 1908, when the Boys' Brigade reached its twenty-first birthday, its founder was knighted. Little did Sir William Smith realize, when he started that first company on 4th October, 1883, that he was starting an organization that would help millions of boys to learn some of the greatest lessons in life.

O God our Father, bless all who work among boys and girls, teaching them the true values of life. Fill the leaders of youth organizations with your patience: let your Spirit be with all Sunday School teachers and club leaders. Bless this school, that those who teach may do so with sincerity and those who learn with enthusiasm so that we may better ourselves and be true and loyal servants of our heavenly Father. *Amen.**

Closing prayer No. 57

Go ye into all the world . . . (1)

The last command which Jesus gave his disciples was to preach the Gospel throughout the world.

Bible Reading: St. Matthew 28: 16–20

So the Gospel spread from Jerusalem to neighbouring lands, to Rome and from there to Britain. This came about because Pope Gregory, remembering the fair-haired slaves in the market place, sent Augustine and other monks to preach the Gospel to the English.

We must remember that this mission was to the English—the Angles and Saxons—and not to the Britons who had been pushed west and were already Christian people.

In spite of hair-raising stories, Augustine sailed for Kent and landed at Ebbsfleet, where he was received by King Ethelbert, whose wife, Bertha, was already Christian.

The King listened but would not change his religion. However, he allowed the monks to use a small church in Canterbury and to preach anywhere in his kingdom. Eventually, Ethelbert and many of his subjects, won over by the sincerity of the monks, believed and were baptized. Augustine then visited France, where he was declared 'Bishop of the English'.

His attempt to win over the British bishops to the Pope's idea of having two archbishops in England, one at London and one at York was unsuccessful but in other respects, Augustine had remarkable results, especially when we recall that he died after only seven years in England. His feast day is 26th May.

O Lord Jesus Christ, who commanded your disciples saying, 'Go ye therefore, and teach all nations, baptizing them in the name of the Father, and of the Son, and of the Holy Ghost,' we praise you for those who brought the message of the Gospel to our land. Help us to remember our duty and responsibility to spread the Gospel today. We ask it in your Name and for your sake. *Amen.**

Benediction No. 53

Go ye into all the world . . . (2)

A royal wedding is always something a little out of the ordinary and a royal bride has to be well looked after. Perhaps it has always been so. Certainly in the year 625, when Princess Ethelburga, the sister of the King of Kent, was to be married to King Edwin of Northumbria, it was agreed that Bishop Paulinus should travel with her.

This was as well, for the people of Northumbria still worshipped the gods of the Anglo-Saxon people and the new Queen would need all the support the bishop could give. But for Paulinus it was a golden opportunity to preach to those around him. No doubt much of his teaching was done by his example. St. Paul had this to write about the conduct of a bishop.

Bible Reading: Titus 1: 7–9

Paulinus appears to have been very successful for, on the eve of Easter, he not only baptized King Edwin into the Christian faith but many of his nobles and other people too. The tall, dark bishop became well known as he travelled to many places, teaching about Christ and baptizing many. Before long, the Pope recognized Paulinus as Archbishop of York.

Then disaster struck. King Edwin was killed in battle and, fearing for the safety of the Queen and her children, Paulinus felt that his first responsibility was to see her safely home to Kent, and this he did by sea.

Paulinus spent his remaining years as Bishop of Rochester but when he is remembered on 10th October each year it is as St. Paulinus of York.

O God our Father, put into our hearts a desire to serve you and to serve those who are around us. Help us to use each opportunity that we have to speak kindly, to act wisely and to be true to our beliefs, so that we may show ourselves to be true children of our Father in Heaven; through Jesus Christ our Lord, to whom be praise and glory now and for ever. *Amen.**

Benediction No. 43

Go ye into all the world . . . (3)

William Carey

William Carey the cobbler hammered away at the shoes he was mending, glancing occasionally at the map of the world which he had drawn and thinking a great deal of far away places. On Sundays he put away his work, took out his Bible, and travelled to little country Baptist chapels to preach.

All the time he was thinking of the need to preach the Gospel in lands across the sea. Whenever he had the opportunity, he spoke to the clergymen about it. Once he was told, 'When God wills to convert the heathen world, young man, he'll do it without consulting you or me'.

But Will Carey was not to be put off. He called together a small group of Baptist Ministers and they met in the back room of a house in Kettering. The purpose of the meeting was to form a missionary society that would send people overseas to preach.

They agreed that they would start a fund and each put his hand in his pocket. Between them they raised the sum of £13 2s. 6d.—the first funds of the Baptist Missionary Society which they had just formed. The date was 2nd October, 1792.

Before long, Will Carey and another man were on their way to India—the first of many missionaries which the Baptist Missionary Society has sent to preach the Gospel overseas.

Carey was a remarkable man who had a wonderful gift for learning and understanding the Indian languages. In the years that followed, he learned thirty-four different Indian languages, translated the whole Bible into seven of them, the New Testament into over twenty more, and the Gospels into the rest, all in addition to preaching, teaching and visiting the needy.

O God our Father, in whose strength humble folk have been able to do great things for you; take our lives, humble as they may be, and use them as a blessing to others; for Jesus Christ's sake. *Amen.**

Closing prayer No. 4

Go ye into all the world . . . (4)

TO THE FORBIDDEN LAND   *Robert Morrison*

A large square-sailed junk sailed into a harbour in China and a young Englishman stepped ashore. The Chinese who were watching whispered among themselves: 'Look at him. He must be from an uncivilized place. Look at his large hands and the strange shape of his face'. How surprised they were when the stranger spoke to them in perfect Chinese.

He was Robert Morrison, born in Northumberland on 5th January, 1782, and now determined to preach in China about Jesus Christ. But he knew he could not begin at once for anyone found listening to him would be severely punished.

Instead, he set about the task of translating the Bible into Chinese, for he believed that if the Chinese read the Bible they would believe. Night and day he worked but, before long, all foreigners were ordered to leave China. Morrison had to smuggle his work out to the island of Macao, where he continued with it.

Imagine his pleasure one day to open a parcel which contained the first copies of a part of the Bible in Chinese. Soon he had translated St. Luke's Gospel, which was smuggled into China in sacks of rice.

Twenty-five years after his arrival in China, copies of the Bible were reaching all parts of China and no one knew how—except Robert Morrison. Neither was he put off when the Emperor promised death for anyone found printing Christian books in Chinese—he just had to be extra careful.

A few years later, missionaries were allowed into China, where they found people eager to hear the word which they had already read for themselves.

O God, the Father of all men, look upon the nations of the world in your love and mercy so that where there is darkness there may be light; where there is war there may be peace; where there is hatred there may be love; so that people throughout the world may find your true peace and joy; through Christ our Lord. *Amen.**

Closing prayer No. 18

Go ye into all the world . . . (5)

John Williams was born in 1796 in what was then the little village of Tottenham, lying to the north of London. When he was fourteen, he moved into London and became a blacksmith.

At that time he gave up church-going but, one evening when his friends let him down, his master's wife asked him to go to church with her. That night he vowed that the rest of his life would be spent in serving Jesus.

He prayed, he studied his Bible and took the examinations of the London Missionary Society. At the age of twenty, with his wife, Mary, he sailed for the Pacific.

Twelve months after leaving London, they arrived at Tahiti before moving on to other islands. At Rarotonga, Williams built his own ship and sailed in her for thousands of miles.

Wherever he went he was loved and respected. He was called *Wiliamu Tama*—'Williams our father'. Everywhere churches were built to replace the altars on which human sacrifices had been offered. Everywhere he saw how the Christian Gospel was changing men's lives.

After eighteen years, he returned to England on leave. He toured the country, spoke at meetings and raised enough money to buy a fine new ship, the *Camden*. Moreover, when he sailed in her on 11th April, 1838, he took with him sixteen new workers.

Visiting new islands he was thrilled to be welcomed by the islanders. Then, after eighteen months came the end. He was not to know when he landed on one island that the people had been badly treated by some white traders. Williams was clubbed to death.

Throughout the world people were shocked and stunned. Many of the islanders felt they had lost a dear friend. But the work which Williams started went on and it continues to this day.

O thou who didst command thine apostles to go into all the world and to preach the gospel to every creature, let thy name be great among the nations, from the rising up of the sun unto the going down of the same, O Lord our strength and our redeemer. *Amen.*

Prayers in use at Uppingham School

Closing prayer No. 37

Prayers and Bible Readings

Prayers for opening worship

These prayers are suitable for use as part of the opening act of worship. They form a small selection of many which can be found in anthologies of prayers and should not be regarded as a complete list, since a varied opening is essential if the service is to have vitality.

PRAYERS OF PRAISE AND THANKSGIVING

Almighty God, we thank thee that thou hast kept us through the past night and brought us in safety to the beginning of another day. We pray thee to preserve us both in soul and body; to give us health and wisdom; to uphold us in temptation, to keep us from sin, and to help us in all things to please thee; through Jesus Christ our Lord. *Amen.*

Source not known

Almighty God, whose glory the heavens are telling, the earth his power, and the sea his might, and whose greatness all feeling and thinking creatures everywhere herald; to thee belongeth glory, honour, might, greatness, and magnificence now and for ever, to the ages of ages, through Jesus Christ our Lord. *Amen.*

Liturgy of St. James (Second Century)

Creator of life and light, we bless thee for the beauty of thy world; for sunshine and flowers, for clouds and stars, for the first radiance of dawn and the last glow of sunset. We thank thee for physical joy, for the smell of rain on dry ground, for hills to climb and hard work to do, for music that lifts our hearts to heaven, and for friendship. For all the beauty and the joy of home-love, for mother-love, for child-love, for the joy of the sense of thy presence, we thank thee, O Lord. *Amen.*

The Guide Law

Father, we thank you for all your great gifts to us; for food and clothing, for health and strength, for families and friends, for work and play, and for so many blessings that we are quite unable to count them. Help us never to take these gifts for granted but to show our thankfulness in our attitudes to others, knowing that in serving them we are serving you; through Jesus Christ our Lord. *Amen.**

Prayers for opening worship   403

In the morning, O Lord, let our prayer come before thee: Grant, we beseech thee, that we may pass this day in gladness and peace, without stumbling and without stain; that, reaching the eventide victorious over all temptation, we may praise thee, the eternal God, who art blessed, and dost govern all things, world without end. *Amen.*

Mozarabic Liturgy

O Lord, our heavenly Father, almighty and everlasting God, who hast safely brought us to the beginning of this day: defend us in the same with thy mighty power; and grant that this day we fall into no sin, neither run into any kind of danger; but that all our doings may be ordered by thy governance, to do always that is righteous in thy sight; through Jesus Christ our Lord. *Amen.*

Gelasian Sacramentary

We come before you, O Lord our God, at the beginning of the day before we become involved in our many and varied activities. Accept our thanks for all you have given and let your blessing rest upon us. May we endeavour throughout the day, in all our activities, to do and say only those things which are acceptable in your sight; through Jesus Christ our Lord. *Amen.**

We give thee hearty thanks, O Lord, for the rest of the past night, and the gift of a new day, with its many opportunities of pleasing thee. Grant that we may so pass its hours in the perfect freedom of thy service, that at eventide we may again give thanks unto thee; through Jesus Christ our Lord. *Amen.*

Daybreak Service of the Eastern Church (Third Century)

Other prayers suitable for opening worship may be found on the following pages:
5, 11, 17, 28, 49, 51, 53, 54, 60, 73, 76, 80, 90, 92, 94, 112, 116, 118, 119, 120, 121, 123, 126, 127, 130, 133, 146, 160, 163, 170, 172, 232, 357, 359, 364, 387, 389, 392

BEFORE A BIBLE READING

Prayers that could be used before a Bible reading not linked to one of the stories may be found on the following pages:
56, 74, 156, 392

PRAYERS OF CONFESSION AND PENITENCE

Grant, we beseech thee, merciful Lord, to thy faithful people pardon and peace; that they may be cleansed from all their sins, and serve thee with a quiet mind; through Jesus Christ our Lord. *Amen.*

Gelasian Sacramentary (Eighth Century)

O merciful Lord, forgive us
For careless words which have offended other people;
For thoughtless deeds which have hurt other people;
For all our acts of selfishness, unkindness or deceit;
For deliberately avoiding opportunities of helping others;
For breaking your holy laws.
   For these and all our sins, forgive us in the Name of our Lord Jesus Christ. *Amen.**

See also the following pages:
102, 104, 128, 169, 199, 217, 366, 380

Closing prayers

1. Almighty God, unto whom all hearts be open, all desires known, and from whom no secrets are hid: cleanse the thoughts of our hearts by the inspiration of thy Holy Spirit, that we may perfectly love thee and worthily magnify thy Holy Name; through Christ our Lord. *Amen.*

Bishop Leofric

2. Almighty God, whose service is perfect freedom; grant us so to follow the example of thy Son Jesus Christ, that we may find our joy in service all the days of our life. *Amen.*

The Daily Service

3. Father, we thank you for all those whose company we enjoy. Help us to know the love of others for us, and to be loving and kind in all our ways; for Jesus Christ's sake. *Amen.**

4. For freedom, peace, and quiet minds, praise be to you, O God. *Amen.**

5. Give me strength, O God, to do the work of this day: and grant that at its close I may be found worthy of thy trust in me. *Amen.*

The Daily Service

6. Grant, Lord, that what we have said with our lips we may believe in our hearts and practise in our lives; and of thy great mercy keep us faithful unto the end. *Amen.*

John Hunter

7. Grant, O God, that these few minutes with you may send us out again
    More kind to others;
    More honest with ourselves;
    More loyal to you;
   through Jesus Christ our Lord. *Amen.*

Dr. William Barclay

8. Grant to us, O God, the seeing eye, the hearing ear, the understanding mind and the loving heart, so that we may see your glory, and hear your word, and understand your truth, and answer to your love: through Jesus Christ our Lord. *Amen.*

Dr. William Barclay

9. Grant us, O Lord, to pass this day in gladness and peace, without stumbling and without stain, that reaching the eventide victorious over all temptation, we may praise thee, the eternal God, who art blessed and dost govern all things, world without end. *Amen.*

Mozarabic Liturgy

10. Grant, we beseech thee, almighty God, unto us who know that we are weak, and who trust in thee because we know that thou art strong, the gladsome help of thy loving-kindness, both here in time and hereafter in eternity. *Amen.*

Roman Breviary

11. Help us, O God, to know what is right and to do nothing but the right; for Jesus Christ's sake. *Amen.**

12. Help us, O God, to do some little thing today that will make the world a better place because we have been here. *Amen.**

13. Help us, O Lord, to seek you, to find you and to follow you, so that we may walk in wisdom now and all our days. *Amen.**

14. Into thy hands, O God, we commend ourselves this day;
Let thy presence be with us to its close.
Enable us to feel that in doing our work we are doing thy will
And that in serving others we are serving thee;
Through Jesus Christ our Lord. *Amen.*

Prayers in use at Uppingham School

15. Lord have mercy upon all who suffer in body, mind or spirit and let your healing hand rest upon them; through Jesus Christ our Lord. *Amen.**

Closing prayers

P

16. Lord, make me gentle and unselfish.
    Help me to strive manfully for that which is right.
    Make me merciful to all that are broken or bowed down.
    Create in me a clean heart.
    Teach me the way of peace: and let me be of them that make peace.
       For Jesus Christ's sake. *Amen.*

                                                The Daily Service

17. Make us to remember, O God, that every day is thy gift and ought to be used according to thy command; through Jesus Christ our Lord. *Amen.*

                                                Samuel Johnson

18. O God, be our strength and inspiration so that we may be bold to resist temptation and to stand up for all those things which we believe to be right. *Amen.**

19. O God, come and dwell in our hearts so that we may be like you in all our ways; and to you be the glory for ever. *Amen.**

20. O God, give us wisdom to know what is right; strength to do it; and courage to declare it; for the sake of Jesus Christ our Lord. *Amen.**

21. O God, give us humility and meekness, make us long-suffering and gentle, help us ever to esteem others better than ourselves, and so, O Lord, teach us to follow more closely in the steps of our Divine Master, Jesus Christ our Lord. *Amen.*

                                                A Chain of Prayer

22. O God, help us to be the masters of ourselves that we may become the servants of others, and thus follow in the path of thy blessed Son, Jesus Christ our Lord. *Amen.*

                                                Alec Paterson

23. O God, make me to be all that I ought to be, so that your Name may be glorified through me. *Amen.**

24. O God of truth and love, make us strong and courageous so that we may ever uphold your truth and live in your love; for Jesus Christ's sake. *Amen.**

25. O God,
Open my ears that I may hear you speaking to me;
Open my eyes that I may see how to do your will;
And open my heart so that I may think more of you than I do myself; for Jesus Christ's sake. *Amen.**

26. O God our Father, give us work to do, patience to keep at it and perseverance until it be finished; through Jesus Christ our Lord. *Amen.**

27. O Heavenly Father, we pray thee to send into our hearts and into the hearts of all men everywhere, the Spirit of our Lord Jesus Christ. *Amen.*

(Source unknown)

28. O Lord,
Let us not live to be useless;
For Christ's sake. *Amen.*

John Wesley

29. O Lord, make thy way plain before me. Let thy glory be my end, thy Word my rule; and then, thy will be done. *Amen.*

King Charles I

30. Open our eyes, O God, to the beauties of the world around us. May nothing we do spoil it for others; through Jesus Christ our Lord. *Amen.**

31. Open my eyes that I may see
The work that thou hast set for me;
And help me daily by thy grace
Thy will to do, thy steps to trace. *Amen.**

32. Teach us, good Lord, to use our gifts in the service of others. Make our feet willing, our hands useful, our minds active and our hearts pure in thy service; for Jesus Christ's sake. *Amen.**

33. The things, good Lord, that we pray for, give us grace to labour for; through Jesus Christ our Lord. *Amen.*

St. Thomas More

34. Thine, O Lord, is the greatness, and the power, and the glory, and the victory, and the majesty; for all that is in the heaven and in the earth is thine; thine is the kingdom, O Lord, and thou art exalted as head above all. Now therefore, our God, we thank thee and praise thy glorious name. *Amen.*

1 Chronicles 29, 11–13

35. Thou hast given so much to us, give one thing more, a grateful heart; for Christ's sake. *Amen.*

George Herbert

36. Throughout this day, O Father, let us walk with you and talk with you. May your presence be known and your will be done. We ask it for Jesus Christ's sake. *Amen.**

37. We thank thee Lord, for all the saints and heroes who have fought and conquered in thy Name. Fill us with the spirit of adventure and the courage we shall need to follow their example. For Jesus Christ's sake. *Amen.*

Geoffrey Clifton

38. We thank thee, O God, for all that thou hast given us. Help us to use thy gifts better, and to show our gratitude by giving ourselves more truly to thy service. *Amen.*

E. M. Venables

39. We thank you, O God, for all your blessings. Help us to share them with others, knowing that in doing so we are serving you; for Christ's sake. *Amen.**

Benedictions

(dagger symbol † indicates traditional benedictions or source unknown)

---

40. Into the faithful hands of our God we commit ourselves now and always. O Lord, let us be thine and remain thine for ever; through Jesus Christ, thy Son, our Lord. *Amen.*†

41. May God the Father bless us and all men everywhere and fill our hearts with his peace and goodwill. *Amen.**

42. May God the Father bless us.
May Christ the Son take care of us.
The Holy Ghost enlighten us all the days of our life.
The Lord be our defender and keeper of body and soul both now and forever. *Amen.*

    Bishop Aedelward (Ninth Century)

43. May God the Father of our Lord Jesus Christ, bless, direct and keep us, and give us thankful hearts, now and for evermore. *Amen.*†

44. May grace, mercy and peace from the Father, the Son and the Holy Spirit, be with us all this day and always. *Amen.*†

45. May the blessing of God Almighty, the Father, the Son, and the Holy Spirit, rest upon us and upon all God's people everywhere, now and for ever. *Amen.*†

46. May the grace of courage, gaiety, and the quiet mind, and all such blessedness as cometh from the Father to his children, be ours now and ever. *Amen.*†

47. May the Lord grant us his blessing and fill our hearts with the spirit of truth and peace, now and for evermore. *Amen.*†

48. May the Lord lead us when we go, and keep us when we sleep, and talk with us when we wake; and may the peace of God, which passeth all understanding, keep our hearts and minds; through Jesus Christ our Lord. *Amen.*†

---

49. May the Spirit of the Lord Jesus Christ direct our thoughts and help us to learn of him with honest hearts, now and always. *Amen.*†

50. May the strength of God pilot us. May the power of God preserve us. May the wisdom of God instruct us. May the hand of God protect us. May the way of God direct us, and may the shield of God defend us, now and evermore. *Amen.*

St. Patrick

51. Now may God bless us and keep us: may he give us light to guide us, courage to support us, and love to unite us, this day and for evermore. *Amen.*†

52. Now unto the King, eternal, immortal, invisible, the only wise God, be honour and glory for ever and ever. *Amen.*

St. Paul (1 Timothy 1, 17)

53. Our God and Father himself, and our Lord Jesus Christ, direct our ways; and the Lord make us to increase and abound in love towards one another, and towards all men, now and ever. *Amen.*

St. Paul (1 Thessalonians 3: 11–12 adapted)

54. The grace of our Lord Jesus Christ and the love of God, and the fellowship of the Holy Spirit, be with us all, evermore. *Amen.*

St. Paul (2 Corinthians 13: 14 adapted)

55. The peace of God, which passeth all understanding, keep your hearts and minds through Christ Jesus. *Amen.*

St. Paul (Philippians 4: 7)

56. Unto God's gracious mercy and protection we commit ourselves. The Lord bless us and keep us. The Lord make his face to shine upon us and be gracious unto us. The Lord lift up the light of his countenance upon us, and give us peace, both now and evermore. *Amen.*

Numbers 6: 24–26 (adapted)

Prayers for the school

(see also in Prayer index)

57. Prosper with thy blessing, O Lord, the work of this school, and grant that those who serve thee here may set thy holy will ever before them, doing that which is well-pleasing in thy sight and persevering in thy service unto the end; through the might of Jesus Christ our Lord. *Amen.*

Source not known

58. O Lord, bless our school: that working together and playing together, we may learn to serve thee, and to serve one another: for Jesus' sake. *Amen.*

The Daily Service

59. Visit, O Lord, this school with thy mercy; remove far from it all that would stain its honour or destroy its comradeship; let thy holy presence dwell in it to preserve us in peace, and let thy blessing be upon it and upon us evermore; through Jesus Christ our Lord. *Amen.*

Source not known

60. O Almighty God, who hast gathered us together as members of one body, grant that we may realize our responsibility to one another; may truth, honour and kindness abound amongst us; may thy blessing rest upon our work, may thy Name be hallowed in our midst, and thy peace guard our hearts; through Jesus Christ our Lord. *Amen.*

Source not known

Prayers for special occasions

61. *The beginning of term*

O God our Father, we come to you now at the beginning of this new term to thank you for the holiday which we have just enjoyed and to ask your blessing upon all we shall do this term. In our work grant us patience and determination when facing new problems; in our play help us to be fair and show consideration to others; in all things help us to remember that we are your children and to look to you for guidance; through Jesus Christ our Lord. *Amen.**

62. *The end of term or half-term*

O God, we thank you for this short break from our studies. Help us to enjoy ourselves in the company of our families and friends and in the open air. Inspire us to be helpful in the home and careful in the streets, so that nothing we do may spoil this holiday for ourselves or for others; for Jesus Christ's sake. *Amen.**

63. *The end of the school year*

Accept, O God, our thanks for all this year has meant to us:
For the work that we have accomplished;
For the pleasures we have enjoyed;
For the friendships we have formed.
We ask your blessing upon
All who are leaving this school today;
All who will return after a refreshing holiday;
All who will be working to make the school ready for their return.
Grant that the lessons we have learned here may remain with us and enrich our lives in the days to come; through Jesus Christ our Lord. *Amen.**

64. *Before a school journey*

O God our Father, some of our teachers and our friends will be leaving us today on a school journey [to ......]. We pray that you will bless their time together. May they benefit from their journey by seeing much that is of interest and by learning how to live and work together. Watch over and guard them, keep them from harm and danger, and, when their journey ends, bring them safely home; through Jesus Christ our Lord. *Amen.**

65. *After a school journey*

We thank you, O God, for the safe return of those who have been away from the school. Grant that the lessons learned may be of lasting benefit and that happy memories may remain. Now together again, we join to praise your Holy Name. *Amen.**

66. *On Sports Day*

O God, we thank you for fit bodies and active minds. Today as we enjoy our sports, help us to strive hard but fairly and to remember that not all can win. May we not become big-headed if we win nor be unduly disappointed if defeated, but know that our chief reward is the satisfaction of having done our best; through Jesus Christ our Lord. *Amen.**

67. *On Open Day*

O God our Father, we remember today with thankfulness all those who have helped to shape our lives:

Our parents who have watched over us, fed and clothed us, and provided homes for us to live in.

Our teachers who have taught us with patience and skill so that we have grown in knowledge and wisdom.

Our friends, relatives and neighbours, who have often been willing to help us through our difficulties.

Our church, Sunday School or youth organization leaders, who have taught us about you and about your great love for us.

For these and all who have guided us, praise be to you, O God. *Amen.**

68. *Serious illness of children or staff*

O Lord Jesus Christ, who when on earth helped many who were ill or in pain, we remember in prayer many who suffer today. We pray especially for ..... and ask that your healing hand may be upon *him* so that *he* may be restored again to health and strength if it is your will. Bless those who watch over *him* and grant them your strength and patience at this time. In your mercy hear our prayer, O Christ. *Amen.**

69. *Death of a member of staff*

O God of the spirits of all men, we praise thy holy Name for the courage and faithfulness of thy servant who, having fought a good fight, has passed from this life on earth; and we beseech thee that, encouraged by *his* example and strengthened by *his* fellowship, we with *him* may be found ready to share in the life eternal, through the power of Jesus Christ our Lord. *Amen.*

Source not known

70. *Death of a child*

O God, the Father of us all, we thank you for the life and the friendship of . . . . . . who has been taken from us [and no longer has to suffer pain]. Receive *him* into your holy keeping and grant your fatherly comfort to the family which mourns; through Jesus Christ our Lord. *Amen.**

71. *For those who mourn*

Comfort, O Lord, we pray thee, all who mourn for the loss of those dear to them; be with them in their sorrow; give them faith to look beyond the troubles of the present time, and to know that neither life nor death can separate us from the love of God which is in Jesus Christ our Lord. *Amen.*

The Kingdom, the Power, and the Glory

72. *A wedding in the school*

O God, whose nature is love, we thank you for that love which can unite a man and a woman in a bond which can last as long as life itself. Today we rejoice with . . . and . . . as they make their promises to each other and before you; and we ask your blessing on their marriage, praying that every joy might be theirs in their life together; through Jesus Christ our Lord. *Amen.**

73. Confirmation of pupils

Almighty God, by whose Son we were taught the need through baptism to show that we desire to be changed and lead a new life; we thank you for those whose parents brought them to you as children and who now wish to confirm this action by offering themselves for your blessing. Let your Holy Spirit enter their lives to inspire them to serve you faithfully all their days: in the Name of the Father and of the Son and of the Holy Ghost. *Amen.**

74. After a street accident

O God our Father, the roads are so busy and often we do things without thinking. Help us to remember all that we are told about Road Safety so that we cause no accident which will hurt us or others. [Today we pray for ...... who has just been hurt in an accident and ask that *he* may soon be well again and able to return to school.] We ask it in the name of Jesus. *Amen.**

75. Those responsible for our school

Almighty God, as we thank you for our school, we thank you, too, for those responsible for building it and for providing for our daily needs:
The Council responsible for the area in which we live;
The Education Committee, who make decisions about schools and education;
The Education Officer and his staff who carry out these decisions and equip the schools;
The Governors/Managers who are especially interested in this school.
Grant unto them your guidance and wisdom in all the decisions they have to make and let all their actions be those which are in the true interests of education in this district; through Jesus Christ our Lord. *Amen.**

76. School neighbours (differences of opinion)

O God our Father, we pray that we may be good neighbours to those who live near our school. Forgive us if sometimes we do things which annoy them or if we speak rudely or unkindly when they complain. Grant that they may have patience with us and that we may be considerate toward them, so that a happy relationship may exist between us; through Jesus Christ our Lord. *Amen.**

77. *Former pupils*

Heavenly Father, we thank you for all those teachers and pupils who have made this school what it is today. We thank you for those who have still remained interested in the school and its welfare in the years since they left to go their several ways. Grant that we, like them, may enter whole-heartedly into our school life so that for us, as for them, our school may hold many treasured memories; through Jesus Christ our Lord. *Amen.**

78. *Before an election*

O God our Father, tomorow our school will be used for voting and we ask your blessing on all that shall be done. May those who vote do so wisely, and may those candidates who are elected be those who will be able to serve our *country/town/ community/* . . . faithfully and well. We ask it in Jesus Christ's name. *Amen.**

79. *A special event*

Almighty God, we commend into your hands *the event (which should be named)* for which we have been working. We thank you for all the enjoyment which we have had in preparing for it and we pray that it may be a success, bringing pleasure to all who attend and satisfaction to all taking part; through Jesus Christ our Lord. *Amen.**

Sources of prayers

Sources of prayers   419

Bible readings linked to stories

Bible readings linked to stories   423

Q

Bible readings linked to stories

Additional Bible readings

The following readings, which have not been used in conjunction with any of the stories, would be suitable for inclusion in the opening act of worship on days when no Bible reading is indicated.

READINGS FROM THE OLD TESTAMENT

2 Samuel 22: 2–7

1 Chronicles 16: 8–14
              31–34

Psalm   1
          17; 4–7
          18; 30–31
          47; 5–9
          51; 9–12
          72; 18–19
          84; 8–12
          86; 8–12
          89; 15–18
          96; 7–10
              11–13
          104; 1–9
               31–35
          105; 1–4
          111
          113
          134
          135; 1–3 & 5–6
          145; 3–7
          147; 1–2 & 5–7
          148; 1–6

Proverbs 3; 1–7
         4; 20–27

Isaiah 12; 4–5

Daniel 2; 20–23

INCIDENTS IN THE LIFE OF JESUS AND THE APOSTLES

St. Matthew	3; 13–17	Baptism of Jesus
	4; 23–25	Curing illnesses
	8; 14–17	Healing Peter's mother-in-law
	9; 18–19 & 23–26	Jairus's daughter
	10; 1–4	The twelve apostles
	17; 14–20	The epileptic healed
St. Mark	2; 1–12	Palsied man lowered through roof
	7; 31–37	Healing the deaf
	8; 22–26	Healing the blind beggar
	10; 13–16	Blessing the children
	46–52	Blind Bartimaeus
St. Luke	4; 31–37	Jesus speaks with authority
	7; 1–10	Centurion's servant healed
St. John	4; 1–15	The Samaritan woman at the well
Acts	3; 1–10	Peter heals the cripple
	5; 12–16	Peter's shadow heals

TEACHINGS OF JESUS AND THE APOSTLES

St. Matthew	5; 17–20	Upholding the Law
	23–24	Reconciliation with brother
	10; 28–31	A lesson concerning sparrows
	11; 28–30	'Come unto Me'
	18; 1–7	Lesson of the little child
	21–22	Forgiving 70 x 7
	25; 1–13	Wise and foolish virgins
St. Mark	3; 1–6	Doing good on the Sabbath
	12; 28–34	The Great Commandment
St. Luke	5; 36–39	Parables of the new and the old
	11; 11–13	God's fatherly care
	33–36	The lamp under the bushel (meal tub)
St. John	10; 1–14	The Good Shepherd
	14–18	The Good Shepherd
	15; 1–10	The Vine and the branches

Romans	8;	1–4 (8)	*Living in God's ways*
		26–30	*Things work together for good*
		31–34	*God's love*
		35–39	*Assurance of presence of Christ*
	10;	11–15 (17)	*The universal Gospel*
	13;	7–10	*On the Commandments*
	16;	17–18	*Avoid troublemakers*

| 1 Corinthians | 13 | | *Sermon on love* |

| Galatians | 6; | 1–5 | *Help rather than condemn* |

| Ephesians | 3; | 14–21 | *Christ in our hearts* |
| | 4; | 25–32 | *Right attitudes* |

| 1 Timothy | 6; | 17–19 | *Trust God, not riches* |

1 John	1;	5–10	*God is Light*
	2;	7–11	*A command to love*
	4;	6b–21	*Love God: love brother*

Index of Prayer Subjects

Accident, 417
Achievements, 102
Actions, 18, 187, 295
Active minds, 93, 225, 242, 409
Activities of the day, 404
Actors and actresses, 48
Admitting faults and mistakes, 269, 303, 353, 361, 377
Advent, 150
Adventure, 81, 83, 87, 114, 254, 310–312, 410
Advice, 261, 353
Africa, 343
Aiming high, 89, 234
Air travellers, 84
Alertness, 42, 44, 84
Ambition, 115, 234, 289, 315
Ambulance workers, 243
Amusements, 112, 126
Anger, 381
Animals and birds, 35–6, 38–9
Annoyance to others, 417
Appreciation of gifts, 47
Armour of God, 202
Art and craft, 51, 69, 172, 226
Arrogance, 283
Ascension, 154
Asia, 343
Authority, positions of, 136, 197
Authors, 56, 67
Autumn, 127, 130

Bad feelings, 13
Ballet, 46
Baptism, 417
Beauty of the world, 39, 51, 53, 94, 110, 116, 118, 120, 127, 130, 226, 338, 359, 403, 409
Beginning of term, 414
Behaving openly, 269, 303, 377
Beliefs, 275, 283, 285, 332
Believing, 134, 354
Benedictions, 411–2
Better world, 88, 192, 196, 224, 339, 407
Bible, 56, 64, 74, 98, 156–60
Bible societies, 98, 158
Bible study, 56, 64, 156, 392

Big-headedness, 415
Birth of Christ (see *Christmas*)
Blessing of God, 63, 411–3
Blessings, 11, 57, 60, 62, 97, 100, 126, 127, 146, 214, 307, 404
Blind, 35, 110, 338, 363
Blind eye, a, 279
Body, human, 42, 246, 248, 250
Boldness, 78, 122, 347
Books, 12, 49, 56, 67
Braille, 338
Bravery, 71, 288, 376
Brotherhood, 190, 192–3, 195–6, 210, 316

Called by God, 78, 341–2
Care for others (see *Service*)
Care of bodies, 225, 248
Cares, 31, 99, 166
Caretaker, school, 414
Challenges, 43, 311, 312, 371
Changelessness of God, 80, 125, 232
Charity, 284, 374
Cheer, 224
Cheerfulness, 61, 121, 259
Children, 13, 164, 236, 305
Children's homes, 164
Choice, free, 271
Choosing right, 271, 346
Christian Church, 16
Christian unity, 147, 148, 210
Christmas, 94, 138–40, 151, 335
Church, 16, 147, 148, 210
Church leaders, 415
Cinema, 49
Citizenship, 12
Cleaners, school, 8, 414
Cleanliness, 248, 250
Close of the day, 404, 407
Closing prayers, 406–10
Clothing, 403, 415
Clowns and comedians, 45, 48
Club leaders, 395
Comfort, 7, 100, 112, 165, 171, 284, 345, 383
Commands of God, 40
Common sense, 294
Commonwealth, The, 181, 185

Evil, 66, 77, 202, 204, 253, 352
Evil spirits, 132
Example, Christ's, 29, 43, 87, 89, 94,
 160, 200, 205, 221, 263, 277, 324,
 333, 373, 380, 392, 406
Example of others, 133, 134, 263,
 266, 285, 337, 341, 349, 369, 379,
 410
Experiments, 85, 358, 362
Eyes, 130, 279, 308, 338, 361, 406,
 409

Facing problems, 19, 114
Failure, 87, 115, 234, 289, 358, 380,
 387
Faint-hearted, 300
Fairness, 40, 41, 198, 414, 415
Faith, 24, 81, 311, 353
Faith in God (see *Trust in God*)
Faithfulness, 14, 41, 134, 222, 230,
 253, 274, 275, 277, 278, 285, 286,
 287, 298, 344, 386, 405, 406
Families and friends, 3, 7, 14, 65,
 100, 272, 320, 403, 406, 414
Faults, 29, 30, 269, 302, 303
Fear, 43, 71, 87, 261, 296, 351, 380
 freedom from, 132, 197, 235, 282,
 323, 347
Feeding our minds, 225
Fighting evil, 77
Finding God, 280, 308, 389, 407
Finishing our tasks, 41, 228, 314, 409
Firemen and fires, 240
Firm foundations, 101
Fishermen, 70, 79, 103
Fitness, 42, 44, 246
Floods, 101
Flowers, 118, 119, 130, 403
Following God, 29, 31, 64, 99, 229,
 265, 331, 332, 408
Food, 129, 130, 403, 415
Foolishness, 294
Forgiveness sought, 30, 104, 107,
 199, 217, 328, 380, 387, 405
Forgiving others, 8, 23, 187, 205, 221
Former pupils, 407
Freedom, 68, 183, 189, 212–14, 216,
 235, 282, 347, 406
 from fear (see under *Fear*)
 to choose, 271
Friendless, the, 229, 331, 335
Friends, 22, 262, 272, 320, 414
Friendship, 22, 179, 182, 185, 198,
 205, 403, 414

Full lives, 291, 382
Future, 25, 81, 107, 309, 391

Games, 415
Generosity, 138, 218, 284
Gentleness, 171, 218, 284, 332, 407
Gifts, 108, 118, 130, 151, 217, 403
Give and take, 21
Giving, 23, 96, 138, 206, 284
Giving in, 213
Giving of our best, 307, 322, 356
Giving ourselves, 4, 153, 410
 (see also *Talents*)
Giving pleasure, 366
Gladness, 139, 404, 407
Glory to God, 63, 89, 139, 148, 154,
 324, 364, 403, 409
Good name, 27
Good relationships, 59
Goodness, 219
 of God, 99, 232
Goodwill, International, 179–83
Goodwill to men, 138–40
Gospel, 16, 64, 145, 159
Government, 124, 136, 197, 216
Gratefulness, 47, 53, 410
Greatness of God, 90, 123
Greed, 13, 96, 381
Guidance, 18, 74, 107–9, 114, 125,
 155, 163, 167, 188, 203, 204, 218,
 232, 271, 346, 349, 355, 388, 414
Guide dogs, 35, 338

Half-term, 414
Hands, 409
Happiness, 65, 126, 231, 233, 301,
 304, 306, 319
Hardship, 82, 116, 286, 371
Harmony, 20, 205
Harvest, 117, 127, 129, 130
Hatred, 13, 24, 26, 104, 190, 191,
 197, 201, 399
Healing, 171, 242–7, 407, 415
Health, 116, 126, 225, 242, 248, 390,
 403
Healthier world, 290
Hearing, 75–6, 78, 288, 341, 363, 406
Heart, 251, 406, 408, 409
Help of God, 19, 43, 80, 125, 168,
 232, 313, 317
Helping hand, 6, 19, 61, 71, 100,
 112, 141, 186, 291, 292, 334, 335,
 345, 372, 376, 393
Heritage, 47, 60, 63

Heroes, 410
Holidays, 126, 414
Holy Spirit, 155–7, 181, 207, 288, 355, 367, 382, 386, 406
Holy Week, 152
Home, 3, 6, 7, 44, 100, 116, 403, 415
Homeless, 7, 335, 340
Honest with ourselves, 344
Honesty, 18, 269, 300, 303, 406
Honourable things, 230, 250, 253
Hope, 24
Hopes, 261
Hospitals, 242, 243, 247
Humility, 208, 252, 254, 264, 324–7, 398, 408
Humour, sense of, 45
Hunger, 129, 186, 305, 335, 340
Hurting others, 405
Hymns, 139, 170, 384
Hymn writers, 170

Ice and snow, 112, 116
Ideals, 271, 272
Illness, 242–9
  in school, 415
Imagination(s), 296, 358
Impossible, The seemingly, 86, 87
Injustice, 197, 220
Inspiration of God, 43, 88, 155, 181, 288, 304, 351, 352, 355, 408
Interesting things of life, 58
International friendship, 179–86, 192–3, 195–6
Intolerance, 201, 203
Introspection, 29
Invention, 62, 97

Journey of life, 309–14
Journeys, 84
Joy, 55, 59, 83, 86, 95, 154, 207, 249, 261, 276, 323, 362, 365, 403, 406
Judges and magistrates, 72, 227, 299
Judging others, 183, 283, 302
Justice, 124, 197, 210, 220, 299

Keeping Commandments, 153
Keeping fit, 44
Kindness, 15, 22, 71, 96, 138, 203, 219, 229, 264, 266, 284, 331, 376, 406, 413
Kingdom of God on earth, 82, 85, 89, 140, 148, 193, 286, 317, 336
Knowing what to do, 293, 348
Knowledge, 10, 52, 113, 415

Labour (see also *Work*), 4, 206
Laughter, 45, 52, 121
Law and order, 256, 299
Law breakers, 299
Laws, God's, 72, 382
Leaders, 72, 181, 188, 216, 227
Leadership, 210
Learning, 87, 236, 395
  Men of, 72
Leisure, 321
Leprosy, 337
Less fortunate, The, 7, 75, 100, 117, 129, 164, 165, 186, 231, 282, 334, 335, 340, 363, 390
Lessons, 38, 414
Letters, 55
Life, Full, 306
Life's adventure (see *Adventure*)
Lifeboats, 239, 255
Light, 24, 107, 109, 111, 137, 224, 293, 297, 368, 399
Lighthouses and lightships, 238
Likeness to God, 284, 331
Listening to God, 40, 76, 78, 341, 392, 406, 408
Literature, 47, 51, 172
Little things, 82
Lives, 250, 332
Living Christ, 154
Living well, 40, 60, 134, 235, 237, 279, 300, 319, 344
Local government, 124, 136, 417, 418
Losing heart, 222, 358
Love, 23, 24, 26, 71, 96, 148, 181, 219, 221, 297, 332, 399
  of God, 90, 123, 137, 140, 154, 188, 221, 263, 345, 354, 364, 407
  of others, 100, 406
  towards God, 132, 153, 162, 207, 265, 280, 387, 406
  towards others, 77, 149, 182, 193, 205, 263, 269, 303, 376, 406
Loving-kindness, 407
Loyalty: to friends, 8, 270, 272
  to God, 270, 271–2, 287, 320, 378, 406
  to ideals, 270–3, 320
  to others, 269–73, 303, 377
  to school, 270

Making room for Christ, 151, 152
Making our mark, 61, 233
Making up one's mind, 271, 275, 349
Mankind, 317

Index of Prayer Subjects

435

Using talents (see *Talents*)

Values, True, 319–23
Village, 28, 391
Violence, 104
Visions, 88
Voices, 50, 53, 75, 91

Wages, 215
Wales, 384
Walking with God, 31, 99, 114, 133, 149, 166, 223, 309, 323, 355, 410
Want, 305
Watchfulness, 84, 200
Way of God, 199, 235, 409
Weaknesses, 163, 260, 293, 407
Weather, 112
Wedding, 416
Whitsun, 155
Whole armour of God, 202

Wild life preservation, 39
Willingness, 150, 264, 342, 365, 391
Winter, 112, 116
Wisdom, 60, 107, 136, 161, 173, 203, 208, 210, 234, 282, 294, 295, 298, 353, 403, 407, 408, 415
Wonder, 91, 123
Word of God, (see *Bible, Gospel*)
Words, 250, 387
  Hurtful, 187
Work, Daily, 10, 41, 44, 49, 59, 60, 215, 305, 321, 403, 406, 409, 414
Working together, 18–21, 44, 179–183, 352
World Council of Churches, 148
Worry, Freedom from, 323
Worship of God, 150, 223, 282
Writers, 56, 67

Youth work, 395, 415

General Index

Duffield, George, 169
Dumbness, 363
Dunmow Flitch, 15
Dunstan, St., 5
Dunstan's St., 338
Dutch in the Medway, 204
Duty, 65, 252, 277, 285

Easter, 154
Eddystone Lighthouse, 109, 238
Edgehill, Battle of, 13
Edmund, St., 285
Education Act, 1870, 8
Edward I, King, 187
Edward III, King, 227
Edward VI, King, 147
Edward the Confessor, St., 388
Eliot, George, 27
Elizabeth I, Queen, 146, 159, 269, 304
Engineers, 62, 234, 238, 289, 357, 358
English Bible (see *Bible*), 158
Enjoyment, 55–9
Enmity, 205
Entertainment, 45–9, 128
Enthusiasm, 357
Epiphany, 108, 151
Europe Day, 184
European Economic Community, 184
Eve of St. Mark, 296
Everest, Mount, 19
Everyday things, 62
Evil, 202, 352
Evil Spirits, 132
Explorers 7, 16, 58, 114–16, 163, 309–10, 314, 343, 353
Eyam, 373

F.A. Cup, 166
Factory Acts, 339
Fair weather or foul, 311
Fairs, 128, 322, 344
Fairy tales, 67
Faith—church cat, 37
Faithfulness, 260, 274–8
Faraday, Michael, 97
Farming, 117, 126, 128, 129
Father Christmas, 138
Fawcett, Henry, 110
Fawkes, Guy, 245
Fielding, Henry, 302
Fire, 123, 240, 276
    Brigades, 240
    of London, 240

First Actress, 48
Fishermen, Deep-sea 79
Fishers of men, 341
Flag Days (see *Appeals*)
Flamsteed, John, 92
Fleming, Cox'n William, 255
Fleming, Sir Alexander, 290
Floods, 101
'Flora Day', 120
Flowers, 118
Flying, 85–9, 318
Fonteyn, Dame Margot, 46
Food, 129
Foolishness, 294–6, 428
Football Association, 40
Forgiveness, 104, 428
Four-minute mile, 42
Fox, George, 344
Francis de Sales, St., 324
Francis of Assisi, St., 24, 321
Francis Xavier, St., 4
Frederick the Great, 208
Free to worship, 68
Freedom, 68, 212–16, 379
French Revolution, 202
Friars, 24, 367, 393
Friends, 24, 269, 333
Froebel, Friedrich, 11
Frost Fair, 112
Fry, Elizabeth, 224
Furry Dance, 120

Gagarin, Yuri, 93
Galileo, Galilei, 92, 361
Gallantry, 286
Gamaliel, 72
Games, 40, 41
Gandhi, Mahatma, 273
Garibaldi, Giuseppe, 371
George, St., 381
George Cross, 254, 255, 286, 352
Germs, 249, 250, 290
Ghoulies & ghosties, 132
Gilbert, Sir W. S., 21
Giles, St., 390
Gipsies, 326
Gipsy Smith, 326
Give and take, 13–17
Giving of one's best, 356–60
Gladstone, William Ewart, 72
Glastonbury, 5
Glencoe massacre, 198
Glory of God, For the, 364
Go ye into all the world, 396–400

General Index   441

General Index   443

Michaelmas, 128, 296
Michelangelo, 226
Midsummer Day, 122
  old, 124
Missionaries, 78, 79, 293, 337, 343, 385, 394, 396–400
Mohammed, 162
Mohr, Joseph, 140
Mollison, Jim & Amy, 87
Mompesson, Rev. William, 373
Monasteries, 5, 17, 161, 243, 360, 368, 388
Monte Cassino, 161
Moon, 94
More, St. Thomas, 348
Morrison, Robert, 399
Motor cars, 318
Mountaineering, 19
Mountbatten of Burma, Earl, 180
Mozart, Wolfgang Amadeus, 359
Museums, 39
Music, 20, 50–4, 57, 61, 172, 359, 364, 366

Nagasaki, Atomic bomb, 190
Names and reputations, 27–31
Nansen, Fridtjof, 7
Napoleon, 129, 210
Nathanael, 267
National Christian Education Council, 236
National Sunday School Union, 236
Natural disasters, 100
Nautilus, U.S. Submarine, 83
Neighbours, Good, 372
Nelson, Lord, 65, 146, 279
New ideas, 233
New Year, 107
New Zealand, 195
Newton, John, 323, 328
Nicholas, St., 138
Nightingale, Florence, 245
Ninian, St., 145
Nobel, Alfred, 192
Nobel Prizes, 192, 194, 271, 365
North Pole, 83, 115, 116
Nothing but the best, 318, 322
Nothing is impossible, 351–5
Novello, Ivor, 27
Now thank we all our God, 167
Now the day is over, 170
Nuns, 321, 322, 392
Nursery schools, 12
Nursing, 243, 245, 272

O God, our help in ages past, 168
Oates, Captain, 374
Old Midsummer Day, 124
Onward Christian Soldiers, 170
Open air school, 12
Opera, 21, 52
Orchestra, 20, 51
Order of the Garter, 227
Orders of Chivalry, 227
Ordinary & extraordinary, 132–6
Orphanages, 149, 164
Osmund, St., 174
Oswald, St., 266
Owen, Robert, 306
Oxfam, 340

Pacific Ocean, 58
Paderewski, Ignace Jan, 346
Padres, 277
Paganini, Nicolo, 366
Pageantry, 135, 136
Palm Sunday, 152
Pantomime, 48
Parables, 428
Parachute, 237, 372
Park, Mungo, 310
Parliament, 70, 135, 216
Parsons, Charles, 358
Pasteur, Louis, 249
Patience, 261
Patrick, St., 383
Patriotism, 271
Paul, St., 22, 55, 133, 171, 386
Paulinus, St., 397
Peace & brotherhood, 192–6
Peace of Westphalia, 167
Pearl Harbor, 200
Pearson, Sir Arthur, 338
Peary, Robert, 115
Peel, Sir Robert, 299
Pen friends, 182
Penicillin, 290
Penn, William, 193
Penny Postage, 55
Pentecost, 155
People in authority, 207–11
Perseverance, 222, 225, 289–93
Peter, St., 341, 382
Pets, 35
Pharisees, 30, 72, 152, 155
Phillip, Capt. Arthur, 82
Pianists, 172, 346
Pilgrim Fathers, 68
Pilgrim's Progress, 355

True values, 319–23
Tull, Jethro, 117
Turbinia, 358
Tutankhamun's treasure, 95
Twain, Mark, 27
Tyndale, William, 158
Tynwald Day, 124
Tyrrel, Sir Walter, 26

Uncle Tom's Cabin, 77
Unemployment, 305
United Nations, 186
Universal Postal Union, 182
Universities Boat Race, 44
Unselfishness, 284

Vaccination, 248
Valentine, St., 14
Van Alstyne, Frances Jane, 307
Verne, Jules, 56, 83
Vespucci, Amerigo, 28
Vianney, John Baptist, 261
Victoria, Queen, 63, 211, 278
Victoria Cross, 252, 278, 286
Vikings, 370
Vincent de Paul, St., 331
Violin, 366,
Virginia settlers, 81
Volcano, 100
Vulgate, 157

Wagner, Wilhelm Richard, 52
Waitangi, Treaty of, 195
Walker, Rev. George, 66
Wall paintings, 74
War and peace, 187–91
Washington, George, 303
Water Babies, The, 218
Waterloo, Battle of, 210
Watt, James, 173
Watts, Isaac, 168
Weathering the storms, 312
Webb, Captain Matthew, 43
Wellington, Duke of, 146, 210
Wesley, Charles, 139

Wesley, John, 139, 276
Westminster Abbey, 53
When a knight won his spurs, 228
When I needed a neighbour, 336–340
When I survey the wondrous cross, 168
Whitby, 392
Whitsun, 155
Whittle, Sir Frank, 88
Why me? 334
Wilberforce, William, 219
Wild life preservation, 39
William II, King, 26, 280
Williams, John, 400
Wind in the Willows, 29
Winstanley, Henry, 109
Winter, 137
Wisdom, 297–8, 428
Wolfe, General James, 179
Wolsey, Cardinal Thomas, 274
' Woodbine Willie ', 277
Wordsworth, William, 118
Work, 59
Working together, 16
World Council of Churches, 148
World Hunger, 129, 334, 335, 340
World War I, 188, 191, 272, 277
World War II, 189, 190, 191, 200, 213, 352
Worst journey in the world, 113
Wreckers, 130
Wren, Sir Christopher, 69
Wright, Orville & Wilbur, 86
Wyclif, John, 74

X-rays, 251
Xavier, St. Francis, 4

Yeoman of the Guard, 135
Your kind of music, 50
Youth work, 395

Zeppelins, 85
Zutphen, Battle of, 231